T0221041

Blockchain for Real World Applications

Blockchain for Real World Applications

Rishabh Garg
Birla Institute of Technology and Science - Pilani, India

This edition first published 2023

© 2023 John Wiley & Sons, Inc. All rights reserved.

Published by John Wiley & Sons, Inc., Hoboken, New Jersey.

No part of this publication may be reproduced, stored in a retrieval system, or transmitted in any form or by any means, electronic, mechanical, photocopying, recording, scanning, or otherwise, except as permitted under Section 107 or 108 of the 1976 United States Copyright Act, without either the prior written permission of the Publisher, or authorization through payment of the appropriate per-copy fee to the Copyright Clearance Center, Inc., 222 Rosewood Drive, Danvers, MA 01923, (978) 750–8400, fax (978) 750–4470, or on the web at www. copyright.com. Requests to the Publisher for permission should be addressed to the Permissions Department, John Wiley & Sons, Inc., 111 River Street, Hoboken, NJ 07030, (201) 748–6011, fax (201) 748–6008, or online at http://www.wiley.com/go/permission.

Trademarks

Wiley and the Wiley logo are trademarks or registered trademarks of John Wiley & Sons, Inc. and/or its affiliates in the United States and other countries and may not be used without written permission. All other trademarks are the property of their respective owners. John Wiley & Sons, Inc. is not associated with any product or vendor mentioned in this book.

Limit of Liability/Disclaimer of Warranty

While the publisher and author have used their best efforts in preparing this book, they make no representations or warranties with respect to the accuracy or completeness of the contents of this book and specifically disclaim any implied warranties of merchantability or fitness for a particular purpose. No warranty may be created or extended by sales representatives or written sales materials. The advice and strategies contained herein may not be suitable for your situation. You should consult with a professional where appropriate. Neither the publisher nor author shall be liable for any loss of profit or any other commercial damages, including but not limited to special, incidental, consequential, or other damages. Further, readers should be aware that websites listed in this work may have changed or disappeared between when this work was written and when it is read. Neither the publisher nor authors shall be liable for any loss of profit or any other commercial damages, including but not limited to special, incidental, consequential, or other damages.

For general information on our other products and services or for technical support, please contact our Customer Care Department within the United States at (800) 762–2974, outside the United States at (317) 572–3993 or fax (317) 572–4002.

Wiley also publishes its books in a variety of electronic formats. Some content that appears in print may not be available in electronic formats. For more information about Wiley products, visit our website at www.wiley.com.

Library of Congress Cataloging-in-Publication Data

Names: Garg, Rishabh, author.

Title: Blockchain for real world applications / Rishabh Garg.

Description: Hoboken, New Jersey : John Wiley & Sons, 2023. | Includes index.

Identifiers: LCCN 2022041346 (print) | LCCN 2022041347 (ebook) | ISBN
    9781119903734 (hardback) | ISBN 9781119903741 (pdf) | ISBN 9781119903758
    (epub) | ISBN 9781119903765 (ebook)

Subjects: LCSH: Blockchains (Databases) | Electronic funds transfers.

Classification: LCC QA76.9.B56 G37 2023 (print) | LCC QA76.9.B56 (ebook)|
    DDC 005.74--dc23/eng/20220920

LC record available at https://lccn.loc.gov/2022041346

LC ebook record available at https://lccn.loc.gov/2022041347

Cover image: © Yuichiro Chino/Getty Images

Cover design by Wiley

Set in 9.5/12.5pt STIXTwoText by Integra Software Services Pvt. Ltd, Pondicherry, India

Contents

Illustrations

List of Figures

Code Cells

Tables

Foreword

Mistaken identity has often produced many delightful works in literature starting from the *Comedy of Errors* by Shakespeare. Alas, the complex world of today does not admit of that luxury. The modern systems developed by governments and businesses all over the world use individual identities for a large number of functions and delivery of services. Every day, millions of people sign up online to carry out a wide range of activities. Users are routinely coerced to disclose their personal identifiable information before allowing access to online services. With each transaction, the user leaves his digital footprints behind, which have the potential to compromise specific personal information. This is why an identity system that is error free and impervious to manipulation and fraud is a prerequisite for the real world.

Blockchain technology, while ensuring a self-sovereign identity, offers a robust and tamper-proof ecosystem to conduct real-world activities, such as education, health care, real estate, transportation, banking, business, trade/finance, supply-chain management, e-commerce, and decentralized streaming.

The present book expounds the multifaceted nature of blockchain technology, its architecture, and key characteristics, such as irreversibility and persistence. The readers will discover the potential use of blockchain technology in all significant walks of life and learn to handle transactional procedures. The narrative is lucid, with great art-work, and is sure to enthuse readers.

The book also provides associated code cells for IPFS commands, creation of digital IDs, encryption and decryption, a decentralized voting process, auction process, e-commerce with a practical stepwise mechanism for readers to attain breakthrough proficiency in the thrust area.

Rishabh Garg, BITS – India has envisioned blockchain as a panacea for building robust identity systems. Though the technology is in its nascent stage, the present book will serve as a beacon to those seeking crystallized knowledge on blockchain. I have no doubts that with its simple handling of a complex subject this book will find inroads to American and European Universities.

Indraneel Shankar Dani
Former Additional Chief Secretary
Chairman, Land Reforms
Government of Madhya Pradesh, India

Preface

The "Tragedy of the Commons" is a long-held belief that people cannot serve their personal interest and the common good simultaneously. Holding to this concept, millions of people worldwide continue to scavenge for basic necessities in the absence of formal identity, despite incomparable technical advancements.

Identity is the nucleus of all human endeavors across the globe, including education, jobs, banking, finance, health care, business, e-commerce, national security, etc. Nevertheless, 1.1 billion people worldwide have no proof of identity, and 45% of those without an identity are among the poorest 20% on the planet. This problem overly affects children and women in rural areas of Asia and Africa. Given this, the author came up with the current concept for an all-inclusive ID in 2016 and originally called it "Generic Information Tracker" (*Dainik Bhaskar*, 2016). During the platinum jubilee celebrations of the Council of Scientific and Industrial Research (CSIR) at Vijnana Bhawan, New Delhi, India, the author discussed his concept with Mr. Narendra Modi, the prime minister of India. Mr. Modi praised the author's work and encouraged him to develop the idea for India Vision, 2020.

After working through the complexities, the author presented the breakthrough to scientists, corporate stalwarts, and policy makers at the India International Science Fest, 2016. The author was honored with the Young Scientist Award by the Ministry of Science and Technology, Earth Science, and Vijnana Bharti (*Times of India*, New Delhi, 2016).

To make the title more explicit, the prototype was renamed as Digital ID with Electronic Surveillance System (*Dainik Jagran*, 2017). The National Innovation Foundation, Department of Science & Technology, Government of India, registered the inventive project (NIF, 2018), and the author was conferred with the National Award for Outstanding Innovation, 2017 by the honorable president of India, Mr. Ram Nath Kovind at Rashtrapati Bhawan, New Delhi.

During the last five years, the author deliberated upon the feasibility, benefits, and privacy concerns of a single identity model against multiple identity documents. Following an analysis of the security concerns associated with a centralized database, a number of digital identity models were examined with respect to data security, decentralization, immutability, revocation, accountability, auditability, speed, and user control over personally identifiable information. Finally, blockchain seemed to be the most promising solution to readdress nearly all the issues affecting digital identity and access management.

The book provides a thorough understanding of the blockchain ecosystem, framework, essential features, Ethereum, Hyperledger, and cryptocurrencies. This is followed by a comprehensive discussion on the prospective uses of blockchain cryptography, cybersecurity, identity management, credential verification, job validation, health care, remote health monitoring, organ transplantation, genomics, drug supply chain, food and civil supplies, etc. Vibrant illustrations and corresponding code cells have been provided to help readers to comprehend banking, trade, finance, decentralized finance, prediction markets, portfolio management, quadratic funding, crowd funding, e-commerce, etc.

The very purpose of the book is to help readers adopt this embryonic stage of blockchain technology for multiple use cases, whether they are a budding technologist, a start-up enthusiast, or a nontechnical user of decentralized apps.

The author accords his special thanks to Mr. Hari Ranjan Rao, joint secretary, Ministry of Telecom, Government of India; and Mr. Manish Rastogi, principal secretary, Department of Science and Technology, Government of MP for informal discourses, which helped him to resolve the prevalent inadequacies and put together a coherent picture of the decentralized framework.

The foreword of the book has been written by Mr. Indraneel Shankar Dani, former additional chief secretary, and chairman of Land Reforms, Government of Madhya Pradesh, India, to whom the author is deeply grateful.

1

Introduction

Dating back to Babylonian era, the ledger appears to be a bedrock of civilization as the exchange of value always required two unknown people to trust each other's claims. Even today, we need a common system, which can provide order to the society, keep track of our transactions, establish public trust in it, and maintain it forever.

A blockchain is fundamentally a digital ledger that carries a list of transactions, that could, in principle, represent almost anything – money, digital stocks, cryptocurrencies, or any other asset. Blockchain can follow instructions to buy or sell these assets and implement inclusive set of terms and conditions through so-called smart contracts.

Blockchain differs from a simple ledger in that all transactions are stored in multiple copies on independent computers, individually within a decentralized network, rather than managed by a centralized institution, such as a bank or government agency. Once a consensus is reached, all computers on the network update their copies of the ledger simultaneously. If a node attempts to retroactively add or subtract an entry without consensus, the rest of the network automatically invalidates the entry.

Unlike a traditional ledger, it is governed by complex mathematical algorithms and impregnable cryptography that adds a layer of integrity to the ledger, what Ian Grigg (2005) referred to as triple-entry accounting – one entry on the debit side, another on the credit side, and a third on an immutable, undisputed, shared ledger.

Thus, Distributed Ledger Technology (DLT) is a technical infrastructure and protocol that allows simultaneous access, verification and updating of records in an irreversible manner over a network spanning multiple entities or locations. Blockchain is one of its many forms – Directed Acyclic Graph (DAG), Hashgraph, Holochain, or Tempo (Radix). It is a sequence of blocks containing a complete list

Blockchain for Real World Applications, First Edition. Rishabh Garg.
© 2023 John Wiley & Sons, Inc. Published 2023 by John Wiley & Sons, Inc.

of transactions in the form of a digital public ledger that is replicated and distributed throughout the network. The blockchain ecosystem includes blocks – the data structure used to keep records of transactions, which are distributed among all nodes in the network, and nodes – a user or computer that holds a complete copy of the record or ledger.

The blockchain technology was first mentioned by Stuart Haber and W. Scott Stornetta in 1991. However, Satoshi Nakamoto, a person who goes by the alias, popularized it in 2008 to operate as the public transaction ledger of Bitcoin. Over the past one decade and a half, there have been innovations around blockchain consensus mechanisms, constitutional design, programmable smart contracts, and tokens. Blockchain 1.0 applications were mainly limited to digital currencies, which were used in commercial transactions, foreign exchange, gambling, and money laundering. The expansion of Blockchain 2.0 applications enabled smart-contracts, decentralized applications (dApps), and Decentralized Autonomous Organizations (DAO). Blockchain 3.0 was able to register its presence in areas, such as education, health, science, transportation, and logistics in addition to currency and finance, and now Blockchain 4.0 is evolving as a business-friendly ecosystem for the world of commons. The integration of blockchain with emerging technologies like Internet of Things, cloud, artificial intelligence, and robotics is one of the biggest promises of the times to come.

Blockchain is typically classified into public, private, and consortium blockchain. A public blockchain is a permissionless blockchain in which any user, whosoever wishes to transact with the network, can participate and write on the blockchain. A private blockchain only allows nodes coming from a specific organization to participate in the consensus process. That's why it is also called permissioned blockchain. A consortium blockchain is a semi-private system in which a group of like-minded companies leverage cross-company solutions to improve workflow, accountability, and transparency.

Blockchain, irrespective of its type, uses an asymmetric cryptography mechanism to validate the authenticity of transactions. It is basically a network of participants that share nodes for common business purpose and process. Each block of the blockchain contains about 1 MB of data. This block stores the information chronologically until its 1 MB data capacity is occupied, and then the second block repeats the same process. All these blocks join in a sequence, and to do this, each block gets a unique hash that exactly matches the string of data in that block. If anything inside a block changes, even to a little extent, the block gets a new hash.

In a blockchain, this hash is created by a cryptographic hash function. A cryptographic hash function is a complex algorithm that takes any string of input and turns it into a 64-digit string of output. A hash is not always qualified. A block on the blockchain will only be accepted if its hash starts with at least ten consecutive zeros. A small, specific piece of data is added to each block called a nonce. The process of repeatedly altering and hashing a block's data to find a suitable hash is called mining, and this is what miners do. Miners spend a lot of electricity in the form of computational power by constantly changing the block structure (nonce) and hashing it until a qualified signature (output) is found. The more computational power they have, the faster they can hash different block compositions to find a qualified hash.

The process (hash function) used here that converts any information into a string of alphanumeric values (hash), is called encryption. There are mainly two types of encryption – asymmetric encryption and symmetric encryption, depending on whether the same or different keys are used for encryption and decryption. Cryptocurrencies use blockchain to achieve the benefits of a public ledger as well as an advanced cryptographic security system so that online transactions are always chronicled and secure. Transactions are simply data that indicate the flow of cryptocurrency from one wallet to another.

In order to record the flow of currency or data from one wallet to another in an immutable form, nodes communicate with one another to reach consensus on the records of the ledger. However, the transaction is accepted only if majority of the nodes agree on its validity. When all nodes reach a consensus, transactions are recorded on a new block and added to the existing chain. While Bitcoin focused on decentralized payments, Vitalik Buterin and his collaborators introduced arbitrary computer code into the blockchain using transactions. Thus, Ethereum came into being as a peer-to-peer network where each node runs an operating system called the Ethereum Virtual Machine. This securely executes and verifies application code, hitherto called smart contracts, and allows participants on the blockchain to transact with each other without a trusted central authority.

Smart contracts are used for the automation of common centralized processes, such as conditional transfer of digital assets, multisig asset exchange, or waiting for a specific amount of time to execute a transaction. It allows the creation of decentralized applications for B2C trades whereas B2B transactions, which need to keep their data secure and confidential, can adopt Hyperledger. Hyperledger offers a modular architecture that delivers a high degree of privacy, resilience, and scalability. It is an enterprise-level private blockchain network that enables several business entities – such as banks, corporate institutions or trade establishments – to transact with each other.

Thus, digital transactions can be decentralized, encrypted, and held securely on a distributed ledger. It has the potential to cut millions of hours spent on administrative processes every year and bring efficiency through smart contracts in all walks of life. The present book explicates the unrestrained functionality of blockchain and its application in the real world.

It's a well-known fact that identity is the nucleus of all the activities in the world. In a civilized society, identity entitles the individual to discharge his rights and responsibilities. Over the centuries, governments around the world issued a variety of identity documents to enable citizens to make access to education, health care, business activities, pensions, banking, social benefits, and state welfare schemes.

Many countries issued identity numbers for a singular purpose, but in due course of time, they became a de facto national identification number. In order to provide an official identity to every citizen of India, the Department of Information Technology, Government of India, introduced a biometric-enabled, unique identification number (UID). This project has listed over a billion users with an estimated expenditure of 130 billion INR, till date (UIDAI, 2022). India's Unique Identification System, called Aadhaar, has been taken as a case study to deliberate over the advantages and disadvantages of a centralized identity model in light of privacy issues, unconstitutional access, absence of data-protection laws, involvement of private partners, etc.

The UID project was expected to portray a more accurate picture of Indian residents and enable them to have hassle-free access to government schemes and public services, but the ground reality has been far from such claims. First of all, the technological framework for such a large database is not available in the country; and second, the Indian bureaucracy is not technically smart enough to handle such big data with burgeoning privacy and data-security issues in India. Also, the lack of interoperability between departments and government levels takes a toll in the form of excess bureaucracy, which, in turn, increases processing time and cost.

At present, the system preserves the personally identifiable information (PII) of millions of users on a centralized government database, supported by some legacy software, with numerous single points of failure (SPoF). Such a centralized system, containing PII, acts like a honeypot to hackers. Following the reports of prevalent data breaches and continuing threats to online data over the past decade, the security of digital identities has emerged as one of the foremost concerns on the national front. Today, a user has to juggle various identities associated with his username across different websites. There is no consistent or homogenous way to use the data generated by one platform on the other. The most threatening and frustrating experience is that a digital identity arises organically from the personal information available on the web or from the shadow data created by a user's online activities, on a day-to-day basis. The fragile links between digital and offline identities make it relatively easy to create pseudonymous profiles and fake identities, for enactment of fraud.

In a world where a number of vulnerable citizens, not having an identity or bank account, but own a smartphone, echoes the possibility of a mobile-based, digital-identity solution. Due to the increasing sophistication of smartphones, advances in cryptography, and the advent of blockchain technology, a new identity management system can be built on the concept of decentralized identifiers (DID).

Decentralized identity is an approach to identity management that allows individuals to store their credentials and personally identifiable information in an application called a wallet. In such a system, passwords are replaced with non-phishable cryptographic keys that validates identities for business activities while securing users' communications.

Detailing the models of decentralized identity – federated, user-centric, and self-sovereign – the present book explores the likelihood of storing and managing identity credentials and information in an interplanetary file system or wallet through a blockchain-based solution. Blockchain assures citizens, organizations, and service providers that big data is never stored in a single repository, rather distributed among decentralized databases. Users, without being physically present, can share their digital ID with the service provider through a personal device, such as a smartphone, and receive appropriate services without jeopardizing their privacy.

Further, all the documents that identify users get stored on their personal devices backed by IPFS, making them safe from data breaches. No transaction of user's information would occur without the explicit consent of the user. It will permit the user to control his personally identifiable information, make the system more interoperable, allow the user to employ data on multiple platforms, and protect the user from being locked into one platform. Thus, blockchain would allow people to enjoy self-sovereign and encrypted digital identities, replacing the need for creating multiple usernames and passwords.

Blockchain identity management can help people to create, manage, verify, and authenticate their identity in real-time. It can provide relief to billions of people holding multiple cards for specific purposes. A single ID (*One World – One Identity*) comprising 20 digits could be provided to all on the day of census. The Digital ID System (IPFS/Private Ledger) would record all substantive data of a citizen, like digital identity number, citizen name, date of birth, family details, photo, biometric details, digital signature, educational progress, employment details, driver's license, financial details, passport, visa, medical records, etc. in a distributed ledger like blockchain. While millions of transactions are recorded across hundreds of nodes scattered over thousands of financial institutions, notwithstanding any geographical or political boundaries; likewise, all identity documents from different administrative organizations can be recorded using a private key (Garg, 2019, 2021). The difference between a private key and a public key is that a private key, also called a secret key, is a variable that can be used to both encrypt and decrypt data, whereas a public key is a big numerical number that can only be used to encrypt data.

The main purpose of encryption is that it allows only the actual sender of the message and the intended recipient to read the pertinent information. There has been several milestones in the history of cryptography that led to the formation of the fundamentals of modern algorithms. In early times the cipher was the fundamental component for communicating secret messages, which included letters as a basic element. A few of its variants include Simple Substitution Cipher, Caesar Cipher, Vigenere Cipher, Transposition Cipher, Playfair Cipher, and Hill Cipher. In addition, many cryptographic algorithms, such as the RSA algorithm, Multiple Precision Arithmetic Library, GNU Multiple Precision Arithmetic Library, Chinese Remainder Theorem, and Secure Hashing Algorithm (SHA-512) Hash in Java have also been popular.

Just as encryption protects any data from misuse, cybersecurity protects systems and networks from digital attacks. The cyber-attack landscape has grown exponentially in the last few years. Cyberattacks are carried out by using various malware like Trojans, Rootkits, Virus, etc. and are known as Distributed Denial of Service (DDoS) attack, Man in the Middle (MITM) attack, phishing, Ransomware attack, and Structured Language Query (SQL) injection. Blockchain has emerged as a promising mitigation technology for cybersecurity.

Once an identity management is set up and cryptographically protected, the Ethereum blockchain can allow a credential holder to share all his academic credentials with validators in an encrypted format. The system uses smart contracts, and thus, no document can be shared without the explicit consent of its holder. Thus, blockchain can prove to be a good tool for background verification of a candidate, thereby saving time, cost, and human resources spent on verification and evaluation.

Apart from academic verification, blockchain has a wide range of applications and uses in health care as well. It helps secure the transfer of patient medical records, manage drug supply chains, and unlock biological and genetic codes for health researchers. Besides, there has been a spurt in efforts to scale-up the capabilities of blockchain for decentralized voting and the food supply. Blockchain lets the journey of food items to be tracked directly from the farm to the shelves of the superstore. Many issues, such as food fraud, security recalls, and supply chain inefficiencies, can be solved through blockchain-enabled food traceability.

There has also been an unprecedented boom in the banking and finance industry in the wake of blockchain technology. Blockchain makes it easy for remote untrusted parties to build consensus on the state of a database, without the intervention of gatekeepers. It can handle all financial transactions like payments, settlement systems, fundraising, securities management, loans, credit, and trade finance, etc. like a bookkeeper. This is the reason why it surpasses the traditional system in terms of identity verification, payments, withdrawals, settlements, credits and loans, asset transfers, peer-to-peer transfers, hedge funds, safety, and accountability.

Another area that is poised for a blockchain revolution is trade finance. Trade finance relies heavily on paper-based business operations involving information transmission, asset transfer, and payment processes. Instead of legal terms, these contracts may be better described in Python programming language so that traders can better understand them. Thus, blockchain, along with smart contracts, provides a secure, transparent, auditable, and automated transaction environment for business investors. It has a potential to revolutionize trade finance by rationalization of the processes of smart contracts, enterprise resource planning, lightning network, pre- and post-trade processes, accounts and audits, loyalty rewards, etc.

Beyond the precincts of existing financial networks, decentralized finance (DeFi) is a blockchain-based fintech, which is altogether open and programmable. In the present book, the product and potential of myriad use-cases of decentralized finance, such as asset management, tokenization, token derivatives, decentralized autonomous organization, data analysis and assessment, payments, lending and borrowing, insurance, margin trading, market place, gaming, and yield farming have been delineated. It also outlines Ethereum as a platform for DeFi to transfer funds, streaming money, programmable currency, lending, borrowing, no-loss lotteries, exchange tokens, advance trading, fund aggregation, portfolio management, quadratic funding, crowd funding, and insurance.

The blockchain landscape is expanding quickly, spanning over all facets of the real world, such as agriculture and natural resources, animal husbandry, air travel, billing and payments, construction, drugs supply, entertainment, fisheries, food and drink, gambling, human resource management, information and communications, infrastructure and energy, insurance, Internet of Things, legal enforcement, public assistance, medical claim settlement, messaging, hospitality, postal services, production, public transport, real estate, ride hailing, shipping and freight transport, taxation, travel and mobility, vaccination and community health, vehicles, welfare distribution, and wills and inheritances.

Many nations have tried to create their own e-governance systems to deliver essential civic services during the past few decades, but majority of them ran into privacy and security issues. Blockchain can resolve these issues and assist government agencies to lower labor costs, save time, and enhance operational efficiency.

Another area, the supply chain, is also becoming increasingly more complex, more elaborate, and more global. Due to a serious business restriction called supply chain visibility, most businesses have little to no awareness about their second- and third-tier suppliers. Better results may be expected if blockchain technology is implemented in the supply chain. To trace the product's origins and manufacturing processes, the supply chain can use a shared, consensus-based public ledger. Blockchain may offer certification and documentation, including information about the product lifecycle, and make it instantly available to all parties. Products can be tracked from factory to storage, transit, delivery, and sale.

Further, e-commerce establishments can leverage the advantages of Ethereum. It is a platform for those e-commerce brands who desire to manage their own blockchain through apps that accept Bitcoin payments. The introduction of blockchain technology into e-commerce will help users to track their purchase orders, store product, and service warranties, and gain access to the data. At the same time, it enables businesses to combine services like payment processing, inventory control, product description, etc. to evade the cost of buying and maintaining separate systems. It can speed up tracking, compliance, maintenance, and delivery of goods by integrating the Internet of Things.

The main advantage of blockchain applications is that almost all of the software, including Hyperledger fabric, are open source, and most of them are designed to work on Linux. Virtual machines or Docker containers can also be used to execute them on Windows. In the present book, blockchain operations have been explained in a vivid and engaging way. By using their private key, a user can quickly create an account on the blockchain. They may then download the smartphone application from the Play Store. The user can self-certify their information using this software, which will retrieve personal information from the supplied ID. Alternately, the user may submit their credentials, which include name, date of birth, location, parents' names, address, and biometric data (DNA map, finger impression, retinal image, blood sample, etc.).

A government agency may at any moment access the user's information for authentication purposes. The authorities may use text messages to ask the identity holder for access to certain information. Business logic in smart contracts will produce a credibility score for the user. The higher the score, the higher is the credibility of the individual. Consequently, a banker and a customer, sitting on two sides of the globe, can automate the transfer of money on their decentralized software, thanks to cryptography and smart contracts that run on Ethereum. Distributed record-keeping and algorithmic consensus, two of blockchain's fundamental properties, are thus primed to allow entrepreneurs to create and implement decentralized apps that have the potential to change the world.

References

Garg R, 2019. Multipurpose ID: One Nation – One Identity, Annual Convention – Indian Society for Technical Education (ISTE). National Conference on Recent Advances in Energy, Science & Technology, (39). doi: 10.6084/m9.figshare. 16945078. https://www.researchgate.net/publication/337398750_Multipurpose_ ID_One_Nation_-_One_Identity.

Garg R, 2021. Global Identity through Blockchain. Proceedings of the International Webinar on Blockchain, Scholars Park, India, 01–60. doi: 10.13140/RG.2.2.27803.18728. https://www.researchgate.net/publication/353141617_Global_Identity_through_Blockchain.

Grigg I, 2005. Triple Entry Accounting. https://iang.org/papers/triple_entry.html

UIDAI, 2022. https://uidai.gov.in.

2

Distributed Ledger Technology

The concept of Distributed Ledger Technology (DLT) encompasses how cryptography and an open distributed ledger can be integrated into a digital business. DLT refers to the technical infrastructure and protocols that allow simultaneous access, verification, and updating of records in an irreversible manner over a network spanning multiple entities or locations. It could be a blockchain, Directed Acyclic Graph, Hashgraph, Holochain, or Tempo (Garg, 2017).

2.1 Different Types of Distributed Ledger Technology

2.1.1 Blockchain

Blockchain is a type of DLT where transaction records are saved, in the ledger, as a chain of blocks. All the nodes maintain a common ledger, so the overall computational power gets distributed among them, which delivers a better outcome.

- Enhanced Security: Every single data is deeply encrypted (hashed) that allows a higher level of security. It renders hacking impossible.
- Faster Disbursement: Relatively faster than typical payment systems, although bigger networks may have slower transaction rates.
- Consensus: Supports a wide range of consensus algorithms that help the nodes to make the right decision.

Once a transaction takes place, the nodes on the network verify it. After verification, the transaction gets a unique hash ID and gets stored in the ledger. Once it gets added to the ledger, no one can mutate or delete the transaction.

Blockchain for Real World Applications, First Edition. Rishabh Garg.
© 2023 John Wiley & Sons, Inc. Published 2023 by John Wiley & Sons, Inc.

2.1.2 Directed Acyclic Graph

Every transaction is entered on the ledger in a sequential order. However, to validate it, the transaction needs to endorse two previous transactions to call itself valid. Here, a sequence of transactions is called a "branch," and the longer it goes, the more valid all the transactions become.

- Virtually Infinite Scalability: The more users use the network, the less time it takes for validation. That's how it can reach an infinite level of scalability.
- Quantum-resistance: The use of one-time signatures makes it quantum-resistant.
- Parallel Transactions: All transactions align in a parallel line after validation.

2.1.3 Hashgraph

Hashgraph employs a Gossip protocol to relay the information about a transaction. Once a transaction takes place, the adjoining nodes share that information with other ones, and after sometime all the nodes would know about the transaction. With the help of the "Virtual Voting" protocol, every node validates the transaction and then the transaction gets added to the ledger.

- There can be multiple transactions stored on the ledger with the same timestamp. All transactions are stored in a parallel structure. Here every record on the ledger is called an "Event."
- The ledger logs down every gossip sequence on the network in an ordered fashion.
- Random Gossip: Nodes randomly gossip about what they know with other nodes to spread the information until every node knows the information.

2.1.4 Holochain

In Holochain, every node on the network maintains its own ledger. Though the system does not prescribe any global validation protocol, yet the network maintains a set of rules called "DNA" to verify every individual ledger.

- Holochain moves on from the data-centric structures to agent-centric structures. Agent-centric nodes can validate individually without any forced consensus protocol.
- Energy Efficient: The different nature of the ledger makes the system more energy efficient than its other equivalents.
- True DLT: Every node on the network maintains their own ledger, which creates a true distributed system.

2.1.5 Tempo (Radix)

- Logical Clocks: The system relies on the sequence of the transactions, rather than timestamps, to reach consensus.
- Sharding: Every node on the network keeps a shard (smallest section of the global ledger) with a unique ID.
- Gossip Protocol: Nodes broadcast all their information to synchronize their own shards.

From the foregoing comparison, blockchain, owing to some of its properties, like its decentralization, information transparency, openness, and tamper-proof construction, seems to be a good fit for identity management.

2.2 Chronological Evolution

Blockchain has revolutionized a number of arenas since its inception (see Figure 2.1). A review of literature makes it clear that the scope of blockchain applications has extended from virtual currencies to financial applications, education, health, science, transportation, and government. So far, three generations of blockchain have been identified, namely Blockchain 1.0 for digital currency, Blockchain 2.0 for digital finance, Blockchain 3.0 for digital society, and Blockchain 4.0 as business-friendly ecosystem for the real world. (Garg, 2022a).

2.2.1 Blockchain 1.0

Blockchain 1.0 was limited to virtual currencies such as Bitcoin, which was the first and most widely accepted digital currency (Menelli and Smith, 2015). Most

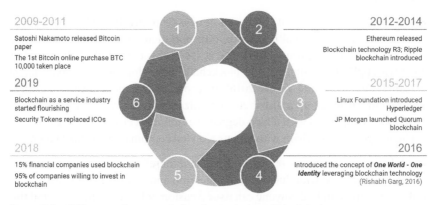

Figure 2.1 Different milestones during the evolution of blockchain.

Blockchain 1.0 applications were digital currencies, used in commercial transactions and relying on the cryptocurrency ecosystem for small-value payments, foreign exchange, gambling, and money laundering.

Initially, virtual currencies relied on encryption techniques to generate, transact, and validate their values. Cryptocurrency transactions are written in a blockchain that verifies and approves each transaction by leveraging the resources of a large peer-to-peer network. The major advantage of using blockchain for digital currency is that it provides a reliable platform to transfer an asset without the involvement of trusted intermediaries or counterparties.

The first block was created by Nakamoto (2008), who introduced the first cryptocurrency, Bitcoin (Nomura Research Institute, 2016). Its current market capitalization is over US$ 140 billion. Other cryptocurrencies – Litecoin (2011), Namecoin (2011), Dogecoin (2013), and Peercoin (2012) – all maintain their presence with a total market cap of over US$ 30 billion. At the moment, there are over 18,000 cryptocurrencies in the market with a total market capitalization of US$ 3.2 trillion.

2.2.2 Blockchain 2.0

This level of blockchain primarily includes Bitcoin 2.0, smart contracts, decentralized applications (dApps), Decentralized Autonomous Organizations (DAOs), and Decentralized Autonomous Corporations (DACs) (Swan, 2015). However, it was used to disrupt traditional currency and payment systems in exclusive areas of finance, primarily banking, stock trading, credit systems, supply chain finance, payment clearing, anti-counterfeiting, and mutual insurance. Certain cryptocurrencies based on programmable smart contracts were introduced such as Ethereum, Codius, and Hyperledger.

2.2.3 Blockchain 3.0

Blockchain is regarded as the blueprint of new economy. It can be employed in sectors like education, health, science, transportation, and logistics, apart from currency and finance (Swan, 2015). The scope of this type of blockchain and its potential applications suggest that blockchain technology is an ongoing target (Crosby, Pattanayak, and Verma, 2016). It encompasses a more advanced form of smart contracts to set up a distributed organizational unit, which formulates its own laws and operates with a high degree of autonomy (Pieroni et al., 2018).

The merger of blockchain with tokens is a vital combination of Blockchain 3.0.

- A token is an attestation of digital rights, and therefore, blockchain tokens are widely recognized with due credit to Ethereum and its ERC20 standard.
- Based on this standard, anyone can issue a custom token on Ethereum, and this token can indicate any right or value.

- Tokens denote economic activities created through the encrypted tokens, which are basically but not exclusively based on the ERC20 standard.
- Tokens can serve as a form of validation of any number of rights, including personal identity, educational diplomas, currency, receipts, keys, rebate points, vouchers, stocks, and bonds.
- It can be stated that tokens are its front-end economic face while blockchain is the new age back-end technology.

2.2.4 Blockchain 4.0

Blockchain 4.0 is now emerging as a business-friendly ecosystem for building and operating applications in the real world. The system can achieve infinite scalability by exploring the possibilities of a virtual blockchain within a blockchain. Blockchain 4.0 describes solutions and approaches that rationalize the technology for business demands, particularly Industry 4.0 and commerce.

Industry 4.0 embodies the integration of automation, enterprise resource planning, and various execution systems, and this is what makes blockchain useful for real-life applications of the future. The amalgamation of blockchain with industry and business allows for cross-system business processes, ensuring data security and privacy with automation, counterparty exclusion, and transparency.

The integration of blockchain with emerging technologies like Internet of Things (IoT), cloud, artificial intelligence, and robotics is one of the biggest promises of the times to come. Blockchain will automate processes by gaining trust, transferring value, and storing data securely. Supply chain management, business workflow, financial transactions, IoT-data collection, health management, asset management, and credit systems are some examples of areas that can be empowered by blockchain technology.

Thus, by using blockchain technology, a digital architecture can be introduced that can combine automation, accountability, and privacy protection to generate a frictionless experience in the real world (Garg, 2021a).

2.3 Blockchain Architecture

Blockchain is a sequence of blocks, which holds a complete list of transaction records like a conventional public ledger (Wang et al., 2018). With the previous block hash contained in the block header, a block has only one parent block (see Figure 2.2). The first block of a blockchain is called a "genesis block," which has no parent block.

The internal details of blockchain are described hereunder.

Figure 2.2 Blockchain – a continuous sequence of blocks.

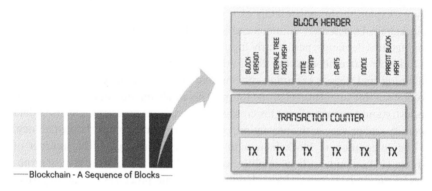

Blockchain - A Sequence of Blocks

Figure 2.3 An illustration of a block.

2.3.1 Block

A block comprises a block header and a block body (see Figure 2.3). The block header contains:

- Block version that signifies the set of block validation rules to be followed.
- Merkle tree root hash that indicates the hash value of all the transactions in the block.
- Timestamp that depicts the current time in universal time since January 01, 1970.
- nBits that target the threshold of a valid block hash.
- Nonce that denotes a 4-byte field, which typically starts from 0 and goes up for every hash calculation.
- Parent block hash with a 256-bit hash value that points to the previous block.

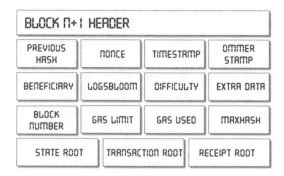

Figure 2.4 Components of a block.

The block body is a unit composed of a transaction counter and a transaction. The maximum number of transactions that a block can hold depends on the size of the block and the size of each transaction. Blockchain uses an asymmetric cryptography mechanism to validate the authentication of transactions (NRI, 2016). Digital signatures based on asymmetric cryptography are used in untrusted environments.

The block body comprises (see Figure 2.4):

1) Transaction Hash
2) Transaction Root
3) State Hash
4) State Root

To check the integrity of the block, the hashes of all the components are used. To validate the block, additional conditions are checked.

2.3.2 Hash Function

As described above, each block contains hashed information (see Figure 2.5).

Hash function, used in cryptography, depicts a mathematical algorithm that transforms information bits to a string of alphanumeric values. Unique in itself, the hash indicates whether the information of input and output is the same. Hash functions have a high avalanche effect i.e., a small change in the input string results in an entirely different output string. This makes it almost impossible to reverse engineer unless sophisticated machine learning algorithms are applied (Garg, 2021b, 2022b).

Common hashing functions are SHA-3, SHA-256, and Keccak. There are two types of hashing methods:

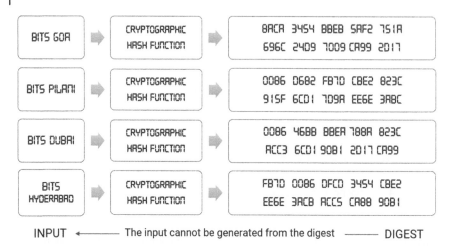

Figure 2.5 A cryptographic hash function.

1) Simple Hash: Hashing is done by a brute-force approach. It is suitable for documents/blocks with fixed amounts of content/transactions, e.g. block header.
2) Merkle Tree Hash: Data is arranged as leaf nodes (binary tree), and hashing is done in sets of two leaves. Used for variable size of arguments in the hash function. For example, composite block integrity; $O(n) = \log n$.

2.3.3 Encryption

The first instance of encryption was presented as symmetric key encryption. In this, the same key (rule) is used for encryption and decryption. For example, Caesar encryption; wherein alphabets (ASCII values) are shifted by a fixed amount.

2.3.3.1 Problems

1) Easy to derive the original message.
2) Passing the key for decryption is difficult.

In order to solve the above-cited problems, public-key cryptography or asymmetric encryption was introduced. In this, each user has a pair of keys. The message encrypted with the private key of the sender, together with the public key of the receiver, is decrypted with the private key of receiver and public key of the sender. This authenticates both the sender and the recipient.

The Rivest Shamir Adelman (RSA) algorithm uses the concept of asymmetric encryption to help users log in to a virtual machine on the cloud, such as Amazon Web Services. However, in blockchain, Elliptic Curve Cryptography (ECC family) algorithms are used to construct the public and private key pair, as they are much stronger than RSA (256 bits ECC key pair $\equiv$ 3072 bits RSA pair).

2.3.4 Keys: Public and Private

To secure decentralized identities, private keys are known only to the owner, while public keys are widely disseminated. This pairing achieves two purposes (see Figure 2.6). The first is authentication, where the public key verifies that the holder of the paired private key has sent the message. The second is encryption, where only the holder of the paired private key can decrypt the message encrypted with the public key. This process is called "cryptography."

Nodes on a network are identified by their account addresses that are generated as follows:

1) A 256-bit random number is generated and designated as a private key.
2) The ECC algorithm is applied to the private key to generate a public key.
3) Hash function is applied to the public key to generate a 20-byte account address.

Transaction data, which is hashed and encrypted, acts like a digital signature. The receiver receives the original copy of the data and a secure hash of the data. The

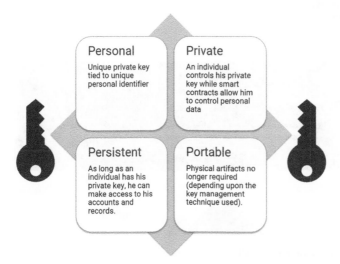

Personal
Unique private key tied to unique personal identifier

Private
An individual controls his private key while smart contracts allow him to control personal data

Persistent
As long as an individual has his private key, he can make access to his accounts and records.

Portable
Physical artifacts no longer required (depending upon the key management technique used).

Figure 2.6 Asymmetric key encryption in blockchain.

receiver decrypts the secure hash and recomputes the hash of the original data received. If both are same, it entails that no modification has happened in the data obtained.

2.3.5 Decentralized Identifier

A decentralized identifier (DID) is a pseudo-anonymous identifier for a person or company. Each DID is secured by a private key. Only the private key owner can establish that they own or control their identity. One person can have multiple DIDs, which limits the extent to which they can be tracked across the multiple activities in their life.

Each DID is often associated with a series of verifiable credentials (attestations) issued by other DIDs, which confirm the distinctive characteristics of that DID (such as age, diplomas, pay slips, address). These credentials are cryptographically signed by their issuers, which allow DID owners to store these credentials themselves as an alternative to a single profile provider.

A DID is stored on the public ledger together with a DID document, which contains the public key for the DID, any other public credentials (which the identity owner wishes to disclose publicly), and the network addresses for interaction (see Figure 2.7).

Figure 2.7 Decentralized identifier (DID).

Coming Up

The foregoing account has dealt with the need and evolution of blockchain from a mere cryptocurrency to a fully developed decentralized system equipped with programmable logic. It also summarized some technical terms that would be used while explaining the practical use cases of blockchain in the real world.

The upcoming chapter will introduce readers to blockchain architecture and its alternative representations, along with a proper rationale behind choosing one type of consensus algorithm over the other on a blockchain.

References

Crosby M, Pattanayak P, and Verma S, 2016. Blockchain technology: beyond Bitcoin. *Applied Innovations*, 2: 6–19.

Garg R, 2017. Hi-Tech ID with Digital Tracking System, National Conference on Application of ICT for Built Environment, India. doi:10.5281/zenodo.4761329. https://www.researchgate.net/publication/325248504_Hi_-_Tech_ID_with_Digital_Tracking_System.

Garg R, 2021a. Blockchain Based Decentralized Applications for Multiple Administrative Domain Networking. BITS – Pilani, KK Birla Goa Campus India, 1–69. doi:10.13140/RG.2.2.29003.87845. https://www.researchgate.net/publication/351871690_Blockchain_based_Decentralized_Applications_for_Multiple_Administrative_Domain_Networking.

Garg R, 2021b. *Souveräne Identitäten*. Verlag Unser Wissen, Germany, 1–104.

Garg R, 2022a. A Technological Approach to Address Deficiencies in UID (Aadhaar). 3rd International Conference on Big Data, Blockchain and Security, Copenhagen Denmark. doi:10.5281/zenodo.5854732. https://zenodo.org/record/5854732#.YvYODaBBzIU.

Garg R, 2022b. Distributed ecosystem for identity management. *Journal of Blockchain Research* 1 (1) (In Press).

Mainelli M and Smith M, 2015. Sharing ledgers for sharing economies: An exploration of mutual distributed ledgers (Blockchain technology). *The Journal of Financial Perspectives*, 3 (3): 38.

Nakamoto S, 2008. Bitcoin: A Peer-to-Peer Electronic Cash System. https://bitcoin.org/bitcoin.pdf.

Nomura Research Institute, 2016. Survey on Blockchain Technologies and Related Services. Technical Report. https://www.nri.com/-/media/Corporate/en/Files/PDF/news/info/cc/2016/160621_1.pdf?la=en&hash=5F190404DE669076B66330D09C4AFBEB4B21C501.

Pieroni A, Scarpato N, Di Nunzio L, Fallucchi F, and Raso M, 2018. Smarter city: smart energy grid based on Blockchain technology. *International Journal for Advances in Science, Engineering and Information Technology*, 8 (1): 298–306.

Swan M, 2015. *Blockchain: Blueprint for a New Economy*. O'Reilly Media, CA US, 152.

Wang H, Zheng Z, Xie S, Dai H, and Chen X, 2018. Blockchain challenges and opportunities: A survey. *International Journal of Web and Grid Services*, 14: 352–375.

3

Blockchain Ecosystem

Distributed ledger technology (DLT), commonly known as "blockchain," refers to the technology of working on decentralized databases that provides control over the evolution of data between entities, through a Peer-to-Peer (P2P) network, where consensus algorithms ensure replication across the nodes of the network.

Nodes

A blockchain system is made up of multiple nodes, each of which has its own copy of the ledger. Nodes communicate with each other to reach consensus on the records of the ledger, eliminating the need of a central authority for coordination or verification.

Nodes also help with the entry of new data as well as the verification and transmission of submitted data on the blockchain (Lewis and Larsen, 2016). Any node can request to add any transaction. However, the transaction is accepted only if majority of the nodes agree on its validity (Boucher, 2017). When all nodes reach a consensus (Lewis, McPartland, and Ranjan, 2017), transactions are recorded on a new block and added to the existing chain (Singh and Singh, 2016). This work is known as "mining."

Miners

Miners create new blocks on the blockchain chain by a process called mining. Each block in a blockchain has its own unique nonce and hash, which refers to the hash of the previous block in the chain.

Mining a block is a cumbersome task, especially on large chains. Miners use specialized software to solve the incredibly complex mathematical problem of finding the nonce that generates an acceptable hash. Since the nonce is only 32 bits and the hash is 256, the probability of perfect mining is formed after mining about four billion possible nonhash combinations.

Blockchain for Real World Applications, First Edition. Rishabh Garg.
© 2023 John Wiley & Sons, Inc. Published 2023 by John Wiley & Sons, Inc.

Thus, after solving a complex cryptographic algorithm, a miner adds each new block to the chain, which is accepted as legitimate data by a majority of nodes in the network. The network rewards miners with digital credits for adding a valid block to the chain. This is an incentive provided for miners to maintain and continuously verify the consistency of data across the network.

Wallets

Wallet is an application that allows end-users to create and maintain private keys and derive public keys or addresses from them. Unlike real-world wallets that store money (cash or credit cards), it's only the private key that acts as an indicator to your tokens in the blockchain. If the private key is lost or compromised; the same will happen with the token too, and the holder will not be able to make any claim on it.

Wallets can be of two types, deterministic and nondeterministic. The main difference between the two is that deterministic wallets allow you to recover a private key from a seed. The seed is a pass-phrase or a set of words, written on a piece of paper and stored in an offline medium. If the private key is lost, it can be recovered through the seed. However, with nondeterministic wallets, if the private key is lost, there is no way to recover the same.

Two more factors to be considered when choosing a wallet are the platform where it operates and how it preserves the private keys. Wallet can be a web wallet, a mobile wallet, or a hardware wallet. Wallets that do not give you direct access to your keys are known as custodial wallets.

3.1 Working of Blockchain

Blockchain realizes trust by validation, verification, and consensus algorithms. Garg (2021a, 2021b) has illustrated its working in the following manner (see Figure 3.1):

- The user, who wants to join the blockchain network, first creates an account (see Figure 3.2).
- Then a genesis file is created and a genesis block is initialized (see Code Cell 3.1).
- After starting nodes, peers are added using the blockchain APIs (see Figure 3.3).
- Peer accounts addition may be confirmed (see Figure 3.4; Code Cell 3.2) and the account balances may be checked (see Figures 3.5) by clicking the given options.
- Using these unlocked accounts, transactions can be initiated on the blockchain (see Figure 3.6).
- Transactions, the fundamental elements of the blockchain, are validated and broadcast.
- Multiple transactions form a block.
- Several blocks form a chain through a digital data link.

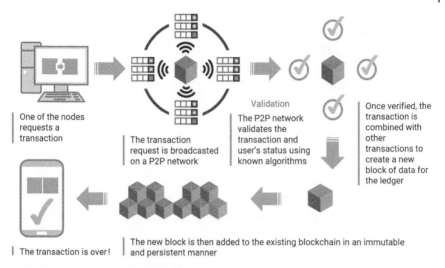

Figure 3.1 Working of blockchain.

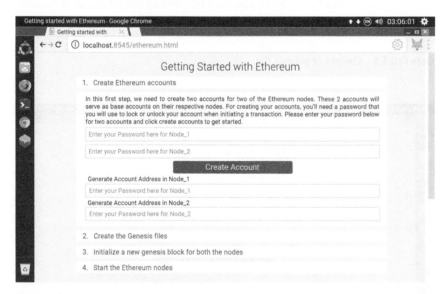

Figure 3.2 Creating blockchain account.

- Blocks go through a consensus process to select the next block to be added to the chain.
- The chosen block is verified and added to the current chain.
- The validation and consensus processes are carried out by special peer nodes called miners.

```
{
    "config":{
        "chainId": 12,
        "homesteadBlock": 0,
        "eip155Block": 0,
        "eip158Block": 0
    },
    "difficulty": "0x20000",
    "gasLimit": "0x2feed8",
    "alloc": {},
    "nonce": "0x0000000000000041",
    "timestamp": "0x0",
    "parentHash": "0x0000000000000000000000000000000000
000000000000000000000000000000",
    "extraData": "",
    "mixhash": "0x0000000000000000000000000000000000000
000000000000000000000000000",
    "coinbase": "0x0000000000000000000000000000000000000
00000"
}
```

Code Cell 3.1 Content of genesis file.

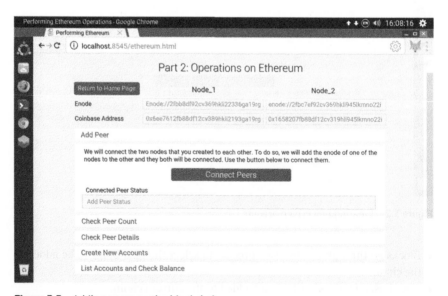

Figure 3.3 Adding peers on the blockchain.

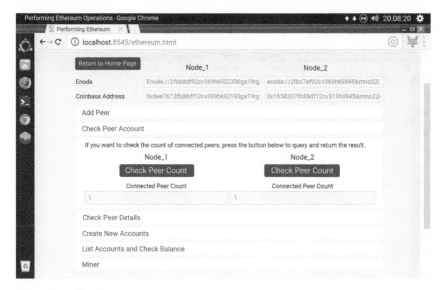

Figure 3.4 Checking peer account.

```
[
    {
      "id": "85eae04bb7cc52c04ddc78b37e564055098dbc6a
6118f469d9187428e2f3802202ed147ccb44aca7a824b8fa171c8
f2d28131ef4d12aa92e56241dd0a6448a68",
      "name": "Geth/v1.8.2-stable-4bb3c89d/linux-amd64/
go1.9",
      "caps": [
        "eth/63"
      ],
      "network": {
        "localAddress": "[::1]:35849",
        "remoteAddress": "[::1]:30302"
      },
      "protocols": {
        "eth": {
          "version": 63,
          "difficulty": 131072,
          "head": "0x5e1fc79cb4ffa4739177b5408045cd5
d51c6cf766133f23f7cd72ee1f8d790f0"
        }
      }
    }
  ]
```

Code Cell 3.2   Connected peer node – 1.

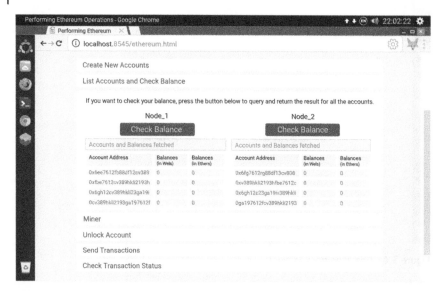

Figure 3.5   Checking account balances.

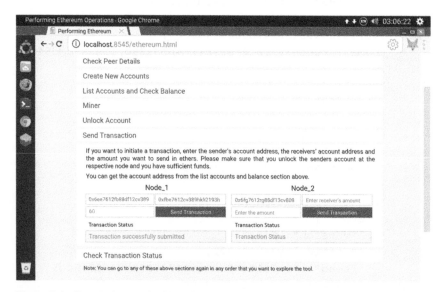

Figure 3.6   Transacting on the blockchain.

- Miners are powerful computers executing software defined by the blockchain protocol.
- Blocks are joined together with links created by referenced hashes.

3.2 Key Characteristics

Blockchain has the following key characteristics (Garg, 2021c) (see Figure 3.7):

3.2.1 Decentralization

In a blockchain, no centralized authority is required to validate the transactions. Consensus algorithms sustain data consistency in distributed networks.

3.2.2 Persistence

It is virtually impossible to delete or rollback a transaction once it is added to the blockchain. Transactions are validated quickly, and invalid transactions are not admitted by honest miners. Therefore, blocks that contain invalid transactions can be detected immediately.

3.2.3 Anonymity

Each user can transact in the blockchain using a generated address, which does not disclose the real identity of the user.

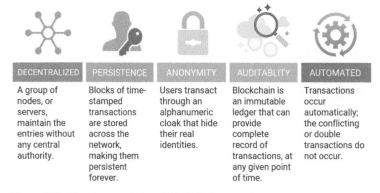

DECENTRALIZED	PERSISTENCE	ANONYMITY	AUDITABLITY	AUTOMATED
A group of nodes, or servers, maintain the entries without any central authority.	Blocks of time-stamped transactions are stored across the network, making them persistent forever.	Users transact through an alphanumeric cloak that hide their real identities.	Blockchain is an immutable ledger that can provide complete record of transactions, at any given point of time.	Transactions occur automatically; the conflicting or double transactions do not occur.

Figure 3.7 Key characteristics of blockchain.

3.2.4 Auditability

Blockchain stores data about user balances based on the Unspent Transaction Output (UTXO) model (Nakamoto, 2008). Any transaction has to refer to some previous unspent transactions.

3.3 Unspent Transaction Output

- Used to maintain the state of blockchain
- Referenced as inputs and outputs in a transaction
- Stored by all participant nodes
- Transaction is transmitted from one/more input Unspent Transaction Outputs (UTXOs) to output UTXOs (see Figure 3.8).

3.4 Classification of Blockchain on Access Management

Current blockchain systems are generally classified into three broad categories: public blockchain, private blockchain, and consortium blockchain (Buterin, 2015).

3.4.1 Public Blockchain

In a public blockchain, all records are visible to the public and each node can participate in the consensus process. Public blockchains are also known as permissionless

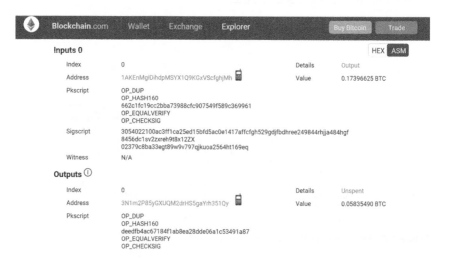

Figure 3.8 Input and output UTXOs references.

blockchains. In a public blockchain, any user, whoever wishes to transact with the network, can participate and write on the blockchain. This is quite useful for those who do not rely on any single central authority. Blockchain technology adopts a decentralized consensus mechanism to ensure the reliability and consistency of data and transactions. In an unlicensed blockchain, miners use different algorithms to validate transactions. Transactions are recorded and added to the blockchain when a majority of nodes reach consensus and approve it.

A public blockchain uses proof-of-work because it ensures that transactions cannot be tampered with as long as no single miner controls more than 50% of the network's hash power. An automated consensus mechanism allows each copy of the ledger to be updated almost instantly. Once a transaction is added to the blockchain, as all nodes share a copy of the ledger, all ledgers reflect the change.

3.4.2 Private Blockchain

In contrast, private blockchains only allow nodes coming from a specific organization to participate in the consensus process. These are also called "permissioned blockchains." Being fully controlled by one organization, it is often thought of as a centralized network. In a permissioned blockchain, the power to access, verify, and add transactions in the ledger is delegated to a limited group. There is also a possibility that in a permissioned blockchain, some users may be allowed to view all transactions in the ledger but may not have rights to write any transaction. Users can view information and transactions in the ledger, depending on their level of access.

In a permissioned blockchain, the access levels and roles of users are predetermined. Once submitted by the parties involved in a transaction, it is validated by other permitted members of the blockchain. Since private blockchain mechanisms are limited to just an organization or a group of people involved, it is easy to build consensus.

In order to make the best use of both public and private blockchain solutions, a hybrid blockchain model can also be adopted.

3.4.3 Consortium Blockchain

The consortium blockchain enables a group of pre-selected nodes to participate in the consensus process. Since only a small fraction of nodes are selected to determine consensus, the consortium blockchain built by multiple organizations is somewhat decentralized. A comparison between the three types of blockchains is listed in Table 3.1.

Table 3.1 Comparisons among public blockchain, consortium blockchain, and private blockchain.

Property	Public blockchain	Consortium blockchain	Private blockchain
Centralized	Decentralized	Partially centralized	Fully centralized
Consensus process	Permissionless (anyone can join the consensus process)	Permissioned	Permissioned
Consensus determination	All miners (each node could take part in the consensus process)	Only a selected set of nodes are responsible for validating the block	Fully controlled by one organization that could determine the final consensus
Read permission	Public	Depends, could be public or restricted	Depends, could be public or restricted
Immutability	Nearly impossible to tamper since records are stored with a large number of participants	Could be tampered easily as there is only limited number of participants	Could be tampered easily as there is only limited number of participants
Efficiency	Low (transaction throughput is limited and the latency is high because of the large number of nodes on the public blockchain network).	High (with fewer validators, the system is more efficient).	High (with fewer validators, the system is more efficient).
Examples	Bitcoin, Dash, Ethereum, IOTA, Litecoin, Monera, Steemit, Stellar, Zcash, etc.	Quorum, Hyperledger, and Corda	R3 (banks), EWF (Energy), B3i (Insurance Corda)
Miners	Don't know each other	May or may not know each other	Know each other

3.5 Consensus

A consensus mechanism is a fault tolerant mechanism, used to achieve agreement on the state of the blockchain to ensure the validity and authenticity of transactions.

In order to understand the ideology behind the creation of blockchain, one must begin with the classical problem, in the distributed system, popularly known as the Byzantine Generals Problem (BGP). According to the BGP scheme, several armies congregate to attack a castle. The castle may only be conquered if all armies attack at the same point of time. Suppose the principal army orders all the other armies to attack at a pre-determined time through a messenger. The messenger can be captured during transit and thus the message to attack the castle would never be distributed. To make sure that the message has been delivered, the sender may call for an acknowledgment, but here again, there is a possibility that the deliverer of the acknowledgment may also be detained.

Therefore, a consensus has to be reached, certifying that (i) the sender of the attack message knows that all other armies have received this message; and (ii) each army that receives this message confirms that all other armies have received this message. Now presume that instead of sending a messenger, the general sends this attack message through a blockchain. The attack is scheduled for six hours from now. The Proof-of-Work, used on this blockchain, is that if all armies work toward solving the problem at the same point of time, it will take about ten minutes for the first solution to appear. Once the general, who has sent the attack message, finds valid Proof-of-Work solutions, appearing nearly every ten minutes, he could be assured that all other armies have received the message. It is unlikely for a few armies to be producing valid Proof-of-Work solutions at this rate. At the same time, all other armies would be fully assured that every other army has seen the attack message, given the rate at which Proof-of-Work solutions are being produced.

The same logic applies to the idea of a distributed ledger. Just as the blockchain solution to the BGP ensures all parties to know that all other parties have seen a message, this rationale can be used to verify that all parties agree on the current state of a ledger (Mahmoud, Lescisin, and Taei, 2019).

In order to achieve consensus, following approaches are used:

3.5.1 Proof-of-Work

Proof-of-Work (PoW) is a consensus strategy used in the Bitcoin network (Nakamoto, 2008). In a decentralized network, some strategy has to be selected to record the transactions, for which random selection is the easiest way. However, random selection is susceptible to attacks. So, if a node wants to publish a block of transactions, a lot of work (computation) has to be done to prove that the node is not expected to attack the network.

In PoW, each node of the network calculates a hash value of the block header. The block header contains a nonce, and the miners would change the nonce recurrently to get different hash values. The consensus requires that the calculated value must be equal to or lesser than a certain given value. When one node reaches the target value, it would broadcast the block to other nodes, and all other nodes must mutually confirm the accuracy of the hash value. If the block is validated, other miners would attach this new block to their own blockchain. Nodes that calculate the hash values are called "miners," and the PoW procedure is called "mining."

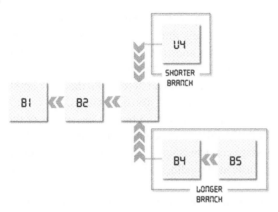

Figure 3.9 Proof-of-work – Fault tolerance mechanism.

In a decentralized network, valid blocks can be generated concurrently when multiple nodes find the appropriate nonce nearly at the same time. As a result, branches may be generated (see Figure 3.9). Even so, it is unlikely that two competing forks will form the next block concomitantly. In PoW protocol, a chain that becomes longer is judged as the authentic one. Consider two forks created by simultaneously validated blocks U4 and B4. Miners keep mining their blocks until a longer branch is generated. As B4–B5 forms a longer chain, so the miners on U4 would switch over to the longer branch. As miners need to do a lot of computer calculations in PoW, these works waste plenty of resources.

3.5.2 Proof-of-Stake

Proof-of-Stake (PoS) is an energy-saving alternative to PoW. Miners in PoS have to prove the ownership of the currency. It is assumed that people with more currencies are less likely to attack the network. However, this assumption does not seem reasonable because the single richest person can dominate the network. Consequently, several solutions were proposed with the combination of stake size to decide which one to forge the next block. Blackcoin, for instance, uses randomization to predict the next generator (Vasin, 2014). It employs a formula that looks for the lowest hash value in conjunction with the stake size. Many blockchains adopt PoW in the beginning and gradually switch to PoS (Wood, 2014; Zamphir, 2015).

3.5.3 Peercoin

Peercoin promotes coin-based selection (King and Nadal, 2012). Here, the older and larger set of coins have the greater probability of mining the next block. But, since the mining cost is almost zero, possibilities of attacks cannot be ruled out.

3.5.4 Practical Byzantine Fault Tolerance

Practical Byzantine Fault Tolerance (PBFT) is a replication algorithm to tolerate Byzantine faults (Miguel and Barbara, 1999). A new block is determined in a round. In each round, a primary would be selected according to certain rules, which is responsible for ordering transactions. The entire process can be divided into three phases: pre-prepared, prepared, and committed. In each phase, a node will enter the next phase if it has got more than two-thirds of the votes of all nodes. It's a precondition that each node is known to the network. Similar to PBFT, Stellar Consensus Protocol (SCP) is also a Byzantine agreement protocol (Mazieres, 2015). PBFT mandates each node to query other nodes while SCP provides participants the right to choose which group of other participants to trust.

3.5.5 Delegated Proof-of-Stake

Delegated Proof-of-Stake (DPoS) is representative democratic and is different from PoS, which is direct democratic. Stakeholders elect their representatives to create and validate the block. Since there are fewer nodes to validate the block, the block can be confirmed more quickly, leading to faster confirmation of transactions. Meanwhile, parameters of the network, such as block size and block interval, can be tuned by delegates. In addition, users do not have to worry about unscrupulous representatives as they can be voted off easily.

3.5.6 Ripple

It is a consensus algorithm that uses trusted sub-networks collectively within a larger network (Schwartz, Youngs, and Britto, 2014). In the network, nodes are divided into two types: servers for participating in the consensus process and clients only for transferring funds. Each server has a unique node list (UNL), which is important to the server. When deciding whether to put the transaction in the ledger, the server will query the nodes in the UNL, and if the received agreement has reached 80%, the transaction will be packed into the ledger. For a single node, the ledger will be correct, given that the percentage of faulty nodes in the UNL is less than 20%.

3.5.7 Tendermint

It is a Byzantine consensus algorithm (Kwon, 2014). In round one, a new block is determined, and a proposer will be selected to broadcast an unconfirmed block. It can be divided into three phases: pre-vote, pre-commit, and commit. During the pre-vote phase, validators choose whether to broadcast pre-votes for the proposed block. In the pre-commit phase, it is determined that if a node has received more than two-thirds of the pre-votes on a proposed block, it broadcasts a pre-commit for that block. If the node receives more than two-thirds of the pre-commit, it enters the commit phase. To finish, the node validates the block and broadcasts a commit for that block (commit phase). If the node receives two-thirds of the commit, it accepts the block. Unlike PBFT, nodes have to lock their coins in order to become validators. Once the verifier is found to be dishonest, they will be penalized.

3.5.8 Consensus Algorithms: A Comparison

Different consensus algorithms have different advantages and disadvantages (Vukolic, 2015) (see Table 3.2).

3.5.8.1 Node Identity Management
PBFT needs to know the identity of each miner in order to select a primary in each round, while Tendermint needs to know the validators in order to select a proposer in each round. For PoW, PoS, DPOS, and Ripple, nodes can connect to the network independently.

3.5.8.2 Energy Saving
In PoW, miners hash the block header nonstop to reach the target value. As an effect, the electricity requirement touches maxima on scale. In PoS and DPOS, miners have to hash the block header to find the target value, but the work is largely

Table 3.2 Comparisons among Typical Consensus Algorithms.

Property	PoW	PoS	PBFT	DPOS	Ripple	Tendermint
Node identity management	Open	Open	Permissioned	Open	Open	Permissioned
Energy saving	No	Partial	Yes	Partial	Yes	Yes
Tolerated power of adversary	<25% computing power	<51% stake	<33.3% faulty replicas	<51% validators	<20% Faulty nodes in UNL	<33.3% Byzantine voting power
Example	Bitcoin (Nakamoto, 2008)	Peercoin (King and Nadal, 2012)	Hyperledger Fabric (HPL, 2015)	Bitshares	Ripple (Schwartz, Youngs, Britto, 2014)	Tendermint (Kwon, 2014)

reduced due to limited search space. For PBFT, Ripple, and Tendermint, since there is no mining in the consensus process, an enormous amount of energy is saved.

3.5.8.3 Tolerated Power of Adversary

In general, 51% hash power is considered as the threshold for gaining control over the network. But selfish mining strategy in PoW systems could help miners to gain more revenue with hardly 25% of the hashing power (Eyal and Sirer, 2014). PBFT and Tendermint can handle up to one-third faulty nodes. Ripple is capable of maintaining correctness, if the faulty nodes in a UNL are less than 20%.

3.5.9 Advances in Consensus Algorithms

A good consensus algorithm means efficiency, security, and convenience. In recent times, there has been a tremendous surge in efforts to improve consensus algorithms in blockchain. More and more consensus algorithms are being devised to solve some of the specific problems of blockchain (Zheng et al., 2017).

One of these new ideas is peer census (Decker, Seidel, and Wattenhofer, 2016). It aims to decouple block creation and transaction confirmations in order to increase the speed of consensus. Besides, Kraft (2016) has suggested a new consensus scheme to ensure that a block is generated at a fairly stable speed, assuming that a high rate of block generation may compromise Bitcoin's security.

In a further advancement, Sompolinsky and Zohar (2013) have recommended a Greedy Heaviest-Observed Subtree (GHOST) chain selection rule to solve this problem. In this method, instead of the longest branch scheme, GHOST weighs the branches, and the miners can choose the better one to follow. Chepurnoy, Larangeira, and Ojiganov (2016) also introduced a new consensus algorithm for peer-to-peer blockchain systems, where anyone who provides non-interactive proofs of retrievability for the past state snapshots, is allowed to generate a block. In such a protocol, the miners have to store the old block headers only, and not the entire blocks.

3.6 Payment Verification in Blockchain

3.6.1 Simple Payment Verification

Simple payment verification (SPV) is a process that enables a lightweight client to verify whether a transaction is on the Bitcoin blockchain without having to download the entire blockchain. An SPV client only needs to download the block headers, which are much smaller than the entire block. The SPV client requests the Merkle branch to test whether the transaction has been included in the block. SPV clients provide better security than web wallets.

3.6.1.1 Key Features

- It is easy and more practical to know the longest chain without becoming a miner.
- A user has to preserve just a copy of the longest proof-of-work chain's block headers and retrieve the Merkle branch that connects the transaction to the block.
- Although a user cannot test a transaction for himself, he can still see if it has been approved by a network node. He can tie the transaction to a point in the chain and stop it.
- Thus, as long as the network is controlled by honest nodes, verification is reliable, although it becomes vulnerable as soon as an attacker takes control of the network.
- The simplified approach can be adulterated or destroyed as long as the attacker is successful in maintaining dominance over the network.
- The singular way to defend the process is to accept warnings from network nodes when they identify an incorrect block, force the user's program to download the whole block, or notify transactions to validate the discrepancy.

3.6.2 Full Payment Verification

Payment verification, in its totality, requires a complete copy of the blockchain, often referred to as a coarse or heavyweight wallet. It helps to verify whether the Bitcoins used in the transaction came from a mined block. Here, the blockchain is scanned transaction by transaction in retrospect, until they find the source.

3.6.2.1 Key Features

These wallet applications act as active players in the Bitcoin network. They not only manage the user's transactions but also verify and relay the trades of other individuals. In such situations, computers executing these applications are called full nodes.

Full nodes are all Bitcoin miners, which means they need a complete copy of the blockchain to mine.

So far, the blockchain has grown to ≥15 GB in size and included 35 million transactions within five years. The technology is likely to grow over hundred times in the next five years.

Depending on its bandwidth, it can take several days for the blockchain network to be downloaded through the Bitcoin wallet application.

This requires all parties (all nodes) on the network to be connected to present their individual findings and to determine which blockchain has the highest proof-of-work to reach consensus.

3.7 Hashgraph

It addresses the problem of efficient consensus algorithms from the point of view of security and power consumption. It uses an Asynchronous Byzantine Fault Tolerance algorithm that can confirm transactions within five seconds (no transaction records required) as opposed to about 70 minutes for Proof-of-Work in Bitcoins.

3.7.1 Elements of Hashgraph

1) Event
2) Transaction
3) Directed acyclic graph
4) Round
5) Participant node
6) Witness: both famous and nonfamous witnesses
7) Consensus (derived or computed) by voting.

3.7.2 Diagrammatic Representation

Hashgraph also uses timestamps to order transactions after the round. The vertical bars indicate the time dimension in the hashgraph. The direction of the time axis is from bottom to top. Rounds of events assist in the virtual voting process. The round number is accessed as the round-Created value.

The event is depicted as a filled circle (see Figure 3.10) and has the following characteristics:

1) Event ID
2) Hashes of sender and receiver parents

The lines joining the events are known as transactions.

3.7.3 How Does Hashgraph Work?

1) The first event in a round created by each participant is called a witness. It may later qualify to become a famous or nonfamous witness, depending on what is witnessed by subsequent events.

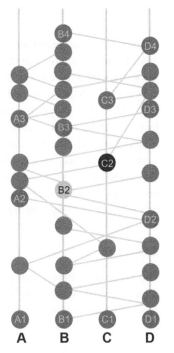

Figure 3.10 Limenberg's representation of hashgraph.

2) "Seeing" means that there is a path down to all witnesses from an event. By "strongly seeing," it is indicated that one event outperforms the other event by the supermajority of participants.

3) If the event can see all or a supermajority of witnesses of a round R, then roundCreated is incremented by one.

4) After creation of a new round, the fame of the previous witnesses is categorized as famous or not-famous.

5) Votes are counted on the basis of fame status, graph structure, and results of perseverance.

6) Events are arranged i.e., roundReceived and Median timestamps are assigned, which in turn arrange transactions.

3.8 Scalability

With the ever-increasing volume of transactions, the blockchain becomes heavy. Due to the inherent restrictions of block size and the time lag for generating a new block, the Bitcoin blockchain can process around seven transactions per second, failing to meet the need to process millions of transactions on a real-time basis. Therefore, there can be only two alternatives: one is storage optimization and the other is redesigning.

Bruce (2014) proposed a new cryptocurrency scheme, in which old transaction records are deleted (or forgotten) by the network. This is important because it is not so easy for a node to operate a full copy of the ledger.

Eyal et al. (2016) proposed Bitcoin-Next Generation to decouple the conventional block into two parts: the major block to elect the leader; and the microblocks for transaction storage. Time is divided into epochs, and in each epoch, miners have to hash, in order to create a major block. Once a key block is generated, the node becomes the leader, responsible for generating the microblock. Bitcoin-NG also expanded the longest chain strategy with microblocks carrying no weight. Thus, by redesigning the blockchain, the trade-off between block size and network security is being addressed.

Coming up

The preceding chapter has provided an outline of the blockchain architecture, design, and representation. The next chapter deals with the in-depth analysis of blockchain at the transaction level from financial and programmable perspectives.

References

Boucher P, 2017. How blockchain technology could change our lives. *European Parliamentary Research Service*, 1–24. https://epthinktank.eu/2017/03/01/how-blockchain-technology-could-change-our-lives/Accessed on 01 March 2017.

Bruce JD, 2014. The Mini Blockchain Scheme (Revised 2017). https://cryptonite.info/files/mbc-scheme-rev3.pdf/.

Buterin V, 2015. A Next-Generation Smart Contract and Decentralized Application Platform. White paper, 1-36. https://blockchainlab.com/pdf/Ethereum_white_paper-a_next_generation_smart_contract_and_decentralized_application_platform-vitalik-buterin.pdf/Accessed on 03 June 2020.

Chepurnoy A, Larangeira M, and Ojiganov A, 2016. A Prunable Blockchain Consensus Protocol Based on Non-Interactive Proofs of past States Retrievability. https://www.researchgate.net/publication/301878891_A_Prunable_Blockchain_Consensus_Protocol_Based_on_Non-Interactive_Proofs_of_Past_States_Retrievability/.

Decker C, Seidel J, and Wattenhofer R, 2016. Bitcoin Meets Strong Consistency. Proceedings of the 17th International Conference on Distributed Computing & Networking Singapore, 13.

Eyal I, Gencer AE, Sirer EG, and Van Renesse R, 2016. Bitcoining: A Scalable Blockchain Protocol. Proceedings of the 13th USENIX Symposium on Networked Systems Design and Implementation, Santa Clara CA, 45–59.

Eyal I and Sirer EG, 2014. Majority Is Not Enough: Bitcoin Mining Is Vulnerable. Proceedings of International Conference on Financial Cryptography and Data Security, Berlin, 436–454.

Garg R, 2021a. *Distributed Framework for Real World Applications*. Barnes & Noble, Basking Ridge, New Jersey US, 1–126.

Garg R, 2021b. Ethereum Based Smart Contracts for Trade and Finance. International Conference on Blockchain and Smart Contracts, Bangkok Thailand. doi: 10.5281/zenodo.5854730 https://www.researchgate.net/publication/357510533_Ethereum_based_Smart_Contracts_for_Trade_Finance/Accessed on 02 February 2022.

Garg R, 2021c. *Identités Auto-souveraines*. Editions Notre Savoir, France, 1–104.

Hyperledger, 2015. Hyperledger: Open Source Blockchain Technologies. https://www.hyperledger.org/ Accessed on 01 December 2020.

King S and Nadal S, 2012. PPCoin: Peer-to-Peer Cryptocurrency with Proof-of-Stake, 19. https://decred.org/research/king2012.pdf.

Kraft D, 2016. Difficulty control for blockchain based consensus systems. *Peer-to-Peer Networking and Applications*, 9 (2): 397–413.

Kwon J, 2014. Tendermint: Consensus without Mining. https://tendermint.com/static/docs/tendermint.pdf.

Lewis A and Larson M, 2016. Understanding blockchain technology and what it means for your business. DBS Asian Insights. https://www.dbs.com/.

Lewis R, McPartland J, and Ranjan R, 2017. Blockchain and Financial Market Innovation. In *Economic Perspectives*, 41: 7. https://www.chicagofed.org/publications/economic-perspectives/2017/7.

Mahmoud QH, Lescisin M, and Taei MA, 2019. Research Challenges and Opportunities in Blockchain and Cryptocurrencies. *Internet Technology Letters. Wiley US*, 2 (93): 01–06.

Mazieres D, 2015. *The Stellar Consensus Protocol: A Federated Model for Internet-Level Consensus*. Stellar Development Foundation. http://www.scs.stanford.edu/17au-cs244b/notes/scp.pdf.

Miguel C and Barbara L, 1999. Practical Byzantine Fault Tolerance. Proceedings of the 3rd Symposium on Operating Systems Design and Implementation, New Orleans, (99) 173–186.

Nakamoto S, 2008. Bitcoin: A Peer-to-Peer Electronic Cash System. https://bitcoin.org/bitcoin.pdf.

Schwartz D, Youngs N, and Britto A, 2014. *The Ripple Protocol Consensus Algorithm*. Ripple Labs Inc. White Paper, 5. https://ripple.com/files/ripple_consensus_whitepaper.pdf.

Singh S and Singh N, 2016. Blockchain: Future of Financial and Cyber Security. 2nd International Conference on Contemporary Computing and Informatics, India, 463–467.

Sompolinsky Y and Zohar A, 2013. Accelerating bitcoins transaction processing. Fast money grows on trees, not chains. *IACR Cryptology e-Print Archive* . https://eprint.iacr.org/2013/881.

Vasin P, 2014. Blackcoins Proof-of-Stake Protocol. https://blackcoin.org/blackcoin-pos-protocol-v2-whitepaper.pdf.

Vukolic M, 2015. The Quest for Scalable Blockchain Fabric: Proof-of-Work vs BFT Replication. International Workshop on Open Problems in Network Security, Zurich, 112–125.

Wood G, 2014. Ethereum: A Secure Decentralized Generalized Transaction Ledger. Ethereum Project Yellow Paper. https://ethereum.github.io/yellowpaper/paper.pdf.

Zamfir V, 2015. Introducing Casper the Friendly Ghost. Ethereum Blog. https://blog.ethereum.org/2015/08/01/introducing-casper-friendly-ghost/.

Zheng Z, Xie S, Dai H, Chen X, and Wang H, 2017. An Overview of Blockchain Technology: Architecture, Consensus, and Future Trends. IEEE 6th International Congress on Big Data, 01–08.

4

Transactions in Bitcoin Blockchain

Cryptocurrencies are digital tokens or currencies transacted on a blockchain, such as Bitcoin, Ethereum, or Litecoin, which can be used to purchase assets, goods, and services, just like cash. However, cryptocurrencies use blockchain to achieve the benefits of a public ledger as well as an advanced cryptographic security system so that online transactions are always chronicled and secure.

Cryptocurrencies can be used digitally to pay for everything from ordinary goods to real estate. Goods can be bought or transferred digitally using a digital wallet or trading platform. Blockchain creates an undisputed, timestamped, and secure track by recording buyer-sellers and transactions in a public ledger.

At present, there are over 18,000 cryptocurrencies in the world with a total market cap of approximately US$ 3.2 trillion. These currencies have gained incredible popularity over the years, with the result that today one Bitcoin is worth US$ 45,410.50.

4.1   Coinbase Transactions

All transactions that occur on a cryptocurrency network are not necessarily a consequence of payment between two people. Some of these transactions are somewhat different. The first transaction in the blockchain took place in Bitcoin. It was a special transaction that allocated reward transactions for miners inside the first block of the blockchain, called the "genesis block." These reward transactions are typically given to miners as an incentive or reward for their work. This type of transaction is known as a Coinbase transaction. These transactions generate new currencies, which have never been spent (for example, the printing of fiat currencies).

Blockchain for Real World Applications, First Edition. Rishabh Garg.
© 2023 John Wiley & Sons, Inc. Published 2023 by John Wiley & Sons, Inc.

When the first genesis block of Bitcoin was mined by Nakamoto (2008, he created a coinbase with a value of 50 BTC based on the halving factor prevailing at that time and made the payment to the Bitcoin address "1A1zP1eP5QGefi2DMPTf TL5SLmv7DivfNa." However, this block was never confirmed, and the reward paid at the given address could not be spent. Although blockchain developers and experts could not find the reason, it can be safely assumed that the first Coinbase transaction was encoded in the source code of Bitcoin's genesis block, on which the entire blockchain is built. Hence, the concept of confirmation is not applicable for this block.

4.1.1 Structure

In the event of a Coinbase transaction, new currencies are created but are never spent. As a result, the input remains blank in such transactions. Such a single blank input of a coinbase transaction is called "The Coinbase."

Let us take an example of a coinbase transaction. The screenshots show the demo data (see Figure 4.1) and its different credentials (see Figure 4.2). The data given in the figures do not indicate any factual transaction.

Unlike the other cryptocurrency transactions, the coinbase (transaction entry) is not linked with the address of any other holder or sender (see Figure 4.3). The transaction points to the cryptocurrency wallet address of the original miner and can point to more than one wallet address as per the miner's choice. The block reward is collected that includes the fees charged by the user for each transaction (see Figure 4.4).

Figure 4.1 Input of raw data.

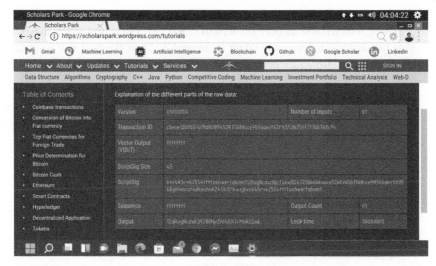

Figure 4.2 Different subdivisions of the raw data.

a0a3466328807cdca1cda1a4b0232a8ed602f0a24dcc6ad3096b818		0 Satoshi SV Byte	Fee: 0 BTC
Input (1)	0BTC	Output	6.48096601 BTC
		12dRugNcdxK39288NjcDV4GX7rMsKCGn68	6.48096601
		SegWit commitment output	0
Coinbase	0	Unable to decode output address	0
		Unable to decode output address	0

Figure 4.3 Instance of a real coinbase transaction.

4.1.2   Key Features of Coinbase Transactions

- A Coinbase transaction is usually the first transaction in a new block. Like a normal cryptocurrency transaction, the reward generated from this transaction can also be sent to one or multiple wallet addresses.
- After a certain number of successful blocks are added to the blockchain, the reward for each successful block added is halved, or 50% (see Figure 4.5). In Bitcoin, this event occurs after every 210,000 successful blocks are mined. By reducing the rewards of mining Bitcoins or by limiting the number of Bitcoins, the supply of coins is limited, thereby keeping demand strong and increasing the potential for prices to rise.

- At the very outset, the reward for each successful block of Bitcoin was 50 BTC per block, which has since been reduced to 25 BTC, 12.5 BTC, and now 6.25 BTC. This rate is expected to come down to around 3.125 in the next two to three years. In early 2020, 12.5 new Bitcoins were added to the network every ten

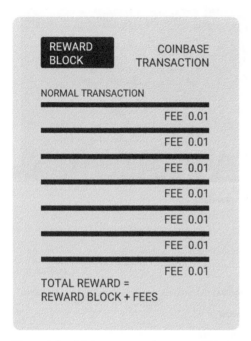

Figure 4.4 Coinbase transaction: reward block.

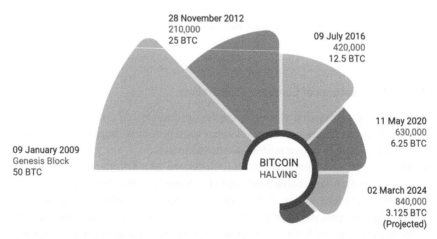

Figure 4.5 Bitcoin halving.

minutes through virtual mining and this process would continue until all 21 million coins are mined. The reward for each Coinbase transaction is determined by the corresponding value.

- Rewards earned by Coinbase transactions cannot be spent until they reach a certain number of confirmations in the blockchain. In the case of Bitcoin, this number is 100. This means, a Bitcoin earned through Coinbase transactions can only be spent if it has received a minimum of 100 confirmations on the blockchain.

- This precondition is set to avoid an event called a fork. In the absence of a certain number of confirmations, a miner will be able to make as much BTC as he can. To prevent the blockchain from being forked, a condition has been placed so that a Coinbase transaction can only be spent if it receives more than or equal to a certain number of confirmations.

4.1.3 Computation of Transaction Value

- To calculate the value of a Coinbase transaction, the value of each input and output of a transaction validated by a specific block is summed.

- The number of transactions in the block, that is, the height of the block, is taken into account. The more transactions there are, the higher are the commissions and fees.

- The miner creates the Coinbase transaction, which includes the fees and the total reward.

- Fees are calculated based on the current pricing tier at the time the order is placed (you are in) and not the tier after the trade has ended (you will be in it). The reward is roughly equal to half the relative.

- Finally, miners have to wait for a certain number of confirmations to produce and complete the value of a Coinbase transaction.

4.2 Transactions Involving Fiat Currency

Bitcoin is not a legal tender issued by the government. It is a cryptocurrency backed by blockchain technology and independent of any central authority. There can be several reasons for exchanging Bitcoins for fiat currency:

- Fiat currency is the most common and popular form of currency around the world, which leads to more liquidity and flexibility with the money.

- One can fetch profit from the favorable market conditions like a bull run on Bitcoin's price.

- Ease of trade and payment of liabilities with fiat currency.

For exchange with fiat currency, for example US$ – the first party sends its money to the second, and the other party receives Bitcoins. This process goes through the blockchain.

There can be several ways to convert Bitcoin to fiat currency, some of which are listed here:

4.2.1 Cryptocurrency Exchanges

Cryptocurrency exchanges are decentralized systems that do not collapse to a single point of failure. This is a forex counter-like scenario, where a person exchanges money while moving from one country to another. Cryptocurrency exchanges are commonly used to convert Bitcoin into local currency, such as US$, euros, etc. Although the operation and adoption of digital coins is increasing rapidly, the number of transactions processed each day is still not very encouraging. Moreover, high exchange rates, lack of liquidity, difficulty in withdrawing money even after the completion of the transaction, go against crypto exchanges.

Cryptocurrency exchanges have an inherent crypto converter feature that depicts how much fiat currency one can get with the Bitcoins that he holds. Some of these exchanges like Gemini, Coinbase Exchange, Binance, etc. have user-friendly interfaces. However, in the event of a bull run, these exchanges run down with technical hitches. Coinbase Exchange is a better option as it has overcome the problem of downtime by increasing its infrastructure capacity. It ensures a hassle-free remittance of converted fiat money directly into the user's bank account.

4.2.2 Bitcoin Debit Card

The Bitcoin debit card is the fastest way to convert Bitcoin into cash or fiat currency. Know Your Customer (KYC) for a Bitcoin debit card can be done by contacting the bank. For easy exchange, there are user-friendly websites. The user can deposit Bitcoins through the user interface, and the website automatically converts the Bitcoins to the desired fiat currency. Bitcoin debit cards can be used on sites where debit cards are accepted (see Figure 4.6). It differs from a bank exchange in that the funds are transferred from a crypto wallet instead of a bank account. Bitcoin debit cards charge transaction fees on each purchase and set a maximum transaction limit.

4.2.3 Bitcoin ATMs

A Bitcoin ATM, also known as a Bitcoin teller machine, operates like a normal ATM. It differs from normal ATMs in that it allows the user to buy and

Figure 4.6 Bitcoin debit card.

exchange cryptocurrencies with fiat money. It operates blockchain-based transactions and often sends the cryptocurrency to a user's digital wallet via a QR code.

It is a fast and convenient way to withdraw cash from a Bitcoin wallet, with additional security features like text messages to ensure easy and secure transactions. However, BTMs levy heavy fees on conversions and allow a limited amount of transactions per card.

4.2.4   Metal Pay

Metal Pay is a money transfer app for blockchain-based payments and reward wallets for digital assets. It provides the facility to buy and sell over 50 cryptocurrencies, including Bitcoin. Through this app, users can link their bank account, complete their KYC, add cash, and start trading. Metal Pay users can buy crypto instantly without waiting for the bank to finish their transaction.

4.2.5   Peer-to-Peer Exchanges

Since Bitcoin has no centralized authority, funds can be transferred from one peer to another. Instead of using an order book to match up buy and sell orders, and thus controlling all the funds being used on the exchange platform itself, peer-to-peer exchanges match buyers and sellers without holding any funds during the trade. It basically involves a buyer who will buy your Bitcoins and give you cash in return.

Transferring Bitcoins is as easy as a bank fund transfer. All you need to do is copy the recipient's address and paste this address into the send field of the Bitcoin wallet app you are using. But, be careful! Transactions in Bitcoin are irreversible, so choose a buyer who you can trust to remit cash after a Bitcoin transaction.

4.3 Top Fiat Currencies for Bitcoin Transactions

The most traded national currencies (see Figure 4.7) for trading Bitcoin are:

4.3.1 US Dollar

The US dollar consistently ranks first on the list of fiat currencies trading Bitcoins, with around 85.5% of the market share. The major reason for this is the huge user base in the blockchain-based Bitcoin network, which has rapidly penetrated the country. While other countries are yet to gain momentum in the Bitcoin arena, the USA hopped far ahead in this race.

4.3.2 Japanese Yen

With around 7% market share, the Japanese yen is the second most widely used fiat currency in Bitcoin trading. Japanese regulators were also some of the earliest adopters and were quite proactive in introducing the necessary regulations, enabling it to grab a decent share of the global market.

Figure 4.7 Top fiat currencies in the world.

4.3.3 Euro

The euro, the currency of Europe, ranks third in the order with approximately 4.7% market share in Bitcoin trading. But Europeans are confined to certain regions only while buying Bitcoins. The German city of Berlin, the Netherlands, and Belgium have been large hubs for cryptocurrency, while some other European nations are on the verge of acceptance.

4.3.4 Korean Won

The South Korean won (KRW) ranks fourth with 3.2% of the market share in Bitcoin trading. The trading has declined significantly over the last three years since the country's regulators have banned cryptocurrency traders from using anonymous bank accounts in Korea.

4.3.5 Chinese Yuan

Interestingly, the Chinese yuan no longer ranks among the top fiat currencies used to trade Bitcoins. In 2014 and 2015, China devalued its yuan that surged it to the top, thrashing the Japanese yen as well as the US dollar. Due to multiple bans imposed by the Chinese government on China-based Bitcoin exchanges since 2017, all those Bitcoin trading activities from China swiftly moved to other venues, helping Japan the most, followed by Hong Kong.

4.3.6 Indian National Rupee

In India, regulators were slow to adopt the development of Bitcoin. Furthermore, individuals who hold Bitcoins, either directly or through intermediaries, need to first convert INR to US$ to buy Bitcoins.

4.4 Price Determination for Bitcoin in Transactions

Bitcoin is neither issued nor regulated by any central authority and is therefore not subject to monetary policies, inflation rates, and economic measures that typically apply to currency. The price of Bitcoin is primarily influenced by its supply, market demand, availability, and competing cryptocurrencies. It is fundamentally different from fiat currency or stocks. Buying stock gives you ownership in a company, whereas buying Bitcoin gives you ownership of that cryptocurrency. Therefore, the price of Bitcoin is influenced by a few technical factors apart from the regular financial factors:

- The cost at which Bitcoin is mined
- Bitcoin supply and market demand for it
- Rewards payable to Bitcoin miners for verifying transactions in the blockchain
- The exchanges on which it trades
- Number of competing cryptocurrencies, such as Ethereum, Dogecoin, XRP, etc.
- Regulatory provisions for sale and use
- Internal governance

4.4.1   Cost of Mining Bitcoin

The cost of one Bitcoin is estimated by computing the average marginal cost of producing a Bitcoin at a given time, based on the block reward, the price of electricity, the energy efficiency of the mining hardware, and indirect costs related to the difficulty level of its algorithm.

The cost of electricity is a major factor as miners use vast amounts of electricity for computation power; low electricity price supports and benefits the miners. Algorithms constitute an indirect cost because different difficulty levels of an algorithm can speed up or slow down the rate of mining and thus affect its price.

4.4.2   Market Supply and Demand

As the value of the US dollar is determined, so is the price of Bitcoin supply and demand. Similar to fiat currency, when the demand for Bitcoin increases, the price rises, and conversely as the demand for Bitcoin decreases, so does the price.

However, Bitcoin is a unique asset because its flow is absolutely rigid. When most goods, including gold and fiat currency, are in high demand, producers bring prices back into equilibrium by increasing production and taking corrective measures. But in the case of Bitcoin, its fresh supply schedule is completely resistant to fluctuations in demand. When the demand for Bitcoins increases, the production of new Bitcoins does not increase.

When Nakamoto created Bitcoin, he established a strict limit on the number of Bitcoins, known as hard caps that could ever exist. The total number of Bitcoins cannot exceed 21 million at any one time. Thus, it is possible to create new Bitcoins only at a fixed rate, which is bound to decrease over time. This hard cap causes demand to exceed supply and puts more pressure on the price. This enhances the confidence of investors that inflation will begin in the upcoming times.

4.4.3   Bitcoin Rewards

The Bitcoin protocol allows the mining of Bitcoins at a group rate. Bitcoin block rewards are new Bitcoins awarded to a miner for being the first to solve a complex puzzle and for creating a new block of verified Bitcoin transactions. The miner uses computational power to do this and is paid in terms of transaction fees and block rewards. A block reward is the amount of Bitcoin rewarded for completing a block on the blockchain.

As miners process blocks of transactions, new Bitcoins are added to the market, and the rate at which new coins are introduced is programmed to decrease their creation-flow over time. The rewards of Bitcoin mining halve roughly every four years. In 2009, when Bitcoin was first mined, the value of reward or incentive was 50.00 BTC, which was slashed down to 25.00 BTC in 2012 and further halved to 12.50 BTC in 2016. Since May 2020, this price is prevailing at 6.25 BTC. The value of the reward has an effect on pricing.

4.4.4 Exchanges

The sum of Bitcoins traded on exchanges represents a small share of the aggregate supply in circulation, which affects its price. Popularity of money raises prices, while less demand for money causes prices to fall. In addition, due to the lack of efficient management of money in exchanges, compensation is sometimes required. This prevents traders from maintaining a uniform arbitrage across exchanges, and thus reflects variations in the market price.

4.4.5 Competing Cryptocurrencies

Although Bitcoin is the most popular cryptocurrency, many other cryptocurrencies such as Dogecoin, XRP, and Ethereum are threatening its dominance. During the initial phase, Bitcoin trading conquered the cryptocurrency markets, but now it is losing its dominance over time.

Bitcoin, the world's largest cryptocurrency, which accounted for more than 80% of the total market cap of the crypto market in 2017, has shrunk to less than 40% in 2022, following the popularity of Ether.

Ethereum's Ether (ETHUSD) has emerged as a formidable competitor to Bitcoin, thanks to the boom in decentralized finance (DeFi) tokens. Ether, a cryptocurrency used as "gas" for transactions on its network, accounts for over 17% of the overall market capitalization of the crypto market.

Ripple's XRP (XRPUSD) and Cardano's ADA (ADAUSD) have also risen, with Stablecoins drawing investors to Binance's BNB token (BNBUSD).

4.4.6 Regulatory Provisions

Bitcoin exists in a nonregulated market with no centralized issuing authority. It does not demand a Social Security number (SSN), a standard bank account, a tax account number, or a unique identification number as proof of address. The absence of regulation allows cross-border transactions without government-imposed restrictions, as is the case with other currencies. But it also invites criminal consequences in many financial jurisdictions.

In this sense, regulation appears to be the most important factor affecting the price of a cryptocurrency. Every time a government, be it China or South Korea, tried to introduce regulations for cryptocurrency trading, Bitcoin declined.

4.4.7 Internal Governance

Bitcoin is not a stable protocol that is controlled by a central authority. It is a decentralized process implemented at the developer level to decide which changes are eligible to be incorporated and how. This is quite different from the centralized system prevalent in the nations of the world, where decisions are made in a top-down manner.

In fact, the process of developing or refining the Bitcoin protocol is a consensus formation, where deliberation and coercion are important, but participants always have the option to opt-out. In general, unless the majority of participants agree to make the change, the change cannot be made, and even then, those who wish to go along with the change are always free to go their own way. This implies that anyone who is able to submit a Bitcoin Improvement Proposal (BIP) can do so for consideration, and if the proposed changes are not appreciable, the entire protocol can be forked with relative ease.

Furthermore, all nodes and miners are free to choose the clients they wish to run. The client, with greater mutual consent, becomes the canonical chain. While it has many advantages, there are some disadvantages too. Since the changes can be introduced through a process of consensus, it takes too long to solve fundamental issues like scalability. At present, Bitcoin software processes hardly three transactions per second, which is too slow. Whenever the community innovates on technologies to speed up transaction rates, an entirely new cryptocurrency often emerges.

4.4.8 Value of Bitcoin

An intrinsic value of a product is the value that it possesses in itself and that it does not require any supplementary sources to earn it. Every item earns its value if there is a price people would pay to obtain it. Bitcoin is a commodity limited to only 21 million, and this limit makes Bitcoin valuable to the extent that it is extremely rare compared to fiat currency or gold. For example, the total value of all the Bitcoins in circulation is just US$ 175 billion while the total value of gold that exists is US$ 8,800 billion. So, it is likely to sustain value (see Figure 4.8 for its

Figure 4.8 Bitcoin value.

value in April 2022). Investors are crying out for a share of the ever-increasing profit that may result from trading its limited supply.

Yet more important is the fact that Bitcoin operates on an imminent technology – the blockchain. Blockchain is a publicly available distributed ledger in which all transactions are held in an immutable, auditable, and tamper-proof manner. These transactions are verified by so-called miners who add only valid transactions to the blockchain and are thus rewarded with Bitcoins. It is a technology that has the potential to solve fundamental problems in countless domains, such as identity management, education and employment verification, health care, transportation, real estate, securities trading, and so on. Bitcoin is one of its applications.

4.4.9 Can the Bitcoin Price Be Zero?

Assuming the price of Bitcoin to be absolutely zero is a huge task that seems almost impossible. Bitcoin has mostly gone up and to the right, with its price rising from basically zero to as high as US$ 60,000 in a decade. Bitcoin, the native cryptocurrency, is now one of the largest currencies in the world, and in a very short time has become one of the most lucrative assets of all time.

Despite its unmatched growth, Bitcoin skeptics believe that it is only a matter of time that Bitcoin will eventually fall to zero. This incredulity is based on the fact that Bitcoin has neither the backing of physical commodities nor an administrative system. Some even argue that Bitcoin will collapse to zero because it has no intrinsic value (not backed by a physical commodity like gold). But the question arises whether fiat currencies like the US$ and GB£, which were once backed by gold, are still backed by any valuables today? Bitcoin enthusiasts opine that the cryptocurrency is backed by consumer confidence and mathematics – the number of users.

In recent years, there's been a gush of institutional investment in Bitcoin, with companies including Aker ASA, MicroStrategy, Square, and Tesla buying Bitcoin for their corporate reserves. Such institutional investment can be viewed as an indication of its looming stability.

Another point of concern is that Bitcoin could be superseded by a more advanced cryptocurrency or a parallel payment system, which could render it useless as an asset or as a method of payment. But it will take many years for such conditions to be created, and then such possibilities can be a threat to any currency or payment method. In addition, Bitcoin has a lot of deployment potential, such that there could be an option to universally hold or transfer Bitcoin's reserves underground, or one could use its reserves in tranches. In any case, the value of Bitcoin will remain, if not in the form of money, then at least as a historical artifact for future generations.

One possibility, which points to the near-zero value of Bitcoin, is that all governments in the world may outright invalidate the ownership, use, or transaction of Bitcoin. At present, the governments of many countries have taken such steps. But this would require them to bring down the entire Bitcoin network, rendering all nodes offline, including the ones that are in space, and then setting up the network anew. All of this would be very difficult.

Critics also claim that Bitcoin is actually an elaborate scam, coined by some unethical entities with the aim of siphoning off users' hard-earned money. Some scholars, including Warren Buffet and Mark Cuban, believe that Bitcoin has been overvalued while its utility is little or none at all.

Characterizing network effects, Metcalfe's law states, "the value of a telecommunications network is proportional to the square of the number of connected users of the system." This implies that with the exponential growth of Bitcoin wallets, Bitcoin's utility is likely to grow faster. The cryptocurrency that was initially used for peer-to-peer barter and online trading, now has an entire ecosystem of DeFi tools, with myriad use-cases that increase its usefulness even further.

4.4.10 Why Is Bitcoin's Price Volatile?

Bitcoin is in its infancy when compared to other types of investment instruments and currencies. It takes time for any new concepts to settle down and behave accordingly, and the same is true for cryptocurrencies.

Cryptos have gained global prestige or notoriety over the past decade, but as an asset class, they are not as welcomed as other traditional assets, such as equities or gold. Market acceptability and maturity complement each other. Since investors are still moving with the market, it is not possible to have steady prices at such an early stage.

Unlike fiat currency, some cryptocurrencies are in limited supply. Bitcoin has a maximum supply of 21 million, Litecoin's supply is limited to 84 million, while

Chainlink's (Ethereum-based) maximum limit is one billion. Given the limited supply, some organizations tend to go for major holdings and thus inflate the prices. Sometimes institutions holding coins in large quantities start selling them, which leads to a fall in the prices. Such accounts are called "whales" because they have a large holding and have the ability to influence the market. Since Bitcoin is one of the most popular cryptocurrencies, demand and supply play an important role in pricing.

Furthermore, investors are constantly trying to experiment with their funds to predict the dynamics that are responsible for volatility in cryptocurrency prices. Investors place bets when prices go up or down, and these speculations cause sudden inflows or outflows, leading to high volatility. As cryptocurrencies become more popular, more and more investors will be able to understand the factors that determine their impetus. Until then, these undercurrents will remain speculative as investors are buying and selling according to the market sentiments.

For instance, a new investor, in anticipation of a rise in price, buys Bitcoins before the price increases, in the excitement that when the price rises, he will be able to sell these Bitcoins at a higher profit per share. This type of consumer speculation leads to an increase in the market cap of Bitcoin.

Conversely, when the price of Bitcoin begins to drop, people anticipate bearishness and want to sell their Bitcoins before the price drops further and a massive sell-off occurs. The price of Bitcoin often falls in parallel as consumer confidence declines. Investors, who own Bitcoins, are scared to see the price falling and often want to sell their Bitcoins before they make a loss without examining the market, and in turn, the price keeps falling.

4.5 Controlling Transaction Costs in Bitcoin

Bitcoin was a peer-to-peer cryptocurrency used for daily transactions. Over the years, as it gained mainstream traction and price escalation, Bitcoin became an investment vehicle rather than a currency. The blockchain platform on which it worked was seen to lack scalability as it was inherently incapable of handling large numbers of transactions. The MB block size limit for Bitcoin led to an increase in the confirmation times and fees for transactions on the Bitcoin blockchain. The inordinate delay in waiting for confirmations caused transactions to become queued, as the blocks could not handle the increase in transaction size. Hence, another cryptocurrency was created which shared many features with Bitcoin and also solved such problems – Bitcoin Cash.

The main purpose of creating Bitcoin Cash was to create larger block sizes in the blockchain from 8 MB to 32 MB so that more transaction records could be held in a single block than the original Bitcoin. The average number of transactions per block on Bitcoin was around 1,000 and 1,500 when the Bitcoin Cash proposal was introduced. The number of transactions on Bitcoin Cash's blockchain was estimated at 25,000 per block during a stress test in September 2018.

Bitcoin Cash is a transactional cryptocurrency primarily designed to be spent rather than held as an asset. It works as an electronic cash payment system. It is a type of fork of Bitcoin that has a lower transaction cost than Bitcoin. Originating in August 2017, Bitcoin is split into two separate cryptos – Bitcoin and Bitcoin Cash.

The cryptocurrency underwent another fork in November 2018 and split into Bitcoin Cash ABC and Bitcoin Cash SV (Satoshi Vision). Bitcoin Cash ABC is referred to as Bitcoin Cash now because it uses the original Bitcoin Cash client.

Although Bitcoin Cash is an upgraded version of the original Bitcoin, Bitcoin Cash and Bitcoin share many technical similarities. They use the same consensus mechanism, and their supply volume is capped at 21 million Bitcoins. Both of them use the Proof-of-Work mechanism to mine new Bitcoins and generate transactions. Bitcoin Cash also uses the same mining difficulty algorithm – Emergency Difficulty Adjustment (EDA) which adjusts the difficulty approximately every two weeks or every 2016 blocks. Miners take advantage of this similarity by alternating their mining activity between Bitcoin and Bitcoin Cash. Though the practice was gainful for miners, yet it had an adverse effect on the increasing supply of Bitcoin Cash in the markets. Hence, Bitcoin Cash has revised its EDA algorithm to ease miners to generate the cryptocurrency.

Thus, Bitcoin Cash is able to handle many more transactions per second than the Bitcoin network and process them more quickly, which also saves confirmation times and reduces processing fees.

4.5.1 History of Bitcoin Cash

In 2010, Bitcoin launched its own blockchain, which was vulnerable to hackers and operated mostly low-value transactions that allowed the system to be crawled somehow. The average size of a block on Bitcoin's blockchain was less than 100 KB, and the fee per transaction was hardly a few cents. Also, the time taken to mine new Bitcoins was much more than other cryptocurrencies, which took hardly ten minutes. Therefore, the original Bitcoin was outperformed in every department.

Bitcoin Cash is considered a fork of Bitcoin that was created in a situation when participants were not agreed on how to scale cryptocurrency in the Bitcoin ecosystem (Bitcoin, 2022). The major cause of contention was the size of the block, which accounts for the volume of transactions processed per second. Since transactions are processed as data, a larger block size enables more transactions to be contained, thereby achieving higher throughput.

The Bitcoin protocol was limited to blocks of 1 MB in size for years. But such security measures proved to be a deterrent when Bitcoin gained mainstream traction due to its potential and matchless efficiency. With the increase in number of Bitcoin users, the settlement times also increased due to limited block size, and the competitors began to impose high transaction fees in the pursuit of higher earnings. As a result, it retained its relevance for high-value transactions, in which transaction speed is of little importance but lost its traction on low-value transactions, where both fees and speed are vital. This meant that Bitcoin became less useful as cash.

Two solutions were offered by developers to solve the problem: either to increase the average block size or to delete some parts of the transaction in order to accommodate more data in the blockchain. The Bitcoin core team, which was responsible for developing and maintaining the algorithm that powers Bitcoin, insisted on keeping the 1 MB block size as such. They contended to scale Bitcoin off chain, on a second layer solution, while maintaining status quo for large transactions on-chain. The other party strived to increase the block size, allowing faster transactions per block and keeping the fees low.

As consensus was not being reached by the Bitcoin community, a hard fork resulted in the separation of the two versions of Bitcoin – the upgraded version of the block size was called Bitcoin Cash, while the unchanged version was named Bitcoin (BTC). Bitcoin Cash originated as an entirely new cryptocurrency operating on a separate blockchain.

In August 2017, Bitcoin Cash made its high-profile debut on cryptocurrency exchanges at an impressive price of $900. Each Bitcoin holder received an amount equal to Bitcoin Cash, leading to an unprecedented increase in the number of coins in existence. Major cryptocurrency exchanges, such as Coinbase and itBit, embargoed Bitcoin Cash and did not allow it to be listed on their exchanges. Under such circumstances, Bitcoin Cash received significant support from Bitmain, the world's largest cryptocurrency mining platform. This ensured the supply of coins for trading on cryptocurrency exchanges when Bitcoin Cash was launched. The price of Bitcoin Cash rose to US$ 4,091 at the height of the crypto frenzy in December 2017.

Ironically, Bitcoin Cash underwent another fork after a gap of almost one year (see Figure 4.9). In November 2018, Bitcoin Cash split into Bitcoin Cash ABC and Bitcoin Cash Satoshi Vision (SV). This time, the discord was over a proposed protocol update that incorporated an increase in the average block size and the use of smart contracts on Bitcoin's blockchain. Bitcoin Cash ABC uses the original Bitcoin Cash client but has incorporated several changes to its blockchain, such as the Canonical Transaction Ordering Route (CTOR), which rearranges the transactions in a block into a specific order.

Bitcoin Cash SV is led by Craig Wright, who claims to be the original Nakamoto. He rejected the use of smart contracts on a platform meant for payment transactions. Whatever be the circumstances in which the dispute

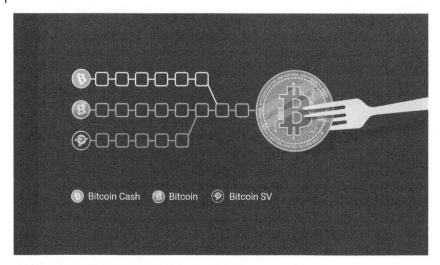

Figure 4.9 Bitcoin hard forks.

started, at the end, more and more money has flowed into the cryptocurrency ecosystem and has resulted in large number of coins available to investors. Since the launch, both cryptocurrencies have gained respectable valuations at crypto exchanges.

4.5.2 Concerns about Bitcoin Cash

Bitcoin Cash has not yet met the criteria on which it was envisioned. The most important of these is the block size, which is much smaller than the Bitcoin block-chain. The smaller block size means that the idea of enabling more transactions through larger blocks is yet to be technically tested.

The drop in the transaction fees for Bitcoin has made it a viable competitor to Bitcoin Cash. Other cryptocurrencies, which harbor similar drives of becoming a medium for daily transactions, have dashed the original objectives of Bitcoin Cash. Many have even ventured into partnerships with organizations and govern-ments at home and abroad. Even if such claims are doubtful, Litecoin has started working with event organizers and professional associations, and Dash has tried to gain traction in a turbulent economy, such as Venezuela.

Although its split from Bitcoin was extremely high-profile, Bitcoin Cash did not achieve the same fame as Bitcoin enjoys today. Bitcoin is still far ahead of the competition, based on the level of transactions on the blockchain. Bitcoin Cash is not known to many people outside the crypto community and has not found a patron yet.

Bitcoin Cash's first fork on the blockchain was acceptable, but the second fork puts the board of its developer pool under suspicion. A large faction believes that Bitcoin Cash is undermining its original vision, paving the way for further splits in the future. Smart contracts are an essential feature of all cryptocurrencies, and thus, it is to be seen whether Bitcoin Cash remains merely a platform for payment systems or can also be a means to incorporate smart contracts for transactions.

Bitcoin Cash does not have a clearly defined governance protocol, while other cryptocurrencies, such as Dash and VeChain, have well-elaborated governance protocols that assign voting rights. Bitcoin Cash's vision for development and design seems to be centralized with its development team that does not divulge whether investors, without substantial cryptocurrency holdings, have voting rights or privileges to decide the future direction of Bitcoin Cash.

4.5.3 Bitcoin Cash Core Features

Bitcoin Cash is a decentralized, peer-to-peer electronic cash system that does not rely on a central authority, such as a government or financial institution. It is completely decentralized and independent and works with the help of a distributed ledger – commonly known as blockchain. No third party is involved in the process of the transaction. It represents a fundamental remake of the currency.

Some salient features of Bitcoin Cash are:

- Bitcoins are outside the purview of governments and other central authorities that can neither block user transactions nor restrict Bitcoin accounts.
- Bitcoin Cash is open to everyone. It does not require any identification or authorization for use. It is neither possessed nor controlled by anyone. Anybody can transact it without censorship. The user experiences more freedom as compared to dealing in national currencies.
- Similar to Bitcoin, a block stores transactions chronologically until its 1 MB of data capacity is occupied and then another block repeats the same process. All these blocks are joined in a sequence to form a global public ledger called a blockchain.
- All transactions are done in a secure and transparent manner, and a copy of the ledger is available at all times so that one can easily access the entire record at any point of time.
- The ledger is publicly stored and distributed in discrete silos by a network of participants called nodes. This not only evades the honeypot problem (all data in a centralized repository) but also reduces the chances of a Single Point of Failure (SPoF).
- Even though the mechanism is not under the control of any central authority, all nodes follow a pre-determined protocol to achieve consensus on the state of the ledger. Bitcoin Cash also uses a proof-of-work consensus mechanism to process transactions.

- Although protocols can be developed on demand from participants, changes are implemented after a high level of consensus. The consensus, as a quasi-political system, constitutes the truth, wherein the participants form a sort of social contract.
- Bitcoin Cash works on an immutable technology. Once a transaction is recorded in the blockchain, it becomes perpetual, i.e. it cannot be changed. All transactions are recorded as per predetermined protocol, leaving no room for manipulation of any transaction processes.
- Like Bitcoin, miners compete to add new blocks to the chain, through a proof-of-work (PoW) process, which constitutes the ledger. Thus, by espousing the principles of game-theory, the hardware and energy costs associated with PoW mining play an important role in keeping the network secure. Since the cost of the first two is exorbitant, it is extremely expensive to attack the network, and the attacker can never take advantage.
- Bitcoin's hard cap of 21 million coins makes Bitcoin Cash a hard asset like land, property, or gold, giving people the opportunity to store value in a digital form for long periods of time.
- Every transaction in Bitcoin Cash is a public record that can be audited by anyone. The investor's private key is the only link between him and his Bitcoin Cash. As long as the private key is secure, the investor's money is safe.
- Bitcoin Cash enables fast and affordable transactions of any value across geographic or political boundaries. Due to its ease of operation, it can be an effective alternative to payment networks, such as Visa and MasterCard.

4.5.4 Utility of Bitcoin Cash

Bitcoin Cash provides an eccentric form of money that supports economic freedom. Unlike fiat currencies prevalent around the world, Bitcoin Cash protects money against (i) monetary forfeiture, (ii) censorship, and (iii) devaluation by uncapped inflation.

As discussed earlier, Bitcoin transactions are relatively faster than traditional bank transfers in fiat currencies. These transactions are done with nominal or sometimes zero fees, making it a good fit for petty transactions, such as paying restaurant bills or buying groceries. It involves immediate settlement regardless of the physical location of the participants. It is a better option for transfer of currency as compared to normal cash or credit cards.

4.5.5 Advancements over Bitcoin

Bitcoin Cash was built from the same code base as Bitcoin. This is why the hard fork resulted in the emergence of Bitcoin Cash – a currency that shares many technical characteristics with Bitcoin. Nevertheless, since the forking in 2017, independent teams of developers working on the Bitcoin Cash protocol have made several innovations to improve the usability of Bitcoin Cash that make Bitcoin Cash superior to the original Bitcoin in a number of ways:

4.5.5.1 Maximum Block Size

By using hard fork technology, Bitcoin Cash has upgraded the block size to around 8 MB to 32 MB, which not only provides faster transaction rates per second but also records the transaction details within each block.

This has resulted in an unsurpassed processing volume and speed of Bitcoin Cash. Bitcoin Cash effectively addresses scalability issues by supporting 116 transactions per second, while the Bitcoin network has a capacity of ten transactions per second.

4.5.5.2 Cost Efficiency

Consequent upon the increased volume and velocity, there has been a tremendous reduction in the cost of Bitcoin Cash transactions. Bitcoin Cash transactions usually cost less than a penny. Overall Bitcoin Cash is cheaper and faster than Bitcoin, allowing more people to execute transactions on the blockchain at the same time. An average on-chain Bitcoin transaction fee is around US$ 0.03, while the cost of a BTC transaction is around US$ 20.

4.5.5.3 Smart Contract Support

With Bitcoin Cash, it is possible for developers to use smart contract languages, such as CashScript to enable more complex operations than Bitcoin. CashScript allows writing cash contracts in a more straightforward manner. This is essentially the ticket of Bitcoin Cash going face-to-face with BTC and ETH on the DeFi front.

Bitcoin creates a smart contract that can only send money to a specific address and nowhere else. The word *covenant* originates in property law, where it is used to restrict the use of a commodity or to limit the use of money in the Bitcoin Cash context. Bitcoin Cash covenants use an opcode called OP_CHECKDATASIG, which allows you to verify the digital signature on any message. It opens avenues for decentralized finance (synthetic derivatives trading), private payments (CashFusion and CashShuffle), and issue of tokens.

4.5.5.4 Issue of Token

BCH is the digital asset token of the Bitcoin Cash network. Similar to Bitcoin, the smallest subunit of BCH is equal to 10^8 BCH or one hundred millionth of BCH (0.00000001 BCH). Bitcoin Cash can be exchanged with fiat currency or other digital currencies. Using the Simple Ledger protocol, developers can also issue new tokens that reside on the Bitcoin Cash blockchain such as ERC-20 tokens that reside on the Ethereum blockchain or USDT tokens on the Bitcoin Cash chain. It enables people to send and receive USDT per transaction using a noncustodial digital wallet, such as the Bitcoin.com wallet.

4.5.5.5 Nonfungible Tokens

The Simple Ledger Protocol also supports Nonfungible Tokens (NFTs), which are functionally similar to Ethereum's ERC-721 standard (Garg, 2022). NFTs are digital tokens that are distinct from each other and qualify for a wide range of potential use cases, from digital artwork marketplaces to in-game items.

4.5.5.6 No Replacement-by-Fee

Replacement-by-fee (RBF) refers to swapping an unconfirmed transaction stuck on the blockchain with a different version of the same transaction at a higher fee.

One school of opinion holds that some users may misuse RBF to double-spend the same fund. For instance, if a buyer uses RBF to transfer money to a seller for a small fee in exchange for a product, and if the seller does not allow sufficient time for confirmation, the buyer can route the transaction to a different wallet by paying higher fees.

However, most RBF versions essentially match the output of both transactions. Furthermore, if the recipient agrees to hold off until confirmation, the RBF will not be required, as the original transaction will execute. The RBF protocol has been deprecated since the delisting of the Bitcoin Cash network in August 2017.

In the Bitcoin Cash protocol, since unconfirmed transactions are irreversible, the lack of replacement-by-fee makes Bitcoin Cash more secure. With the May 2021 Bitcoin Cash protocol upgrade, the unconfirmed on-chain transaction limit (previously set at 50) was abolished and double-spend tests were introduced. This further enhanced the utility of Bitcoin Cash as a payment solution where high volumes of small-value transactions have to be processed in a short amount of time.

4.5.5.7 Schnorr Signatures

The Schnorr signature is a lightweight signature scheme introduced by Claus Schnorr. Typically, a digital signature consists of a single public key, a message to be attested, and a signature, which attests that the owner of the public key has signed the given message. When more than one party is involved in the same transaction and they want to sign the same message, each of them must include their own public key and signature. This mean that if three parties are involved in a transaction, the document would include three public keys and three signatures, which appears to be suboptimal for computation and storage reasons. This would require each node to perform signature verification three times and store them with three sets of public keys, which is an extremely expensive task.

Key aggregation eliminates the need for multiple public keys and signatures. Under the Schnorr scheme, if three parties wish to sign a transaction, they can irreversibly combine their three public keys to form a public key. Then, using each of their three private keys, they can sign the same message. A verifier only needs to verify a signature and the public key to ensure that all three parties have signed the message.

4.5.5.8 Difficulty Adjustment Algorithm

Due to fork technology, Bitcoins exist simultaneously without any disruption. Both the BTC and BCH coins use a Difficulty Adjustment Algorithm (DAA). The network difficulty for BTC is adjusted every 14 days or after each block of 2016, while for BCH, it is adjusted every ten minutes or after each block. The difficulty tells us how much computing power the miner will need for each block.

Bitcoin Cash deploys an exponentially moving target difficulty adjustment algorithm called "aserti3-2d." For every two days when blocks are behind schedule, the difficulty is halved, while every two days when blocks are ahead of schedule, the difficulty doubles. Accordingly, SHA256 miners move their hashing power from BTC to BCH and back. Bitcoin Cash's DAA ensures that blocks continue to be produced at the desired consistent rate.

4.5.6 Bitcoin Cash – Ease of Use

The transaction fee for Bitcoin Cash is around US$ 0.28. The major reason for such a low transaction fee is that it is able to store large transaction details, owing to its large block size, and work faster due to its high speed. A transaction fee applies only when one transfers cryptocurrency to someone else's address. Bitcoin Cash is the most popular cryptocurrency among people due to its low-cost fees and secure, transparent transactions.

4.5.7 Challenges to Bitcoin Cash

In 2017, Bitcoin Cash supporters also divided into two factions. Supporters of Bitcoin Cash wanted to use it as a medium of exchange in goods and commerce, while opponents sought it to be a means of storing value. Therefore, in 2018, it created another off-shoot crypto: Bitcoin SV.

The second split of Bitcoin Cash began as a confrontation between the two camps. One group, backed by Bitmain's Roger Ver and Jihan Wu, wanted to restrict the block size to 32 MB. The other side was supported by Steven Wright and Calvin Ayre who wanted to increase the block size to 128 MB, and they formed Bitcoin SV.

Coming Up

The previous chapter discussed the financial perspective for understanding transactions on the Bitcoin blockchain. In the next chapter, readers will delve into the programmable aspect of blockchain transactions, which are the backbone of modern business use cases.

References

Bitcoin, 2022. https://news.Bitcoin.com.

Garg R, 2022. Ethereum based Smart Contracts for Trade and Finance. International Conference on Blockchain and Smart Contracts, Bangkok Thailand. doi: 10.5281/zenodo.5854730 https://www.researchgate.net/publication/357510533_Ethereum_based_Smart_Contracts_for_Trade_Finance/ Accessed on 02 February 2022.

Nakamoto S, 2008. Bitcoin: A Peer-to-Peer Electronic Cash System. https://bitcoin.org/bitcoin.pdf.

5

Ethereum and Hyperledger Fabric

Ethereum is a variant of blockchain that was conceived by Russian–Canadian developers, Buterin (2014) and his co-workers. Bitcoin focused on decentralized payments, while Buterin and his collaborators aimed to improve the decentralized finance system with apps powered in the blockchain and to address the various limitations present in Bitcoin. They made an initial proposal that recommended users or applications to push arbitrary computer code into the blockchain using transactions. This is how the concept of smart contracts (or contracts for short) first emerged.

Thus, Ethereum came into being as a peer-to-peer network that works on a decentralized platform called blockchain. This securely executes and verifies application code, hitherto called smart contracts, and allows participants on the blockchain to transact with each other without a trusted central authority. Transactions are sent and received through user-created Ethereum accounts. The sender signs each transaction and incurs Ether (Ethereum's native cryptocurrency) toward the cost of processing the transaction on the network. Transaction records are immutable, auditable, and securely distributed across the network, giving participants full ownership and visibility of transaction data.

But the thing that makes Ethereum so exciting for users is its network's ability to do more than just process financial transactions. Ethereum further enhances the merits of the Bitcoin blockchain as it allows developers to run programs that represents the core logic of decentralized applications or dApps.

In this way, the Ethereum network provides a more flexible environment than the Bitcoin blockchain and derived special-purpose blockchain. It can also process smart contracts without the need to create any special-purpose blockchain infrastructure. Unlike Bitcoin and other single-purpose blockchains, Ethereum decoupled this smart contract layer, which now runs on top of the underlying

Blockchain for Real World Applications, First Edition. Rishabh Garg.
© 2023 John Wiley & Sons, Inc. Published 2023 by John Wiley & Sons, Inc.

Ethereum blockchain, making it easy to create smart contracts with a few lines of code.

Ethereum, like other cryptocurrencies, can be used to send and receive value globally, without the involvement of a third party that stores data, transfers collateral, and keeps track of complex financial instruments. Ethereum also has the feature that any participant can broadcast requests to perform arbitrary computations that other participants on the network verify, validate, and execute. This causes a change in the state of the Ethereum Virtual Machine (EVM), which is committed and propagated across the network. The said state of the EVM, which is generated by the consensus of all the nodes, is stored in the blockchain. The cryptographic mechanism assures that all transactions are signed and executed with the proper authorizations.

5.1 Early Attempts to Program Cryptocurrencies

Bitcoin Scripts

Scripts can be considered as one of the initial concepts in the implementation of the business logic layer in the blockchain. The script was an optional feature in transactions, used to limit the spending of cryptocurrency for specific purposes. Later, they were removed because of a bug in the script's opcodes (such as OP _ LSHIFT). Some examples of OPCODES in Bitcoin scripts are given in the tables (see Tables 5.1 and 5.2).

Buterin, who was involved in such projects for some time, realized that these adaptations of the Bitcoin blockchain were feasible but were neither efficient nor flexible enough. Subsequently, he introduced the idea of decoupling the smart contract functionalities from the blockchain functionalities and started the Ethereum project.

Table 5.1 Constants.

Word	Opcode	Hex	Input	Output	Description
OP_0, OP_FALSE	0	0x00	Nothing.	(Empty value)	An empty array of bytes is pushed onto the stack. (This is not a no-op: an item is added to the stack.)
N/A	1-75	0x01– 0x4b	(Special)	Data	The next *opcode* bytes is data to be pushed onto the stack
OP_PUSH-DATA1	76	0x4c	(Special)	Data	The next byte contains the number of bytes to be pushed onto the stack.

Table 5.2 Flow control.

Word	Opcode	Hex	Input	Output	Description
OP_NOP	97	0x61	Nothing	Nothing	Does nothing.
OP_IF	99	0x63	<expression> if [statements] [else [statements]]* endif		If the top stack value is not False, the statements are executed. The top stack value is removed.
OP_NOTIF	100	0x64	<expression> notif [statements] [else [statements]]* endif		If the top stack value is False, the statements are executed. The top stack value is removed.

5.2 Smart Contracts

A smart contract is an application code that resides on a blockchain at a specific address known as a contract address. Applications can call smart contract functions, change their state, and initiate transactions. Smart contracts are written in programming languages, such as Solidity (which is like an object-oriented programming language) and Viper. In order to execute smart contracts in any hardware or software, an abstraction layer is required. It is provided by EVM that converts high-level language into EVM byte code.

Smart contracts satisfy conditions by following a computer's simple "if... then" statements that are programmed on a blockchain. These terms may include payment, transfer of goods, or issue of bills when a specified condition is met. Once the transaction is completed, the blockchain is updated after which the transaction cannot be altered. Only the permitted party can see the result.

In practice, participants do not write new code each time a computation is requested on the EVM; rather, application developers upload reusable snippets of code to the EVM storage, and then users make request for the execution of these code snippets according to various parameters.

Smart contracts are used for the automation of common centralized processes, such as conditional transfer of digital assets, multisig asset exchange, or waiting for a specific amount of time to execute a transaction.

A smart contract is represented by a contract account. This can be implemented by an Externally Owned Account (EOA) that is required to participate in the Ethereum blockchain. The invitation process is done using transactions sent by the EOA in the form of Ether and gas. When the target address in a transaction is a smart contract, the execution of the smart contract occurs upon verification (such as checking a nonce combination and fee) and validation of the transaction (see Table 5.3).

Table 5.3 Computation Fee in Gas Points.

S. no.	Operation name	Gas Cost
1.	Step	1
2.	Load from memory	20
3.	Store into memory	100
4.	Transaction base fee	21000
5.	Contract creation	53000

Transaction in Ethereum contains:

1) Amount of Wei (1 Ether = 10^18 Wei)
2) STARTGAS (max computational steps)
3) GASPRICE (fees per different steps of code execution)

Around 21,000 gas points are paid to miners for adding a transaction to a block.

Note: Computation requirements are specified in gas, as it is a standard cryptocurrency. Unlike Ether, its value does not change as per market swings.

The state of an Ethereum blockchain changes when state hash and receipt hash of smart contract changes.

Like a programming language, the Solidity class contains a state of variables and methods to access the public variables. When methods are called during smart contract execution, the values of variables change, which in turn changes the state of the smart contract. This change is recorded in the form of state hash. The final result of the execution is stored in the form of receipt hash. The following sample shows a smart contract implemented with Solidity.

```solidity
pragma solidity >=0.8.4;
contract MyCoin {
  mapping (address => uint) balances;
  event Transfer(address indexed from, address indexed
_to, uint256 _value);
  constructor()  {
    balances[tx.origin] = 10000;
  }
  function sendCoin(address receiver, uint amount)
public returns(bool success) {
    if (balances[msg.sender] < amount) return false;

    balances[msg.sender] -= amount;
    balances[receiver] += amount;
```

```
    emit Transfer(msg.sender, receiver, amount);
    return true;      }
  function getBalance(address addr) public view returns
(uint) {
    return balances[addr];
  }
}
```

The given sample represents a simulated token or coin transferred between addresses in the blockchain. Now, let's examine each part in depth.

```
pragma solidity >=0.8.4;
```

The Pragma directive specifies which version of Solidity can be used to compile the contract. If someone compiles the contract with any version that is not in that range, he gets a compilation error.

```
contract MyCoin {
```

MyCoin is the name for the contract definition and is only used to refer to this contract in code by other contracts. Contracts are invoked by knowing the public address, so it is impossible to have a collision by name.

```
mapping (address => uint) balances;
```

Mapping is a particular construct in Solidity that acts as a dictionary or hash for key pairs. Address is a specific data type that represents a public address, and uint is an unsigned integer.

```
event Transfer(address indexed _from, address indexed _
to, uint256 _value);
```

Transfer is an event arising out of a contract whose payload contains the address of the owner or sender (from), recipient (s), and a value. Since contracts run asynchronously and concurrently after validation, they do not emit any feedback. One way to emulate reactions is to emit events. Those transactions are recorded in the log, which can either be queried by any node connected to the network or by appending to the client library, which may be an option.

```
constructor()   {
        balances[tx.origin] = 10000;
}
```

The contract constructor is invoked only once when deployed on the blockchain and a public address is assigned. It assigns an arbitrary number of tokens to the contract owner. Here, "tx" is an implicit variable that provides an access to information about the current transaction.

```
function sendCoin(address receiver, uint amount) public
returns(bool success) {
        if (balances[msg.sender] < amount) return false;
        balances[msg.sender] -= amount;
        balances[receiver] += amount;
        emit Transfer(msg.sender, receiver, amount);
        return true;
}
```

This method moves tokens from the sender's address to the receiver's address. As would be the case with "tx", "msg" is another variable that provides access to the execution context. This implementation checks whether the sender has tokens available in the balance and accordingly moves it to the recipient's address if tokens are available. Otherwise, if no token is available, it returns false to complete the transaction.

```
function getBalance(address addr) public view
returns(uint) {
    return balances[addr];
}
```

getBalance returns the balance at the associated address. The node executing this method can only query the ledger without submitting any transactions, so gas is not required.

5.3   Working of Ethereum

When a transaction triggers a smart contract, all nodes in the network faithfully execute each instruction. To make it happen, Ethereum implements an execution ecosystem through a single canonical computer called the EVM. As part of the block verification protocol, all nodes in the network operate the EVM (see Figure 5.1). In block verification, each node goes through the transactions listed in the respective block they need to verify and runs the computer code, triggered by the transaction in the EVM. All nodes on the network perform the same computation in order to keep their ledgers in sync. Each transaction includes a gas limit and a fee that the sender voluntarily pays for the transaction. If the total amount of gas required to process the transaction is less than or equal to the gas limit, the transaction is processed. Otherwise, the transaction is aborted, and the fee is lost. The gas balance, which remains unused after the transaction, is reimbursed to the sender in the form of Ether. Hence, it is always better to have a higher gas limit than expected for safe transactions. Further, the higher the price, the higher will be the priority to verify transactions in the execution queue. Verifiers would obviously prefer those who pay more.

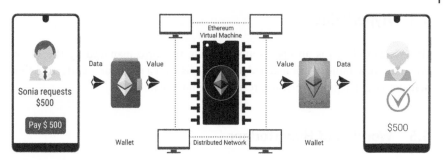

Figure 5.1 Working of Ethereum.

5.3.1 Gas

Gas is consumed in executing lines of code or allocating storage space. Both computing resources and storage are scarce and have their own cost. Hence, running code in EVM comes at a cost, which is expressed in a unit known as "gas." Gas represents a unit and not a price, and it signifies a tiny fraction of Ether (Wei or 10x18). Thus, for every transaction on Ethereum, it is mandatory for the user to pay gas. The sender can set a gas limit on each transaction as he wishes, which expresses how much he is willing to spend on execution. If the transaction costs more than this, it is aborted and the tokens are lost. Otherwise, the balance is refunded to the sender.

5.3.2 Ether

The purpose of Ether is to establish a market mechanism for computation that provides an economic incentive for participants to execute transaction requests and to provide computational resources to the network. The broadcast requires giving some amount of Ether, which is eventually received as a reward to those who verify the transaction, execute it, commit it to the blockchain, and broadcast it over the network.

Since all participants are continuously charged, this discourages malicious participants from intentionally shutting down the network by requesting the execution of infinite loops or resource-intensive scripts, as doing so is heavy on their wallets.

Ether and gas are two aspects. Ether is a currency that has an inherent value. On the other hand, gas is a fuel, which is an inevitable cost of using the system. However, those who have the system (gas) can trade it with those who wish to use the system in exchange for the same intrinsic value. If occasionally, the user does not have gas to transact, he can convert any Ether around him into gas. This is why the Ether market and the gas market are different. The price of one can fluctuate without affecting the price of the other.

5.4 Hyperledger

Hyperledger (HPL) is an open-source private platform managed by the Linux Foundation, to build distributed ledger solutions with a modular architecture that delivers a high degree of privacy, resilience, and scalability.

5.5 Working of Hyperledger

5.5.1 Components

Hyperledger Fabric is an enterprise-level private blockchain network in which various business organizations – such as banks, corporate institutions, or trade establishments – transact with each other to achieve their business goals.

Each organization has a fabric certificate authority, on the basis of which it is identified as a member. Each member of the fabric can set up one or more authorized peers to participate in the network, using their own fabric certificate authority.

There is a network-connected client-side application, written with a Software Development Kit (SDK) of a particular programming language.

5.5.2 Workflow

Each transaction in fabric takes place in the following steps:

5.5.2.1 Proposal

A transaction is initiated by offering or invoking a transaction request with the help of a member organization client application or portal. The client application then sends the received proposal to peers in each organization for endorsement.

5.5.2.2 Endorsement

After reaching out to peers in each organization to endorse the proposal, the peer checks the requesting member's fabric certificate authority and other details required to authenticate the transaction. Then it executes the chain code (a piece of code that is written in one of the supported languages, like Go or Java) and returns a response. This response indicates acceptance or rejection of the following transaction. The response is carried out to the client.

5.5.2.3 Transmission to Ordering Service

After receiving the endorsement output, the approved transactions are transmitted to the ordering service by the client-side application. The peer responsible for the ordering service includes the transaction in a specific block and sends it to the peer nodes of various members of the network.

5.5.2.4 Updating the Ledger

After receiving the specific block, the peer nodes of the organizations update their local ledger with this block, thereby committing new transactions (see Figure 5.2).

5.5.3 Industrial Applications of Hyperledger Fabric

Hyperledger Blockchain is one of the foremost open-source blockchain technologies that provides the tools and framework for enterprise-grade blockchain deployment. It assures a credible system for implementation of various administrative processes of the government, which can be scaled up as and when required, without compromising on security and transparency.

Fabric provides a permissioned blockchain for administrative operations of federal schemes. If the government wants, it can also make modules for digital identity and connect people to the system. Being a licensed network, it may also provide a membership identification service, which can be used to authenticate and manage digital identities for network participants.

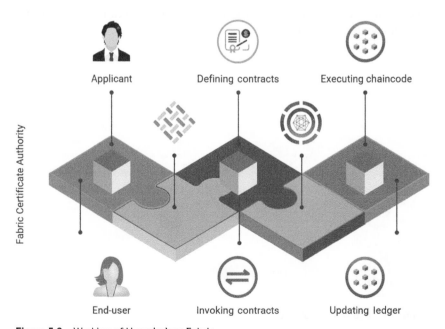

Figure 5.2 Working of Hyperledger Fabric.

5.5.3.1 Production

Production is one of the topmost applications of Hyperledger Fabric. The final assembler can use Fabric to create a supply chain network that can be a great medium between part suppliers and manufacturers to keep up with demand and supply. Using Fabric means more responsiveness in the system, and hence, blockchain in manufacturing has amazing potential to change the current landscape forever.

Also, the use of the standard protocol among the participants means that each one of them follows the same rules and regulations, creating a standard approach.

5.5.3.2 B2B Contract

Under a business-to-business (B2B) contract, two parties automate contracts in a mutually trusted environment. To ensure that both parties' privacy and security is maintained, Hyperledger Fabric provides a permissioned way to manage contracts. Thus, sensitive business information is not shared with anyone other than those two parties. This way B2B contracts can ensure the protection of sensitive information from outside parties who have access to the ledger (see Figure 5.3).

This proves even more useful when it comes to making contracts traceable to the parties in the account. This way, the parties can scrutinize the contract and bid accordingly. Hyperledger Fabric ensures that the approach is standardized, where bidders can find and bid on contracts without the need to engage directly with another business party.

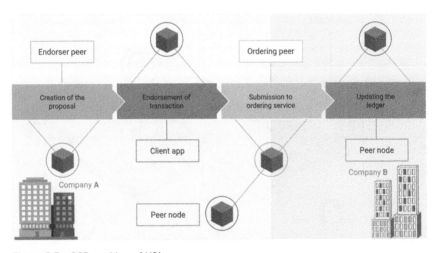

Figure 5.3 B2B working of HPL.

5.5.3.3 Supply Chain

A supply chain can be a global or regional network of manufacturers, suppliers, and retailers of a particular product. The Hyperledger Fabric network can improve the clarity and accountability of transactions within Fabric by reducing the risk of counterfeit transactions. On the Fabric network, enterprises holding authentication to access the ledger can view data from past transactions. Product status can be tracked in a very fast, simple, and efficient manner by updating the real-time production, transaction, and shipping status in the ledger.

Hyperledger Fabric can maintain an immutable track record of all participants in the supply chain network by managing all aspects, such as raw material input and track sourcing, manufacturing telemetry, origin of goods and warehousing, and shipping of the finished product.

5.5.3.4 Asset Depository

Another use case of Hyperledger Fabric is asset depository in which assets can be dematerialized on the blockchain network.

In this way, all stakeholders can directly access the asset, use it to trade and interact with the market in real time, without intermediaries. Additionally, businesses or stakeholders can reduce operating costs by adding business rules to stored assets.

Hyperledger Fabric provides companies, stakeholders, and end users the ability to convert one asset type to another, where one party owns one asset type, and the other party does not accept it.

5.5.3.5 Trading and Asset Transfer

Trading and asset transfers are executed between organizations or members working in tandem like importers, exporters, banks, brokers, etc. Hyperledger Fabric can add a layer of trust in the form of a document signed by a trusted authority in place of a paper document. It also improves system performance.

Hyperledger Fabric enables the trader or stakeholder to have direct access to their financial securities and trade it at any time. Another advantage is that assets on the blockchain network can be dematerialized with the help of Hyperledger Fabric.

5.5.3.6 Insurance

Frauds and scams are a common occurrence in the insurance industry. The industry spends billions of dollars each year to debunk insurance fraud and false claims. The KYC process and verification can be simplified by using a private blockchain such as Hyperledger Fabric. Along with this, the insurance company can also refer to the transaction data, which is stored inside the ledger. Hyperledger

Fabric can accelerate claims processing and automate payments, using on-chain code. This can further automate the process of recovery of erroneous payments made to the insured. This process will also be helpful in processing multi-party settlement claims.

5.5.3.7 Real Estate

Real estate is another industry where Hyperledger Fabric can be used to increase liquidity in the market. Actually, it has become a big issue due to the volatility of the market. The market, being limited to the reach of only the high-end buyer, is getting out of reach for middle-class citizens.

The use of blockchain can bring about a dramatic change in the real estate sector. By using Fabric, real estate can offer fragmented ownership, which is a great way to invest in this business. Moreover, it can also streamline international property deals without any compacting process.

5.5.4 Benefits of Hyperledger Fabric

5.5.4.1 Open Source

Hyperledger Fabric, hosted by the Linux Foundation, is an open-source blockchain framework designed by an active community of developers to make the code publicly accessible. Any participant in the community, who has an interest or expertise in programming, can help develop the source code. Any person in the world may audit, develop, modify, or distribute the code as he deems fit.

5.5.4.2 Private and Confidential

In a public blockchain network, each node in the network receives a full copy of the ledger. Thus, keeping confidentiality becomes a matter of grave concern as everything is open to all. Being a public blockchain, the identities of all participating members are not authenticated. But this is not the case with Hyperledger Fabric. The identities of all participating members are verified, and the ledger is accessible to the certified members only. It is more advantageous in industry-level cases, such as banking, insurance, etc., where customer data needs to be kept private.

5.5.4.3 Access Control

Hyperledger Fabric provides a virtual blockchain network over and above the physical blockchain network, thus enabling access and control of data. It has its own access rules and mechanisms for ordering transactions. These act as additional tools for access control and help to make data private, hide information from competitors, or limit the broadcasting of data between associates.

5.5.4.4 Chaincode Functionality

Chaincode uses a container technology to host application codes or smart contracts, which define the business rules of the system. It accommodates the complexity present in the economy and supports a variety of pluggable components.

5.5.4.5 Performance

Hyperledger Fabric is a private blockchain network, so transactions are executed quickly without the need for verification. It also provides parallelism and concurrency as the transaction are executed separately from the transaction commit and order.

5.5.4.6 Modular Design

The modular architecture of Hyperledger Fabric enables it to be used with other systems and to modify its functionality over time.

5.6 Ethereum Versus Hyperledger

The key differences between Ethereum and Hyperledger are as follows:

5.6.1 Purpose

- Ethereum is a platform to build B2C business and decentralized applications with the aim of running smart contracts on the EVM. With Ethereum, decentralized apps can be created for mass consumption.
- Hyperledger Fabric is managed by the Linux Foundation. Hyperledger has been designed to build B2B and cross-industry applications. It helps businesses or industries to collaborate with developers, who work with DLT. This allows for the creation of customized blockchain apps with limited access.

5.6.2 Cryptocurrency

- Ethereum has its own native cryptocurrency called Ethereum (ETH). Any participant node can mine ETH by paying for gas.
- Hyperledger does not have any such cryptocurrency that can be involved in mining.

5.6.3 Participation

- Ethereum is a public (permissionless) network in which anyone who has access to the internet can download the software and start mining.

- Hyperledger is a limited-participation network in which only authorized members and participants, selected by authorized members, can make access to the Hyperledger platform and its tools. It keeps its valuable and confidential information safe and does not allow any tampering.

5.6.4 Privacy

- Ethereum is a public network in which all transactions are absolutely transparent. Any person who has an access to the internet can view these transactions.
- Hyperledger is a permissioned and limited-access blockchain network in which only organizations or individuals holding an authorization certificate can view transactions on the network. It is extremely secure and confidential.

5.6.5 Governance

- The Ethereum network is governed by the Ethereum developers only. It's a product of in-house development rather than a collaboration.
- Hyperledger Fabric is a product of successful collaboration between the Linux Foundation and IBM.

5.6.6 Computer Code

- Ethereum often uses Solidity to write smart contracts, while a high-level language like JavaScript, Python, Golang is used to develop applications.
- Go is widely used to write chaincode, and to some extent Java and JavaScript in Hyperledger.

5.6.7 Smart Contracts

- An Ethereum smart contract is a set of conditions, written in a programming language, that automatically starts the implementation when certain conditions are met. It is irreversible, which, once created, cannot be changed by any third party. It governs the transfer of digital assets between two or more parties under a contract.
- Like smart contracts, Hyperledger Fabric also allows member organizations to run some code on peers that create transactions on a specific state. These are known as Chaincodes.

5.6.8 Consensus Mechanism

- Ethereum, being a decentralized network, has a Proof-of-Work (PoW) mechanism or consensus mechanism that runs throughout the blockchain. This allows all participating nodes of the decentralized network to reach consensus on certain parameters, such as account balances, the order of transactions, etc., preventing participants from making fake transactions or double-spending coins

- Hyperledger, being a private and permissioned network, does not require any PoW or consensus mechanism to validate transactions. If two participants agree on a particular transaction, no third participant can view or interfere with that transaction. This improves the scalability and transaction rates of the system as well as the overall performance of the network.

5.6.9 Rate of Transactions

- Being a public domain, Ethereum's massive PoW mechanism slows down its transaction speed. It barely manages 20 transactions in a second.
- To be a permissioned blockchain network, Hyperledger Fabric does not require heavy PoW mechanisms like Ethereum. With this, the transaction speed touches about 2,000 transactions per second, which is much higher than Ethereum.

5.6.10 Use-cases

- Ethereum smart contracts can be used publicly or for B2C when developers or developing organizations intend to build decentralized applications for customer use. With the Ethereum network, anyone who has access to the internet can create a node, and each such node possesses a complete copy of the blockchain. Community-led open-source applications that are developed and hosted by blockchain developer communities around the world can be created using Ethereum. Such applications do not require any confidentiality.
- Businesses, such as private or B2B, which do not wish to keep their confidential data on a public blockchain such as Ethereum, can adopt Hyperledger as a permissioned blockchain network. It keeps the organization's information completely secure and confidential. Hyperledger's flexibility can prove to be an exceptional tool where an organization or business needs to define its own customized blockchain algorithms. In Hyperledger projects, the entire fundamental infrastructure of the blockchain can be modified to create customized blockchain applications for business purposes.

5.7 Decentralized Applications

In a centralized scheme, the application software resides at one or more central locations, depending on the size of the installed client base. In a decentralized scheme, the application software resides on each client machine (see Figure 5.4).

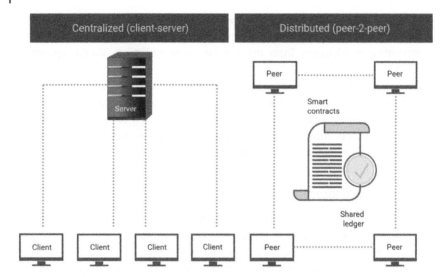

Figure 5.4 Comparison between centralized and distributed systems.

Decentralized applications (dApps) address the problem that requires block-chain services and blockchain infrastructure (Garg, 2021). dApps consist of a front-end, a blockchain back-end, and middleware, that is, the code that connects the two. The dApp front end is used to implement functions/methods on the smart contract, which, in turn, change the state of the smart contract. The front-end can be a sophisticated web app or mobile app that can employ technologies, such as HTML, CSS, and JavaScript frameworks like React. It can be thought of as an embedded web client with web3.js scripts communicating over the RPC pipeline. The token is used to maintain the standards of the dApp.

5.7.1 Merits of Decentralized Applications

5.7.1.1 Zero Downtime
Relying on a peer-to-peer system ensures that dApps continue to function even when individual computers or parts of the network fail. Once smart contracts are deployed on the blockchain, the contracts would be implemented by default. This forbids malicious actors to launch Denial-of-Service (DoS) attacks, targeting individual dApps.

5.7.1.2 Privacy
No real-world identification is required to deploy or interact with the dApp.

5.7.1.3 Resistance to Censorship

With a single point of failure, it is very difficult for governments or powerful individuals to control the network. No entity on the network can block users from submitting transactions, deploying dApps, or reading data from the blockchain.

5.7.1.4 Absolute Data Integrity

The data stored on the blockchain is immutable and encrypted. Once added to the blockchain, it cannot be changed.

5.7.2 Demerits of Decentralized Applications

Although dApps promise to address many of the major problems faced by regular apps, they also come with a few hiccups.

5.7.2.1 Maintenance

Decentralized applications can be difficult to maintain because once deployed, it is not possible for developers to update their dApps (or the underlying data stored by dApps). If a bug or vulnerability has been introduced in a previous version, it will be difficult to resolve, even after it has been identified.

5.7.2.2 Performance Overhead

Scaling is a serious problem in the face of large performance overhead. In order to achieve the level of security, integrity, transparency, and reliability that Ethereum seeks, each node runs and stores each transaction. On top of this, proof-of-work also takes time.

5.7.2.3 Network Congestion

When a dApp uses a lot of computational resources, the entire network is backed up. Currently, the network can only process about 10 to 15 transactions per second; that is, if the transaction speed exceeds this, the pool of unconfirmed transactions can grow rapidly.

5.7.2.4 User Experience

Due to network effects, dApps often struggle with low user numbers, which makes them less interactive. It can also make them less secure, as the security of a dApp often depends on how many users it has.

5.7.2.5 Centralization

User-friendly and developer-friendly solutions built on top of Ethereum's base layer are analogous to centralized services. Centralization may offset the advantages of blockchain.

5.8 Tokens

In the Ethereum system, tokens represent a diverse range of digital assets, such as vouchers, IOUs, or even real-world, tangible objects. Essentially, Ethereum tokens are smart contracts that use the Ethereum blockchain.

Tokens can be of two types – fungible or nonfungible. Fungible tokens are of equal value and can be exchanged for each other. The ERC20 guidelines are considered to be the standard for exchangeable tokens, for example – voting tokens, staking tokens, or virtual currencies (Garg, 2022). The standards for nonfungible tokens are inherited from the ERC721 guidelines, for instance, rights to an artwork or a song. ERC-777 allows additional functionality on top of the token, such as mixer contracts for better transaction privacy or an emergency recovery function to bail out if one's private keys are lost. ERC-1155 allows for more efficient trades and transaction bundling. This token allows the creation of both standard utility tokens (such as $BNB or $BAT) and nonfungible tokens, such as Cryptopunk.

Decentralized Apps built on Ethereum, such as Augur and Grid+, make extensive use of the token for market prediction and dispute settlement in terms of payment for electricity usage.

Ethereum also allows the creation of unique and indivisible tokens, called nonfungible tokens (NFTs). Their ownership information is recorded and maintained on the blockchain network. These are unique and indivisible tokens, useful for proving the provenance of rare assets, both digital and tangible, for example, for representing collectibles, digital art, sports memorabilia, virtual real estate, and objects within games. NFTs are gaining popularity as more companies seek to tokenize assets and provide users with tamper-proof lineage information about their assets.

Coming Up

In further chapters, we will explore specific use cases for Ethereum-based smart contracts and tokens, including identity management, cybersecurity, banking, finance, and more. Personal identity is a prerequisite for any individual, public, or business enterprise. A sophisticated identification system enables enterprises to conduct digital transactions in the real world. With this ideology in mind, the very next chapter focuses on the development of a system that not only allows the identities to be digital, universal, and multi-purpose, but also assures the privacy and security of personal sensitive information.

References

Buterin V, 2015. A Next-Generation Smart Contract and Decentralized Application Platform. White paper, 1–36. https://blockchainlab.com/pdf/Ethereum_white_

paper-a_next_generation_smart_contract_and_decentralized_application_
platform-vitalik-buterin.pdf/ Accessed on 03 June 2020.

Garg R, 2021. Blockchain Based Decentralized Applications for Multiple
Administrative Domain Networking. BITS – Pilani, KK Birla Goa Campus India,
1–69. doi :10.13140/RG.2.2.29003.87845. https://www.researchgate.net/
publication/351871690_Blockchain_based_Decentralized_Applications_for_
Multiple_Administrative_Domain_Networking.

Garg R, 2022. Distributed Ecosystem for Identity Management. *Journal of Blockchain
Research*, 1 (1) (In Press).

6

Identity as a Panacea for the Real World

Identity entitles a person to exercise his rights and responsibilities fairly and equitably in a civilized society. It provides access to education, health care, business activities, pensions, banking, social benefits, and welfare schemes of the state. Through enrollment, accurate population figures are available to the government for meticulous planning and policy preparations.

The use of paper documents to establish identity of users is cumbersome and involves a high risk of data loss. In comparison, advanced electronic capture and storage of data has been found to reduce costs as well as human error and increase administrative efficiency (World Bank, 2020). The core idea in a citizen's digital registration and identification system is to link a randomly generated unique identification number with the identity while keeping all relevant details in a secure and distributed database.

However, it is extremely difficult to register the population and reach all across various physical and geographical barriers. Consequently, over one thousand million people, including 21 million refugees, still do not have access to an authorized identity, presumably due to exorbitant fees, indirect costs, intermediaries, and complex procedures.

6.1 Identity Systems

All over the world, residents have several forms of identity documents for specific purposes, such as a voter card for election purposes, a driver's license, a passport for traveling abroad, or a Social Security number to record the covered wages or self-employment earnings (Garg, 2016). It dates back to 1803, when the world's first identity system was introduced by Napoleon Bonaparte.

Blockchain for Real World Applications, First Edition. Rishabh Garg.
© 2023 John Wiley & Sons, Inc. Published 2023 by John Wiley & Sons, Inc.

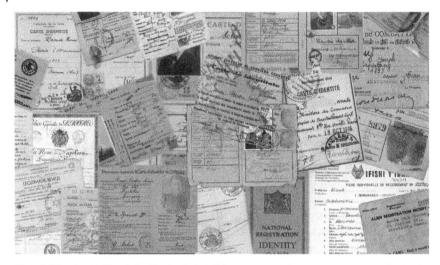

Figure 6.1 Paper identities across the world.

The contemporary era of ID cards began with World War II (see Figure 6.1). In 1938, the United Kingdom passed the National Registry Act, which required all residents to have an identity card (Whitley and Hosein, 2009). In 1940, the Vichy government of France established an ID system with Greece and Poland, which is more or less retained until now. Barring a few exceptions, hardly any country with common law in the world has adopted a peacetime identification system.

The adoption of ID cards in Asia was reflected in a boom after World War II. The Hong Kong government introduced an identity card in 1949 to prevent immigration from mainland China and strengthen its sovereignty. Taiwan in 1949 and South Korea and Singapore in the 1960s followed the suit in pretext of economic transformation.

6.1.1 Contemporary ID Systems

In the United States, a nine-digit Social Security number (SSN) is issued to all US citizens, permanent residents, and temporary residents over the age of 18 (see Figure 6.2). Although it was originally intended to identify individuals for social security purposes, it is now also used to track individuals for taxation purposes. In practice, it has become a de facto national identification number due to its wide range of applications, such as opening a bank account or applying for a driving license.

Social Insurance numbers were introduced in Canada but ended in 2004 with the introduction of the Personal Information Protection and Electronic Document as real ID numbers.

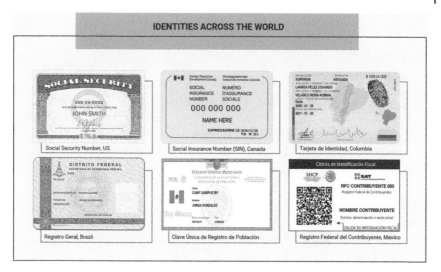

Figure 6.2 Digital identities across the world – North and South America.

Within the European Economic Area and Switzerland, the European Health Insurance Card is issued for health-care purposes. This card lists a code called an identification number. In Finland, the personal identification code, henkilotunnas (HETU or Swedish Personbeteckning) has been in vogue since 1964 and is used to identify citizens for government and corporate transactions.

In France, the INSEE code that originated during the Vichy regime is used for identification, social insurance, employment, and taxation purposes. In Germany, as of 2007, only a decentralized database was maintained by social insurance companies, which allocated a social insurance number to almost every person. After 2008, the former tax file numbers were replaced by new taxpayer identification numbers, Steuerliche Identifikationsnummer or SteuerIdNr. Individuals who are both employee and self-employed at the same time can get two taxpayer identification numbers. The corresponding number for organizations is issued by the Federal Central Tax Office, and is named Wirtschafts-Identifikationsnummer.

In Italy, a financial code (Codicefiscale) is issued in the format SSSNNN YYMDDZZZZX at the time of birth (see Figure 6.3). SSS are the first three consonants in the family name (if there are not enough consonants the first vowel, then X are used); NNN is the first name, from which the first, third, and fourth consonants are used. YY are the last two digits of the year of birth, M is the letter assigned to the month of birth, and DD are the last two letters of birth. ZZZZ is the specific area code for the municipality where the person was born; X is a parity character calculated by adding together the letters in even and odd positions. The

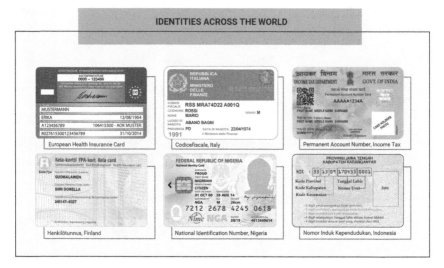

Figure 6.3 Digital identities across the world – Europe, Asia, and Africa.

letters of the month are used alphabetically, but only the letters A to E, H, L, M, P, and R to T are used (thus, January is A and October is R). To differentiate between genders, 40 is added to the day of birth for females; and for foreigners, a country-wide code is used in place of a municipal code.

The Gambia and Nigeria allot 11-digit identification numbers to their citizens called National Identification Numbers (National Identity Management Commission (NIMC), 2012).

In the People's Republic of China, an 18-digit ID card in the format RRRRR-RRYYYMMDDSSSC is mandatory for all citizens above 16 years of age. RRRRRR is a standard code for the administrative division of the county or city where the holder is born; YYYYMMDD is the date of birth of the holder; and SSS is a sequential code to differentiate people with the same date of birth and place of birth (Shaw, 1996; Perry, 1997). The sequential code is odd for males and even for females.

Indonesia has rolled out a 16-digit RFID card with electronic signature, iris scan, ten-finger fingerprint scan, and a high-resolution passport under the name of e-KTP (Electronic Kartu Tanda Penduduk) since 2012. This program has been designed on the basis of UIDAI of India.

In India, countless IDs have been floated and rolled back so far, leading to a state of flux and confusion among the citizens (Garg, 2017, 2019). These include photo-IDs, licenses, permits, registrations, certificates, and documents, which are basically derivatives of the services being offered by various agencies, such as the EPIC, issued by the Election Commission of India.

The Electors Photo Identity Card (popularly known as EPIC or Voter ID) was implemented in the year 1993 to bring transparency in the electoral process and to enable voter's identification on election day. Up till now, more than 450 million voters hold election identity cards across the country. The EPIC also acts as an identity proof and address proof to open a bank account, make an online reservation for travel, and to book an accommodation. However, it could not become an all-purpose National ID, owing to its limited operations.

As of now, more than one hundred identity documents are operational to transact and receive government benefits, in lieu of any National ID (Garg, 2021a), such as:

- Indian passport
- Overseas passport
- Electoral photo identity card (EPIC) issued by ECI
- Overseas citizenship of India (OCI)
- Person of Indian origin card (PIOC)
- Permanent account number (PAN) issued by IT department
- Driving license, issued by individual states

It is not just about procuring the documents; the matter gets more complicated, as these documents have to be renewed periodically, and the process gets complicated with long queues, lengthy procedures, bulk formalities, and the intervention of proxies and agents (Garg, 2021b).

Even during the online process, every e-site generates and requires a new ID and password with erratic captchas in the midst of heavy traffic and server issues. This is how, instead of making things simple, the online processes make things more cumbersome. Government officials also get bogged down handling piles of applications for processing services.

Verification of these documents, at each level, is another tedious exercise. An average Indian has to carry at least three to five different documents to prove his identity. The limitation of existing IDs is that they serve dissimilar and limited purposes only. Further, it is not uncommon to find discrepancies in the citizen's profile among different repositories, causing confusion and error (Garg, 2021c).

Catering to the needs of different identity cards, Estonia has developed the most advanced National ID system on the planet. It substitutes travel documents, medical tokens, and bank accounts. Singapore is another country that follows a National Digital Identity (NDI) system. From 2020, the NDI was expected to work alongside SingPass – Singapore's online account management, through the citizen's cellphone – to access hundreds of digital government services (Govtech, 2022).

6.2 Centralized Model

6.2.1 A Case Study of World's Largest Biometric ID System – Aadhaar

For more than a decade, India has been striving to provide an official identity to all its citizens. The idea of a universal identity cropped up in 2006, with a primary objective to provide a biometrics-enabled unique number to every resident of India. The flagship project of the Unique Identification Authority of India (UIDAI), prevalently known as Aadhaar, has been in vogue for past decade. It is the world's largest biometric identification program in which a 12-digit personal identification number is issued by UIDAI on behalf of the government of India. The government perceives the Aadhaar card as a tool for better governance, as each Aadhaar number is unique to an individual and remains valid until death. It aims to:

- achieve social inclusion with more efficient public and private service delivery;
- curb the number of masquerading and fake identities; and
- facilitate direct benefit transfer.

Aadhaar was conceptualized to offer an identity to those residents who did not have any individual identity or who had multiple identities. The basic idea was to create a super identity, which is traceable and less susceptible to being misused. The government came up with an idea of creating a single biometric identification system that could be monitored by UIDAI and may allow Indian residents to make access to the public services.

In 2010, the National Identification Authority of India (NIAI) was created with the objective of issuing unique identification numbers – Aadhaar – to all residents of India and to certain other classes of individuals. The NIAI Bill did not define certain other persons but stipulated that the central government may, from time to time, notify such other categories of persons, who may have an Aadhaar number. The information, so collected, shall be stored in the Central Identities Data Repository (CIDR) and used for providing authentication services.

6.2.1.1 Salient Features of Aadhaar

Some of the salient features of Aadhaar project as mentioned in the UIDAI draft (UIDAI, 2009) are enumerated here under:

- The UID, a randomly generated number, without any intelligence, will function to reduce the possibility of fraud but will not be an indication of citizenship status.
- The enrollment process for a UID number will be voluntary, upon providing the demographic and biometric information by the resident.
- The UIDAI will only issue a number to the individual that can be printed on a card like PAN card or voter's ID. The number will remain the same until death.

- In order to prevent frauds, UIDAI will set Know Your Resident (KYR) parameters for the UID enrollment process.
- The UIDAI will form a Central Identity Data Repository (CIDR) and ensure core services like storage, verification, authentication, and amendment of the UID-linked resident data.
- In order to expedite the enrollment process, the UIDAI planned to partner with the existing government and nongovernment agencies across the country and took leverage of their infrastructure to process UID application, connect to the CIDR database for verification and de-duplication, and finally, to receive the UID numbers.

6.2.1.2 Biometric and Demographic Standards

The data used in Aadhaar encompasses biometrics and demographics (Sharma and Kumar, 2013).

a) Demographic

UIDAI collects the following demographic details for Aadhaar (i-Government Bureau, 2009):

- Personal details
- Address details
- Parents' details
- Introducer details
- Contact details (see Figure 6.4)

b) Biometric

UIDAI has adopted a multi-modal biometric system on the basis of three different biometric data: (i) all ten fingerprints; (ii) iris scan; and (iii) facial recognition of every individual (see Table 6.1; Li and Jain, 2011). Multimodal system allows the integration of two or more types of biometric recognition and verification in order to meet stringent performance requirements. It helps to overcome the restrictions imposed by a single biometric system, like calloused fingerprints or problems in facial detection due to change in ambient light (Kant, Nath, and Chaudhary, 2008).

c) Supporting Documents

In order to verify the information submitted by residents, three distinct methods of verification were employed (Dass and Bajaj, 2008):

- Support documents
- Personal introducer
- National population register (NPR)

Figure 6.4 Aadhaar – An identity based on biometric and demographic data.

Table 6.1 Demographic and biometric details collected by UIDAI.

Demographic Information	Name, address (permanent and present), date of birth/age, gender, mobile number, email address, relationship status, UID number of parents (optional for adult residents), and information-sharing consent.
Biometric Information	Iris, fingerprints, and facial identity through photograph

6.2.1.3 Enrollment Set-up

A standard enrollment architecture involves a network of registrars and enrollment agencies. A registrar is a unit, authorized by UIDAI, for the purpose of enrolling individuals, which in turn, appoints the enrollment agencies that are

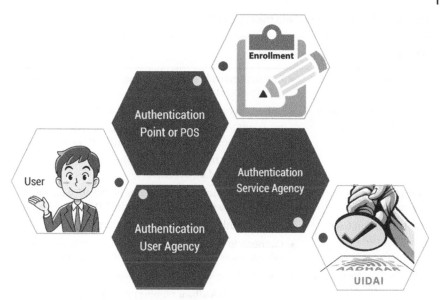

Figure 6.5 Entities involved in UID project.

responsible for collecting biometric and demographic information during the enrollment process. The latter completes its task by involving certified operators/supervisors (see Figure 6.5).

The Unique Identification Project includes unique entities like UIDAI, an enrollment station, and a Central Identities Data Repository (CIDR), which co-exist and function in close harmony. The UIDAI has also appointed a number of Authentication Service Agencies (ASAs) and Authentication User Agencies (AUAs) from various government and nongovernment organizations.

6.2.1.4 Entities and Their Roles

The brief description of key factors and the manner in which they are associated to each other have been depicted in the ensuing table (see Table 6.2).

The UIDAI, for the purpose of instant authentication of residents, has set up a scalable ecosystem. The Aadhaar authentication ecosystem is capable of handling multi-million authentications, on a day-to-day basis.

Since the authentication service is provided in real-time, two data centers function simultaneously, one where authentication is done and, second, where the online services like e-KYC are available in active-active mode to ensure prompt response. The financial institutions and payment network operators have embedded Aadhaar authentication into their micro-ATMs, to permit branchless banking all over the country in a real-time, accessible, and interoperable manner.

Table 6.2 Different entities and their role in UID cycle.

Entities	Functions
Enrollment Station	• Captures individual's demographic and biometric details for enrollment in Aadhaar database.
Authentication Point or Point of Sale (PoS)	• Collects personal identity data from Aadhaar holders. • Prepare the information for transmission and authentication and to receive the authentication results.
User	• Enrolls with UIDAI and receives the UID (Aadhaar number), issued by UIDAI.
Authentication Service Agency (ASA)	• Transmits authentication requests on behalf of one or more AUA, as per formal bond with UIDAI.
Authentication User Agency (AUA)	• Provides authentication services to the users. • Connects to the CIDR and uses Aadhaar authentication to validate users for enabling services like PDS, NREGS, etc.
The Unique Identification Authority of India (UIDAI)	• Provides basic identification and authentication services. • Issues a UID (Aadhaar number) to each resident. • Maintains biometric and demographic data in a Central Identities Data Repository (CIDR). • Monitors the said repository (CIDR).

6.2.1.5 Process of Authentication

- After procuring the Aadhaar number, together with necessary demographic and/or biometric details and/or an OTP from the user's cellphone, the client application packs and encrypts these input parameters into PID block instantly, before any transmission.
- The PID block is forwarded to the requesting entity's server, using a secure protocol as per the prescribed norms and specifications.
- The requesting entity's server, after verification, sends an authentication request to the CIDR through the ASA's server, as per the specified norms and procedures. The authentication request is digitally signed by the requesting entity and/or by the ASA, based on the mutual agreement between them.
- Thereafter, the CIDR, reverts a digitally signed, "Yes" or "No" authentication response with encrypted e-KYC data, as the case may be, along with other technical details, based on authentication request, after validating the input parameters against the data stored therein (see Figure 6.6).
- The authentication is reduced to a 1:1 match as the Aadhaar number, along with all the input parameters, is a necessary prerequisite for submission.

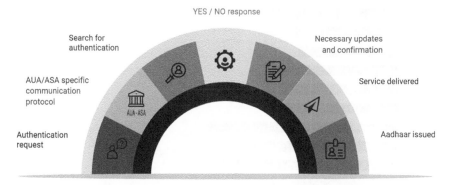

YES / NO response

Search for authentication

Necessary updates and confirmation

AUA/ASA specific communication protocol

AUA-ASA

Service delivered

Authentication request

Aadhaar issued

Figure 6.6 Process of authentication.

The key factors could engage with each other in many ways. For example, an AUA could choose to become its own ASA, or an AUA could access Aadhaar authentication services through multiple ASAs for reasons, such as business continuity planning, or an AUA could transmit authentication requests for its own service delivery needs or also on behalf of multiple sub-AUAs.

A biometric system adopted by UIDAI is mainly a pattern recognition system that obtains biometric data from an individual, then extracts a feature set from the acquired data, and finally, compares this feature set against the standard template set in the database. As a result, a random number, irrespective of any classification, is generated as a unique identity of an individual. In response to identification queries, the UIDAI authenticates as a "Yes" or "No" (Patnaik and Gupta, 2010).

To establish an individual identity, the system hunts all the templates of the users in the database to find a good match. Therefore, the system conducts a one-to-several comparison. Identification is a critical component in negative recognition applications, where the system establishes whether the person is who he denies to be. Negative recognition helps to prevent a person from using multiple identities.

In the verification mode, an individual's identity is validated by equating his biometric template stored in the database with that of the captured biometric data. In such a case, a person who needs to be recognized claims an identity through a personal identification number (PIN), a user name, or an IC enabled card, and the system conducts a one-to-one comparison to ascertain the validity of the claim. Identity verification, commonly termed as positive recognition, is normally used to prevent more than one person from using the same identity.

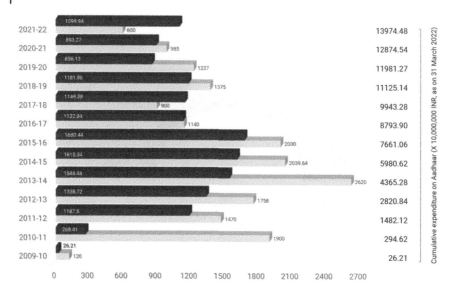

Figure 6.7 Budget and expenditure of UIDAI (in 10,000,000 INR).

6.2.1.6 Budget and Outlay

Figure 6.7 depicts the total budget allocation and expenditure incurred on UIDAI for enrollment and authentication.

6.2.1.7 Enrollment Status and Saturation

To date, 1.33 billion citizens have been enrolled in the system, with a total expenditure of 139.75 billion INR toward the issue of Aadhaar numbers (UIDAI, 2022) over the last 13 years (see Figure 6.8), .

Thus, it is apparent that India has not yet achieved the target of delivering Aadhaar cards to all concerned. So far only 1.26 billion Aadhaar cards have been issued (see Figure 6.9) with an overall saturation ratio of 92.35% (UIDAI, 2022). The saturation ratio is the number of Aadhaars issued with respect to the projected total population of the country, in percentage. Here, the projected total population is the population that has been estimated in 2022 on the basis of census figures.

$$\text{Saturation Ratio} \ (\%) = (A \ / \ B)*100$$

Where A = Number of Aadhaar Cards issued, and
　　　 B = Total Population.

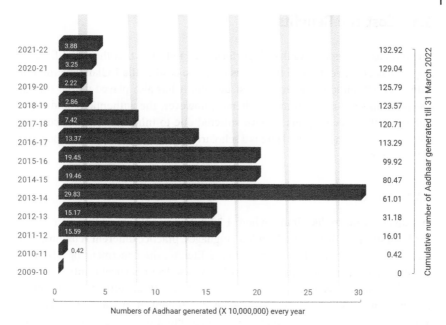

Figure 6.8   Numbers of UID (Aadhaar) generated (X 10,000,000).

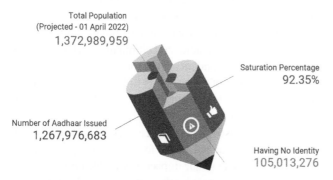

Figure 6.9   Saturation status (in percentage).

The picture that emerges from the saturation ratio, as on date, is that despite an expenditure of ≥139.74 billion INR, the government has not been able to achieve 100% targets over a period of thirteen years. This implies that 105 million marginalized residents who are in dire need of access to limited benefits provided by the State, are still living dispossessed. There must be certain lapses, which need to be probed further.

6.3   Cost and Benefits

A careful assessment of Aadhaar's performance indicates that this identification system has effectively roped in billions of users, costing the Indian government with over 130 billion INR for the last decade. It has also played a vital role in speeding up several government schemes; however, the authenticity and functioning of the system seems to have suffered due to inherent malpractices and fake identities in the system. Here is a scholarly appraisal of the costs and benefits of the system.

6.3.1   Merits

In a diverse country like India, where 1.37 billion people are spread over 3,287, 263 km^2, speak 22 different scheduled languages, practice different religions, and merely three quarters of the population is literate, the enactment of UID was indeed a challenge at socioeconomic, political, and technological fronts.

Aadhaar started as a unique identification tool, with an authentication infrastructure in its first phase, evolved as an instrument of public sector delivery reforms in its second phase, and transformed into a tool for e-KYC and direct benefit transfer in the third phase (Prasad, 2019). In the first two years, it saved to the government treasury a sum of 361.44 billion INR in a few welfare schemes.

Aadhaar, with a portable ID, has empowered the excluded and deprived sections of the society, such as migrants, transgenders, and tribals. The Jan Dhan-Aadhaar-Mobile (JAM) trinity served as a bridge to connect public funds, mobile numbers, and Aadhaar cards to transfer subsidies and eliminate intermediaries to stop leakages. It enabled banking correspondents to approach rural areas to facilitate banking transactions with the use of micro-ATMs linked to Aadhaar. Bank accounts were opened with free accident insurance, a zero balance savings account, a RuPay card, and many more benefits.

State governments have been advised to implement Aadhaar-based Direct Benefit Transfer (DBT) to individual beneficiaries for all central government wholly or partially funded schemes. The major impact was visible on the people who rely on food subsidies and food grains under the National Food Security Act, 2013. Aadhaar-based DBT not only weeded out ghost beneficiaries but also facilitated direct transfer of funds to the bank account of the target person.

One of the major breakthroughs of Aadhaar was evident in the passport procurement process. This has significantly slashed down the time-consuming police verification process and paved the way for issuance of passports within ten days. Perhaps, this is the reason why the Aadhaar card has emerged as a mandatory document to obtain a passport.

Similarly, Aadhaar has simplified the process of monthly pension and provident fund withdrawal for individuals who have registered their Aadhaar numbers with their bank accounts and with the Employees Provident Fund records. Aadhaar is also being linked with voter ID to eliminate bogus voters and those having more than one voter ID.

Aadhaar has also initiated the process of shifting from relational to personal identity for women as individuals. Women are now authorized to receive their cash transfers directly into their bank accounts, and this process has given them greater mobility (Kelkar et al., 2015). Overall, Aadhaar, being an identity proof for every individual, is a big leap toward the financial inclusion and socioeconomic development of the country.

6.3.2 Demerits

The UID project was a critical initiative for India and in all possibilities, the government had to ensure that the future of this project would not be like the other mega exercises, such as the launch of EPIC in the country. Unfortunately, the over-enthusiastic political and administrative fraternity never ventured into the pros and cons, which a common man managed to see, probably as a hindsight effect.

6.3.2.1 Waste of Resources

The saga of Aadhaar's pitfall begins with the National Identification Authority of India Bill (NIAI, 2010) itself. The Standing Committee on Finance, in its 42nd Report, questioned the need of adding yet another form of identity, i.e. Aadhaar, without exploring the possibility of using the existing forms of identity like passports, voter IDs, driving licenses etc. and referred to it as a potential waste of resources. In response to the query, the government clarified that the project was not meant to do away with the existing forms of identification. Those IDs would remain pertinent to a domain and service. This was, perhaps, the first indication of its downfall.

The Aadhaar number, which was imagined by the government as a general proof of identity and proof of address could not hold ground because various existing forms of identity still continue and the requirement of furnishing other documents for proof of address, even after the issue of Aadhaar number, make its existence superfluous.

6.3.2.2 Lack of Neutrality

According to the Bill, Aadhaar number is not linked to citizenship, and therefore, every resident of India is entitled to it, provided they furnish their demographic and biometric information. Though demographic information does not include information related to nationality, religion, language, income, or health by the documentary proofs that are collected for it, such sensitive information is automatically brought forth, questioning the neutrality of information.

6.3.2.3 Technical Glitches

Further, the NIAI, as per the framework of the Bill, is responsible for protection and privacy of information. The Bill stipulates that sharing of data is prohibited, except by the consent of the resident, by a court order, or for national security when it shall be directed by an authorized official. However, the term national security, having an unstipulated and indefinite meaning, has not been defined anywhere in the Bill.

The Standing Committee voiced some of the security concerns coming from civil society groups and recommended the government to introduce a new bill, and a national data protection law, as a prerequisite.

The committee also criticized that no comprehensive assessment has been done regarding the data security, practical aspects, and financial implications of the project. It was envisioned that the project was a pro-poor one, which would stop leaks in the welfare system, and the technology would fix rest of the things. However, on the technical side itself, the flaws have to be rectified. The use of biometrics as an authentication mechanism has several drawbacks, for which similar projects in developed countries, such as the UK and the US, were halted after public scrutiny. According to the National Research Council in the US, biometric technology is suitable for a small scale only. It is inherently fallible for large-scale biometrics, and the results are often probabilistic.

6.3.2.4 Security Procedures

A question arises that what are the security measures taken by the government of India to protect the private and confidential information of citizens?

UIDAI has drawn up a comprehensive security policy that enunciates that:

- The Aadhaar number should never be used as a domain-specific identifier.
- In the case of operator-assisted devices, the operators must be authenticated using mechanisms of password, Aadhaar authentication, etc.
- Personal Identification Data (PID) needs to be encrypted after the block is initially captured for Aadhaar authentication.
- Encrypted PID blocks should not be stored unless buffer authentication is required; that, too, for a maximum period of 24 hours.
- Biometric or other personal data, captured for Aadhaar authentication, cannot be kept in any permanent storage device or database.
- The responses and metadata should be logged for audit purposes.
- A secure network should exist between AUA and ASA.

Have these measures been effective in declining the occurrence of data breaches?

6.3.2.5 Unauthorized Access

Over the last decade, there have been multiple instances of Aadhaar data leaking online. Three Gujarat-based websites were found disclosing the Aadhaar numbers of the beneficiaries on their websites (ToI, 2018). Further, a website hosted by Jharkhand Directorate of Social Security disclosed Aadhaar details of about 1.6 million people due to a technical anomaly (The Quint, 2017). The problem is so rampant that a single Google search can reveal colossal amounts of demographic data and personal information.

An IIT graduate was arrested for building an app called Aadhaar e-KYC, by hacking the servers related to an e-Hospital system, created under the Digital India initiative. He allegedly accessed the Aadhaar database for the period from 01 January to 26 July 2017 and procured the same without any authorization (The Hindu, 2017a).

UIDAI has regularly shut down fraudulent websites and mobile apps that claimed to render Aadhaar services to users. Having become conscious of the fact that the Aadhaar portal could be accessed without authorization, UIDAI blocked around 5,000 officials from accessing the portal (Tech2, 2018). The saga does not end here, as another racket was unearthed by a reporter from *The Tribune*, who offered access to the Aadhaar data on payment of Rs. 500 to individuals via WhatsApp. The report indicates that the agents hacked into the website of the Government of Rajasthan to gain access to the software and fetched the details of all users listed by UIDAI, including name, address, email ID, as well as the mobile phone number.

Apart from the typical hackers breaching the security of the Aadhaar database, some miscreants also created fake Aadhaar cards, posing a threat to UIDAI. According to a report, a gang in Kanpur was running a racket to generate fake Aadhaar cards (The Hindu, 2017b). UIDAI stated that the system detected abnormal activities and lodged a complaint. It spelled out that a big scam to generate the fake cards was blocked by the system, and it did not affect the database of the processing system.

As the data records have no secure encryption, they are easily exchanged by the illegal companies and utilized at their convenience. According to the Breach Level Index (BLI), computed by a digital security firm, almost one billion data records have been compromised in India, which includes the name, address, and other personal information since 2013. BLI is a global database of public data breaches. It has exposed 945 data cracks that led to about 4.5 billion data records either stolen, lost, or negotiated worldwide during January to July 2018. It is a matter of grave concern that hardly 8.33% of data is encrypted to render the information useless for hackers.

Of late, the privacy concerns about Aadhaar attracted public attention when a French security researcher pointed out flaws in the mAadhaar app, available on the Google Play Store. The government mobile app, with flaws, can potentially allow attackers to access the Aadhaar database while accessing the demographic data.

Following the reports of prevalent data breaches and the continuing threat to online data, the security of digital identity has emerged as one of the most important concerns on a national front.

6.3.2.6 Absence of Data Protection Act

Ab initio, Aadhaar was optional and was mandatorily linked to few government schemes for disbursement of LPG and food. It was targeted at the disadvantaged sections of the society who could not have bank accounts or access to public services due to lack of official identity. Of late, Aadhaar has served as a tool to make data-driven reforms in the service sector. The Planning Commission of India prepared a UIDAI Strategy Overview, which assures that such identification will facilitate vulnerable groups to have easier access to government and private sector services.

The UIDAI Strategy Overview asserts that the project is about identity and is a single-stage identity-verification document. But if one examines the approach of the UIDAI system to collect, maintain, and use information, it becomes apparent that the project aims to ensure identification more than identity. Else, how different is it from a driver's license, PAN card, passport, ration card, or voter ID? All these documents are likewise valid and acceptable forms of confirming one's identity. In order to address all such queries, the Bill must be examined thoroughly.

India does not have a data protection law at the moment, and the right to privacy is not cited anywhere in the Constitution. However, the Supreme Court has derived the right to privacy from the rights stated under Articles 19(1)(a) and Article 21 of the Constitution. Besides the Constitution, the only legal instrument to protect privacy is the Information Technology Act, 2000, Section 43-A that prescribes compensation when a person, who holds sensitive personal data or information in a computer resource, fails to retain its sanctity and loses it to an individual who gains out of it in an unlawful manner.

Though the right to privacy does not find any explicit mention in the Constitution, India is a co-signer of all major international conventions which defend the right to privacy, such as the UN Charter (1945), Universal Declaration of Human Rights (1948), and the International Covenant on Civil and Political Rights (1966).

In the present milieu, UIDAI cannot share personal data without the consent of the individual. As per the interim orders issued by the Supreme Court of India, no service provider can make Aadhaar mandatory. The government and the private vendors can make access to the user's information only in his presence.

Despite the Court's verdict, confusion persists as to whether the information provided to UIDAI is voluntary or not, as the National Identification Authority of India (NIAI) Bill is silent on this issue. However, subsequent clarifications in official responses state that the information furnished to the agency is voluntary in nature. Obviously, this voluntariness extends to the disclosure of information to the registrar or enrollment agencies. Nonetheless, it is still uncertain who will access it, to what extent it will be retrieved, and how much of this information will be utilized at the other end. In absence of a clear legislative and judicial verdict in India, the UIDAI project needs to be effectively safeguarded. In other countries, information privacy is protected by comprehensive data protection laws (US Privacy Act, 1974; UK Data Protection Act, 1998; US Computer Matching and Privacy Act, 1988).

It is quite unfortunate that despite the intervention of the Court, the issue of data privacy in India has not been resolved. On the contrary, the government has made an amendment to the Income Tax Act to coerce linking of Aadhaar numbers with PANs for tax returns to be processed. Failure to do so may lead to invalidation of the respective PAN. These regulations are a forced compulsion upon the citizens to cede their Aadhaar to these documents. Since Aadhaar holds a lot of personal and private information like biometrics, fingerprints, etc., it eventually defies data privacy.

6.3.2.7 Involvement of Private Players

There is additional fear concerning the involvement of private players in the Aadhaar process. Since most of the enrollment centers are run by private agencies, there is an apparent threat to data security. As Aadhaar is linked to several government services and subsidies, the chances of misuse in order to avail those services cannot be ruled out.

Not only this, the issue of data security also applies to the private companies, service providers, financial institutions, and other private players who have access to the user's biometric information. They preserve a copy of Aadhaar as a precondition to processing and getting access to their services. A website called magicapk had leaked data of existing Reliance Jio Customers, indicating a potential risk for citizens' private information (Livemint, 2017).

Time and again, Aadhaar is compared with the Social Security number (SSN) system in the USA (Medianama, 2019). However, its provisions are objectively different from that of Aadhaar. The US provides every citizen with a unique number (SSN), which requires an ID proof. It is a much better format in terms of data security; it is stored separately and matched to the name only for security reasons. Over the years, the US government has tried to restrict its use to federal agencies only, for the purpose of identification, which is in contrast to the Indian government's constant efforts for increasing its usage. In India, Aadhaar is applicable to commercial purposes, too, and has the involvement of private parties in its data access, which imposes a huge risk of data breaches, given that there are no existing privacy laws.

Another major concern is about the cyber ecosystem of the UIDAI, where citizen's privacy is the utmost crucial. This raises a doubt whether the Indian bureaucracy is equipped enough to manage something like the UID database. Else, the lack of competence to handle such big data will only make it easier for the hackers to target the honeypot (UID system).

So far, it has been a practice to capture the user's information provided to government offices, financial institutions, and service providers in discrete towers (silos). Each silo holds specific information for a specific purpose so that no single institution or agency could amass interrelated data with it, as far as possible. But in the case of Aadhaar, UIDAI has merged all these silos together for convenience and one-step solutions. The standing committee on the NIAI Bill has rightly recommended that in the absence of sufficient safety measures, with respect to privacy of information, the storing and sharing of sensitive data in centralized agencies must be stopped to prevent an Orwellian state (The Economic Times, 2019).

6.3.2.8 Freedom of Choice as an Illusion

Romer describes the UID project as the most sophisticated ID program in the world (Rodrigues, 2017). Nilekani also argued that enrollment in Aadhaar is voluntary, and individuals are granting permission for data collection for their own convenience and benefits. Therefore, it hardly qualifies as a violation of their right to privacy (Nilekani, 2015).

However, Nilekani's argument seems to be hypocritical because individuals truly have no choice but to enroll if they wish to continue to access basic social and financial services (Chandrasekhar, 2015). This echoed an ideological belief that individuals made choices only after assessing the cost benefit, and therefore, they were responsible for it. This philosophy validates virtually all user agreements employed by technology companies that directly or indirectly collect users' personal data, such as Google and Facebook (Hoofnagle and Urban, 2014). As a result, individuals themselves, and not governments or corporations, become the locus of privacy decisions in such matters (Baruh and Popescu, 2017).

Holding users responsible for privacy in their dealing with technology companies and government-backed data projects in the name of alleged autonomy or freedom of choice is a form of hoax or the best trick at worst. Personal choice is an illusion in the politico-economic environment; the government takes one-time consent and continues to extend the project on a fractional basis (Shahin and Zheng, 2018).

In a country where 412 million people are illiterate and impoverished, it is unfair to hold citizens accountable for their decisions or choices. This leads to speculation that social and cultural institutions, the so-called "data intermediaries" (Sawicki and Craig, 1996), who shape public understanding of technology services and data projects, have played their role faithfully and presented the costs and benefits of big data in a transparent manner.

In general, big data is viewed as a technological marvel of the information age. The three Vs – volume, velocity, and variety, which refer to the unprecedented scale of data sets, the unmatched speeds at which data is produced and the unparalleled range of data types (Ward and Barker, 2013) – persuade a common man to rely upon them. That's why NAIA envisioned that technology would fix everything. However, the privacy threats are not due to the volume of the data, but to the technologies that are being applied to collect, analyze, and make use of data (Andrejevic and Gates, 2014).

These days, websites, social media, telecom operators, sensor networks, government organizations, credit card companies, and public profile managers all collect users' personal information from a variety of data points with or without users' knowledge. If one data set does not have personal indicators, then big data enables cross-referencing with other sites to create them. For instance, one can easily match anonymous profiles on dating sites with public pictures on Instagram or Facebook, through facial recognition techniques (Ohms, 2010; Acquisti, Gross, and Stutzman, 2011).

Despite the unprecedented surge of public information on social media, a large number of users are unaware of how technology services compromise their privacy (Srinivasan et al., 2018). Those who are aware want more regulations on the activities of governments and corporations providing such services (Elueze and Quan-Haase, 2018). The legal framework within which governments and corporations operate often holds users accountable for their privacy. Even in the United States, it is imperative for individuals to evaluate their choices and take onus for the decisions they make (White House, 2012).

India's data privacy landscape follows the same logic. The Information Technology Act, 2000, and the IT Rules, 2011, warn citizens about biometric data as sensitive data that is to be shared only with consent (Roy and Kalra, 2011). But the consensus itself is so vague that it has little (Dixon, 2017) or no practical value. One-time consent may have the potential to abuse and affect the privacy of an individual.

It is recommended that the individual should be asked to give consent at each stage of receiving a service. The government must recognize all dimensions of the right to privacy and address concerns about data security, protection against unauthorized interception, access to personal identity, and surveillance. Privacy ought to be treated as an inalienable right rather than a market commodity that individuals can trade for data-oriented services or facilities. In addition, governments and corporations that provide such services should be held accountable for violations of privacy rights.

The government must assure citizens that it will prevent unauthorized disclosure and access to such data. This could be the first step toward changing the governmental and corporate tendency to view data and technology services as tools of surveillance and a means of expanding their social control.

6.3.2.9 Implicit Coercion

Another debatable aspect of the project has been voluntary as opposed to the implied mandatory nature of enrollments. Although the project document does not make it mandatory for an individual to obtain an Aadhaar number, it also

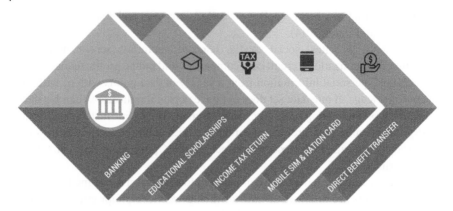

Figure 6.10   Areas, where Aadhaar is mandatory.

does not prohibit an agency from demanding an Aadhaar number for availing a service. Taking advantage of this, in recent years, the government has made it obligatory to cede Aadhaar with PAN, passport, and ration cards, as a prerequisite to access the service (see Figure 6.10).

Nowadays, linking of Aadhaar with social schemes has ironically created more barriers for the unprivileged section of the society, who are in dire need of access to limited benefits provided by the State. This remarkably differs from the United States, where a government agency cannot deny a benefit to an individual if he or she does not possess a Social Security number or refuses to disclose it, unless there is an express necessity under the law to do so.

In September 2013, the very statement that an Aadhaar card has to be a prerequisite for public services suffered a setback, when the Supreme Court of India passed an interim order in a case, challenging the constitutional validity of the UIDAI. On March 16, 2015, the Apex Court made it clear that no person shall be denied any benefit or suffer for not having an Aadhaar card issued by the UIDAI. In light of the Court's verdict, Aadhaar has lost its ground (The Economic Times, 2018).

6.4   Quest for *One World – One Identity*

In this wake, it seems worthwhile to have a *One World – One Identity*, leveraging the advantages of a decentralized identity system. The unique identification number comprising 20 digits may be provided to one and all, at the time of birth or on the day of census. The Digital ID System (using an Interplanetary File System (IPFS) or the so-called Private Ledger) would record all substantive data of a citizen, including digital identification number, name of the citizen, date of birth, family details, photograph, biometric details, digital signatures, educational progress, extra-academic achievements, employment details, transfers and switch-overs, driving license, vehicle registration, mobile phone, PAN, LPG, bank accounts, financial assets, liabilities, passports, visas, foreign travel, legal and medical records, rewards, and punishments from time to time in distributed ledgers (Garg, 2021d).

Obviously, it would replace all possible documents procured by an individual during his lifetime and save the system from fake accounts, forged identity, and data breaches. Though provision of multiple services to a massive population by government and private organizations is a gigantic task; however, *One World – One Identity* would help in improved educational, banking, investment, health care, public distribution schemes and other services, where a single card with unique number would hold all the substantive data of a citizen, whether it be personal, biometric, educational, extracurricular, vocational, medical, legal, or financial, in different silos, in a duly encrypted manner (Garg, 2022a). A single ID would reinforce national and social security for citizens and serve as an instrument to allow access to varied government and private services (i-Government Bureau, 2009).

Introduction of a *One World – One Identity* could also hand over the control of personal data to the citizens. By sharing the optimum amount of personal data, one could minimize the risks of hacks and breaches associated with sensitive data. According to Scalar Decisions, individual Canadian organizations face an average 440 cyberattacks per organization per year, with 3% amounting to a breach (Scalar, 2019). By confining to a distributed digital identity model, there wouldn't be centralized databases, and organizations would curtail the costs that accompany a data breach. At the same time, users would be able to restrict access to the pertinent information and avoid the problem of oversharing their personal information.

Moreover, distributed models assure the consumers, organizations, and service providers that the bulk of information is never stored in a single repository, rather distributed among decentralized databases. Consumers, without being physically present, can share their digital ID with the service provider through a personal device, such as a smartphone, and receive appropriate services without jeopardizing their privacy.

Another strong advantage of such an identity system is its capability to streamline administrative processes, thereby enhancing the productivity of departments and services. Subsequently, the system can work on a global level to connect different service providers across multiple countries through use of Distributed Ledger Technology. Organizations can minimize the time spent on tedious tasks that include customer service calls or entering data from the application forms submitted by the citizens (Garg, 2022b).

Coming Up

This chapter considered the cost and benefits of a centralized identity management model through the case study of the world's largest biometric project, Aadhaar. This led to the conclusion that a centralized identity system could fail on data security and privacy issues by becoming a honeypot for hackers and unauthorized entities.

With the rampant exploitation and recurrent threat to online data, the security of digital identities has emerged as one of the foremost concerns on the global front. For privacy and security of personal data, decentralized identity may be a great solution, and the technology that has risen to the top of the list is blockchain. The upcoming chapter discusses how blockchain can syndicate authentication technologies with advanced privacy features to provide a robust and frictionless identity management.

References

Acquisti A, Gross R, and Stutzman F, 2011. Faces of Facebook: Privacy in the Age of Augmented Reality. Paper presented at Black Hat Conference, Las Vegas, NV.

Andrejevic M and Gates K, 2014. Big Data Surveillance: Introduction. *Surveillance & Society*, 12: 185–196.

Baruh L and Popescu M, 2017. Big Data Analytics and the Limits of Privacy Self-Management. *News Media and Society*, 19: 579–596.

Chandrasekhar R, 2015. A Shaky Aadhaar. *The Indian Express*.

Dass R and Bajaj RK, 2008. Creation of a Single National ID: Challenges & Opportunities for India.

Dixon P, 2017. A Failure to Do No Harm – India's Aadhaar Biometric ID Program and Its Inability to Protect Privacy in Relation to Measures in Europe and the U.S. *Health Technology*, 7: 539–567.

The Economic Times, 2018. Aadhaar Verdict: Legal, but Limit Use to Government Benefits, Says Supreme Court.

The Economic Times, 2019. Personal Data Protection Bill Can Turn India into Orwellian State.

Elueze I and Quan-Haase A, 2018. Privacy Attitudes and Concerns in the Digital Lives of Older Adults: Westin's Privacy Attitude Typology Revisited. *American Behavioral Scientist*, 62 (10) 1372–1391.

Garg R, 2016. Generic Information Tracker. 2nd India International Science Festival, New Delhi India. doi: 10.5281/zenodo.3474609. https://zenodo.org/record/3474609#. YvZkCaBBzIU.

Garg R, 2017. Hi-Tech ID with Digital Tracking System, National Conference on Application of ICT for Built Environment. doi:10.5281/zenodo.4761329. https://www.researchgate.net/publication/325248504_Hi_-_Tech_ID_with_Digital_Tracking_System.

Garg R, 2019. Multipurpose ID: One Nation – One Identity, Annual Convention – Indian Society for Technical Education (ISTE). National Conference on Recent Advances in Energy, Science & Technology (39). doi: 10.6084/m9.figshare.16945078. https://www.researchgate.net/publication/337398750_Multipurpose_ID_One_Nation_-_One_Identity.

Garg R, 2021a. *Digital Identity Leveraging Blockchain.* Barnes & Noble, Basking Ridge, New Jersey US, 1–124.

Garg R, 2021b. *Souveräne Identitäten.* Verlag Unser Wissen, Germany, 1–104.

Garg R, 2021c. *Identità Auto Sovrane.* Edizioni Sapienza, Italy, 1–104.

Garg R, 2021d. Blockchain Based Identity Solutions. *International Journal of Computer Science & Information Technology.* (In Press).

Garg R, 2022a. Distributed Ecosystem for Identity Management. *Journal of Blockchain Research.* (In Press).

Garg R, 2022b. A Technological Approach to Address Deficiencies in UID (Aadhaar). *3rd International Conference on Big Data, Blockchain and Security, Copenhagen Denmark.* doi:10.5281/zenodo.5854732. https://www.researchgate.net/publication/325247615_A_Technological_Approach_to_Address_Deficiencies_in_UID_Aadhaar.

Govtech Singapore, 2022. Digital Identity. https://www.tech.gov.sg/singapore-digital-government-journey/digital-identity.

The Hindu, 2017a. Fake Aadhaar Card Network Busted in Kanpur.

The Hindu, 2017b. Techie Arrested in Bengaluru for Accessing Aadhaar Data.

Hoofnagle C and Urban J, 2014. Alan Westin's Privacy Homoeconomicus. *Wake Forest Law Review*, 49: 261–309.

i-Government Bureau, 2009. India Plans Multi-purpose National ID Cards for Citizens. *International Covenant on Civil and Political Rights, 1966. General Assembly of the United* Nations. https://treaties.un.org/doc/publication/unts/volume%20999/volume-999-i-14668-english.pdf.

Kant C, Nath R, and Chaudhary S, 2008. Challenges in Biometrics. International Conference on Emerging Trends in Computer Science & Information Technology.

Kelkar G, Nathan D, Revathi E, and Sain Gupta S, 2015. Aadhaar: Gender, Identity and Development, Academic Foundation. http://www.ihdindia.org/Aadhar-Gender-Identity-and-Development.pdf.

Li SZ and Jain AK, 2011. *Handbook of Face Recognition.* Springer Link.

Livemint, 2017. Reliance Jio data leaked on website: report https://www.livemint.com/Industry/ucK2SJDM4Ws8k36ovZVj6H/Reliance-Jio-customer-data-allegedly-compromised-report.html.

Majumdar S, 2019. Unique Identification Initiative: An Evaluative Study on World's Largest Project Aadhaar in India. *International Journal of Research in Management. Economics and Commerce*, 08 (3): 45–50.

Medianama, 2019. Key Differences Between The U.S. Social Security System and India's Aadhaar System. https://www.medianama.com/2019/08/223-differences-between-the-u-s-social-security-system-and-indias-aadhaar-system/.

National Identity Management Commission (NIMC), 2012. About the NIN.https://nimc.gov.ng/about-nin/.

NIAI, 2010. The National Identification Authority of India Bill, Forty-second Report. https://uidai.gov.in/images/report_of_the_departmental_standing_committee_on_finance_on_the_bill_13012017.pdf.

Nilekani N, 2015. Why Supreme Court Judgment on Aadhaar Calls for an Appeal? *The Indian Express.* https://indianexpress.com/article/opinion/columns/why-supreme-court-judgment-on-aadhaar-calls-for-an-appeal/ Accessed on 15 September 2015.

Ohms P, 2010. Broken Promises of Privacy: Responding to the Surprising Failure of Anonymization. *UCLA Law Review*, 57: 1701.

Patnaik A and Gupta D, 2010. Unique Identification System. *International Journal of Computer Applications*, 7 (5): 46–48.

Perry EJ, 1997. From Native Place to Workplace: Labor Origins and Outcomes of China's Danwei System. In Lu X and EJ P (Eds.) *Danwei: The Changing Chinese Workplace in Historical and Comparative Perspective.* M.E. Sharpe, New York, 42–59.

Prasad RS, 2019. Aadhaar in national interest, does not violate privacy. *Business Standard.* https://www.business-standard.com/article/news-ani/aadhaar-in-national-interest-does-not-violate-privacy-rs-prasad-119062400785_1.html/ Accessed on 24 June 2019.

The Quint, 2017. Shocking Data Breach: Aadhaar Details of over a Million Leaked. https://www.thequint.com/news/india/shocking-data-breach-million-aadhaar-number-details-leaked-online-jharkhand-directorate-of-social-security/ Accessed on 23 April 2017.

Rodrigues J, 2017. India ID Program Wins World Bank Praise despite 'Big Brother' Fears. Bloomberg. https://www.bloomberg.com/news/articles/2017-03-15/india-id-program-wins-world-bank-praise-amid-big-brother-fears#xj4y7vzkg/ Accessed on 16 March 2017.

Roy C and Kalra H, 2011. The Information Technology Rules. PRS Legislative Research, Center for Policy Research. https://prsindia.org/files/bills_acts/bills_parliament/2011/IT_Rules_and_Regulations_Brief_2011.pdf.

Sawicki DS and Craig WJ, 1996. The Democratization of Data: Bridging the Gap for Community Groups. *Journal of the American Planning Association*, 62: 512–523.

Scalar Security, 2019. The Cyber Resilience of Canadian Organization, Results of the 2019 Scalar Security Study. https://tucu.ca/wp-content/uploads/2020/02/Scalar_Security_Study_2019.pdf.

Shahin S and Zheng P, 2018. Big Data and the Illusion of Choice: Comparing the Evolution of India's Aadhaar and China's Social Credit System as Technosocial Discourses. *Social Science Computer Review*, 38: 25–41.

Sharma N and Kumar S, 2013. Unique Identification System: Challenges and Opportunities for India. 7th International Conference on Advanced Computing and Communication Technologies, Panipat, India.

Shaw VN, 1996. *Social Control in China: A Study of Chinese Work Units*. Praeger Publishers, Westport Connecticut, 14: 82–228.

Srinivasan J, Bailur S, Schoemaker E, and Seshagiri S, 2018. Privacy at the Margin. The Poverty of Privacy: Understanding Privacy Trade-offs from Identity Infrastructure Users in India. *International Journal of Communication*, 12: 1228–1247.

Tech2, 2018. UIDAI blocks 5,000 officials from Aadhaar portal following reports of unauthorised usage. https://www.firstpost.com/tech/news-analysis/uidai-blocks-5000-officials-from-aadhar-portal-following-reports-of-unauthorised-usage-4294143.html.

Times of India, 2018. Three Gujarat Websites Including Government Portal Made Aadhaar Details Public. https://timesofindia.indiatimes.com/city/ahmedabad/three-gujarat-websites-including-govt-portal-made-aadhaar-details-public/articleshow/62406648.cms.

UIDAI, 2009. https://uidai.gov.in.

UIDAI, 2022. https://uidai.gov.in.

UK Data Protection Act, 1998. 1–86. https://www.legislation.gov.uk/ukpga/1998/29/pdfs/ukpga_19980029_en.pdf.

UN Charter, 1945. Charter of the United Nations and Statute of the International Court of Justice. San Francisco, 1–55. *Universal Declaration of Human Rights, 1948. The UN General Assembly.* https://www.un.org/en/about-us/universal-declaration-of-human-rights.

US Computer Matching and Privacy Act, 1988. 81 FR 8053-8054.

US Privacy Act, 1974. Public Law, 93–579.

Ward JS and Barker A, 2013. Undefined by Data: A Survey of Big Data Definitions. https://citeseerx.ist.psu.edu/viewdoc/download?doi=10.1.1.705.9909&rep=rep1&type=pdf.

White House, 2012. Consumer Data Privacy in A Networked World: A Framework for Protecting Privacy and Promoting Innovation in the Global Digital Economy.

Whitley EA and Hosein G, 2009. *Global Challenges for Identity Policies. Technology, Work and Globalization*. Palgrave Macmillan, Basingstoke, UK.

World Bank Group, 2020: Digital Financial Services, 54. https://pubdocs.worldbank.org/en/230281588169110691/Digital-Financial-Services.pdf.

7

Decentralized Identities

7.1 Identity Models

Since the advent of the internet, the models for online identity have advanced through four broad stages (see Figure 7.1; Garg, 2022a):

7.1.1 Centralized Identity

The first model of digital identity management is extensively being used worldwide. It is controlled by a single authority. Each organization issues a digital identity credential to users to allow them to access their services. Each user is required to have a new digital identity credential for each new organization he/she engages with (see Figure 7.2). Aadhaar (UID) is an eloquent testimony of this prototype.

7.1.2 Federated Identity

The second model of digital identity management is called the Federated Model. The poor user experience of the first model led third parties to issue digital identity certificates that allow users to log into services and other websites.

It is regulated by multiple federated authorities. Microsoft's Passport (1999) was the first to visualize federated identity, which allowed users to utilize the same identity on multiple sites. Federated identity permits users to wander from site to site under the system. However, each individual site remains an authority.

The best examples of this are "login with Facebook" and "login with Google" functionalities. Facebook, Google, and others became the intermediaries. Companies outsourced their identity management to major corporations who have an

Blockchain for Real World Applications, First Edition. Rishabh Garg.
© 2023 John Wiley & Sons, Inc. Published 2023 by John Wiley & Sons, Inc.

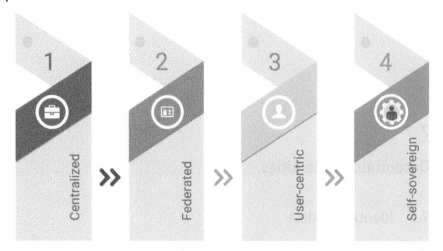

Figure 7.1 Online identity models: Stages of evolution.

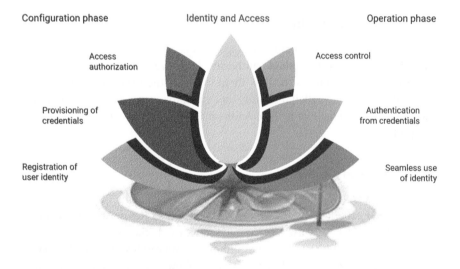

Figure 7.2 Centralized identity.

economic interest in amassing such large databases of personal data. This, of course, raised privacy and security concerns.

7.1.3 User-centric Identity

It is controlled by an individual, across multiple authorities, without requiring a federation. This identity model is based on the assumption that every individual

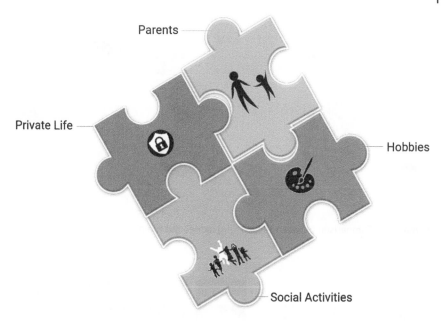

Figure 7.3 User-centric identity.

has the right to control his or her own online identity. A user can theoretically register his own Open ID that he can use independently (see Figure 7.3).

7.1.4 Self-sovereign Identity

Self-sovereign identity (SSI) is the next step after user-centric identity where the user is central to the administration of identity across any number of authorities (see Figure 7.4). A self-sovereign identity can be transportable and interoperable across multiple locations. Since self-sovereign identity confers full authority and control of identity to the users across multiple authorities, it is best suited to the contemporary needs of identification and access management.

This evades the honeypot problem too. There is no centralized storage of digital identity that may be subject to breaches (see Figure 7.5). Since every individual carries his identity details in his own identity wallet – Interplanetary File System (IPFS) – a hacker would have to hack those one billion people individually to steal one billion profiles, which is highly improbable.

7.2 Blockchain-based Solutions

Blockchain-based solutions provide an exceptional functionality in resolving issues related to the following (see Figure 7.6; Garg, 2021a):

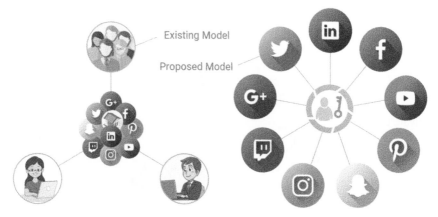

Figure 7.4 Comparison between the existing model and the proposed model.

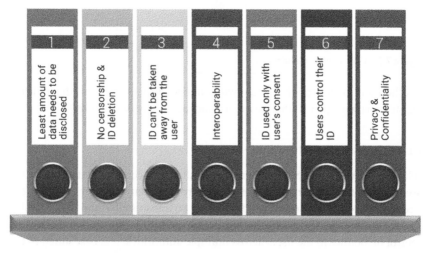

1. Least amount of data needs to be disclosed
2. No censorship & ID deletion
3. ID can't be taken away from the user
4. Interoperability
5. ID used only with user's consent
6. Users control their ID
7. Privacy & Confidentiality

Figure 7.5 Characteristics of self-sovereign identity.

1) Identity management (Single ID for lifelong activities)
2) E-verification of documents related to education and employment
3) Crowd operations (e.g., electronic voting)
4) Government services, such as health care, education, public distribution, welfare schemes, taxation, bill payments, and legal enforcement
5) Financial services, such as bank transactions, crowd funding (such as raising startup funds), investments, e-banking, credit history, and currency exchange
6) Predicting markets and trading (e.g., automated auctions)

Figure 7.6   Use cases of blockchain.

7) Distributed resources and the Internet of Things (such as power generation and distribution)
8) Goods transfer (e.g., supply chain) and remote services delivery (e.g., post, travel, and tourism)

7.3   Identity Management

As discussed in the previous chapter, the current identity management system is full of flaws. To bring in an endless list of identities and documents, one has to face long queues, lengthy processes, bulk formalities, proxies, and the intervention of agents. Moreover, the verification of these documents at each level is another dreary task. Even during the online process, each app generates or asks for a new ID and password. Users are required to create a unique username and password each time they sign up or register on each site. It becomes difficult for the users to remember these credentials whenever they log into any online platform.

7.3.1 Current Challenges

These challenges render traditional identity management difficult and unsafe:

7.3.1.1 Absence of Compatibility

The apps on which a typical ID management system works are neither updated on a regular basis nor do they comply with the security norms. In addition, diverse administrative models for different applications create inconsistency.

7.3.1.2 Identity Theft

According to the Breach Level Index, 4.5 million records are filched daily (Businesswire, 2018). This happens because people often share their personal information on anonymous forums to avail online services. Such online information falls prey to hackers because it is stored in a central server.

7.3.1.3 KYC Onboarding and Weak Authentication Protocols

The prevalent Know Your Customer (KYC) authentication process is complex and quite expensive, as it involves three stakeholders: (i) verification/KYC companies; (ii) user; and (iii) the third party for whom the user's identity is verified. Since KYC companies have to meet the requirements of banks, health-care providers, immigration officials, etc., they need more resources to expedite their operations. To facilitate this, these KYC companies charge a huge amount for verification, which is charged to the user in the form of hidden processing fees. Despite this, customers have to wait for a long time to get the facility by connecting to third parties.

7.3.1.4 Lack of Control

Currently, users have no control over personally identifiable information (PII). Users are making compromises with their privacy without being aware of how often their data is shared or where it is stored. Therefore, the current identity management system needs an immediate overhaul.

From the preceding account, it emerges as a fact that identity should be portable and verifiable anywhere, anytime. Also, they need to be made private and secure so that they can overcome the shortcomings of existing identity management systems.

- There can be a smooth interactive platform between the government and the complex bureaucratic system to reduce processing time and cost.
- The functionaries in health-care zones – hospitals, clinics, doctors, pharmacies, and insurance organizations under health care – should be intertwined on the operational front for providing quick and efficient health-care facilities to the patients.
- The education structure should be systematized and equipped with a robust certification and verification process.
- Banking should be made safer and more user-friendly by avoiding repeated "sign ins and sign outs" to access the bank accounts for every transaction.

In this context, blockchain technology appears to be a promising tool to address identity issues such as inaccessibility, data insecurity, and lack of control. It facilitates self-sovereign identity (SSI) and assures users that no third party can share their PII without their consent. SSI enables users and trades to store their own identity data on their own devices, with the users selecting the pieces of information they wish to pass on to validators without relying on a central identity data repository. These identities can be created independent of nations, states, corporations, or organizations.

Since SSI confers users with full rights and control of identity across any authorizations, it is best suited to the contemporary needs of identity and access management. It also eliminates the problem of honeypot because there is no centralized store of digital identities that could infringe on an individual's right to privacy. Because each person saves his or her identity credentials in his or her own identity wallet, such as IPFS, a hacker would have to infiltrate each of those 100 million people's personal devices independently in order to obtain 100 million profiles, which appears quite unlikely (Garg, 2019).

A broad outline of the process is summarized hereunder:

- Identity metadata can be hashed and stored on a blockchain.
- Information could be available when people need it.
- Identity data can be safely and securely recorded and accessed through IPFS by authorized parties.
- Trusted partners would provide a secure and immutable network for creating opportunities at the bottom of the pyramid.

7.4 Identity Storage | Interplanetary File System

IPFS uses a peer-to-peer (P2P) network model for file sharing that is decentralized and distributed across multiple computers or nodes. Files are split into different parts and stored in a network of nodes that track the file by hash. When the parts are assembled together, based on their hash value, it recreates the original file. The use of Distributed Hash Tables (DHT) for file system storage and retrieval is the main innovation for IPFS. It is similar to the BitTorrent protocol but differs in the way the file is indicated for sharing. It stores files on a blockchain as key value pairs. The data is split into 256 KB chunks and spread across a network of nodes or computers. It is efficiently coordinated to enable efficient access and lookup between nodes. BitTorrent does not use a blockchain but relies on torrents instead of pointing to files. One can have different torrents pointing to the same file, but in IPFS, one only needs a hash ID that points to a single file.

Files are not posted to IPFS in the same way that a file is posted to the cloud. IPFS uses a secure hash of the file contents for location identification and DHT for location resolution. This is done because the resource or object is not available on the server but on a decentralized platform. When someone requests data, the data is directly represented by its hash ID, not by the actual file. IPFS thus provides an abstraction to the actual location of the file, so the actual physical location does not matter to the application. This abstraction takes away the complexity for the application developers (Garg, 2021b, 2022b).

IPFS differs from location-based storage systems, i.e. the conventional Hyper-Text Transfer Protocol (HTTP) family or the centralized namespaces. When a storage system is location-based, it tracks the host by a logical addressing scheme (such as an IP address) mapped to a user-friendly name. If the host changes its name or address, it must also be modified in the name service table.

Content-based address storage requires a content identifier that determines the physical location of the file. In this case, the data is accessed, based on its cryptographic hash rather than a logical address, almost like a digital fingerprint of a file. Regardless of who uploaded the file, where, and when, the network always returns the same content based on that hash.

Thus, IPFS is a decentralized solution for storing files. The metadata or hash of the contents of the document can be stored on the blockchain server with the original document stored on the IPFS. This is because blockchain uses two types of variables in smart contracts: "memory" and "storage." The crypto-fuel, or gas, required for storage variables is much higher than that required for memory. Significant computation is required for changing the state hash, receipt hash, and transaction hash if entire documents are put on the blockchain server. Moreover, they will have to be processed by all the nodes in the network, leading to huge wastage of computation power and resources on blockchain.

7.4.1 How Does IPFS Access the Documents?

- IPFS does not use the HTTP family of protocols or a centralized namespace for location identification; instead, it uses a secure hash of the file contents and a Distributed Hash Table (DHT) for location resolution. This is done because the resource/object is available on a decentralized platform rather than a server. In DHT, the key is the content-hash, and the value is the file's location.
- The Bitswap protocol is used to incentivize block exchange.
- For version-based file management, the Merkle directed acyclic graph is employed.
- The files to be shared are arranged as objects held by the global network's nodes. The cryptographic hashes of a node's public key are used to identify it (similar to the 20-byte account address in Ethereum blockchain).

7.4.2 Transactions Involved in Accessing Documents on IPFS

- Peer nodes have a want list and a have list. The imbalance in these lists is identified as credit and debit.

- Tokens are used to represent value. When a node sends a block, it receives credit in the form of a token, which it can use to obtain a file from its peer nodes.

7.4.3 IPFS Commands

Following is a project made using IPFS and Ethereum Blockchain for document storage:

```
cd go-ipfs
/install.sh
/ipfs init
ipfs cat <readme file>
cat <filename>
ipfs add <filename>
```

Code Cell 7.1 IPFS commands.

App.js logic

```
import Table from 'react-bootstrap/Table';
import Grid from 'react-bootstrap/Container';
import Form from 'react-bootstrap/Form';
import Button from 'react-bootstrap/Button';
import React, { Component } from 'react';
import logo from './logo.svg';
import './App.css';
import web3 from './web3';
import ipfs from './ipfs';
import storehash from './storehash';

class App extends Component
{
  state =
  {
  ipfsHash:null,
  buffer:'',
  ethAddress:'',
  blockNumber:'',
  transactionHash:'',
  gasUsed:'',
  txReceipt: ''
  };
```

Code Cell 7.2 App.js logic.

```
captureFile =(event) =>
{
  event.stopPropagation()
  event.preventDefault()
  const file = event.target.files[0]
  let reader = new window.FileReader()
  reader.readAsArrayBuffer(file)
  reader.onloadend = () => this.convertToBuffer(reader)
};

convertToBuffer = async(reader) =>
{
  //file is converted to a buffer to prepare for
uploading to IPFS
  const buffer = await Buffer.from(reader.result);
  //set this buffer -using es6 syntax
  this.setState({buffer});
};

onClick = async () =>
{
  try
  {
    this.setState({blockNumber:"waiting.."});
    this.setState({gasUsed:"waiting…"});

    // get Transaction Receipt in console on click
    await web3.eth.getTransactionReceipt(this.state.
transactionHash, (err, txReceipt)=>
{
    console.log(err,txReceipt);
    this.setState({txReceipt});
    }); //await for getTransactionReceipt

    await this.setState({blockNumber: this.state.
txReceipt.blockNumber});
    await this.setState({gasUsed: this.state.txReceipt.
gasUsed});
  } //try
```

Code Cell 7.2 (Continued)

```
  catch(error)
  {
   console.log(error);
  } //catch
 } //onClick

 onSubmit = async (event) =>
 {
    event.preventDefault();

    //bring in user's Metamask account address
       const accounts = await web3.eth.getAccounts();

    console.log('Sending from Metamask account: ' +
accounts[0]);

    //obtain contract address from storehash.js
    const ethAddress= await storehash.options.address;
    this.setState({ethAddress});

    //save document to IPFS,return its hash#, and set
hash# to state
    await ipfs.add(this.state.buffer, (err, ipfsHash) =>
    {
     console.log(err,ipfsHash);
     //setState by setting ipfsHash to ipfsHash[0].hash
     this.setState({ ipfsHash:ipfsHash[0].hash });

     // call Ethereum contract method "sendHash" and .
send IPFS hash to contract
     //return the transaction hash from the ethereum
contract

     storehash.methods.sendHash(this.state.ipfsHash).
send({
        from: accounts[0]
      }, (error, transactionHash) => {
       console.log(transactionHash);
```

Code Cell 7.2 (Continued)

```
    this.setState({transactionHash});
   }); //storehash
  }) //await ipfs.add
 };

 render()
 {
  return(
   <div className="App">
    <header className="App-header">
      <h1>Blockchain Storage</h1>
      <img src="https:ipfs.io/ipfs/QmVqKYfEjdHmbWD4q
ML5RezYakhRQC3aJL5vj2qb4cBu8m" width="90" height="90"/>
    </header>
    <hr/>

   <Grid>
     <h3>Select a file to upload on the Blockchain
Storage</h3>
     <Form onSubmit={this.onSubmit}>
      <input
      type = "file"
      onChange = {this.captureFile}
     />
      <Button
      bsStyle="primary"
      type="submit">
      Submit
      </Button>
     </Form>

     <img src={`https:ipfs.io/ipfs/${this.state.ipfs
Hash}`} alt=""/>

     <hr/>
      <Button onClick = {this.onClick}> Get Transaction
Receipt </Button>
```

Code Cell 7.2 (Continued)

```jsx
      <Table bordered responsive>
       <thead>
        <tr>
         <th>Tx Receipt Category</th>
         <th>Values</th>
        </tr>
       </thead>

       <tbody>
        <tr>
         <td>IPFS Hash # stored on Eth Contract</td>
         <td>{this.state.ipfsHash}</td>
        </tr>
        <tr>
         <td>Ethereum Contract Address</td>
         <td>{this.state.ethAddress}</td>
        </tr>

        <tr>
         <td>Tx Hash # </td>
         <td>{this.state.transactionHash}</td>
        </tr>
        <tr>
         <td>Block Number # </td>
         <td>{this.state.blockNumber}</td>
        </tr>

        <tr>
         <td>Gas Used</td>
         <td>{this.state.gasUsed}</td>
        </tr>
       </tbody>
      </Table>
    </Grid>
   </div>
   );
  }
}

export default App;
```

Code Cell 7.2 (Continued)

IPFS is not built on the blockchain; rather it's designed to work in conjunction with the blockchain protocol. Though IPFS uses the same architectural elements as the Merkle tree, yet storing data on the blockchain could be expensive. For this reason, developers are turning to solutions like IPFS. Such a hypermedia protocol and a distributed file system enable computers around the world to store and distribute information as part of a vast network. Through a client designed by Cloudflare or Protocol Labs, users can store and access data, files, applications and websites for free.

To add an IPFS site to a domain, go to the 'My Domains' section; register an account with UD; and append the IPFS hash. Then, 'Copy' and 'Paste' the IPFS hash provided by the external IPFS upload agency, and click the 'Save' button to update the records associated with your domain.

IPFS
Here web3 is used for sending RPC requests from the blockchain.

IPFS

```
//using infura.io node, otherwise ipfs requires to run a
daemon on computer/server.
const IPFS = require('ipfs-api');
const ipfs = new IPFS({ host: 'ipfs.infura.io', port:
5001, protocol: 'https' });

//run with local daemon
// const ipfsApi = require('ipfs-api');
// const ipfs = new ipfsApi('localhost', '5001',
{protocol: 'http'});

export default ipfs;
```

For storing the hashes

```
import web3 from './web3';
//access our local copy to contract deployed on rinkeby
testnet
//use your own contract address
```

Code Cell 7.3 Storing the hashes.

```
const address =
'0xb84b11953f5bcf01b08f926728e855f2d4a62a9';
//use the ABI from contract
const abi = [
 {
  "constant": true,
  "inputs": [],
  "name": "getHash",
  "outputs": [
   {
    "name": "x",
    "type": "string"
   }
  ],
  "payable": false,
  "stateMutability": "view",
  "type": "function"
 },
 {
  "constant": false,
  "inputs": [
   {
    "name": "x",
    "type": "string"
   }
  ],
  "name": "sendHash",
  "outputs": [],
  "payable": false,
  "stateMutability": "nonpayable",
  "type": "function"
 }
]

export default new web3.eth.Contract(abi, address);
```

Code Cell 7.3 (Continued)

7.5 Biometric Solutions

Biometric authentication is integral to the modern technology landscape. There are a number of biometric authentication solutions available on smartphones, such as thumbprints, fingerprints, hand geometry, voice or facial recognition, thermal mapping, eye pattern – retinal scan, iris scan, etc. Biometric data is stored and processed with database servers, encrypted tokens or physical tokens. More secure devices typically use on-device or on-premises storage of biometric templates that ensure authentication of identity without sending any sensitive biometric information to a different server or location on the internet.

While the internal process of biometric authentication is technology based, it is incredibly easy and quick from the user's point of view. Keeping a finger on a scanner and unlocking an account in seconds is quicker and easier than typing a long password consisting of many special characters. Biometric authentication requires its input to be present upon authorization. You cannot transfer or share biological metrics digitally; the only way most biometric authentication systems are used is through physical applications. Biometrics, such as facial patterns, fingerprints, iris scanning, and others, are not so easy to replicate with current technology. There is a one out of sixty-four billion chance that your fingerprint will match exactly with that of someone else. Nevertheless, fingerprint recognition technology is accepted by a large number of users. At the same time, it is relatively inexpensive and easy to use.

7.5.1 Fingerprint Verification

Fingerprint recognition and iris scanning are the most well-known forms of biometric security. The identification system based on fingerprint recognition looks for features in the line and contour patterns on the surface of the finger. The bifurcation, ridge end, and island that make up this line pattern are stored as an image. But its biggest disadvantage is that it is an image, and this image can be replicated even if it is stored in encoded form. In principle, you could generate code similar to this. In addition, some line patterns are so similar that, in practice, this can result in high false acceptance rates, where there is room for partial matching.

Some common biometric authentication methods rely on partial information to authenticate a user's identity. For example, a mobile biometric device scans the entire fingerprint during the enrollment phase, and converts it into data. However, it uses only parts of the prints while verifying identity. This allows artificial intelligence to fabricate partial fingerprints to match someone else's profile and can deceive the authentication system.

7.5.2   Iris Scan

During an iris scan, the scanner reads the unique characteristics of an iris and converts it into an encrypted (bar) code. Iris scanning is known to be an excellent security technique, especially if it is performed using infrared light. However, users find it an unpleasant experience to have their eyes scanned. Iris scanning provides a high level of security, and more recently, devices have been developed, which can read a person's iris from a distance. Iris or retinal scans reduce the incidence of false positives and also achieve high processing speeds. However, it is not cost effective and may not give high level of accuracy in cases of ophthalmological issues.

7.5.3   Vascular Technology

In vein recognition technology, finger vein end points and bifurcations are captured as an image, digitized, and converted into an encrypted code. Since the veins are found under the skin rather than on the surface, they are far more secure than fingerprint-based identification. Although these techniques are quicker and more convenient, very cold fingers and the dead ones (Raynaud's syndrome) make it extremely difficult to read vein patterns. Perhaps this is the biggest drawback and reason why is this technology still relatively unknown.

7.5.4   Palm Vein Pattern

Another technique, palm vein pattern recognition, is also based on the identification of unique vein patterns. However, it uses more reference points than finger vein pattern recognition, and is simple as well as a safe identification method. Access control systems based on palm vein pattern recognition are relatively expensive. That is why such systems are mainly successful in the government, justice system, and banking sectors.

7.5.5   Facial Recognition

Facial recognition technology analyzes the features of different parts of the face to perform verification. This technology has developed rapidly in recent years, making it an excellent tool for remote identification. It also allows for negative detection or face-out, making it easier to scan for suspicious individuals in a crowd.

Facial recognition can be implemented for ID management, using a powerful identity management tool like BlockID. BlockID can theoretically be integrated with trust-computing technologies on any biometric-capable mobile device, such as a smartphone. It can enhance the user experience by streamlining enrollment, login, and authentication processes while augmenting security and privacy (1kosmos.

com). By generating a digital identity from a government-issued credential, it aids in precisely mapping citizens' information to a blockchain-based transaction system. BlockID uses trust-computing technologies and biometric-based user verification to make sure the data recorded on the blockchain is authentic and has originated from reliable sources.

By leveraging biometrics, such as a fingerprint, retina scan, face, or voice, BlockID eliminates the need for a credential in user transactions and enables quick and safe user authentication. As a result, BlockID offers trusted identities which provide security against identity theft, fraud, and unauthorized disclosure of personal information. However, this technology focuses mostly on the face itself, and recognition usually requires a person to look straight into the camera. Additionally, the smartphone's front-facing camera captures the user's image, which is then compared to the owner's face preserved in the device's memory. Since we don't employ a depth camera or 3D system for this, the system can be tricked by displaying a face that looks like the owner's or any archived image of the owner.

7.5.1.1 Verification of Government ID

A government ID can be verified in a number of ways, such as using the integrated chip, the barcode written on it, the QR code, or the magnetic strip on the back. These can be used with a card reader, scan reader, or barcode scanner to verify the information they carry. The information, once validated, won't need to be verified again and again because it will be permanently stored on the blockchain.

To determine how BlockID can accurately bind or link the image to the data stored on the blockchain, it is necessary to examine its security aspects.

7.5.1.2 Verification of a User

Facial recognition is the most common way for an identity creator to identify a user, as every ID card typically includes a photo of the owner's face. Although there may be several other ways to ensure identity, such as biometric data, these methods can only authenticate digital identity. The picture of the face is the only tool that is found on most identity cards. The identity creator will take a picture of the person to be identified and send it to the government database through a secure channel. If the matching, through artificial intelligence technology, is found to be positive, then the verification becomes successful.

7.5.1.3 Creation of a Digital ID

To generate a digital ID, the user has to unlock his smartphone and enter the government ID and biometrics in it. The identity creator will then generate a public and a private key. The private key can be stored in a processor architecture of the smartphone, such as AppViewX CERT+ or TrustZone for future authentication and/or transactions in the blockchain. The identity maker will now produce a certificate referencing the public key and containing all the user data extracted from the ID card. This certificate will be useful for the user to verify his identity while transacting on the blockchain.

7.5.2 System Overview

BlockID can be divided into two major components – one that creates the identity and the other that is responsible for the management of the identity. There can be four types of participants who can play their roles (see Figure 7.7):

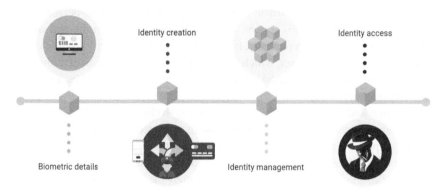

Figure 7.7 Biometric solution – system overview.

7.5.2.1 Identify Creator

A centralized organization, a government agency, or a commercial representative appointed to this role is referred to as an identity creator. It assists the user in developing a digital identity for usage with the blockchain system. Since this authority or representation creates identities for users, its legitimacy is obviously undeniable as it will never let users create fictitious digital IDs on their behalf.

7.5.2.2 Identity User

In order to take part in the transaction, every identity user needs to have a digital ID from the identity creator. The identity creation component, the initial part of the BlockID, assists the user in developing a digital ID that may be used in block-chain-based banking transactions.

For all commercial dealings, the user will go by this identity. Let's say the user is in charge of transferring money at a bank counter. The second component (identity management component) of BlockID keeps track of how issued digital IDs are used (see Figure 7.7). If the user is not trusted, they can attempt to use the digital identity of someone else.

7.5.2.3 Identity Manager

The identity manager can be a group of nodes other than a single identity. No single node is trusted as part of identity management; they work together to submit identity-related transactions to the blockchain system.

7.5.2.4 Identity Device

A smartphone is owned by a single user and is used to establish the user's identity to transact on the blockchain. Being tamper-resistant, smartphones always follow a pre-determined protocol and store the information faithfully while transacting with blockchain.

Blockchain is a powerful instrument to manage information in cyberspace. To unleash the potential of this system, a reliable mapping between the real world and the cyberworld is a prerequisite. In this affair, from the security point of view, the digital identity of the user, which he receives from any government authority, plays a significant role. Blockchain-based identification systems can be a reliable tool in bridging this gap.

Although Radio Frequency Identification (RFID) technology or other equivalent digital labeling systems can serve this purpose in restricted areas; but for the supply chain, mapping is done either manually or using expensive, dedicated equipment. In the present state of affairs, when people need a cost-effective solution to map the cyberworld, the user can easily transact through the cost-effective blockchain system by keeping the digital identity on their own device, such as a smartphone. As a result, each access event is associated with a real, verified identity.

7.5.3 Blockchain Identity Protocol

7.5.3.1 Creation of Digital ID

In order to create a digital ID to be used in a blockchain-based system, the user must have a government issued ID and a biometric authentication device, in addition to their smartphone (Gao et al., 2018). (see Code Cell 7.4).

If the step 1 becomes successful, certificate is user's digital identity that can be used in the blockchain's system for other individuals to recognize the user.

7.5.3.2 Use of Digital ID

The user can now use the code (see Code Cell 7.5) that represents his digital ID to log in.

A user needs to utilize their smartphone to use their digital identity. Step 2 shows the workflow of using the digital identity.

Other blockchain users who receive signatures find the relevant certificate and utilize embedded public key to verify the signature. These users utilize a consensus technique to decide how to add transaction together with signature to the blockchain if signature and transaction are compatible.

```
user sends government id to creator;
creator checks;
cd 1: the validity of government id;
cd 2 : consistency of government and user;
if cd 1= cd 2 = true, then;
user provides smartphone to creator;
if user can unlock smartphone using biometric
information, then;
creator and smartphone together run (public key, private
key) ← KeyGen;
private key is securely stored in smartphone;
creator collects information about user from government
id;
creator generates a certificate with both public key and
information, and authenticate certificate with its
private key;
return certificate;
end if;
end if;
return fail;
```

Code Cell 7.4 Creation of Digital ID.

```
user receives a transaction tx from blockchain;
if user recognizes tx and wants to authorize it, then;
user unlocks smartphone using their biometric
information;
if smartphone accepts user's biometric, then;
smartphone uses private key to generate a digital signa-
ture of tx and returns it to user;
user submits signature to blockchain;
return 1;
end if
end if return 0;
```

Code Cell 7.5 Use of Digital ID.

7.5.3.3 Digital ID Management

A group of nodes control digital IDs, allowing a small number of nodes to act as management nodes. A government agency, for instance, which is adept at checking the data entered in the certificate, would function well as a management node. They can also aid in more effective decision-making during the consensus-building process.

The primary duties of managing digital identities include creating new ones while deactivating the ones that already exist. Only when a digital identification certificate is integrated into the blockchain system can it be used. The group of nodes conduct a consensus mechanism to decide whether to accept a certificate into the blockchain after it is created and submitted to the system. If the data contained in the certificate is accurate, the system will revoke the current identity and reach agreement to adopt it.

A user can send a request transaction to the blockchain to have the related certificate revoked if they misplace their smartphone's private key that is kept on their smartphone. One or more groups of nodes must agree with this request before they can decide whether to put the repeal in the blockchain. Without assistance, a user cannot submit a revocation request since denial-of-service attacks could then be launched. Participants won't recognize signatures produced, using private key after the revocation transaction has been added to the blockchain.

7.5.4 Security Audit

BlockID solely serves to confirm that the digital ID is being used on the blockchain system by its rightful owner. The contact with blockchain systems is handled by the four components of digital identity – identity creator, identity manager, user, and smartphone. The binding attribute may be compromised, and the attacker may be able to access the system using the government ID of another individual if any one of the four connections is lost.

With expanded access comes a higher danger of fraud for users. A gadget in the wrong hands might approve unauthorized transactions and cause financial harm. Hackers enter user accounts to steal money as well as data, which gives them an immediate reward. Users need a system that can quickly mitigate all potential frauds while still being able to meet the demands of instant access, remote identity proof, and user authentication.

In order to defend against attempts to input an illegitimate device or phone numbers on a user's account, BlockID may compare a user's mobile number to the number registered with his or her financial institution. Only users who have a registered phone number can pair their device as an authenticator to approve or reject transactions, thanks to the BlockID app. The use of binding by BlockID lessens fraud, especially in the area of online retail banking where unsuspecting consumers can be persuaded to allow unauthorized parties to register the app and seize control of the account.

7.5.4.1 Binding

Binding means the conjugation of the digital identity used in the blockchain with its smartphone and its biometric information. The digital identity won't be able to display the right user information if the binding attribute is not secured.

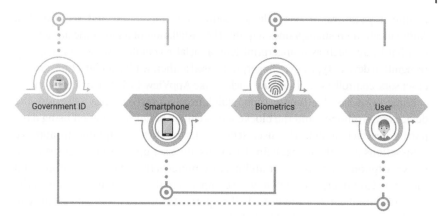

Figure 7.8 Security audit – binding.

Only legitimate users are able to verify themselves using biometric data, such as a retinal scan, fingerprint, facial recognition, voice, or thermal mapping on their smartphone device through Connections 2 (smartphone) and 3 (biometrics), which rely on built-in biometric-based authentication (see Figure 7.8). It gives the gadget the ability to sign contracts on behalf of the users.

7.5.4.2 Privacy

The smartphone communicates with the blockchain technology and stores all the confidential data. A smartphone's private key, for example, can be extracted through privacy intrusion, and the attacker can use that ID to complete transactions in the blockchain system. Even if they are unsuccessful in stealing the confidential information after obtaining the smartphone, they can still attempt to change or remove it. In such a situation, however, the attacker will be able to disguise themself as the user, but they will prevent the legitimate user from using his digital identity in the blockchain system.

The smartphone stores and safeguards the private key using a processor architecture such as AppViewX CERT+ or TrustZone in a secure environment to maintain its secrecy and integrity. The hardware prevents the private key from ever leaving the system and only permits approved software to utilize it to create signatures.

7.5.5 Authentication Protocol

Biometric authentication is a popular scheme that has been in practice on smartphones for many years. In a vast country like India, it is an integral part of the identification system. Compared to conventional authentication techniques that require a password or passcode to secure, it is more safe and sophisticated. Authentication on smartphones requires the installation of a biometric authentication hardware, such as a fingerprint tool, a facial recognition sensor, or a speech recognition device. Typically, a fingerprint-based authentication architecture consists of sensors, controllers, and a secure enclave like AppViewX CERT+ or TrustZone.

Fingerprint-based authentication, which involves three parties – the user, the device (smartphone), and the blockchain – can be better understood using a tripartite abstract model. The user seeks to utilize his smartphone to approve transactions from the blockchain. To do this, the user uploads his fingerprints to the smartphone; the processor architecture protects the saved fingerprints, and the uploaded fingerprints will now be compared to the stored fingerprints. If the match is found correct, the user shall be permitted to use his digital identity to conduct transactions on the blockchain.

Any smartphone with a processor that functions with a fingerprint biometric sensor can use the AppViewX CERT+ or TrustZone technology. While such technology is not implemented in the earlier ARM architecture, the CPU must be ARMv6KZ or later in order to be fingerprint-capable. Refactoring a fingerprint image from this enclave is virtually impossible. Only when the smartphone needs to confirm whether the fingerprint provided by the user matches the fingerprint placed in the processor architecture, it uses sensitive biometric data, which is itself encrypted.The smartphone throws an FIQ (Fast Interrupt) exception to enter the secure mode when a user starts a transaction from the blockchain. In this mode, the blockchain application is placed in an isolated environment where malware infections are not a concern. The application will now ask the user to submit a fingerprint for verification because it is still in security mode. The verification will fail if the score returned by the controller after processing the fingerprint is less than a predetermined threshold. In this situation, the transaction is finished, and the smartphone will return to its default setting. The user is now free to approve any further transactions they receive from the blockchain.

A basic Swift code for the iPhone has been displayed henceforth (see Code Cell 7.6). The function verify() will be called to begin verification if the device supports biometric ID. The phone will provide an error code (e) if the user is unable to authenticate.

Once an FIQ exception is thrown under the hardware process, the Advanced Peripheral Bus Bridge (AXI to APB) will request the I/O controller to enable the fingerprint sensor. The processor and controller then collaborate to produce a score. If this score is higher than a predetermined threshold, the processor will produce a signature that will be posted to the blockchain through a direct register write. The transaction can then be verified and completed on the blockchain.

```
context . verify ( . . .
reply : {
[unowned self] (s,err)
-> Void in
if ( s ) {
// fingerprint supplied by user matches
// Process the transaction from blockchain
} else {
// Display err
}
} )
```

Code Cell 7.6 Fingerprint authentication code for iPhone.

7.6 Identity Access

The entire process and technology of identification, authentication, and authorization, delegated to a body to access services or a system in any organization is called "Identity and Access Management (IAM)".

IAM involves an administrative set up, where employees make use of software or hardware with specific access, privileges, and restrictions for the issue and verification of birth certificates, national ID cards, passports, or driver's licenses that allow the user to prove his identity and access specific services from the government or service providers (see Figure 7.9).

7.6.1 Identity Encryption

The identity of a person needs to undergo a two-step method, an authentication and verification process, to avail services or facility. To prove that the identity is of the same person who has approached the office, his name and identifying documents are checked by the authentication process. To know whether the documents indicating name, address, or passport number submitted by the person are correct or not, there is a process of verification. That means that a verifying entity confirms that the data that is claimed by the individual as his own is genuine or not. This is usually done through the verification of identifying documents.

Certain privacy concerns arise at this stage, such as whether the verifying authority should get access to other information from the document when seeking to verify only primary information. This is quite debatable as information, more often than not, contains extra personal details that tag with the basic information, infringing the user's right to privacy.

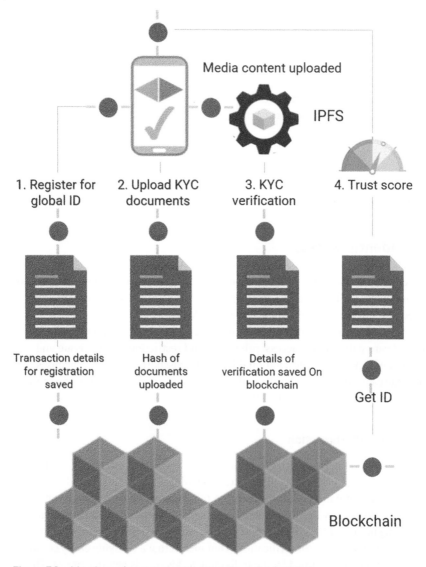

Figure 7.9 Identity and access management through blockchain.

7.6.2 Zero Knowledge Proof

Identity management can utilize a Zero Knowledge Proof authentication method, by which one entity, through encryption, masks details of information received, yet proves to another entity that it has the concerned information without having to disclose any personal information to the other to support that proof. The verification entity, despite zero knowledge, gets convinced of its validity about the information supporting the proof. To make it more explicit, an identity management system can be compared to a distributed ledger. Like it, each entity of the block in the network has the same source of truth about the validity of credentials and the information about the attesting authority also, without getting hold of the actual data of the identity. This is especially useful when and where the authentication entity does not trust the verifying entity but still has to convince it about possessing specific information.

Therefore, an identity management case with blockchain scenario allows a person to state his personal details, to fulfill certain requirements, without the obligation to reveal all his actual details (Garg, 2021c).

For example, if the proof of someone's date of birth has to be verified, the verifying entity will verify the signatures of the attesting entity, which issued the credential but cannot demand proof of date of birth from the identity owner. Hence, the verifier attempts to judge the reliability of the attester to decide validation of a proof.

7.6.3 Revocation

In order to ensure trustworthiness of the system and eliminate the possibility of fraud, credentials are immutable, i.e. once it is issued, no one (not even the issuer) can change the information inside the credential. Nevertheless, attributes, such as house address, telephone number, number of children, and those credentials that have an expiry date, for example a passport or driving license, can change over time.

Revocation means deleting or updating a credential. The possibility for an issuer to revoke a credential is crucial to an identity infrastructure for the very reason that identities are dynamic.

Whenever attributes change, a new credential needs to be issued, and the old one needs to be declared invalid. Each credential in the registry has a recent status, which indicates either the credential has been revoked (deleted or updated) or that the credential is still valid. (Garg, 2021d).

7.7 Merits of a Proposed System

7.7.1 Seamless Navigation

Unlike centralized frameworks, access rights are granted according to one interpretation of policy and all individuals, including services, are properly authenticated, authorized, and audited. Automated identity and access management allows trades to operate more professionally by decreasing the effort, time, and cost than that required to manage access to those networks manually.

7.7.2 Accessibility

Users can present the verified identifier in the form of a QR code to establish their identity and make access to certain services. The service provider verifies the identity by verifying the proof of control or ownership of the presented attestation, which has been linked with a decentralized identifier (DID), and the user signs the presentation with the private key belonging to that DID. If they match, access is granted.

7.7.3 Easy and Secure

MetaMask allows users to run Ethereum dApps on their browser with a secure identity vault. It provides a user interface to manage identities on different sites, making Ethereum applications more accessible and easier to use for all.

7.7.4 Decentralized Public Key Infrastructure

Blockchain enables decentralized public key infrastructure (DPKI), by creating a trusted platform to distribute the asymmetric verification and encryption keys of the identity holders. DPKI also enables everyone to create or anchor cryptographic keys on the blockchain in a tamper-proof and chronologically ordered way. DPKI is an enabler for cases, such as verifiable credentials.

7.7.5 Decentralized Storage

Decentralized storage is one of the core components of secure identity data management. In a decentralized structure, credentials are usually stored straight on the user's device or distributed data storage systems like IPFS or identity hubs such as u-Port's Trust Graph or 3Box (Consensys, 2020). Decentralized storage solutions diminish an entity's ability to unauthorized data access in order to gain an individual's confidential information (see Table 7.1).

7.7.6 Manageability and Control

In centralized identity systems, the entity providing the identity is usually accountable for safekeeping of data. However, in a decentralized identity framework, security becomes the responsibility of the user, who may determine their own security measures or outsource the task to some service app like a password-manager or a digital bank vault. Thus, blockchain-powered decentralized identity solutions compel hackers to target discrete data stores, which is expensive and cumbersome.

Table 7.1 Comparison between a Typical ID Management and a Blockchain ID Management.

Typical IAM	Comparative characters	Blockchain IAM
Honeypots – treasure of information is likely to be attacked by hackers		Provides anonymity and privacy through permissioned blockchain network
Users use the same password for different sites. If one password is stolen, all apps will be compromised with.	Password protection	Encrypted public key creates a secure digital reference about the identity of the user (a secured alternative to password)
The use of cloud computing for various purposes has led to the challenge of tracking usage of resources across environments.	Cloud Applications	May augment existing single sign on solutions or be designed to track activity across platforms.
Multifactor authentication acts as a challenge to manage due to the infrastructure requirements to support it.		Blockchain technology can enable MFA without the need for additional infrastructure
Introduces a challenge of having a single source of truth, which makes audits difficult to conduct.	Centralization	Transactions are immutable by nature, they can be used to both store and retrieve data that needs to be regulated by various compliance standards.

7.7.7 Data Portability

The European Union General Data Protection Regulation, Article 20 (EU GDPR, 2018), entitles users to transmit their personal data directly from one controller to another, subject to technical feasibility. This right helps to enhance user experience, cutting down on the need to reverify their identity across various services and platforms. With DIDs and verifiable credentials, it is likely to transfer identities that were anchored on one target system to another with ease. Data portability reduces friction for the user, while making the sign-up process simple, which increases user adoption.

DID data portability also permits reusable credentials, where a user can quickly reverify himself to meet the regulatory KYC requirement. This will skip the cumbersome identity verification process where a lot of documents are required and checked, which would successively curtail customer's time onboard, avoid dropout rates, and reduce cost in the financial sector.

7.7.8 Prevention of Identity Theft

In blockchain identity management, each user can store his identity credentials on a digital identity wallet on a device, like his smartphone. Digital identity credentials are only valid if they are used from a device that was authorized to do so. If under any circumstances, the device is lost, stolen, or stops working, the user can use any other authorized device, such as his desktop, laptop, or cellphone, to write on the blockchain that the authorization of his device has now been revoked.

This would take instant effect and stop anyone from using the digital identity credentials on the cellphone. The burglar would not be able to impersonate the user, even though he has his passwords, biometrics, or the device because the immutable and secure chain (blockchain) would now hold a revocation registry for the phone. Thus, the thief will not be able to create new relationships.

In the next step, the existing relationship keys (pairwise connections where each of them has a unique key) are to be revoked. This prevents the thief from exploring the existing relationships between the device and other people or organizations.

7.8 Disadvantages of the Proposed System

Despite unlimited prospects, blockchain has had some teething problems, which restricts its wide range of applications (see Figure 7.10). Apart from these drawbacks, there are some other pitfalls as well, which are as follows:

7.8.1 Privacy Leakage

For the reason that users transact with their private key and public key, without any real identity exposure, blockchain helps to preserve privacy to a significant

Figure 7.10 Disadvantages of blockchain in ID management.

extent. Nonetheless, Meiklejohn et al. (2013) and Kosba et al. (2016) have revealed that blockchain cannot promise the transactional privacy since the values of all transactions and balances for each public key are publicly visible. Besides, Barcelo (2014) has shown that a user's Bitcoin transactions can be linked to disclose user's information. Biryukov, Khovratovich, and Pustogarov (2014) also worked out a way to link user pseudonyms to IP addresses even when users are behind the firewalls or Network Address Translation (NAT). Employing the given technique, each client can be distinctly identified by a set of nodes it connects to, and the origin of a transaction can be easily traced through.

7.8.2 Selfish Mining

Blockchain is vulnerable to the attacks of conspiring selfish miners. Eyal and Sirer (2014) have clearly indicated that the network is at risk, even when a very small fragment of the hashing power is used to cheat. In a selfish mining approach, selfish miners keep their mined blocks without being broadcasted and reveal the private branch in public, only if some requirements are satisfied. As the private branch is longer than the current public chain, it would be admitted by all miners. Until the private blockchain publishes, honest miners waste their resources on a useless branch, and the selfish miners mine their private chain without competitors.

Based on selfish mining, many other attacks have been suggested to show that blockchain is not completely secure. In stubborn mining, miners could intensify their activity by nontrivially composing mining attacks with network-level eclipse attacks (Nayak et al., 2016). The trail stubbornness is one of the persistent strategies that miners still mine the blocks even if the private chain is left behind.

7.8.3 Admin Conflicts

In digital identification, besides privacy, blockchain compels a flexible framework since the secretarial structures and models vary greatly (Garg, 2021d). For example, users sign up to an SSI and data platform to create and register a DID. During this process, the user creates a pair of private and public keys. Public keys associated to a DID can be stored on-chain in case keys are compromised or are rotated for security reasons. Additional data associated with a DID, such as attestations, can be fastened on-chain, but the full data itself cannot be stored on-chain to maintain scalability and compliance with privacy regulations.

7.9 Challenges

In order to overcome flaws, like scalability, privacy leakages, selfish mining, and administrative disparities, the technology needs some fine tuning.

7.9.1 Storage Optimization and Redesign

Enhancing scalability is the major pain point with blockchain-based ID management, but there are two alternatives: storage optimization and redesign. Bruce (2014) proposed a novel cryptocurrency scheme, in which the old transaction records are removed by the network. It is significant because running a full copy of the ledger is rather challenging for a node.

Bitcoin-Next Generation was introduced by Eyal et al. (2016) to decouple conventional blocks into key blocks for leader election and microblocks for transaction storage. The time has been divided into epochs, and the miners must hash to produce a key block in each epoch. The node becomes the leader after a key block is formed, and the leader is likely to produce microblocks. Bitcoin-NG also extended the longest chain strategy in which microblocks carry no weight. This is how the trade-off between block size and network security can be resolved by redesigning blockchain.

7.9.2 Privacy Protection

Several methods have been proposed to improve anonymity of blockchain. Miers et al. (2013) used zero-knowledge proof (Zerocoin). Miners do not have to validate a transaction with a digital signature but to validate coins from the list of valid coins. A payment's origin is separate (unlinked) from transactions to avoid analysis of the transaction graph, but it shows the amount and destination. In order to resolve this issue, Sasson et al. (2014) came forward with Zerocash, wherein the amounts of transaction and the values of coins, held by users, remain veiled.

7.9.3 Random Beacons and Timestamps

To fix the selfish mining problem, Heilman submitted a novel scheme for honest miners to choose a branch to follow (Heilman, 2014). With random beacons and timestamps, honest miners would select more fresh blocks.

7.10 Solutions with Hyperledger Fabric

Hyperledger Fabric (Androulaki, Barger, and Bortnikov, 2018) is intended to resolve these issues as it is a framework for implementing blockchains with the support for channels. A channel, in Hyperledger Fabric, is simply a ledger that is distributed only to a select group of parties.

7.10.1 Warning Pointers

- A red flag indicates when private data is introduced in the blockchain ledger, and that ultimately affects the privacy of the users under breaching or hacking activity.
- It violates current privacy regulation (e.g., GDPR; right to be forgotten).
- Personal data is not static, and so it is not advisable to put an entry in the ledger (attributes are dynamic and can change over time, e.g. phone number, house address).

7.10.2 Safety Protocols

In order to have safe, secure, and tamper-proof transactions, the following norms must be complied with:

- No personal data should ever be put on a blockchain.
- Only users' verified credentials, after attestation, should be reflected.
- Public DID or unique identifiers, procured for digital identity and controlled by the identity owner, should be retained in the network. DIDs should be permanent in nature, unchangeable, and nontransferrable to some other entity.
- Identifiers, other than DIDs, like IP addresses and e-mail IDs, can be assigned to entities who are supposed to look after the concerned part.
- Proofs of consent for sharing of content by the identity owner can be kept.
- Revocation registers should be indicated in the blockchain, as they are records in which the issuers have the right to withdraw a credential.
- Each DID is resolvable and maintains a DID document or a manual containing trustworthy operations of DID with public keys, authentication protocols, and service endpoints. Through the DID document, an entity should understand how to use that DID.
- Decentralized identifiers should be cryptographically verifiable and decentralized from the central register. Trust forms the basis of distributed ledger technology, as every entity has the same source of truth about the data in the credentials.
- New speculation has arisen in recent times, where the individual will possess and control his identity, without any dependency on the central service to resolve DIDs. They would be able to share information through peer DIDs. It would then increase security and the privacy of the owner's information. Ultimately, they will turn digital identities into SSIs as they allow each individual to own and control their identity without depending on other parties.

Coming Up

In this chapter, different identity models were compared which led to the conclusion that self-sovereign identity gives the highest degree of freedom and ease of operation among different departments. Technical details of blockchain-based ID management along, with its merits and demerits, were explained in detail, followed by optimizations to solve some of the challenges posed by the technology.

The next chapter covers the different types of cryptography and cybersecurity aspects of blockchain, including some real-world examples of using blockchain in cybersecurity.

References

Androulaki E, Barger A, and Bortnikov V, 2018. Hyperledger Fabric: A Distributed Operating System for Permissioned Blockchains. Proceedings of the 13th EuroSys Conference, NY, 30 (15) 1–30.

Barcelo J, 2014. User privacy in the public Bitcoin blockchain. *Journal of Latex Class Files*, 6 (1). https://www.upf.edu/-jbarcelo/papers/20140704_user_privacy_in_the_public_bitcoin_blockchain/paper.pdf.

Biryukov A, Khovratovich D, and Pustogarov I, 2014. Deanonymisation of Clients in Bitcoin P2P Network. Proceedings of the 2014 ACM SIGSAC Conference on Computer & Communications Security, NY US, 15–29.

Bruce JD, 2014. The Mini-blockchain Scheme. https://cryptochainuni.com/wp-content/uploads/The-Mini-Blockchain-Scheme.pdf.

Businesswire, 2018. Data Breaches Compromised 4.5 Billion Records in First Half of 2018. https://www.businesswire.com/news/home/20181008005322/en/Data-Breaches-Compromised-4.5-Billion-Records-in-First-Half-of-2018/ Accessed on 09 October 2018.

Consensys, 2020. Blockchain in Digital Identity. https://consensys.net/blockchain-use-cases/digital-identity/.

EU GDPR, 2018. Regulation (EU) 2016/679 of the European Parliament and of the Council, L 119/1-88. https://eur-lex.europa.eu/legal-content/EN/TXT/PDF/?uri=CELEX:32016R0679.

Eyal I, Gencer AE, Sirer EG, and Van Renesse R, 2016. Bitcoining: A Scalable Blockchain Protocol. Proceedings of the 13th USENIX Symposium on Networked Systems Design and Implementation, Santa Clara CA, 45–59.

Eyal I and Sirer EG, 2014. Majority Is Not Enough: Bitcoin Mining Is Vulnerable. Proceedings of the International Conference on Financial Cryptography and Data Security, Berlin, 436–454.

Gao Z, Xu L, Turner G, Patel B, Diallo N, Chen L, and Shi W, 2018. *Blockchain-based Identity Management with Mobile Device*. CryBlock, Germany.

Garg R, 2019. Multipurpose ID: One Nation – One Identity, Annual Convention – Indian Society for Technical Education (ISTE). National Conference on Recent Advances in Energy, Science & Technology, 39. doi:10.6084/m9.figshare.16945078. https://www.researchgate.net/publication/337398750_Multipurpose_ID_One_Nation_-_One_Identity.

Garg R, 2021a. Blockchain Based Decentralized Applications for Multiple Administrative Domain Networking. BITS – Pilani, KK Birla Goa Campus India, 1–69. doi :10.13140/RG.2.2.29003.87845. https://www.researchgate.net/publication/351871690_Blockchain_based_Decentralized_Applications_for_Multiple_Administrative_Domain_Networking.

Garg R, 2021b. *Identidades Auto-soberanas*. Ediciones Nuestro Conocimiento, Spain, 1–104.

Garg R, 2021c. Blockchain based identity solutions. *International Journal of Computer Science & Information Technology* (In Press).

Garg R, 2021d. *Identità Auto Sovrane*. Edizioni Sapienza, Italy, 1–104.

Garg R, 2022a. Distributed ecosystem for identity management. *Journal of Blockchain Research*, 1 (1) (In Press).

Garg R, 2022b. Decentralized Transaction Mechanism Based on Smart Contracts. 3rd International Conference on Blockchain and IoT, Sydney Australia. doi:10.5281/zenodo.5708294. https://www.researchgate.net/publication/325336102_Decentralized_Transaction_Mechanism_based_on_Smart_Contracts.

Heilman E, 2014. One Weird Trick to Stop Selfish Miners: Fresh Bitcoins, a Solution for the Honest Miner. https://eprint.iacr.org/2014/007.pdf.

1kosmos, 2022. Passwordless MFA with verified identity. 1kosmos.com. Accessed on 11 August 2022.

Kosba A, Miller A, Shi E, Wen Z, and Papamanthou C, 2016. Hawk: The Blockchain Model of Cryptography and Privacy-Preserving Smart Contracts. Proceedings of IEEE Symposium on Security and Privacy, San Jose CA, 839–858.

Meiklejohn S, Pomarole M, Jordan G, Levchenko K, McCoy D, Voelker GM, and Savage S, 2013. A Fistful of Bitcoins: Characterizing Payments among Men with No Names. Proceedings of the 2013 Conference on Internet Measurement, NY US.

Miers I, Garman C, Green M, and Rubin AD, 2013. Zerocoin: Anonymous Distributed e-Cash from Bitcoin. Proceedings of IEEE Symposium Security and Privacy, Berkeley CA, 397–411.

Nayak S, Kumar K, Miller A, and Shi E, 2016. Stubborn Mining: Generalizing Selfish Mining and Combining with an Eclipse Attack. Proceedings of 2016 IEEE European Symposium on Security and Privacy, Saarbrucken Germany, 305–320.

Sasson EB, Chiesa A, Garman C, Green M, Miers I, Tromer E, and Virza M, 2014. Zerocash: Decentralized Anonymous Payments from Bitcoin. Proceedings of the 2014 IEEE Symposium on Security and Privacy, San Jose CA, 459–474.

8

Encryption and Cybersecurity

8.1 Cryptography

Cryptography is the technique of secure communication that allows only the actual sender of the message and the intended recipient to see the relevant content. The word is derived from the Greek root – *kryptos* (hidden).

Claude E. Shannon, who worked for years at Bell Labs, propounding the mathematical theory of cryptography, is considered as the father of cryptography. In this technique, an encrypted message replaces the character with another character. To decode encrypted content, you'll need a grid or table that defines how letters are coded or decoded.

8.1.1 Different Types of Cryptography

In general, there are three types of cryptography:

8.1.1.1 Symmetric Key Cryptography

Symmetric cryptography is an encryption system where the sender and receiver of a message encrypt and decrypt messages using common keys. Symmetric key systems are fast and simple but require the sender and receiver to exchange keys in a secure way. In symmetric cryptography, a secret key (or private key) is a short piece or code from which messages are decrypted and encrypted. The most popular symmetric key cryptography system is the Data Encryption System (DES).

8.1.1.2 Asymmetric Key Cryptography

Asymmetric encryption is also called public key encryption, but it actually results from the simultaneous use of two mathematically coupled keys, one the public key, and the other the private key. In this process, a message is encrypted and decrypted by the respective keys to protect it from unauthorized access or use. The

Blockchain for Real World Applications, First Edition. Rishabh Garg.
© 2023 John Wiley & Sons, Inc. Published 2023 by John Wiley & Sons, Inc.

public key is widely disseminated for encryption, and the private key of the receiver is used for decryption. The public key is known by all, so the intended receiver can only decode it because he alone knows the private key. Therefore, the private key is kept secret and is used only by its owner.

8.1.1.3 Hash Functions

A hash function takes a set of inputs of any arbitrary size and fits them into a table or other data structure that contains elements of a fixed size. Hashing can be used to convert a password into a string of authorized characters, called a "hash value," or "digest."

With this data structure, the data in an array can be searched and stored in an efficient manner. Suppose someone has a table of 5,000 digits, and he needs to find a given number in that list – the software or system will scan each number in the list until a match is found.

The hash function in this algorithm does not use encryption but, instead, calculates a fixed-length hash value according to the plaintext, which makes it impossible to retrieve the contents of the plaintext. Many operating systems use hash functions to encrypt passwords. While it is possible, it is unlikely to produce the original input by reversing the output values.

8.1.2 Cryptographic Schemes

The history of cryptography has several milestones that led to the formation of the fundamentals of modern algorithms. Cipher was a common notion for conveying confidential information in the early times. These ciphers have been conceived on the symmetric key encryption scheme. In contrast to present-day digital systems, which treat data as binary digits, these systems comprise letters as basic elements.

8.1.2.1 Simple Substitution Cipher

The Simple Substitution Cipher is the most commonly used cipher that consists of an algorithm, substituting each plaintext character for each ciphertext character. This cipher makes use of permutation of alphabets. Despite the large number of infallible keys, this cipher has some inefficiencies, such as choosing an explicit permutation, which does not make this cipher secure.

8.1.2.2 Caesar Cipher

The Caesar Cipher is the most candid form of substitution cipher scheme. Employing this cipher, each letter in the plaintext can be swapped with another alphabet letter to form the ciphertext. Even with modest processing power, a hacker can easily decrypt plaintext using one of the 26 potential keys, rendering it highly vulnerable.

8.1.2.3 Vigenère Cipher

In order to provide more strength to the cryptosystem, the Caesar Cipher has been modified to design the Vigenère Cipher. This cipher operates with a text string as the visible cipher key. It converts every single letter of the key to a numeric value to transpose characters in plaintext. It was referred to as an unbreakable cipher because of the difficult level of decryption.

8.1.2.4 Transposition Cipher

In a Transposition Cipher, the positions held by the units of plaintext are shifted so that the ciphertext constitutes a permutation of the plaintext.

8.2 Playfair Cipher

The Playfair Cipher was the first practical digraph substitution cipher, invented by Charles Wheatstone in 1854. It was named after Lord Playfair who promoted the use of the cipher. The Playfair Cipher is rather quick and doesn't necessitate any special equipment. They encrypt a pair of letters (digraphs) instead of a single alphabet, unlike traditional ciphers.

The cipher was used for strategic purposes during the Boer War, World War I (by the British Army), and World War II (by the Australians). Ciphers were used to protect important but noncritical secrets during the actual war. By the time enemies could decrypt the cryptographic information, it was useless to them.

However, the Playfair Cipher is no longer used, after the development of the computer, as computers can quickly and easily decode it, using break codes in a split of seconds. Furthermore, it is a time-consuming and labor-intensive process that does not require a Playfair cipher decoder or calculator. Despite the fact that Python and C both have Playfair Cipher programs, it can be risky for commercial organizations to use the Playfair Cipher.

8.2.1 Encryption Algorithm

The Playfair Cipher consists of a key and a plaintext. The key can be formed as a short or long word, using any 25-letter combination that doesn't recur. This can be illustrated by an example of Playfair Ciphers with encryption and decryption algorithms:

8.2.1.1 Step 1 – Generate Squares (5 * 5)

The key square is a 5 * 5 grid of letters, which serves to encrypt the plaintext. Given that the grid can only fit 25 letters, one letter (J) of the alphabet is dropped from the table. Thus 25 letters are left in the alphabet, without any numerics, punctuation, or nonalphabet character. The cipher begins with the exclusive alphabet of the key in the order of occurrence, then the remaining characters of the alphabet in the same sequence. Thus, a cipher uses a single alphabetic class without repetition and includes a digraphic substitution.

8.2.1.2 Step 2 – Algorithm to Encrypt Plaintext
Plaintext is split into pairs of two letters (digraphs). For example:

Plaintext: "ambidextrous"
After Split: "am" "bi" "de" "xt" "ro" "us"

If the number of letters is odd, a Z is added to the last letter.

Plaintext: "workmanship"
After Split: "wo" "rk" "ma" "ns" "hi" "pz"

If a pair cannot be formed from the same letter, a bogus letter can be added to its previous letter by breaking the letter into singles

Plaintext: "ditto"
After Split: "di" "tx" "to"
Here "x" is the bogus letter.

If a letter stands alone in the pairing process, an additional fictitious letter can be added with the lone letter.

Plaintext: "recurrence"
After Split: "re" "cu" "rx" "re" "nc" "ez"
Here "z" is the bogus letter.

Rules for Encryption:

Consider the letters below each alphabet if both letters in a digraph are in the same column. Accordingly, if one of the digraph letters is the bottom letter in the grid, take into account the top alphabet in the same column (see Figure 8.1).

For example:

Digraph: "xt"
Encrypted Text: "fp"
Encryption: x -> f and t -> p

X	A	R	C	D
F	G	H	M	K
T	L	N	B	I
P	Q	V	U	O
E	W	Y	Z	S

Figure 8.1 Cipher encryption: If both the letters in the digraph are in the same column.

Consider the letters to the right of each alphabet if both letters in a digraph are in the same row. As a result, if one of the digraph letters is represented by the rightmost alphabet in the grid, take into account the leftmost alphabet of the row (see Figure 8.2).

For example:

Digraph: "bi"
Encrypted Text: "it"
Encryption: b -> i and i -> t

X	A	R	C	D
F	G	H	M	K
T	L	N	B	I
P	Q	V	U	O
E	W	Y	Z	S

Figure 8.2 Cipher encryption: If both the letters in the digraph are in the same row.

If none of the preceding rules apply, draw a quadrilateral or rectangle with two letters in the digraph and consider the letters on the parallel opposite corners of the quadrangle (see Figure 8.3).

For example:

Digraph: "ro"
Encrypted Text: "dv"
Encryption: r -> d and o -> v

Now, in totto:

Plaintext: "ambidextrous"
Encrypted Text: "rhitxsfpdvoz"
Encryption: a -> r; m -> h; b -> i; i -> t; d -> x;
e -> s; x -> f; t -> p; r -> d; o -> v; u -> o; and
s -> z (see Figure 8.4).

X	A	R	C	D
F	G	H	M	K
T	L	N	B	I
P	Q	V	U	O
E	W	Y	Z	S

Figure 8.3 Cipher encryption: If none of the rules apply.

Implementation of Playfair Cipher in C

Output (see Code Cell 8.1)

Key text: "Monarchy"
Plaintext: "ambidextrous"
Ciphertext: "rhitxsfpdvoz"

8.2.2 Decryption Algorithm

The Playfair Cipher is decrypted by going reverse through the encryption process. The communication can be decrypted by the recipient, using the same key and the same key table that were used to encrypt it.

8.2.2.1 Step 1 – Generate Squares (5 * 5)

The key is a 5 * 5 grid of square letters, which serves to decrypt the encrypted code. Since the grid can only accommodate 25 characters, at the time of encryption one

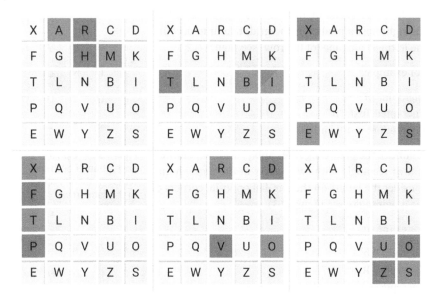

Figure 8.4 Cipher encryption: Plaintext to ciphertext.

```
// C program to implement Playfair Cipher

#include <stdio.h>
#include <stdlib.h>
#include <string.h>
#define SIZE 30

// convert the string to lowercase
void toLowerCase(char plain[], int ps)
{
    int i;
    for (i = 0; i < ps; i++) {
        if (plain[i] > 64 && plain[i] < 91)
            plain[i] += 32;
    }
}

// remove all spaces in the string
int format(char* plain, int ps)
{
    int i, count = 0;
```

Code Cell 8.1 Playfair Cipher – Encryption using C.

```
        for (i = 0; i < ps; i++)
            if (plain[i] != ' ')
                plain[count++] = plain[i];
        plain[count] = '\0';
        return count;
}

// generate the 5x5 key square
void generate(char key[], int ks, char keyT[5][5])
{
    int i, j, k, flag = 0, *dicty;

    dicty = (int*)calloc(26, sizeof(int));
    for (i = 0; i < ks; i++) {
        if (key[i] != 'j')
            dicty[key[i] - 97] = 2;
    }

    dicty['j' - 97] = 1;

    i = 0;
    j = 0;

    for (k = 0; k < ks; k++) {
        if (dicty[key[k] - 97] == 2) {
            dicty[key[k] - 97] -= 1;
            keyT[i][j] = key[k];
            j++;
            if (j == 5) {
                i++;
                j = 0;
            }
        }
    }
    for (k = 0; k < 26; k++) {
        if (dicty[k] == 0) {
            keyT[i][j] = (char)(k + 97);
            j++;
            if (j == 5) {
                i++;
                j = 0;
```

Code Cell 8.1 (Continued)

```
                    }
                }
            }
        }
    }

    // search for the characters of digraph
    in the key square and return their // position
    void search(char keyT[5][5], char a, char b, int arr[])
    {
        int i, j;

        if (a == 'j')
            a = 'i';
        else if (b == 'j')
            b = 'i';

        for (i = 0; i < 5; i++) {

            for (j = 0; j < 5; j++) {

                if (keyT[i][j] == a) {
                    arr[0] = i;
                    arr[1] = j;
                }
                else if (keyT[i][j] == b) {
                    arr[2] = i;
                    arr[3] = j;
                }
            }
        }
    }
    // find the modulus with 5
    int mod5(int a) { return (a % 5); }
    // make the plaintext length even
    int make even(char str[], int ptrs)
    {
        if (ptrs % 2 != 0) {
            str[ptrs++] = 'z';
            str[ptrs] = '\0';
        }
        return ptrs;
    }
```

Code Cell 8.1 (Continued)

```
// perform encryption
void encrypt(char str[], char keyT[5][5], int ps)
{
    int i, a[4];

    for (i = 0; i < ps; i += 2) {

        search(keyT, str[i], str[i + 1], a);

        if (a[0] == a[2]) {
            str[i] = keyT[a[0]][mod5(a[1] + 1)];
            str[i + 1] = keyT[a[0]][mod5(a[3] + 1)];
        }
        else if (a[1] == a[3]) {
            str[i] = keyT[mod5(a[0] + 1)][a[1]];
            str[i + 1] = keyT[mod5(a[2] + 1)][a[1]];
        }
        else {
            str[i] = keyT[a[0]][a[3]];
            str[i + 1] = keyT[a[2]][a[1]];
        }
    }
}

//encrypt using Playfair Cipher
void encryptByPlayfairCipher(char str[], char key[])
{
    char ps, ks, keyT[5][5];

    // Key
    ks = strlen(key);
    ks = format(key, ks);
    LowerCase(key, ks);

    // Plaintext
    ps = strlen(str);
    LowerCase(str, ps);
    ps = format(str, ps);

    ps = make even(str, ps);
```

Code Cell 8.1   (Continued)

```
    generate(key, ks, keyT);

    encrypt(str, keyT, ps);
}

int main()
{
    char str[SIZE], key[SIZE];

    // Key to be encrypted
    strcpy(key, "Monarchy");
    printf("Key text: %s\n", key);

    // Plaintext to be encrypted
    strcpy(str, "ambidextrous");
    printf("Plaintext: %s\n", str);

    // encrypt using Playfair Cipher
    encryptByPlayfairCipher(str, key);

    printf("Ciphertext: %s\n", str);

    return 0;
}
```

Code Cell 8.1 (Continued)

letter (J) of the alphabet was dropped from the table. Thus there were only 25 letters in the alphabet class without any digits, punctuation marks, or nonalphabet characters. The cipher began with the unique alphabet of the key in the order of occurrence; after that, the rest of the letters appear in order. A cipher was thus constructed, using a single alphabetic class without repetition, and it has a digraphic substitution.

Playfair cipher is a type of block cipher, which replaces a particular plaintext character during encryption with a ciphertext character depending on the adjacent character in the plaintext. The easiest way to crack the Playfair cipher is to perform frequency analysis of those letter pairs. Knowing the approximate frequencies for the language used in the message, an attempt can be made to match consecutive ciphertext pairs to consecutive pairs of letters in the language. Albeit this is a colossal task.

8.2.2.2 Step 2 – Algorithm to Decrypt the Ciphertext
The ciphertext is divided into dyads or digraphs – pairs of two letters. This is because at the time of encryption, an extra letter was added to an odd pair (if any)

with a single letter to convert it into an even number. Since decryption itself is the reverse process of encryption, the letters are essentially even in number.

For example:

Ciphertext: "rhitxsfpdvoz"
After Split: "rh" "it" "xs" "fp" "dv" "oz"

Rules for Decryption

Consider the letters above each alphabet if both letters in a digraph are in the same column. Consequently, if one of the digraph letters is the top-most letter in the matrix, take into account the letter at the bottom in the same column (see Figure 8.5).

For example:

Digraph: "fp"
Decrypted Text: "xt"
Decryption: f -> x and p -> t

Consider the letters to the left of each alphabet if both letters in a digraph are in the same row. In this case, take into consideration the rightmost alphabet in the same row if one of the digraph letters is the leftmost letter in the matrix (see Figure 8.6).

For example:

Digraph: "it"
Decrypted Text: "bi"
Decryption: i -> b and t -> i

If none of the above rules apply, draw a quadrangle with two letters in the digraph and consider the letters on the parallel opposite corners of the quadrangle (see Figure 8.7).

For example:

Diagraph: "dv"
Decrypted Text: "ro"
Decryption: d -> r and v -> o

For example:

Ciphertext: "rhitxsfpdvoz"
Decrypted Text: "ambidextrous"

X	A	R	C	D
F	G	H	M	K
T	L	N	B	I
P	Q	V	U	O
E	W	Y	Z	S

Figure 8.5 Cipher decryption: If both the letters in the digraph are in the same column.

X	A	R	C	D
F	G	H	M	K
T	L	N	B	I
P	Q	V	U	O
E	W	Y	Z	S

Figure 8.6 Cipher decryption: If both the letters in the digraph are in the same row.

X	A	R	C	D
F	G	H	M	K
T	L	N	B	I
P	Q	V	U	O
E	W	Y	Z	S

Figure 8.7 Cipher decryption: If none of the rules apply.

Decryption: r -> a; h -> m; i -> b; t -> i; x -> d; s -> e; f -> x; p -> t; d -> r; v -> o; o -> u; and z -> s (see Figure 8.8)

Implementation of Playfair Cipher Decryption in C

Output (See Code Cell 8.2)

Key text: "Monarchy"
Plaintext: "rhitxsfpdvoz"
Deciphered text: "ambidextrous"

8.2.3 Advantages and Disadvantages

8.2.3.1 Advantages
Playfair Ciphers seem to be more secure since the intricate mathematics that is used to create them renders it extremely difficult for the recipient to decrypt the information.

The frequency analysis that works well for simple substitution ciphers does not work here, so it's hard to crack the encryption. However, if one tries to do so by frequency analysis, it will require a lot of ciphertext for 25 * 25 = 625 possible digraphs in a Playfair iteration, as opposed to 25 monographs in a Simple Substitution Cipher.

Playfair Cipher is a manual process that does not need any digital device, such as a calculator or decoder, for encryption and decryption. While implementing

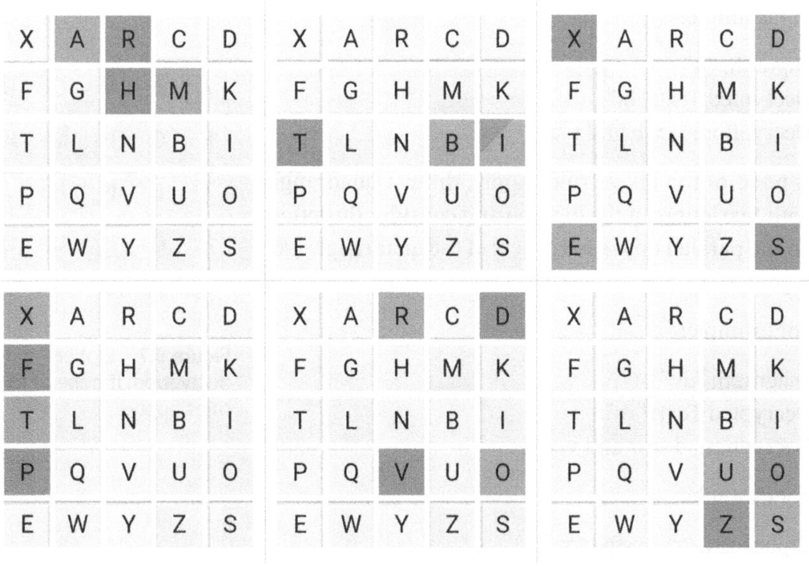

Figure 8.8 Cipher decryption: Ciphertext into plaintext.

```c
#include <stdio.h>
#include <stdlib.h>
#include <string.h>
#define SIZE 30

// convert all characters
of string to lowercase
void LowerCase(char plain[], int ps)
{
    int i;
    for (i = 0; i < ps; i++) {
        if (plain[i] > 64 && plain[i] < 91)
            plain[i] += 32;
    }
}

// remove all spaces in a string
// remove punctuation
int format(char* plain, int ps)
{
    int i, count = 0;
    for (i = 0; i < ps; i++)
        if (plain[i] != ' ')
            plain[count++] = plain[i];
    plain[count] = '\0';
    return count;
}

// generates the 5x5 key square
void generate(char key[], int ks, char keyT[5][5])
{
    int i, j, k, flag = 0, *dicty;

    dicty = (int*)calloc(26, sizeof(int));
    for (i = 0; i < ks; i++) {
        if (key[i] != 'j')
            dicty[key[i] - 97] = 2;
    }
    dicty['j' - 97] = 1;
    i = 0;
    j = 0;
    for (k = 0; k < ks; k++) {
```

Code Cell 8.2   Playfair Cipher – Decryption using C.

```
            if (dicty[key[k] - 97] == 2) {
                dicty[key[k] - 97] -= 1;
                keyT[i][j] = key[k];
                j++;
                if (j == 5) {
                    i++;
                    j = 0;
                }
            }
        }
    }
    for (k = 0; k < 26; k++) {
        if (dicty[k] == 0) {
            keyT[i][j] = (char)(k + 97);
            j++;
            if (j == 5) {
                i++;
                j = 0;
            }
        }
    }
}

// search for the characters of a digraph
// in the key square and return their position
void search(char keyT[5][5], char a, char b, int arr[])
{
    int i, j;
    if (a == 'j')
        a = 'i';
    else if (b == 'j')
        b = 'i';

    for (i = 0; i < 5; i++) {
        for (j = 0; j < 5; j++) {
            if (keyT[i][j] == a) {
                arr[0] = i;
                arr[1] = j;
            }
            else if (keyT[i][j] == b) {
                arr[2] = i;
                arr[3] = j;
            }
```

Code Cell 8.2 (Continued)

```
        }
    }
}

// find the modulus with 5
int mod5(int a)
{
    if (a < 0)
        a += 5;
    return (a % 5);
}

void decrypt(char str[], char keyT[5][5], int ps)
{
    int i, a[4];
    for (i = 0; i < ps; i += 2) {
        search(keyT, str[i], str[i + 1], a);
        if (a[0] == a[2]) {
            str[i] = keyT[a[0]][mod5(a[1] - 1)];
            str[i + 1] = keyT[a[0]][mod5(a[3] - 1)];
        }
        else if (a[1] == a[3]) {
            str[i] = keyT[mod5(a[0] - 1)][a[1]];
            str[i + 1] = keyT[mod5(a[2] - 1)][a[1]];
        }
        else {
            str[i] = keyT[a[0]][a[3]];
            str[i + 1] = keyT[a[2]][a[1]];
        }
    }
}

void decryptByPlayfairCipher(char str[], char key[])
{
    char ps, ks, keyT[5][5];

    // Key
    ks = strlen(key);
    ks = format(key, ks);
    LowerCase(key, ks);

    // ciphertext
```

Code Cell 8.2 (Continued)

```
    ps = strlen(str);
    LowerCase(str, ps);
    ps = format(str, ps);

    generate(key, ks, keyT);

    decrypt(str, keyT, ps);
}
int main()
{
    char str[SIZE], key[SIZE];

    // Key to be encrypted
    strcpy(key, "Monarchy");
    printf("Key text: %s\n", key);

    // Ciphertext to be decrypted
    strcpy(str, "rhitxsfpdvoz");
    printf("Plaintext: %s\n", str);

    // encrypt using Playfair Cipher
    decryptByPlayfairCipher(str, key);

    printf("Deciphered text: %s\n", str);

    return 0;
}
```

Code Cell 8.2 (Continued)

encryption–decryption, using a Playfair Cipher in C, data can travel safely between its source and terminus without making any compromise.

Further, Brute-force attack does not affect the Playfair cipher.

8.2.3.2 Disadvantages

The Playfair Cipher operates with the same key for encryption and decryption, making it possible to crack symmetric cryptography, and it cannot be used to transmit massive amounts of data.

In a Playfair Cipher, since the replacement itself is reverse, one can easily decode an information by employing frequency analysis. If a hacker knows the language of plaintext, he will understand that the ciphertext (RG) and its inverse (GR) have the corresponding plaintext in the digraph, such as HA and AH.

Further, it supports only 25 characters, that too either all upper case or lower case.

It does not support any numeric or special characters, such as symbols, equations, spaces, or punctuation marks.

In addition, it does not allow languages other than English. Doesn't even support encryption of media files.

8.3 Hill Cipher

The Hill Cipher is a polygraphic substitution cipher constructed on linear algebra. Invented by Lester Sanders Hill in 1929, it works impeccably with digraphs (two-letter blocks), trigraphs (three-letter blocks), or other multiple-sized blocks to produce a consistent cipher. It was the first polygraphic cipher in which it was possible to work with more than three symbols at a time.

Each letter in Hill Cipher is represented by 26 modules. Often simple schemes such as A = 0, B = 1 ... Z = 25 are used, but this is not an essential feature of the cipher (see Figure 8.9). The matrix used for encryption is the cipher key and is chosen at random from a set of invertible $n * n$ matrices (module 26). Here, n could be 2, 3, 4, 5 or 6. To decrypt the message, each block is multiplied by the inverse of the matrix encoding.

Examples:

Input: Plaintext: "ACT"
Key: "GYBNQKURP"
Output: Ciphertext: "POH"

Input: Plaintext: "GFG"
Key: "HILLMAGIC"
Output: Ciphertext: "SWK"

A					0				
B	C	D	E	F	1	2	3	4	5
G	H	I	J	K	6	7	8	9	10
L	M	N	O	P	11	12	13	14	15
Q	R	S	T	U	16	17	18	19	20
V	W	X	Y	Z	21	22	23	24	25

Figure 8.9 Letters (left) and corresponding numbers (right) – Hill cipher encryption uses the above scheme of numbers and letters that can be modified as per condition.

8.3.1 Substitution Scheme

Typically, Hill Cipher encryption uses the following structure of alphanumeric (letters and numerals), but this can be modified as per requirement.

8.3.1.1 Encryption

To encrypt a given message, in parallel with modulus 26, each block consists of n letters and these are multiplied in an $n * n$ matrix. Next, for decryption, each block needs to be multiplied by the inverse matrix (see Figure 8.10).

It corresponds to ciphertext of "POH"

8.3.1.2 Decryption

It gives us back "ACT", assuming that all the letters were in uppercase (see Figure 8.11).

Suppose a message 'ACT' (n=3) has to be encrypted. The key is 'GYBNQKURP' which can be written as the nxn matrix:

$$\begin{bmatrix} 6 & 24 & 1 \\ 13 & 16 & 10 \\ 20 & 17 & 15 \end{bmatrix}$$

The message 'ACT' is written as vector:

$$\begin{bmatrix} 0 \\ 2 \\ 19 \end{bmatrix}$$

The enciphered vector is given as:

$$\begin{bmatrix} 6 & 24 & 1 \\ 13 & 16 & 10 \\ 20 & 17 & 15 \end{bmatrix} \begin{bmatrix} 0 \\ 2 \\ 19 \end{bmatrix} = \begin{bmatrix} 67 \\ 222 \\ 319 \end{bmatrix} \equiv \begin{bmatrix} 15 \\ 14 \\ 7 \end{bmatrix} \quad \text{MODULO 26}$$

Figure 8.10 Hill Cipher encryption – ACT encrypts to POH.

The ciphertext is converted back to vector to decrypt the message, and then multiplied by the inverse matrix of the key matrix (IFKVIVVMI in characters). The inverse of the matrix used in the given example is:

$$\begin{bmatrix} 6 & 24 & 1 \\ 13 & 16 & 10 \\ 20 & 17 & 15 \end{bmatrix}^{-1} \equiv \begin{bmatrix} 8 & 5 & 10 \\ 21 & 8 & 21 \\ 21 & 12 & 8 \end{bmatrix} \quad \text{MODULO 26}$$

For the given Ciphertext POH

$$\begin{bmatrix} 8 & 5 & 10 \\ 21 & 8 & 21 \\ 21 & 12 & 8 \end{bmatrix} \begin{bmatrix} 15 \\ 14 \\ 7 \end{bmatrix} \equiv \begin{bmatrix} 260 \\ 574 \\ 539 \end{bmatrix} \equiv \begin{bmatrix} 0 \\ 2 \\ 19 \end{bmatrix} \quad \text{MODULO 26}$$

Figure 8.11 Hill Cipher decryption – POH decrypts back to ACT.

Implementation of the above idea for $n = 3$

Ciphertext: "POH"

```cpp
// C++ code to implement Hill Cipher
#include <iostream>
using namespace std;

void getMatrix(string key, int Matrix[][3])
{
    int k = 0;
    for (int i = 0; i < 3; i++)
    {
        for (int j = 0; j < 3; j++)
        {
            Matrix[i][j] = (key[k]) % 65;
            k++;
        }
    }
}

// encrypt the message
void encrypt(int cipher[][1],
             int Matrix[][3],
             int message[][1])
{
    int x, i, j;
    for (i = 0; i < 3; i++)
    {
        for (j = 0; j < 1; j++)
        {
            cipher[i][j] = 0;

            for (x = 0; x < 3; x++)
            {
                cipher[i][j] +=
                    Matrix[i][x] * message[x][j];
            }
            cipher[i][j] = cipher[i][j] % 26;
        }
    }
}
```

Code Cell 8.3 Encryption and decryption in Hill Cipher using C++.

```cpp
// implement Hill Cipher
void HillCipher(string message, string key)
{
    // Get key matrix
    int Matrix[3][3];
    getKeyMatrix(key, Matrix);

    int message[3][1];

    // Generate vector for the message
    for (int i = 0; i < 3; i++)
        message[i][0] = (message[i]) % 65;

    int cipher[3][1];

    // generate
    the encrypted vector
    encrypt(cipher, Matrix, message);

    string CipherText;

    // generate the encrypted text from
    // the encrypted vector
    for (int i = 0; i < 3; i++)
        CipherText += cipher[i][0] + 65;

    cout << "result:" << CipherText;
}

int main()
{
    // Get the message to be encrypted
    string message = "ACT";

    // Get the key
    string key = "GYBNQKURP";

    HillCipher(message, key);

    return 0;
}
```

Code Cell 8.3 (Continued)

Hill cipher is an example of a classical symmetric encryption algorithm that has succumbed to know-plaintext attacks. In this type of attack, the cryptanalyst had the plaintext of certain messages and the corresponding cipher text of those messages. They try to work-out the algorithm to decrypt any new message encrypted with the same key. Thus its vulnerability to cryptanalysis has made it unfeasible in practice, however it still plays an important pedagogical role in cryptology and linear algebra.

8.4   RSA Algorithm in Cryptography

The RSA Algorithm is an asymmetric cryptography algorithm and hence, works on two different keys – the public key and the private key. It was invented in 1978 by Ron Rivest, Adi Shamir, and Leonard Adelman. It is called the Rivest Shamir Adelman (RSA) Algorithm after their names.

Suppose a client (user) sends his public key to a server (facilitator) to receive some data. Using the client's public key, the server encrypts the data before sending it. The client collects this data but needs to decrypt it first. Since it is asymmetric and only the client (user) has its private key, no third party, excluding the user, can decipher the information, even if he has the user's public key.

The idea of RSA is based on the fact that it is difficult to factorize a large integer. Though it is easy to get a product of two numbers, it does not seem possible to determine the original prime numbers from that product. Let's understand it this way. The public key comprises two figures (numbers), one of which is a multiple of two larger prime numbers. The same two prime numbers are also used to generate the private keys. This implies that if one succeeds in factorizing a large number, the secret or private key can be hacked.

Hence, the defense mechanism behind the RSA Algorithm is that the hacker has to first determine the values p and q by a factorization of N that happens in exponential time. Thus, if N is a 100-digit integer, it would require more than seventy years to factorize. This complexity prevents an attacker from finding the decryption key I for the reason that d rests on p, q and the encryption key e. Therefore, even if the hacker obtains N and e, he will not be able to calculate d from N and e.

Since encryption strength is completely dependent on the key size, doubling or tripling the key size can make the encryption stronger. Typically, an RSA key can be 1024 or 2048 bits long, and currently, breaking such a large amount of encryption appears to be an impossible task.

Using RSA Algorithms, the public and private keys can be generated as follows (Techtarget, 2022):

Pick the two large primes p and q.

Find $n = p \times q$ by multiplying these values, where n is referred to as the modulus for encryption and decryption.

Choose a number e less than n, such that n is relatively prime to $(p-1) \times (q-1)$. This indicates that the only factor in common between e and $(p-1) \times (q-1)$ is 1.

If $n = p \times q$, then the public key is $<e, n>$.

Public key $<e, n>$ is used to encrypt a plaintext message m. The following formula is used to obtain ciphertext C from the plaintext.

$$m^e \bmod n = C$$

In this case, m must be smaller than n. A larger message ($>n$) is treated as a sequence of communications, each of which is encrypted separately.

To find out the private key, the formula, given here, is used to calculate the d, such that:

$$d_e \bmod \{(p-1) \times (q-1)\} = 1$$

Or

$$de \bmod \varphi(n) = 1 \text{ where } \varphi(n) = (p-1) \times (q-1)$$

The private key is $<d, n>$.

A ciphertext message C is decoded using the private key $<d, n>$. To retrieve plaintext m from the ciphertext C, the formula, given hereafter, is used to get plaintext m.

$$m = C^d \bmod n$$

8.4.1 Working Mechanism

8.4.1.1 Generating the Public Key

- Pick two prime numbers. Assume P and Q to be 53 and 59 respectively.
  Now first component of the public key: $n = P*Q = 3127$.
- Here, a minor exponent, say e, is also required

However, e ought to be:

- A whole number.
- Not be an element or factor of n.
- $1 < e < \Phi(n)$ [$\Phi(n)$ is discussed below],

Now, consider it to be equal to 3.
Our public key is made of n and e

8.4.1.2 Generating a Private Key

- Compute $\Phi(n)$ as follows:
  So as $\Phi(n) = (P-1) \times (Q-1)$
  Thus, $\Phi(n) = 3016$

- Then, determine private key, d:
  For some whole number (integer) k, $d = (k*\Phi(n) + 1) / e$
  For $k = 2$, the value of d is 2011.

Thus, we now have: Public key ($n = 3127$ and $e = 3$) and private key ($d = 2011$)
First, encrypt "HI":

- Convert letters to numbers:
  Here, H = 8 and I = 9

- Accordingly, Encrypted Data $c = 89^e$ mod $n = 89^3$ mod (3127)
  In consequence, the Encrypted Data turns out to be 1394

Further, decrypt 1394:

- Decrypted Data $= c^d$ mod $n = (1394)^{2011}$ mod (3127)
  So, the Encrypted Data comes out to be 89 that represents "HI"
  Where, 8 = H and I = 9

C Implementation of RSA Algorithm for Small Values

```
// C program for RSA asymmetric cryptographic
// algorithm.
#include<stdio.h>
#include<math.h>
int gcd(int a, int h)
{
    int temp;
    while (1)
    {
        temp = a%h;
        if (temp == 0)
        return h;
        a = h;
        h = temp;
    }
}

int main()
{
    // random prime numbers
    double p = 3;
    double q = 7;
```

Code Cell 8.4   RSA Asymmetric Cryptography using C.

```c
// first step for public key:
double n = p*q;

// next step for public key.
// e - > encrypt
double e = 2;
double phi = (p-1)*(q-1);
while (e < phi)
{
    // e is co-prime to phi and
    smaller than phi.
    if (gcd(e, phi)==1)
        break;
    else
        e++;
}
// Private key (d - > decrypt)
// choosing d such that it satisfies
// d*e = 1 + k * totient
int k = 2; // any constant value
double d = (1 + (k*phi))/e;

// Message to be encrypted
double msg = 20;

printf("data = %lf", msg);

// Encryption c = (msg ^ e) % n
double c = pow(msg, e);
c = fmod(c, n);
printf("\nEncrypted data = %lf", c);
// Decryption m = (c ^ d) % n
double m = pow(c, d);
m = fmod(m, n);
printf("\nOriginal Message = %lf", m);

    return 0;
}
```

Code Cell 8.4 (Continued)

Data in message: 12.000000
Data encrypted: 3,000,000
Original Message Sent: 12.000000

It seems impossible to factorize RSA-1024 and RSA-2048 for many years to come. Although the ransomware virus also uses RSA-2048 to encode files on infected machines, it is neither possible to decrypt these files without a decoding key, nor to factorize such a large key.

Applications of RSA can be viewed in web browsers, email, VPN, chat and a range of other communication channels. RSA is often used to create a secure connection between a VPN client and a VPN server. RSA algorithms can also be used for under protocols such as OpenVPN, TLS handshake to exchange keys and establish a secure channel.

RSA is an intrinsically fragile cryptosystem containing countless foot-guns that the average software engineer cannot be expected to avoid. Testing for weak parameters can be difficult, if not impossible, and their poor performance coerce developers to take risky shortcuts.

8.5   Multiple Precision Arithmetic Library

Key Generation – Summary

Select p, q p, q both prime
calculate $n = p^*q$
calculate $\o(n) = (p - 1)^*(q - 1)$
select integer e $gcd\,(\o(n),e) = 1; 1 < e < \o(n)$
calculate d
Public Key $KU = e, n$
Private Key $KR = d, n$

Encryption

Plaintext $M < n$
Ciphertext $C = M^e(\bmod\ n)$

Decryption

Ciphertext C
Plaintext $M = C^d(\bmod\ n)$

The three distinct steps of the RSA method are shown in the equations above. N will be a 2048-bit number if a prime number generator produces the 1024-bit primes p and q. The software that processes 2048-bit will take a lot of time because all modulo procedures during encryption and decryption are implemented with regard to N, where N is a 2048-bit number.

Given the needs of the RSA Algorithm, a GNU Multiple Precision Arithmetic Library (GMP) can be implemented to support the creation of large-sized keys. This would expedite encryption and decryption comprising a large-size modulus. This library will facilitate the complete RSA Algorithm to run on a simple 64-bit operating system with no dependence on high-configuration hardware devices.

8.5.1 GNU Multiple Precision Arithmetic Library

GMP is an open-source library used for arithmetic calculations. This includes extraordinary large or highly precise numbers, the majority of which are employed in cryptographic techniques. This makes it possible to execute arithmetic operations on signed integers, rational numbers, and decimal numbers, irrespective of the machine's configuration or any practical limitation (GNU Library, 2022).

The native interface of the GNU library is designed to work with the C programming language. However, wrappers are available for C++, C#, Ada, Julia, OCaml, PHP, Python, Perl, R, Ruby, and the Wolfram language, among others.

8.5.2 RSA Algorithm Implementation Using GMP Library

A C program that shows the functioning of the RSA Algorithm with smaller prime numbers has been given in code cell 8.4. To comprehend the procedure of the actual RSA Algorithm, C code using the GMP library, with large prime numbers, needs to be worked out. The program performs RSA-1024 by creating random prime integers p and q of 512 bits, followed by encoding and decoding. In such a backdrop, the value 1024 is assigned to the variable modulus size. This value can be modified to 2048 in order to produce an RSA key of 2048 bits.

Implementation of RSA Algorithm
RSA Algorithms can be implemented in secure network transmissions and transactions for a variety of e-commerce applications. In addition, it can also be implemented to share credit card details to online traders, to enable voice messages over low bit rate channels, secure key swapping for high-speed IPSec, etc. (see Code Cell 8.5).

8.5.3 Weak RSA Decryption with Chinese Remainder Theorem

RSA decryption takes longer than encryption because at the time of decryption of the private key, the parameter d is inevitably larger. Moreover, the parameters p and q are two exceptionally large prime numbers.

[RSA is quite slow due to the large number of computations. The message is usually much longer than the secret key to encrypt. One way is to use RSA to encrypt only one secret key, which is used in a symmetric encryption algorithm. This can yield the benefits

```c
#include <stdio.h>
#include <gmp.h>

int main {
mpz_t x, y, result;

mpz_init_set_str(x, "7612058254738945", 10);
mpz_init_set_str(y, "9263591128439081", 10);
mpz_init(result);

mpz_mul(result, x, y);
gmp_printf(" %Zd\n"
          "*\n"
          " %Zd\n"
          "--------------------\n"
          "%Zd\n", x, y, result);

/* free used memory */
mpz_clear(x);
mpz_clear(y);
mpz_clear(result);

return 0;
}
```

Code Cell 8.5 RSA Algorithms using C.

of both the security of asymmetric encryption and the speed of symmetric encryption algorithms].

Determine m such that $c = m^e$ mod (p x q), given the whole numbers c, e, p, and q. (RSA decryption for frail integers).

Fundamentals: There is a public key represented by two factors or strictures n (modulus) and e (exponential). The modulus is the multiplication of two extraordinary large prime numbers (p and q as given following). The user must factorize n into two prime numbers (RSA being safe) in order to decrypt this message, and then determine the modular inverse of e, which is a time-consuming job.

A text version is first transcribed into the corresponding decimal value – a parameter m to be found below. Then the message is encrypted by calculating $c = m^e$ mod (p x q), where c stands for the encrypted text.

Here, an attempt is made to generate a private key by finding the values of p, q, and d, taking advantage of the exponent value and weak modulus to crack the encryption. In the present example, small values of p and q have been taken, nevertheless in actual applications, large values of p and q must be taken to protect the RSA system.

So, let's try to find d in the cases that follow, given p and q.

Examples

Input:
$c = 1614$
$e = 65537$
$p = 53$
$q = 31$

Output:
1372

Explanation:

Calculate $c = m^e \bmod (p \times q)$.
Insert $m = 1372$.
On calculating, we get $c = 1614$.

Input:
$c = 3893595$
$e = 101$
$p = 3191$
$q = 3203$

Output:
6574839

Explanation:

As stated above, if we compute $m^e \bmod (p \times q)$
with $m = 6574839$, we get $c = 3893595$

In general, the value of m can be obtained as follows:

(1) Find out the modular inverse of e.
Use the following equation, $d = e^{-1} \bmod (\lambda(n))$,
where n is the number of variables and λ is the Carmichael Totient function.

(2) Now, determine $m = c^d \bmod (p \times q)$

(3) The Chinese Remainder Theorem, as specified in the implementation below, can be used to speed up the calculation.

Python Implementation of Chinese Remainder Theorem

Output
41892906

```
# find the gcd of two
# integers using Euclidean algorithm
def gcd(p, q):

    if q == 0:
        return p

    return gcd(q, p % q)

# find the
lcm of two integers
def lcm(p, q):
    return p * q / gcd(p, q)

# implementing extended
# Euclidean algorithm
def ext gcd(e, phi):

    if e == 0:
        return (phi, 0, 1)
    else:
        g, y, x = ext gcd(phi % e, e)
        return (g, x - (phi // e) * y, y)

# compute the modular inverse
def modinv(e, phi):

    g, x, y = ext gcd(e, phi)
    return x % phi

# Implement Chinese Remainder Theorem
def implement(dq, dp, p, q, c):

    # Message part 1
    m1 = pow(c, dp, p)

    # Message part 2
    m2 = pow(c, dq, q)

    qinv = modinv(q, p)
    h = (qinv * (m1 - m2)) % p
```

Code Cell 8.6 Chinese Remainder Theorem.

```
    m = m2 + h * q
    return m

p = 9817
q = 9907
e = 65537
c = 36076319
d = modinv(e, lcm(p - 1, q - 1))


"""


pow(a, b, c) calculates a raised to power b
modulus c much faster than pow(a, b) % c
use Chinese Remainder Theorem as it
splits the equation to calculate two
values whose equations have smaller moduli and exponent
value, thereby reducing computing time.
"""


dq = pow(d, 1, q - 1)
dp = pow(d, 1, p - 1)
print implement(dq, dp, p, q, c)
```

Code Cell 8.6 (Continued)

8.6 SHA-512 Hash in Java

Secure Hash Algorithm 512 (SHA-512) is a hashing algorithm, each output of which produces an SHA-512 length of 512 bits (64 bytes), i.e. 128 hexadecimal characters. It can convert any size text into a fixed-size string. This algorithm is commonly used to get email address hash, password hash, and digital record verification.

Six hash functions fall into the Secure Hash Algorithm – two families of the cryptographic hash functions:

Hash Algorithm	Hash Value
SHA-224	224-bit hash value
SHA-256	256-bit hash value
SHA-384	384-bit hash value
SHA-512	512-bit hash value

(Continued)

Hash Algorithm	Hash Value
SHA-512/224	512-bit hash value
SHA-512/256	512-bit hash value

The most widely used and accepted hash algorithms of these are SHA-256 and SHA-512, which use 32-bit and 64-bit words, respectively, for computation. SHA-224 and SHA-384 are the short versions of SHA-256 and SHA-512 in that order. These are calculated with different starting values.

The MessageDigest Class, found in the package java.security, is used to compute cryptographic hash values in Java.

To determine a text's hash value, the MessageDigest class offers these cryptographic hash functions:

- MD2
- MD5
- SHA-1
- SHA-224
- SHA-256
- SHA-384
- SHA-512

A static method named getInstance() initializes these algorithms. After choosing an algorithm, the message digest value is determined, and the output is reverted as a byte array. The BigInteger class is applied to change the resulting byte array into its signum representation. This representation is subsequently transformed to hexadecimal format to get the desired MessageDigest.

Input: hello
Output:
309ecc489c12d6eb4cc40f50c902f2b4d0ed77ee511a7c7a9bcd3ca86d4cd86f989
dd35bc5ff499670da34255b45b0cfd830e81f605dcf7dc5542e93ae9cd76f

Input: helloworld
Output:
acc10c4e0b38617f59e88e49215e2e894afaee5ec948c2af6f44039f03c9fe47a9210
e01d5cd926c142bdc9179c2ad30f927a8faf69421ff60a5eaddcf8cb9c

Implementation of SHA-512 hash function

Output (see Code Cell 8.7)
HashCode Generated by SHA-512 for:

hello:
309ecc489c12d6eb4cc40f50c902f2b4d0ed77ee511a7c7a9bcd3ca86d4cd86f989
dd35bc5ff499670da34255b45b0cfd830e81f605dcf7dc5542e93ae9cd76f

```java
// Java program to calculate SHA-512 hash value

import java.math.BigInteger;
import java.security.MessageDigest;
import java.security.NoSuchAlgorithmException;

public class Sha {
    public static String encrypt(String input)
    {
        try {
            // getInstance() method is called with
algorithm SHA-512
            MessageDigest md = MessageDigest.
getInstance("SHA-512");

            // digest() method is called
            // to calculate message digest of the input
string
            // returned as array of byte
            byte[] messageDigest = md.digest(input.
getBytes());

            // Convert byte array into signum
representation
            BigInteger no = new BigInteger(1,
messageDigest);
            // Convert message digest into hex value
            String hashtext = no.toString(16);

            // Add preceding 0s to make it 32 bit
            while (hashtext.length() < 32) {
                hashtext = "0" + hashtext;
            }

            // return the HashText
            return hashtext;
        }

        // For specifying wrong message digest
algorithms
        catch (NoSuchAlgorithmException e) {
```

Code Cell 8.7 Calculating SHA-512 hash value.

```
        throw new RuntimeException(e);
    }
}

    public static void main(String args[]) throws
NoSuchAlgorithmException
    {

        System.out.println("HashCode Generated by
SHA-512 for: ");

        String s1 = "Hello";
        System.out.println("\n" + s1 + " : " +
encrypt(s1));

        String s2 = "hello world";
        System.out.println("\n" + s2 + " : " +
encrypt(s2));
    }
}
```

Code Cell 8.7 (Continued)

helloworld:
309ecc489c12d6eb4cc40f50c902f2b4d0ed77ee511a7c7a9bcd3ca86d4cd86f989
dd35bc5ff499670da34255b45b0cfd830e81f605dcf7dc5542e93ae9cd76f

SHA-1 forms a part of several widely used security applications and protocols, including TLS and SSL, PGP, SSH, S/MIME, and IPsec. These applications can use MD5 as well, as both MD5 and SHA-1 have derived from MD4. SHA-1 was designed by the United States National Security Agency, and is a U.S. Federal Information Processing Standard.

8.7 Cybersecurity

Cybersecurity is a way of defending systems and networks against online attacks that try to access, modify, destroy, or extort money in exchange for sensitive digital information. Cyberattacks can be carried out through several malware like Trojans, Rootkits, Virus, etc. and are known as Distributed Denial-of-Service (DDoS) attacks, Man-in-the-Middle (MITM) attacks, phishing, Ransomware attacks, and Structured Language Query (SQL) injections (IBM, 2022). With the increasing dependence on technology and Big Data, there is an urgent need to address the security concerns with respect to protection of data and transactions.

8.7.1 Common Cyberattacks

8.7.1.1 Denial-of-Service Attacks

A Denial-of-Service Attack is one in which cybercriminals flood a computer system's network and servers with traffic to prevent legitimate requests from being served. This renders the system unusable, preventing an organization from performing important tasks.

8.7.1.2 Malware

Malware, one of the most common cyberthreats, is malicious software designed to gain unauthorized access or harm a computer. This malware is created by a hacker or cybercriminal, for the purpose of making money or politics-driven cyberattacks, to disrupt or damage the computer of a legitimate user. It is often spread through an unsolicited email attachment or downloadable software that looks genuine and legitimate.

Malware can be of many types, such as:

Virus

It is a self-replicating program that fixes itself to an uninfected file and infects the entire computer system with files containing malicious code.

Trojan

This is a sort of malware, disguised as genuine software. Cyberattackers tempt users to upload Trojans to their computers and collect data by harming their systems.

Spyware

It is software that installs itself on a user's computer and starts secretly monitoring their online behavior without their knowledge or permission. It relays the information so received, about an individual or organization, to other parties.

Ransomware

It's a type of malicious malware that locks a user's files and data, threatens to erase information, and blocks access to files or computer systems until a ransom is paid. Despite the ransom, the user is not assured that the files will be retrieved or the system will be restored.

Adware

It is an advertising software capable of spreading malware through billboards.

Botnet

This malware is a network of infected computers, used by cybercriminals to perform tasks online without the user's consent.

8.7.1.3 Man-in-the-Middle Attack

Through a Man-in-the-Middle Attack, a cybercriminal intercepts communication between two individuals to steal data (see Figure 8.12). For example, on an unsecured

Figure 8.12 Cyber threats (Man-in-the-Middle).

WiFi network, an attacker can intercept the data being passed through a user's device and the network.

8.7.1.4 Phishing

Phishing is the practice of sending fraudulent emails that closely resemble those sent from legitimate companies or trusted sources. This is the most common type of cyberattack whose basic objective is to steal sensitive data, such as credit card numbers and login passwords.

8.7.1.5 Structured Language Query Injection

Structured Language Query (SQL) Injection is a type of cyberattack used to steal data from data repositories. Cybercriminals, taking advantage of vulnerabilities in data-driven applications, insert malicious code into the database through malicious SQL statements that give them access to sensitive information contained in the database.

Social engineering is a tactic used by adversaries to disclose sensitive information by soliciting monetary payment to you or by gaining access to your confidential data. To make this happen, they insist the user click on links, download malware, or rely on a malicious source.

8.7.1.6 Latest Cyberthreats
Dridex Malware

It is a financial Trojan malware with wide capabilities. It infects computers through phishing emails or prevailing malware. It specializes in stealing personal data, login information, banking details, etc., which are then used to conduct fraudulent transactions.

To prevent this, it is important that devices are patched, antivirus is turned on and up to date, and files are backed up.

Emotet malware

Emotet is an advanced Trojan that thrives on crude passwords. It is capable of stealing data and loading other malware as well. The only way to avoid this malware, is to create secure passwords.

8.7.2 Key Cybersecurity Features

- Checksums used in cryptography
- Codes for data backup and rectification
- Assess to risks and threats
- Mitigate system vulnerabilities
- Knowledge of malicious software
- Access management and control
- Authentication
- Encryption
- Setting up firewalls
- Implementation of intrusion detection and prevention systems (IDS and IPS)

The cyberattack landscape has grown exponentially in the last few years (IBM, 2022). Just as data breaches have seen an incredible increase and caused significant financial losses, blockchain has emerged as a promising mitigation technology for cybersecurity.

8.7.3 Blockchain for Cybersecurity

1) Data is undoubtedly an imperative tool for the growth of any business. Enterprises collect sensitive data from a variety of sources and store those data smartly and securely. A majority of organizations still store their data in centralized storage that acts like a honeypot for cybercriminals. Organizations can shield their digital information and assets by implementing blockchain-based decentralized storage solutions. Decentralized storage platforms typically distribute users' files across multiple nodes on their network.

2) Internet of Things: IoT and other connected devices are facing security vulnerabilities and challenges over time. With the increasing use of AI, hackers find an easy access to the overall system. The use of blockchain-enabled, device-to-device encryption can be an effective solution for maintaining cybersecurity in IoT systems.

3) Distributed-Denial-of-Service: DDoS is one of the most popular cyberattacks today, which can disrupt normal traffic on a target server or network by creating a flood of internet data, thus affecting the infrastructure around it. Many new forms of DDoS attacks are emerging rapidly, including hide-and-seek malware. It is often seen that connected devices like routers, smartphones, vacuum robots, and webcams are compromised to launch attacks. It remains present even after system reboot. Blockchain, due to its immutability and cryptographic properties, can effectively overcome these anomalies.

4) Better Security for DNS: The Domain Name System (DNS) is just like a public directory that associates domain names with their IP addresses. Hackers exploit the connection between the IP address and the site to crash the domain, resulting in unnecessary losses for merchants and loyal customers. By decentralizing DNS entries, blockchain can provide a preventive solution to foil such attacks. Its decentralized network allows user domain information to be irreversibly stored on a distributed ledger, and connections can be operated by immutable smart contracts.

5) Multi-signature authentication: Tampering with usernames and passwords is a major cyberthreat. By confirming that they have access to numerous devices, blockchain technology enables users to employ a multi-signature authentication mechanism that does not require usernames or passwords.

6) Software Integrity: Blockchain can be used to protect devices from infection with malicious software by verifying installers. The hash of the software can be recorded on the blockchain, and the same may be compared with that of the installer to verify the integrity of the download (Cyber Management Alliance, 2020).

8.7.4 Pros and Cons of Blockchain in Cybersecurity

8.7.4.1 Pros

- User Privacy: Full encryption of blockchain data by public and private keys ensures that data cannot be accessed by unauthorized parties as it flows through untrusted networks.
- Data transparency and traceability: In blockchain, with each subsequent iteration, the preceding state of the system is preserved, and therefore a complete history of transactions is available. Transaction data is digitally endorsed by the participants of the blockchain network, thereby maintaining transparency.
- Data integrity: The inherent characteristics of immutability and traceability help blockchains to keep data intact. In the event of a cybercontrol attack, smart

contracts can be used to check and enforce rules among all participants in order to avert and control account sharing.

- No single point of failure: Blockchain systems are distributed, and a single point of failure cannot bring down the whole network. It nullifies IP-based DDoS attacks. The data remains accessible all the times through different nodes. In this way, the platform and system are made flexible through the use of several nodes and distributed operations.
- Secure data transfer: Public key infrastructure (PKI) in blockchain preserves authentication at the time of data transfers. Though storing private key backups on secondary storage may pose a high risk, this can be avoided if cryptographic algorithms based on key management procedures and integer factorization problems, such as the Internet Engineering Task Force (IETF) or Remote Function Call (RFC), are implemented.

8.7.4.2 Cons

- In order to encrypt a data, blockchain heavily relies on private keys; however if they are lost, the user's access to encrypted data can be lost forever. Because once the private key is lost, it cannot be recovered.
- Adaptability and scalability challenges: Governments and organizations may find it challenging to integrate blockchain technology because it will require a total replacement of all currently used systems. This is because blockchain networks have predetermined block volume and limitations to execute transactions per second. Increasing its scalability may be somewhat puzzling.
- High operating cost: Blockchain applications are more expensive than their non-blockchain counterparts due to the high computing and storage requirements.
- Lack of control: Blockchain perceptions are yet to be governed and regulated globally.
- Blockchain literacy: Despite the countless applications of blockchain technology, there is a sheer paucity of such blockchain developers in the current scenario, who have in-depth knowledge of various programming languages and tools

8.7.5 Real-world Examples

Some prominent examples of using blockchain for cybersecurity:

8.7.5.1 Australian Government

Canberra, Australia: The Australian government is planning to construct a cyber-security network on a distributed ledger platform. The government has made substantial efforts to build a blockchain ecosystem and has teamed up with IBM to protect the storage of federal documents.

8.7.5.2 Barclays

London, England – Conventional Banking: Barclays have recently submitted a patent application that attempts to leverage blockchain technology to optimize safety parameters during fund transfer. Employing distributed ledger technology (DLT), it will aid in regulating cryptocurrency transfers.

Barclays pioneered the use of blockchain to trace financial transactions, adhere to regulations, and fight fraud. It holds a patent for the Know-Your-Customer process, which enables the bank to store all personally identifiable customer information on a secure blockchain.

8.7.5.3 Chinese Military

Beijing, China – Defense and Armed Forces: The Chinese military and government are gearing up to use blockchain cybersecurity to protect critical government, military, and other intelligence data.

8.7.5.4 Cisco

San Jose, California (Internet of Things): Cisco intends to safeguard the IoT devices via blockchain technology because it circumvents a single point of failure and protects data through encryption. Cisco has earlier worked with hardware company, Rockwell Automation, and supply chain company, Flex, on establishing blockchain networks in manufacturing and shipping.

8.7.5.5 Coinbase

San Francisco, California – Cryptocurrency: Coinbase is an exchange for users to buy and sell digital currency. The wallet and password are kept in a safe database, using encryption. To make sure your crypto is secure, the company conducts rigorous background checks of employees. Coinbase has processed over $150 billion in trades so far.

8.7.5.6 Colorado State

Denver, Colorado – Government: As per the bill approved by the Colorado Senate, the government will adopt blockchain technology to ensure the security of records and thwart attempts to attack it.

8.7.5.7 Founders Bank

Valletta, Malta – Cryptocurrency: The bank aims to be the world's first decentralized bank that will be owned neither by buyers nor by central authorities. The bank will be regulated by the holders of its token-based equity. The bank will use discrete silos for storage, large-scale public ledger systems, and encryption techniques to ensure that cryptocurrency trading can be conducted in a secure and orderly manner.

8.7.5.8 Health Linkage

Mountain View – California: is a blockchain network used in the health-care system to preserve and exchange patient data through hospitals, diagnostic laboratories, pharmacy firms, and physicians. The company aims to secure patient medical history and allows only a few personnel to have access to the record. It will keep track of the significant health-related events to help doctors make informed decisions.

8.7.5.9 JP Morgan

New York – Traditional Banking: The largest financial institution in the US, JP Morgan, has developed an enterprise-focused version of Ethereum called Quorum, which uses the blockchain to handle private transactions. The bank deploys smart contracts on the network to process cryptographically secure but transparent transactions. JP Morgan's blockchain-powered trial aims to cover all aspects of the loan lifecycle: origination, execution, and settlement.

8.7.5.10 Mobile Coin

San Francisco, California – Cryptocurrency: MobileCoin is evolving an easy-to-use cryptocurrency for resource-constrained enterprises that are not sufficiently equipped to process ledger information securely. MobileCoin is planning its product to integrate easily with Facebook Messenger, WhatsApp, and Signal.

8.7.5.11 Philips Healthcare

Andover, Massachusetts – Healthcare: Philips Healthcare has teamed up with hospitals around the world to build a blockchain and AI-enabled health-care network. This ecosystem will trace and examine all aspects of the health-care system, including operational, secretarial and therapeutic data. Blockchain is implemented to secure the large amount of data thus stored.

8.7.5.12 Santander Bank

Boston, Massachusetts – International Payments: Santander is the first bank in the United Kingdom to embrace blockchain to secure its international payment gateway. It empowers customers to make transactions between Santander's accounts in Europe and South America. Santander's One Pay FX, in partnership with Ripple, is prevalent in Brazil, Poland, Spain, and the UK.

8.7.5.13 Wall Street

Outdated and centralized cybersecurity protocols and trillions of dollars in cash flow make large banks easy targets of hacking and fraud. Blockchain can decentralize risk and provide a multi-layered security protocol. This is probably why Wall Street's attention is focused on blockchain's bolstered security protocols. Some of Wall Street's biggest financial institutions, such as JPMorgan and Bank of

America, which often lag behind in adopting new technologies, are trying to stay ahead of the curve.

Like banking, the health-care industry constantly faces cyberattacks. Doctors, clinics, hospitals, and health-care syndicates not only keep patient's bank information, but they also keep a lot of sensitive data, such as Social Security numbers, full names, weight, height, diseases, prescriptions, and medical conditions. Hackers extort millions of dollars from health-care syndicates all over the world by threatening to expose private data, and they might do so indefinitely unless new technologies are put in place. Blockchain could be an immediate solution to this problem. The decentralized state of DLT allows for information to be held in discrete silos and desists cybercriminals to access all identifiable aspects of a person's health records.

Coming Up

Beginning with early attempts at symmetric encryption with Playfair and Hill Ciphers, this chapter aimed to describe well-known asymmetric encryption key techniques like RSA. In addition, various types of cyberattacks and their prevention were discussed in depth using real-world examples.

The next chapter explores the possibilities of managing and verifying data and records through blockchain.

References

Cyber Management Alliance, 2020. https://www.cm-alliance.com. Accessed on 03 June 2020.

GNU Library, 2022. https://gmplib.org. Accessed on 01 April 2022.

IBM, 2022. https://www.ibm.com. Accessed on 20 March 2022.

Techtarget, 2022. RSA algorithm (Rivest-Shamir-Adleman). https://www.techtarget.com/searchsecurity/definition/RSA.

9

Data Management

9.1 Data Science

Big data and blockchain are mutually exclusive. The have their own distinct directions and uses. Although data science is focused on using data for proper governance, the decentralized ledger of blockchain ensures data security. However, one can reap benefits from a combination of blockchain and data science.

The decentralization of the blockchain makes access to critical data difficult as it is nearly impossible to compromise all nodes. In addition, nodes that behave suspiciously can be immediately expelled from the blockchain, making the system secure. Due to its encryption and rigorous verification processes, blockchain makes data integral, traceable, and transparent.

Data science provides in-depth data analysis, while blockchain allows for real-time transactions. Both these techniques can be used together to provide real-time data analysis. Data science can be used to evaluate blockchain data to disclose data insights and veiled trends.

9.1.1 Challenges for Data Scientists

- Data scientists collect information from a variety of sources, which are susceptible to tampering and theft. The rising value of data has resulted in an alarming increase in data breaches.
- Data confidentiality is the most important barrier for data scientists working with the personal sensitive information of consumers.
- Access to data is becoming a challenge for data scientists, as many countries have implemented data protection regulations.
- Data scientists spend a lot of their time in filtering the data because no matter how efficiently they analyze it, the imprecise data may not provide them with fruitful results.

Blockchain for Real World Applications, First Edition. Rishabh Garg.
© 2023 John Wiley & Sons, Inc. Published 2023 by John Wiley & Sons, Inc.

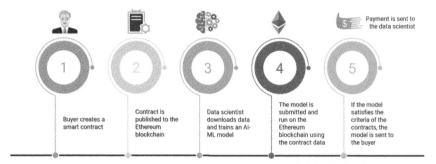

Figure 9.1 Blockchain application for data science.

- Data scientists, while accessing the data, often suffer from an erratic data access process that makes the access and analysis life cycle more difficult.
- Traditional data management systems do not support real-time data analysis, thereby depriving data scientists of taking advantage of real-time analysis.

9.1.2 Blockchain-based Solutions

- Blockchain, being a distributed system, keeps multiple copies of the data so that the authenticity of the data can be easily verified. Each block on the blockchain has its own unique hash or fingerprint, which prevents data manipulation and alteration.
- With its unique protocol, blockchain can help data scientists gain access to privacy-protected data for their research.
- Blockchain can streamline data access processes for data scientists by making them part of a distributed ledger at a specific level (see Figure 9.1).
- The cryptographic authenticity method of the blockchain ensures data consistency. The blockchain has a decentralized consensus method for validating data at the time data is recorded to ensure data accuracy.
- Federated machine learning is a collaborative data analysis technique that allows data to be analyzed across different devices located at a distance.
- Data scientists will undoubtedly benefit from the integrity of database systems, which will allow them to perform real analysis on reliable data.

9.2 Education and Employment Verification

Every year, millions of candidates submit their educational credentials across the world to get admission in higher education institutions or to fetch a dream job. Their grades, certificates, and degrees are verified in order to decide the legitimacy of their education with respect to qualification. An alarming ratio of applicants in every recruitment effort fabricate their educational history or misrepresent their education in a wide variety of ways – either they overstate their academic qualifications or submit fake degrees, procured from unaccredited institutions.

Verification of required documents, such as educational degrees, diplomas, or certificates, is one of the areas where blockchain can provide tangible results. A credential holder may store all of his academic credentials in an encrypted format, supported by the Interplanetary File System (IPFS), on his device and selectively share information with validators for verification or authentication without relying on third parties or central data repositories. No document may be shared without the explicit consent of its owner. Thus, blockchain ensures authentic data exchange and verification without storing any kind of verified credentials on the system. The blockchain ledger, being irreversible and immutable, does not remove the original version of truth, and hence, no tinkering is possible.

9.2.1 Existing Verification Process

Gradesheets, diplomas, and certificates issued by universities and other educational institutions are considered as provenant tools of educational qualifications. For centuries, physical forms of credentials have been the lone instruments to serve the very purpose. Physical certificates are considered as the safest tools of certification because:

- They are difficult to counterfeit due to built-in security features;
- They are held directly by the recipients, giving them complete control over the credentials;
- They are relatively easy to store in a safe vault for a longer time; and
- They can be produced at any time, to any person, and for any purpose by the bearer.

However, physical certificates also have a flip side:

- No physical certificate is immune to the risk of forgery.
- The security of physical certificates comes at a cost. The more secure the certificate, the more expensive it is to create it.
- Certificate details or timestamps can be fabricated by the issuer.
- Once issued by mistake, there is no way to retrieve the certificate without relinquishing control of the owner.
- Certificate registries are a single point of failure as they are maintained in a digital file or physical register. If the record is lost, verification of the certificate is not feasible, even if it is valid.
- Maintaining such a register and updating it from time to time requires substantial manpower.
- The process of verification of physical certificates is time-consuming as each certificate needs to be read and verified manually.

In such a milieu, a hoard of candidates fabricate their credentials to make themselves appear as a good fit. The US churns out an average of 1.98 million graduates annually. Such a large influx of degree holders necessitates a strict verification process to identify unauthorized institutions and fake degrees issued from them. This is probably the reason why a large number of applicants face inordinate delays in the process to get their confirmation letters.

Presently the verification process is conducted as follows:

- Schools, colleges, and universities usually conduct manual verification through their in-house staff.
- The verification process usually takes one to two weeks, but for those students who have graduated years ago, it gets a bit longer.
- Some schools demand a candidate disclosure and release form before starting the verification.
- Female candidates often mention their married name in the application form, while their educational proof shows their maiden name with which they have completed their graduation. A third document, such as a marriage certificate, also needs to be verified to decide analogy between the two.
- It is difficult to verify the degrees and certificates of universities that do not appear as authorized entities on the scrolls of a central regulatory authority, such as the UGC in India.

In a certification system, where multiple people or agencies are authorized to issue certificates, each issuer applies individual or proprietary standards for issuing certificates, resulting in the creation of multiple subsystems. These need to be individually and independently understood and verified in order to generate trust during testing or verification. Therefore, there is a need for a coordinated format and standardization across the network of different issuers to maintain the level of trust inherent across the verification system.

9.2.2 Blockchain as an Option

In blockchain technology, decentralized identifiers (DID) are cryptographically verifiable, and it builds trust in participants when each entity has a single source of truth about the data associated with the credential.

The DID is stored on the public ledger along with a DID document, which contains the public key for the DID, any other public credential that the credential holder wishes to reveal publicly, and network addresses for negotiation. Thus, the credential owner controls the DID document through the associated private key.

To secure a decentralized identity, the private key is owned only by the credential owner, while the public key is widely disseminated. This pairing of keys serves two purposes – first authentication, where the public key verifies that the holder of the paired private key sent the message, and second encryption, where only the holder of the paired private key can decrypt the message encrypted with the public key.

Issuing or verifying certificates on the blockchain requires relatively few resources, as the authenticity of the certificates can be verified without human intervention. The credentials are issued by an issuer, which is typically an educational institution authorized to provide an educational certificate to a candidate who fulfills the criteria to be awarded the relevant diploma or degree. The issuer ultimately acts as a certification-cum-verification authority, which, at the time of issuance of a certificate, affixes the validity of the details contained therein. The blockchain stores certificates with the signature (hash) of the issuer and the name of the receiver on thousands of nodes around the world, making it possible to verify the authority that originally issued the certificate. Credential owners (candidates) can store these credentials in their Pi Wallet and share to prove their eligibility to third parties on demand (see Figure 9.2).

The verifier or third party, which may be a higher education institution or employer, determines the validity of the proof through the validity of the attestation and the credibility of the attesting party, without probing into the validity of the actual data provided in the evidence. It is a zero-knowledge proof authentication method by which one entity masks the details of the information obtained through encryption, yet proves that it possesses the relevant information without disclosing any actual information to the other entity. The verification entity, in spite of zero knowledge, gets convinced of validity about the information supporting the evidence.

In general, a university diploma or degree contains limited information, such as the name of the awarding higher education institution (HEI), name of the awardee, title of the degree, signature of the issuing authority, and the date on which it is issued. Such degrees or certificates can be traded as a hash of the digital certificate or may be transferred from one entity to another as a token. The hash is simply a way of adding a link to the original document, which the user holds. This means that the mechanism permits the signature of the document to be

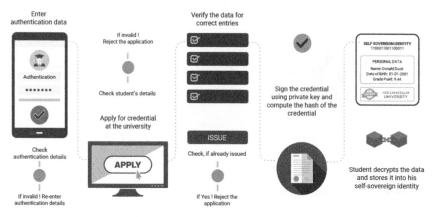

Figure 9.2 Record management process.

published, without the need to publish the document itself, thus keeping the confidentiality of the documents intact.

However, in some cases, these diplomas or degrees contain auxiliary information, such as description of teaching-learning pedagogy, curriculum, and learning outcomes, etc. that run into several pages and cannot be posted on the blockchain. If all the information is stored on the blockchain, the chain would grow enormously, which could lead to high resource consumption. In such cases, auxiliary information may be stored off the chain, and again, a hyperlink may be provided with the main text. Thus, some information may be held in the user's private wallet and some other information may be held in the public domain on the blockchain.

Thus, blockchain registries are tamper-proof, time-stamped, cryptographically secure, and can be updated or revoked for a valid reason by the issuing authority.

9.2.2.1 Enrollment Process

In this system, a student can register using his personal data, such as name, address, email ID, Aadhaar number, PAN card, previous education details, as well as the hash of a secret phrase (Garg, 2021a). The hash of the secret phrase will be stored on the blockchain in the form of a transaction. The student will also retain a copy of this hash. The college will issue the digitally signed degree certificate to a student, using his public key. This signed certificate will be encrypted and uploaded on the IPFS server. The hash of this encrypted, signed certificate will be stored on the blockchain (see Figure 9.3).

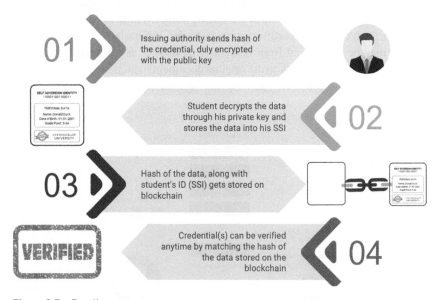

Figure 9.3 Enrollment process.

9.2.2.2 Validation Process

If a student wants to be admitted to another college, he will submit the hash of the secret phrase. The verifying college will retrieve the hash stored on the blockchain. They will compare the hash of the student's secret phrase with the hash stored on the blockchain. If a match is found, the student's identity is valid (see Figure 9.4).

9.2.2.3 Double Layer Encryption

In order to make it more secure, there can be two layers of encryption on the hash generated after uploading the credential on IPFS (see Figure 9.5; Garg, 2021b).

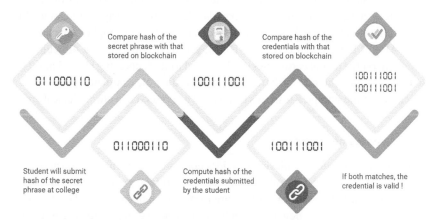

Figure 9.4 Validation process.

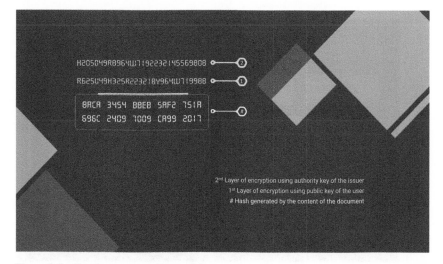

Figure 9.5 Two-layer encryption model.

The first layer of encryption will be implemented by using the public key on top of which, encryption will be implemented using the private key of the issuer (authority). To validate the shared credential, decryption using the private key of the receiver will be done.

The resulting encrypted hash can be compared with the one available on the issuer's database. If both match, the credentials will be considered as valid.

9.2.3 Learner's Console

Although many universities and institutes offer open online courses on a large scale, they have not become overly popular due to third-party certification. Not being universally valid, these certificates create problems in higher education or jobs. Also, if the original certificate is lost, getting a duplicate is a difficult task. Thus, encrypted digital certificates can be issued to students using blockchain. This will also reduce the cost of hardware. By recording all completed courses on a block, with time stamps, a learner's history can be preserved in chronological order.

9.2.4 Assessment Portal

A learner's certificate of achievements does not contain any information about the curriculum or teaching–learning modalities. It deprives a student of transferring his learning achievements or credit score from one platform to another. By using blockchain technology, new tools can be developed to enhance the learning processes and measure their outcome. By providing an assessment dashboard (see Figure 9.6) for the individual student to submit class assignments and projects via

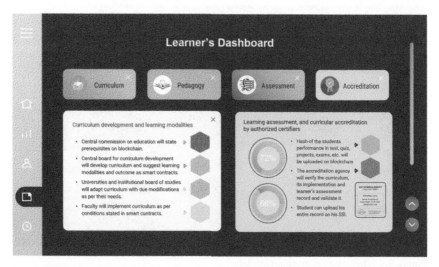

Figure 9.6 Learner's assessment record.

their SSI, employing smart contracts between teachers and students, a detailed record of curriculum, teaching, learning, and assessment can be maintained (Chen et al., 2018; Garg, 2021b).

9.2.5 Background Verification

In order to verify the experience and performance of a candidate, employers can retrieve and verify the information from the data maintained on the blockchain without having to contact the previous employers. When a credential holder (candidate) submits a document, the technology converts or encodes that document into a cryptographic digest or hash. The singularity of the technology is that when the same document is submitted more than once for verification, the hash and the transaction marker essentially match each time. If a change occurs in the document, the markers will never match.

An alternative approach is to check transaction records on the blockchain to verify the existence of a time-stamped document. Returning to the verification page of the original, time-stamped document, the existence of a time-stamped document at an earlier date proves that the document has been verified earlier and is genuine. It can prove to be an ideal tool for educational institutions, human resource managers, and health-care industries for document verification in less time, cost, and effort.

9.2.5.1 Maintenance of Track Record

The concept of blockchain allows the entire history of a candidate from kindergarten to higher education to be stored on the lines of digital ID tracking. From this, we can take stock of the study as well as the participation in other activities by the concerned candidate that transcribes in all respects to his work experience. Traditional background checks are often very slow and expensive, and this is especially a burden for those candidates who do not want to waste their precious time filling out forms. If a candidate's achievements at each stage of his life are accounted for, with privacy and security on a powerful platform, such as blockchain, employers would be able to search for the right candidate, verify their background, and test the documents submitted by them in support of their candidacy. Eventually, the time, cost, and human resources spent on the verification and evaluation can be significantly reduced.

Australian cryptocurrency (Chronobank) has created a blockchain-based platform, Chrono.tech, that allows hiring managers access to the database of freelance workers, along with their verified credentials and work experience. Chrono.tech was established in 2016 with the aim of facilitating short-term employment opportunities, like any other online services. The company empowers HR and recruitment professionals with a blockchain technology platform to help global freelancers find the best jobs and get paid according to their efforts. It is a system that provides a stable token on Ethereum and other participating blockchains. Based on the model of timebanking, workers trade labor hours for goods and services, bypassing the middle men, costs, and inefficiencies of the traditional recruitment sector (Chronotech, 2022).

ValidateMe is a blockchain-based digital vault for individuals to host, share, and validate their educational, employment, and personal documents. However, the documents are always owned by the original holders, and only they have the right to share them. It's a robust SaaS-based platform for issuing certificates and validating documents, having imbibed the features of immutability and transparency from blockchain technology (ValidateMe, 2022). It effectively leverages blockchain technology to provide a platform for information to be irretrievably stored and easily verified by anyone who has the right to view it.

Blockcerts is an open standard for creating, issuing, viewing, and verifying blockchain-based credentials that gives users the ability to keep and share their own authentic records. Its initial prototype was developed by the MIT Media Lab and Learning Machine to facilitate interoperability. It registers cryptographically signed, tamper-proof, and shareable digital records on the blockchain (Blockcerts, 2022).

ProFed is another setup of verified professionals who securely add verified personal data on the platform. Companies charge a commission every time the professionals fetch a job, a business proposal, or a commercial offer based on verified data, scaling the network to a new level (Profed Credit Union, 2022).

9.2.5.2 CV Validation

Often recruiters pay job boards for access to CVs that have been stored in their database for ages. These CVs are sometimes too old to have any relevance or may no longer be representative of that candidate. It has become a common practice to exaggerate achievements or misrepresent the factual information in CVs.

Leveraging blockchain technology, recruiters can have a real database of resumes owned by the candidates. In addition, the achievements counted by the candidate – such as transcripts of the school where he studied, participation in extracurricular activities and sports, awards earned, hours spent in vocation or job, nature of occupation, etc. can be maintained at blockchain and the same may be retrieved and verified, whenever required.

9.2.5.3 Opportunities for Job Aspirants

A blockchain system provides a reliable and transparent platform for both employer and the applicant. Since this system works on a platform in which facts cannot be changed with retrospective effect, it eliminates the possibilities of selection, based on a fabricated resume or false candidature. This will render more opportunities to qualified and proficient candidates and will increase the confidence of the recruiters too.

9.2.6 Bureaucratic Disintermediation

Over the years, universities have become large bureaucracies, where development is more in the administrative area than in the academic landscape, and which manages universities in line with a business management strategy. The hierarchical organization of higher education, where policy makers regulate institutions, institutions regulate departments, and departments regulate faculty members, is extremely slow and inflexible. This also applies to the manner in which professors document their research activities, course evaluation, and accreditation, and apply for funding and reimbursement through the appropriate hierarchy. This is the reason why bureaucracy is stealing precious time and attention from core activities in higher education institutions (HEI). The time and money that could be spent on student learning and research activities is spent on ineffective top-down hierarchies that undermine academic independence and autonomy. In HEIs, time and attention are limited cognitive resources that must be used for educating students and conducting research for the betterment of society and people. Garg (2016, 2017, 2018, 2019, 2022) has introduced many interesting ideas to make access to one's educational records, health history, bank accounts, tax records, land registry, without a central authority. Blockchain-based technology with such a network could also be effective in eliminating bureaucracy from HEIs.

9.2.7 Advantages of Blockchain-based Verification

In the current context, blockchain technology offers the following benefits:

- In a decentralized architecture, credentials are usually stored directly on the user's device or are held securely in private repositories, leaving no risk for data theft or breaches.
- The credential owner has the right to allow or disallow any organization or individual to have access to the document.
- Academic credentials maintained on blockchain are more secure than data stored on centralized servers. With content-based storage systems (CBS or IPFS), they are more capable of keeping the trust and data integrity intact.
- Decentralized public key infrastructure (DPKI) enables everyone to generate or anchor asymmetric cryptographic keys on the blockchain platform in a chronological order.
- Digital document verification will allow educational institutions and business establishments to operate more skillfully while reducing the effort, time, and cost required during manual verification of documents.
- It makes the information interoperable, prevents the credential holder from being locked on a single platform, allows the holder to deploy the data across multiple platforms, and enables them to use the information for various purposes.

- With DID and verifiable credentials, it allows seamless navigation of credentials from one platform to another.
- Although the credentials once issued on a blockchain cannot be changed or tampered with, minor typographical errors and some variables, such as home address, telephone numbers, or e-mail ID, may change over time to render the old credential invalid, and necessitate the reissuing of a new credential. The blockchain allows such mandatory changes, but blockchain preserves the status of each credential, whether revoked or updated.
- In the traditional document management system, if a holder loses their credentials, they have to apply to the concerned institution and wait until the duplicate is issued. In the proposed system, each user would store their credentials on a digital wallet or IPFS, which would be connected globally via blockchain. This leaves no room for losing credentials.

In this way, the process of academic document storage can be made decentralized and interoperable, where any organization or third party can verify one's academic credentials using a blockchain platform. Since it is a distributed system, there will be no single point of failure (SPoF).

9.3 Health Care

Blockchain has a wide range of applications and uses in health care. It helps secure the transfer of patient medical records, manage drug supply chains, and unlock biological codes for health researchers.

9.3.1 Potential Uses in Health Care

9.3.1.1 Digital Health Records

Health-care systems in every corner of the world are grappling with the problem of centralized databases. Having all of the patient's medical records in one place makes them vulnerable to be hacked, and otherwise the patient and their health-care provider may have an incomplete view of the patient's medical history.

One solution to this problem is to create a blockchain-based system that can be integrated with existing electronic medical records software. This allows the comprehensive medical record of the patient to be available as a single view. Each record connected to the blockchain, whether a physician's prescription, a note, or a lab result, is translated into a unique hash function. Each hash function is unique and can be decoded only if the person holding the data gives his consent.

Every time the patient consents to share a part of his medical record, the new information is logged on the blockchain in the form of a transaction – a new disease, a fresh treatment, a new result. Medical insurers can obtain immediate, valid confirmation of health services directly from patients, without the intervention, time, and cost of a third party.

9.3.1.2 Drug Supply Chain

A major challenge across the health-care sector is to ensure the provenance of medical goods to confirm their authenticity. By leveraging blockchain, one can track the item from the manufacturing point through each stage of the supply chain, enabling the customer to have full visibility and transparency of the goods they are going to buy (see Figure 9.7).

MediLedger is a colloquial example of a blockchain protocol that allows companies across the prescription drug supply chain to verify the authenticity of medicines, as well as expiry dates, along with other relevant information.

9.3.1.3 Health Insurance

On the blockchain-based system, pharmaceutical companies, medical device original equipment manufacturers (OEMs), wholesalers, insurers, and health-care providers can authenticate their identities as organizations, log contract details, and track transactions. This type of environment goes a step beyond supply-chain management and enables business partners and insurance providers in the health-care sector to operate digitally and in some cases, as per the terms laid down in smart contracts.

Manufacturers, distributors, and health-care organizations can settle payments and charge-back claims for prescription drugs and other goods, and sharing digital contracts by logging into a blockchain ledger.

9.3.1.4 Remote Health Monitoring

One of the current trends in digital health is the adoption of remote monitoring solutions, whereby physicians are able to provide proactive and preventive care by gaining access to patients' health based on vital signs indicated by sensors.

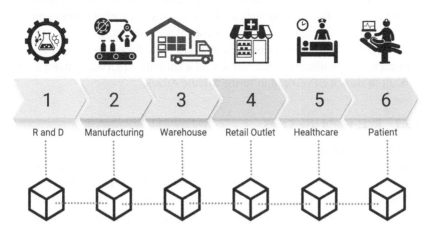

Figure 9.7 Blockchain in healthcare supply chain.

Blockchain cryptography ensures that only permitted parties can gain access to personal data, which is stored on the blockchain as a unique hash function. Any manipulation or alteration in the source data creates an altogether different hash function. Once patient data is entered as a hash on a blockchain ledger, it is nearly impossible to tamper with it, as it would need to gain access to all stored copies.

9.3.1.5 Organ Transplantation

Organ transplantation is a complex process. It is imperative that the donated organ belongs to the person of the respective blood group and should be transplanted on time. While 120,000 people are on the organ transplant waiting list, many donated organs are becoming useless due to nontransplantation on time. Blockchain could be a reasonable solution. Through this, a perfect match can be established between the organ donors, transplant seekers, and health providers who are skilled in organ transplantation. Organtree is the world's first decentralized organ donation database company that provides a blockchain platform to connect organ donors, organ recipients, and health-care facilities.

The United Arab Emirates (UAE) is the first country in the world to use blockchain and AI for organ transplantation. The UAE has partnered with Donor Healthtech, a leading national company focused on global health care, to provide a safe and optimized organ donation process. It aims to improve organ verification, match organs with patients, and optimize the transplantation process using AI and blockchain (Abdul-Malak, 2019).

9.3.1.6 Credential Verification

Similar to tracking the provenance of a medical good, blockchain technology can also track the experience of veteran medical professionals. Trusted medical institutions and health-care organizations can log the credentials of their employees, which in turn, streamlines the recruitment process for health-care organizations. US-based ProCredEx has established such a medical credential verification system using the R3 Corda blockchain protocol (stl partners, 2022).

The decentralized nature of blockchain allows IoT devices to interact directly with each other without the intervention of a centralized server, making it very difficult to launch DDoS or Man-in-the-Middle Attacks.

9.3.2 Real-world Use-Cases

9.3.2.1 Akiri | Foster City

California – Big Data: Akiri operates a network-as-a-service, committed to the health-care industry. It protects patient health data while transmitting it from one health-care center to another. The Akiri system acts as a network as well as a protocol to set policies and configure data layers to verify the sources and destinations of data in real time. Akiri does not store any type of data; rather, it ensures sharing of the duly shareable health-care data with the parties on a need-to-know basis. Subscribers can include any health-care provider, health-insurance payer, or pharmaceutical company.

9.3.2.2 Avaneer Health

Glastonbury, Connecticut – Big Data: Avaneer Health provides a utility network that enables access to secure and shareable data to deliver better experiences and better results. Built on blockchain technology, the digital platform allows data to flow rapidly across patients, providers, payers, employers, and health-care innovators with privacy, security, and control. Backed by Aetna, Anthem, and the Cleveland Clinic, Avaneer supports refining health-care efficiency, better claims processing, and keeping provider directories updated.

9.3.2.3 Block Pharma

Paris, France – Pharmaceuticals, Supply Chain: BlockPharma provides a solution to drug traceability and counterfeiting. Through this app, instant verification of the authenticity of the medicine being purchased by the consumer becomes possible.

BlockPharma relies on the latest machine-learning techniques to improve counterfeit case detection. By verifying the supply chain and all points of shipment, it is extremely easy for a user to know if he is carrying counterfeit medicines.

9.3.2.4 BurstIQ

Colorado Springs, Colorado – Big Data, Cybersecurity, Software: BurstIQ allows digital health establishments, health-care systems, payers, pharmaceutical companies, biotechnology enterprises, and governments to make access to health-related data, through its permissioned blockchain network. The platform ensures strict compliance with blockchain technology HIPAA regulations, in order to protect, sell, share, or license large amounts of patient data. Since BurstIQ's platform includes complete and up-to-date information about patients' health and care activities, it can be effective in preventing the abuse of opioids or other such drugs.

9.3.2.5 Centers for Disease Control and Prevention

Atlanta, Georgia – Government Agency, Health Care, Security: The Centers for Disease Control and Prevention (CDC) leverages IBM blockchain technology to develop an encrypted ledger that collects Electronic Health Records (EHRs), without compromising with data security and regulatory requirements. It uses blockchain to monitor diseases and deliver outbreak reports in real time. By studying the information, scientists can trace the origin and pattern of a disease, which may prove to be effective in its prevention. CDC may also employ blockchain to track the opioid epidemic.

9.3.2.6 Chronicled

San Francisco, California – Supply Chain Management: The Chronicled block-chain network is used to ensure secure and detailed review of drug shipments. Chronicled creates a blockchain network that shows a chain of custody. Chronicled provides automated solutions powered by the blockchain-based Mediledger net-work to eliminate manual processing of transactions, revenue leakages, and cash-flow delays. Mediledger Network is Industry Network 2.0 for the health-care industry, driving solutions for real-time alignment, rule enforcement, and settle-ment of transactions directly between business partners. Thus, it helps drug com-panies ensure that their drugs move without a glitch, and they enable law enforcement to review any suspicious activity, such as drug trafficking.

9.3.2.7 Coral Health

Vancouver, Canada – Health-care IT: Coral Health uses blockchain to automate administrative processes, accelerate the care process, and improve health out-comes. It also implements smart contracts between patients and health-care pro-fessionals to automate processes and ensure that data and treatments are in accordance with the contract.

By incorporating patient information into Distributed Ledger Technology (DLT), the company enables doctors, scientists, lab technicians, and public health officials to connect faster than ever before. The company is exploring the potential of the Smart over FHIR protocol to allow patients track their health files.

9.3.2.8 Embleema

New York – Pharmaceutical Development: Embleema is a health data and analyt-ics SaaS platform that brings innovative treatments to help patients who have no access to treatment. Embleema is a virtual trial and regulatory analytics platform designed to accelerate the availability of treatment to patients through the com-pany's Virtual Studies Suite. This platform is used by the FDA for regulatory eval-uation of health products linked to genomic datasets. In addition to the FDA, the platform is also used by major pharmaceutical companies, biotechs, and patient and clinical research centers.

9.3.2.9 Factom

Austin, Texas – IT, Enterprise Software: Factom creates products that help the health-care industry store digital records on a blockchain platform. Physical papers can be equipped with special Factom security chips that carry patient information and are stored as personal data, accessible only to hospitals and health-care administrators.

9.3.2.10 Guardtime

Irvine, California – Cybersecurity: Guardtime creates a trusted data and information ecosystem for patients, facility providers, payers, regulators, and pharmaceuticals, allowing each stakeholder to access the information necessary to deliver effective patient care. Guardtime uses a blockchain platform for cybersecurity applications and health care. The company has been instrumental in implementing blockchain in Estonia's health-care system, and it recently collaborated with Verizon Enterprise Solutions to deploy multiple platform services based on Keyless Signature Infrastructure (KSI) blockchain.

9.3.2.11 MedicalChain

London, England – Electronic Health Record, Medical: MedicalChain uses blockchain technology to manage health records with a collaborative, smart approach to health care. Doctors, hospitals, or laboratories may request patient information. The system helps to maintain the integrity of the health record while establishing a single point of truth. In May 2018, MedicalChain announced the launch of MyClinic.com – a telemedicine platform that allows the patients to consult their doctors through video and pay their consultation fees with MedTokens.

9.3.2.12 Patientory

Atlanta, Georgia – Cybersecurity, Health Care, IT: Patientory uses blockchain technology for medical supply chain mapping. Once a ledger is created for a drug, it records data at each step, from the point of origin until it reaches the end consumer. This is critical to successfully distributing the product, preventing its hoarding, and protecting it from malpractice. The process can also monitor labor costs and waste emissions.

Patientary's end-to-end encryption ensures that patient data is stored and shared securely and efficiently. The company's platform enables patients, healthcare providers and physicians to access, store, and transfer all vital information via blockchain.

9.3.2.13 Professional Credentials Exchange

Tampa, Florida – Big Data: Professional Credentials Exchange (ProCredEx) provides a network-cum-infrastructure that makes it easy for organizations to securely transfer medical documents between each other. In the health-care system, the practitioner controls and approves that data sharing via a computer, tablet, or mobile app. It uses proprietary verification engines with distributed ledger technology and limits membership to only verified and approved organizations so that the health system can rapidly obtain verified certifications and enhance the quality of patient care.

9.3.2.14 RoboMed

Moscow, Russia – Medicine: RoboMed works to connect patients to providers through clinical guidelines encoded in smart contracts. The company deploys chatbots, telemedicine sessions, and wearable diagnostic devices to collect patient information and share it with the medical team. It combines AI and blockchain to provide a single point of care to patients.

9.3.2.15 Tierion
Mountain View, California – SaaS, Blockchain: Tierion uses blockchain to maintain a clear possession history within the medical supply chain. The company's blockchain platform audits documents, records, and drugs, and uses timestamps and credentials to maintain proof of ownership in the supply chain.

9.4 Genomics

Blockchain can securely hold billions of genetic data points. It is turning into a market where people can trade their encrypted genetic information to create comprehensive databases, giving scientists access to valuable data faster than ever before. Contrary to how existing systems work, if data owners can contact data buyers directly without an intermediary company, analysis costs may come down, and data owners can earn income.

9.4.1 Real World Use-Cases

According to Emergen Research, the global blockchain genomics market size was US$ 40.62 million in 2020 which is expected to reach US$ 2,086 million in the next few years (BioSpace, 2022).

9.4.1.1 doc.ai
Palo Alto, California – AI, Medical Software: doc.ai is a blockchain-based artificial intelligence company. Its digital health platform empowers its users to accelerate insights by integrating real-world medical and life data. Users can join the company's platform to share their medical and genomic data with a community of scientists who use the shared data for predictive modeling. Once the information is uploaded and encrypted on a blockchain, the data is erased, after trials, to ensure confidentiality.

9.4.1.2 EncrypGen
Coral Springs, Florida – Data-Sharing: EncrypGen Gene-Chain is a blockchain-enabled platform that facilitates search, storage, sharing, buying, and selling of genetic information. It stores the raw DNA data file by separating it from the donor's name, email, and other sensitive information. The company protects the privacy of its users by allowing only members to purchase genetic information using traceable DNA tokens. DNA data buyers find suitable gene-chain profiles for their projects and purchase de-identified genomic information with DNA tokens. Member companies can use genetic information to build their genetic knowledge and advance the industry. It is currently working on integrating blockchain platforms by partnering with test companies, analytics software developers, and others.

9.4.1.3 Nebula Genomics

Boston, Massachusetts – Biotechnology, Genetics: Nebula Genomics is all set to introduce DNA sequencing, using blockchain without disclosing customers' personal information. Pharmaceutical and biotech companies spend billions of dollars each year to procure genetic data from third parties. The company strives to eliminate unnecessary costs in the genetic research process through distributed ledger technology. Nebula Genomics is attempting to build a massive genetic database, encouraging users to securely sell their encrypted genetic data.

9.5 Food Supply Chain

The use of blockchain in the food industry is particularly valuable because it allows tracking the journey of various foods, right from the farm to the shelves of superstores. Many issues, such as food fraud, security recalls, and supply chain inefficiencies, can be resolved through blockchain-enabled food traceability.

For example, you go to the supermarket to buy vegetables. The fruits and vegetables that are neatly stacked there look fresh, and hence, you buy them. But do you know whether the fruits or vegetables you are buying are safe to eat? Currently, it is not possible for consumers or retailers to access information related to the cultivation, processing, or transportation of foodstuffs.

Over the years, supply management has faced many problems due to the inadequacy and inefficiency of the system. Seafood is one of the extremely popular categories of the illegal food supply chain. The global fishing industry is faced with numerous challenges, such as unrestricted, unregulated, and illegal fishing. It is the easiest source of infection or allergy in food items.

Often government authorities use food recalls to determine the presence of a potential allergen in foods. Due to the food recall, several prestigious brands such as Cadbury, Nestle, Pepsi, Coca-Cola, Kraft Foods, Blue Bell Creameries, and Peanut Corporation of America have suffered financial losses over the years.

Much of the food we eat today comes from a complex global supply chain that includes production, logistics, processing, packaging, warehousing, inspection, distribution, and more. But with this complex chain comes adulteration, tampering, misrepresentation, or intentional substitution. Food fraud costs the food industry several billions of dollars globally each year. Most of the food categories include milk, tea, coffee, fruit juice, olive oil, maple syrup, seafood, honey, and many other food items without which the common man cannot imagine his day.

With ever-increasing global supply chains, food safety is a serious concern for both consumers and regulators. According to the World Health Organization, food contamination affects one in ten people, which leads to the loss of 33 million healthy life years, and kills about 420,000 worldwide, every year (WHO, 2019). In addition, 125,000 children under the age of five die each year of foodborne contamination.

In this wake, blockchain appears as the only solution that can maintain traceability of immutable records. Let's take a case study of Nestle. Established 150 years ago, Nestle is the largest food manufacturer in the world. The Swiss food giant has 403 factories in about 187 countries around the world, producing food products worth more than US$ 80 billion. It is a trusted pillar of the world's supermarket supply chain due to its popular brands – Nescafe, Perrier, and Milo. It is investing significant resources into innovations through open blockchain technology that makes the product journey as simple, easy, and standardized as flipping a bag of chips and examining its contents (Nestle, 2019).

Through SaaS blockchain, Nestle Group now has an ability to provide information, such as track record, current status, certification, test data, and temperature data of each food item. The consumer can understand that the data uploaded by the producer has not been changed by anyone else later. Other companies, such as Walmart, Golden State Foods, MacLean, Unilever, and Dole, are also experimenting with the potential applications of blockchain in the food supply chain.

Blockchain technology thus gives the food supply chain the ability, reliability, efficiency, and security to quickly trace the entire life cycle of food products from origin through every point of contact throughout their journey from farmer to consumer. The information recorded at each stage in the food supply chain is agreed upon by all members of the food supply network, so once consensus is reached, it becomes an irreversible permanent record. With this technology, the consumer will be able to trace his food from farm to fork by scanning the QR code on the packet (see Figure 9.8).

Outside of the food sector, blockchain is rapidly establishing its dominance in supply chain management of other products too. Though most of the leading companies carry advanced digital infrastructure, such as Enterprise Resource

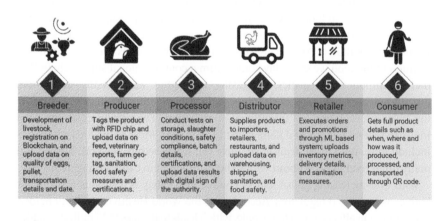

Figure 9.8 Food supply chain management.

Planning (ERP) and Supply Chain Management (SCM) software, the system shows analog gaps, when products are tracked from connected manufacturing equipment (origin) to digital shipping notices and RFID scanning. Even the most sophisticated equipment fails to keep track of product life cycle.

As a result, the visibility and insight of most companies are limited to where their products are at the moment. With blockchain, companies can own a real-time and immutable digital ledger of transactions and movements for all participants in their supply chain network. This makes supply chains reactive to inaccuracies, serving as an alternative to traditional paper-based tracking and manual inspection systems.

Blockchain can be used to collect wealth of data and deploy it in the relevant field. It can become a platform for food suppliers to connect with consumers, providing more verifiable information. Food suppliers, especially those who do not sell their products directly to the end users, hardly get opportunities to interact with the consumers. Often such suppliers struggle to communicate with customers to explain the best practices that they have adopted for processing the product. Blockchain gives food suppliers a tool to get their point across to the consumer at all stages of the supply chain.

Suppliers can provide evidence that the mangoes they are referring to as coming from India have actually been plucked from Indian orchards. Suppliers can state that no inorganic fertilizers or pesticides have been used to grow it and how the methods by which the food is processed are superior to other comparable processing methods. The complex nature of agriculture may not be as easy to explain through a smartphone app.

9.6 Real Estate

Real estate is considered to be the largest asset class in the world. According to a report on global real estate value calculations, the overall value of commercial, residential, and forestry property is approximately US$ 217 trillion, of which non-residential assets account for only one-fourth (Fortune – Savills, a London-based real estate advisor).

Real estate has been a reliable investment option for the rich since time immemorial. There are very few properties that offer the same level of capital appreciation. However, on an international scale, there have been many hurdles, such as citizenship of the respective nation, recognition of a business establishment, international bank accounts, credit scores, matching funds, and access to the right sponsors, financers, and fund managers. All these make real estate business difficult across borders.

According to the United Nations, US$ 800 billion to US$ 2 trillion is processed globally each year, a large portion of which is laundered through real estate. In the coming years, this figure can cross US$ 1.6 trillion annually. A high level of transparency can combat corruption, tax evasion, and money laundering.

Investing in international real estate involves paying a number of additional fees, such as broker fees, attorney fees, exchange charges, transfer charges, investment fees, taxes, etc. Due to such a large number of third-party interventions, investing in foreign real estate becomes a costly affair. Also, even if an investor has an excellent credit score in the country of origin, it may not be valued so in the country where he wants to invest.

Real estate transactions often move at a snail's pace, and sometimes it takes six months to a year to find an ideal investment property. In addition, real estate is not as liquid as cryptocurrency, nor can it be listed on a public exchange and sold quickly during open hours. Hence, buying a property or converting it into cash is a daunting task.

9.6.1 Title Management

Title management is one area in the real estate business that is highly prone to forgery and extortion. Every property owner, in order to protect his property, spends a lot on getting the title registered, freed from encumbrances, and transferring the ownership in his name in the municipality. As a global immutable ledger, blockchain offers all participants a single version of truth about the title of land ownership. As a result, processes, such as double-selling, forged registries, and encroachments that are often associated with real estate can be eliminated.

Blockchain provides the ability to write and maintain an irreversible record of real estate titles in a risk-free and reliable manner. It makes land purchase, sale, and transfer cost-effective by reducing the complexity of the process. Regulating property trading with the help of smart contracts can eliminate the cost of the documentation process, the involvement of middlemen, and property appraisal agents.

9.6.2 Smart Assets

Smart contracts are protocols written in computer language that allow a business transaction to be executed when a set of certain pre-defined conditions are met. These contracts can be automated on the blockchain in the same way that, with a standing instruction, a bank pays interest amounts to its customers' accounts over a period of time or recovers a loan. Smart contracts can introduce the concept of Smart Assets – a notion of transacting all assets on a blockchain-based model. A blockchain-based identity can be created for any hard asset in the physical world, which has been underscored several times in this book. Using these identities, ownership can be controlled through smart contracts.

9.6.3 Trust and Transparency

Blockchain allows each asset to have its own digital address and the details to be saved in the wallet of the respective owner, while maintaining an immutable record of ownership and transfers of assets on the ledger.

These details may include size, location, geographical boundaries, structure, lease, taxes, bill payments, legal disputes, financial transactions, and complete history of transfer of property. Blockchain's hash technique, in which a new hash is added to a block created with the hash value of the previous block, provides a robust security mechanism that makes it impossible to manipulate registries.

9.6.4 Financing

Blockchain is capable of tracking activities from credit origination to loan repayment installments, contract compliance, and other advanced activities. Smart contracts can be used to keep commitments, identify defaults, reduce contract adjustment costs, and more. In the current scenario, India, Sweden, Republic of Georgia, and others are exploring the potential of blockchain in their registry systems with the aim of modernizing record-keeping frameworks.

9.6.5 Cost and Efficiency

The distributed ledger can be customized to suit the needs of the users, which can be permissioned or permissionless. Every information documented on a distributed ledger is saved as a copy on each node connected to the network.

Business terms and conditions can be set through smart contracts, and a payment process can be initiated when those conditions, such as registration of title in the name of the new owner (buyer) or transfer of title in municipal records, etc., are met.

Since all participants in a blockchain network have the same version of the truth, it allows for rapid data processing and verification that would normally require the intermediation of agents and central authorities in a traditional process.

9.6.6 Tokenization

Liquidity of real estate is an arduous task for the traders and the title holders. Blockchain innovations can help reduce assets into real domain tokens as needed. These tokenized resources can be sold in token trades to speculators or buyers rather than selling the entire asset outright.

Tokenization, as a fungible resource, makes the purchase and transfer of assets faster and easier in the real world. It reduces fees and accelerates leasing, buying, and selling. It can develop new facilities and is able to cater to the demands of the specific organization.

Unmatched sources and expanded reach among related organizations opens new avenues for trade and commerce and increases liquidity. A tokenized resource reduces office overheads and agent costs with greater adaptability. The profits earned from investing in these assets, which are divided into tokens, can be shared in proportion to the tokens owned by each shareholder.

9.6.7 Pros and Cons of Tokenization

Tokenization has many benefits. It is a ledger maintained on a blockchain in which the possibility of third-party interference is almost zero, and which does not allow any kind of red tape to enter. It provides unmatched liquidity and secure cross-border exchange across the globe. Tokens allow only fragmented ownership, which often results in a lower cost of trading a real estate asset. With no room for devaluation of tokens, it provides an impeccable protection to speculators and buyers.

The flip side of tokenization is that the blockchain is still in its nascent stage. Malicious programs from hackers pose a tremendous threat to tokens that can create havoc for both buyers and speculators. Until regulations are framed for the purchase and exchange of tokens, a general mindset will not be able to widely accept it as an alternative to real estate.

9.7 Crowd Operations

Decentralized applications (dApps) have the potential to implement smart contracts to automate the processes associated with crowd operations (Garg, 2022). Application Programming Interfaces (APIs) can be used to publish a set of methods and functions to access data, invoke operations programmatically, and store data. The API can help publish a set of services on a dApp.

Categories of APIs in blockchain

1) Management APIs – e.g. admin, miner, personal, txpool
2) Web3 APIs – e.g. web3, eth, net

Examples of APIs in blockchain

1) admin.addPeer(): Here admin is the API and addPeer() is the method/function of the API.
2) debug.dumpBlock(): This can display the block header details of the block number 16.

These APIs can be used to encode the specific operations for common users in the dApp backend and shown as buttons on frontend for intuitive interface and abstraction.

9.7.1 Decentralized Voting (Electoral Process)

The purpose of any electoral process is to conduct elections in a fair, reliable, and transparent manner, for which the bureaucracy often spends billions of dollars and deploys government officials recklessly. The process involves election training, election material, temporary constructions to ensure voter's access to the polling stations, vehicles for polling parties, digital voting machines, voter verifiable paper audit trails and printing of nomination papers, ballot papers, ballot accounts, declarations, three to four dozen documents, their envelopes, training material, etc. that can be eliminated. Instead, all terms and conditions can be pre-defined in smart contracts, and the entire electoral process can be automated.

Blockchain can be effective in making the voting process simple, accessible, transparent, and secure. It will inspire people who often do not exercise their franchise due to living in isolated areas, lack of access to polling station, or suffering from physical infirmity. Being a distributed ledger, it can allow voters to cast their votes from anywhere in the world, without compromising on security. It facilitates the electorate to vote comfortably on the day of polling, sitting at home, without standing in queue or completing redundant formalities. It ensures maximum participation of voters and removes all the uncertainties of the process. It uses decentralized ledger technology to distribute voting data across multiple servers, where it becomes nearly impossible to destroy or change the results.

As cited several times in this book, each citizen can be granted a decentralized identity, referred to as a self-sovereign identity, through which all the important events of the citizen's life can be recorded on a distributed ledger. On the basis of the citizen's data, such as place of usual residence (constituency, where he is eligible to vote), date of birth (when he attains the minimum age prescribed for voting as on January 1), and subject to other conditions (if any), he may be permitted to participate in the election process.

Once a voter has cast his vote after login with his decentralized identity number and credentials, he will not be able to use the same ID number again for the same election. The blockchain will count the votes cast in favor of each candidate by separating the votes of each constituency through software, ensuring the integrity of the votes cast through the individual nodes, by cryptographic hash algorithms. Consequent upon the fulfillment of the pre-determined conditions, as laid down in smart contracts, the election commission shall announce the election results of all the constituencies across the country simultaneously on the stipulated date and time.

At any point of time, a voter can check the ballot (block) and verify for himself if the vote was cast as intended. After declaration of results, anyone can audit the ballots and confirm if the election results are accurate.

Here is a smart contract to automate the voting process (see Code Cell 9.1).

Decentralized Voting System

```solidity
pragma solidity ^0.4.0;
contract Ballot {

    struct Voter {
        bool voted;
        uint weight;
        uint8 vote;
        address delegate;
    }
    struct Proposal {
        uint voteCount;
    }
    enum Stage {Init,Reg, Vote, Done}
    Stage public stage = Stage.Init;

    address president;
    mapping(address => Voter) voters;
    Proposal[] proposals;

    event votingCompleted();

    uint startTime;
    //modifiers
    modifier validStage(Stage reqStage)
    { require(stage == reqStage);
        _;
    }

    /// new ballot with $(_numProposals) different
proposals.
    function Ballot(uint8 _numProposals) public  {
        president = msg.sender;
        voters[president].weight = 5;
        proposals.length = _numProposals;
        stage = Stage.Reg;
        startTime = now;
```

Code Cell 9.1 Voting process using smart contracts.

```
    }
    /// $(toVoter) is given the right to vote on ballot.
    /// only call by $(president).
    function register(address toVoter) public validStage
(Stage.Reg) {
        //if (stage != Stage.Reg) {return;}
        if (msg.sender != president || voters[toVoter].
voted) return;
        voters[toVoter].weight = 1;
        voters[toVoter].voted = false;
        if (now > (startTime+ 30 seconds)) {stage =
Stage.Vote; }
    }

    /// give a single vote to proposal $(toProposal).
    function vote(uint8 toProposal) public
validStage(Stage.Vote)   {
        // if (stage != Stage.Vote) {return;}
        Voter storage sender = voters[msg.sender];
        if (sender.voted || toProposal >= proposals.
length) return;
        sender.voted = true;
        sender.vote = toProposal;
        proposals[toProposal].voteCount += sender.
weight;
        if (now > (startTime+ 30 seconds)) {stage =
Stage.Done; votingCompleted();}
    }

    function winner() public validStage(Stage.Done)
constant returns (uint8 _winner) {
        //if(stage != Stage.Done) {return;}
        uint256 winningVoteCount = 0;
        for (uint8 prop = 0; prop < proposals.length;
prop++)
            if (proposals[prop].voteCount > winningVote-
Count) {
```

Code Cell 9.1 (Continued)

```
                winningVoteCount = proposals[prop].
voteCount;
                _winner = prop;
            }
        assert (winningVoteCount > 0);


    }
}
```

Code Cell 9.1 (Continued)

To avoid visibility of the results during elections, votes can be encrypted with an open source library - eccrypto, which in turn is wrapped in eth-crypto, an open source JavaScript library, and uses the Elliptic Curve digital signature algorithm. To test Solidity code, Truffle and Ganache can be used. Truffle includes a testing framework called Mocha that makes it possible to write JavaScript tests.

Truffle also acts as a package manager, and has built-in functionality to compile Solidity code and deploy it on the blockchain. Truffle provides three different commands: truffle compile, truffle migrate, and truffle test that can be used to compile contracts, deploy them on a blockchain across the network, and perform tests on them. To collect test data, the Ganache CLI version can be used.

Sample Python-Based Frontend

```
pragma solidity 0.4.24;
contract Election {
    struct Candidate {
        uint id;
        string name;
        uint voteCount;
    }
    bool curr = true;
    mapping(address => bool) public voters;
    mapping(uint => Candidate) public candidates;
    uint public candidatesCount;
```

Code Cell 9.2 Decentralized voting process

```
event voted (
    uint indexed _candidateId
);

constructor () public {
    addCandidate("Candidate 1");
    addCandidate("Candidate 2");
    addCandidate("Candidate 3");
    addCandidate("Candidate 4");
    addCandidate("Candidate 5");
    addCandidate("Candidate 6");
    addCandidate("Candidate 7");
    addCandidate("Candidate 8");
}

function add (string memory _name) private {
    candidateCount ++;
    candidates[candidateCount] =
Candidate(candidateCount, _name, 0);
}

function end () public {
    curr = false;
}

function vote (uint _candidateId) public {
    require(!voters[msg.sender],"Already voted");

    require(_candidateId > 0 && _candidateId <=
candidatesCount,"Invalid candidate");
    require(curr,"Election ended");

    voters[msg.sender] = true;

    candidates[_candidateId].voteCount ++;

    emit voted(_candidateId);
}
}
```

Code Cell 9.2 (Continued)

```python
from flask import Flask, render_template, flash,
request, session, redirect, url_for
from wtforms import Form, TextField, TextAreaField,
validators, StringField, SubmitField
import requests;
import json;

backend_addr = "https: //election-backend.net/"

app = Flask(__name__)
app.secret_key = 'helloworld'

@app.route("/", methods=['GET', 'POST'])
def home():
    return redirect(url_for('verify'))

@app.route("/results", methods=['GET'])
def results():
    try:
        req = requests.get(backend_addr+'results')
        if(req.status_code!=200):
            return render_template('confirm.
html',message=req.text),req.status_code
        result = eval(req.text)
        print(result)
        result.sort(reverse=True,key=lambda x: x[2])
        return render_template('results.html',result=result)
    except:
        return render_template('confirm.html',
message="Error processing"),500

@app.route("/verify", methods=['GET', 'POST'])
def verify():
    try:
        req = requests.get(backend_addr+'isended')
        if(not eval(req.text)):
            if request.method == 'POST':
                aid = request.form['aid']
                bio = request.form['biometric']
```

Code Cell 9.3   Python-based frontend

```
                    req
= requests.get(backend_addr+'number_of_users')
                number_of_accounts = int(req.text)
                if(bio == 'yes' and aid.isdigit() and
int(aid)<=number_of_accounts):
                    session['verified'] = True
                    session['aid'] = int(aid)
                    return redirect(url_for('vote'))
            return render_template('verification.html')
        else:
            return render_template('confirm.html',
message="Election ended",code=400),400
    except:
        return render_template('confirm.html',
message="Error processing"),500


@app.route("/vote", methods=['GET', 'POST'])
def vote():
        req = requests.get(backend_addr+'isended')
        if(not eval(req.text)):
            if('verified' in session):
                req
= requests.get(backend_addr+'candidates_list')
                candidates = eval(req.text)
                print(candidates)
                candidates1 = candidates[:int(len
(candidates)/2)]
                candidates2 = candidates[int(len
(candidates)/2):]
                if request.method == 'POST':
                    aid = session['aid']
                    session.pop('verified')
                    session.pop('aid')
                    candidate = request.form['candidate']
                    cid = candidates.index(candidate)+1
                    print(cid)
                    req = requests.post(backend_
addr,json.dumps({'aadhaarID':aid,'candidateID':cid}))
                    print(req)
```

Code Cell 9.3 (Continued)

```
                    return render_template('confirm.
html',message=req.text,code=req.status_code),req.
status_code
                return
render_template('vote.html',candidates1=candidates1,
candidates2=candidates2),200
            else:
                return redirect(url_for('verify'))
        else:
            return render_template('confirm.
html',message="Election ended",code=400),400

if __name__ == '__main__':
    app.run(host="0.0.0.0", port=80, debug = True)
```

Code Cell 9.3 (Continued)

Coming Up

In the foregoing chapter we considered how blockchain can securely and efficiently manage data, create tamper-proof logs of sensitive activities, such as education, employment, health care, drug delivery, remote health care, organ transplantation, food supply, decentralized elections, etc.

In the next chapter we will look at how blockchain allows banks and trade finance to reduce the current level of complexity, eliminate excessive paperwork, and strengthen the possibilities of decentralized finance in the real world.

References

Abdul-Malak L, 2019. UAE First Country in the World to Use Blockchain for Organ Donation. https://www.unlock-bc.com/news/2019-02-01/uae-first-country-in-the-world-to-use-blockchain-for-organ-donation. Accessed on 3 February 2019.

Blockcerts, 2022. The Open Standard for Blockchain Credentials. https://blockcerts.org/guide. Accessed on 2 February 2022.

BioSpace, 2022. https://www.biospace.com/article/blockchain-in-genomics-market-size-to-reach-usd-in-2-086-26-million-in-2028-growing-at-a-cagr-of-65-8-percent-/ Accessed on 10 January 2022.

Chen G, Xu B, Lu M, and Chen NS, 2018. Exploring Blockchain Technology and Its Potential Applications for Education. *Smart Learning Environments*, 5: 1–10. https://doi.org/10.1186/s40561-017-0050-x.

Chronotech, 2022. Blockchain HR Software Solutions. https://chrono.tech.

Garg R, 2016. Generic Information Tracker. 2nd India International Science Festival, New Delhi India, 2:1-34. doi: 10.5281/zenodo.4762602. https://zenodo.org/record/4762602#.YwG8_qBBzIU.

Garg R, 2017. Hi-Tech ID with Digital Tracking System, National Conference on Application of ICT for Built Environment. doi:10.5281/zenodo.4761329. https://www.researchgate.net/publication/325248504_Hi_-_Tech_ID_with_Digital_Tracking_System.

Garg R, 2018. Digital ID with Electronic Surveillance System. Innovation registered with National Innovation Foundation, Autonomous Body of Department of Science & Technology, Government of India. doi: 10.5281/zenodo.4760532. https://www.researchgate.net/publication/325247403_Digital_Identity_with_Electronic_Surveillance_System.

Garg R, 2019. Multipurpose ID: One Nation – One Identity, Annual Convention – Indian Society for Technical Education (ISTE). *National Conference on Recent Advances in Energy, Science & Technology*, 39. doi: 10.6084/m9.figshare.16945078. https://www.researchgate.net/publication/337398750_Multipurpose_ID_One_Nation_-_One_Identity.

Garg R, 2021a. Blockchain Ecosystem for Education and Employment Verification. 13th International Conference on Network & Communication Security, Toronto Canada. doi:10.5281/zenodo.5702685. https://www.researchgate.net/publication/325336225_Blockchain_Ecosystem_for_Education_and_Employment_Verification.

Garg R, 2021b. Interplanetary File System for Document Storage and e-Verification. 2nd International Conference on Software Engineering, Security & Blockchain, Sydney Australia. https://figshare.com/authors/Rishabh_Garg/5261744.

Garg R, 2022. Decentralized Transaction Mechanism Based on Smart Contracts. 3rd International Conference on Blockchain and IoT, Sydney Australia. doi: 10.5281/zenodo.5708294. https://www.researchgate.net/publication/325336102_Decentralized_Transaction_Mechanism_based_on_Smart_Contracts.

Nestle, 2019. Nestlé breaks new ground with open blockchain pilot. https://www.nestle.com/media/pressreleases/allpressreleases/nestle-open-blockchain-pilot Accessed on 02 July 2019.

Profed Credit Union, 2022. https://profedcu.org.

STL Partners, 2022. https://stlpartners.com.

ValidateMe, 2022. https://validateme.online.

WHO, 2019. Food Safety Is Everyone's Business, Report.

10

Banking and Finance

10.1 Banking and Investment

A close review of the distinctive features of blockchain makes it clear that the banking industry can effectively adopt this technology. Perhaps, the very purpose of setting up the banking industry has a lot in common with the nature of blockchain. Banking institutions came into existence to make all kinds of trade and commerce possible by connecting groups of people together. Blockchain has the potential to implement this concept on a global scale with complete security, integrity, and transparency.

It can make business more efficient by introducing streamlined and automated processes in place of manual and paper-based processes. Therefore, blockchain is more than just the underlying technology for cryptocurrencies like Bitcoin or Ethereum.

Blockchain, in the credit and debit industry, makes it easy for remote untrusted parties to build consensus on the state of a database, negating the interference of gatekeepers. It is a bookkeeper that conducts all financial transactions, such as payments, settlement systems, fundraising, securities management, loans, credit and trade finance, etc. without being subject to any government, organization, or institution.

10.1.1 Identity Authentication

Banks cannot conduct online financial transactions without identity verification. However, there may be several different steps in the verification process that consumers may not like. This can be face-to-face verification, a form of authentication (for example, every time you log in to the service), or authorization. For security reasons, all these steps need to be taken for each new service provider. With blockchain, consumers and companies will benefit from quick verification

Blockchain for Real World Applications, First Edition. Rishabh Garg.
© 2023 John Wiley & Sons, Inc. Published 2023 by John Wiley & Sons, Inc.

processes. This is because the blockchain will make it possible for other services to securely reuse identity verification.

The most popular innovation in this field is Zero Knowledge Proof (ZKP). Many countries and large corporations are now working on solutions based on ZKP (The Wire, 2019). Thanks to the blockchain, users will be able to choose how they want to identify themselves and with whom they agree to share their identity. They only have to register their identity on the blockchain once. There is no need to repeat that registration for each service provider – as long as those providers are also powered by the blockchain. Naturally, storing this type of information on the blockchain also ensures its security.

10.1.2   Banking Charges

One of the benefits of blockchain for banks is the cost reduction. By implementing mechanisms, such as smart contracts within a single platform, banks can reduce the interference of counterparties and middlemen. This can significantly reduce transaction fees by eliminating the overhead costs payable on creating, executing, and exchanging assets manually. The elimination of the middleman has also made processes, such as cross-border payments, trade, and settlements faster, more reliable, and less expensive. Moreover, blockchain does not require expensive proprietary infrastructure that further curtails the maintenance expenditure. It also reduces risk due to enhanced data integrity, thereby cutting costs associated with regulatory compliance in areas, such as Know Your Customer (KYC) initiatives.

10.1.3   Fast Payments

With the decentralized ledger feature, blockchain can provide fast payments at low bank fees. Any transaction can be done by blockchain in a split second, and it is more secure than other traditional methods. This will enable the bank to avoid middlemen, which will allow the customer and the bank to be able to complete and process more transactions.

Banking institutions can make payments easier and cheaper by establishing a decentralized channel for payment. By offering higher security and lower costs, banks can launch a new level of service, bring new products to market, and finally be able to compete with innovative fintech startups.

10.1.4   Withdrawal and Settlements

Moving money around the world is a huge logistical challenge. A simple bank transfer needs to bypass a complex system of intermediaries, such as custodial services before it reaches its destination. In addition, bank balances need to be reconciled across the global financial system, which includes an extensive network of asset managers, traders, and more.

Suppose, a customer wants to transfer money from a bank account in the US to an account in India; that transfer has to be moved through Society for Worldwide Interbank Financial Telecommunications (SWIFT). SWIFT officials send about a quarter billion messages daily to approximately 10,000-odd organizations.

The centralized SWIFT protocol only processes payment orders. Real money is transacted through a system of intermediaries, each of whom has to pay an additional cost. It also takes a lot of time.

Distributed ledger technology like blockchain can ease direct settlement of bank transactions and keep their track better than the existing protocols like SWIFT. An average bank transfer takes a few days to settle as it operates through the functionalities embedded in our financial infrastructure. But blockchain accelerates withdrawal and settlement systems where distributed ledgers can reduce the cost of operations and enable real-time transactions between financial institutions.

10.1.5 Credit and Loans

Traditional banking institutions underwrite loans, using a system of credit reporting. Faster and more secure lending processes, including syndicated loan structures or mortgages, can be executed efficiently on a blockchain platform with the capability of peer-to-peer lending.

Banks processing loan applications often assess risk by assessing factors, such as credit scores, land ownership, or debt-to-income ratios provided by credit agencies. Such centralized systems are sometimes harmful to banks or consumers as they can contain sensitive financial information. Perhaps this is the reason why blockchain claims to be a more secure, efficient, and cost-effective option for processing loan applications.

10.1.6 Transfer of Assets

Blockchain creates a more efficient capital market. The volatility of the traditional securities market can be mitigated by placing securities, such as stocks, bonds, and alternative assets on a public blockchain. By eliminating middlemen and asset rights transfers, blockchain asset exchange fees can be reduced substantially.

Buying and selling assets, such as stocks, commodities, or debt, is based on who has what and what they need. Financial markets accomplish this through a complex network of brokers, exchanges, clearing houses, custodian banks, and central security depositories. This system is not only slow but also perforated with flaws and tricks, as it has still not been able to give up its old practice of paper ownership.

The transfer of ownership is so complex that the order is executed by passing through several third parties. Most of the time, buyers and sellers do not trust the same broker or custodial bank. Therefore, each party wants to keep its version of the truth in a separate ledger and has no reliable alternative but to maintain paper documents, sale contracts, and sale deeds.

Blockchain could revolutionize financial markets by creating a decentralized database of digital assets. A distributed ledger allows the transfer of rights of an asset, via cryptographic tokens, that can represent the assets off-chain.

10.1.7 Peer-to-Peer Transfers

Peer-to-peer (P2P) transfers allow customers to transfer funds online from their bank accounts or credit cards to any other person. Although there are many applications for P2P transfer available in the market, they all come with some limitations. Certain apps allow financial transactions in a given geographic area only. Some other apps do not allow money transfers if both parties are located in the same country. In addition, P2P services may also charge a substantial amount as commission for providing their services and are not secure enough to store sensitive customer data.

Blockchain technology can help peer-to-peer transfers through decentralized applications. Since the blockchain has no geographic restrictions, it enables P2P transfers all over the world. Besides, blockchain-based transactions can happen in real time and don't levy charges.

10.1.8 Hedge Funds

A hedge fund is a type of investment partnership in which a group of investors work in a limited partnership. Traditional hedge funds are controlled by fund managers who operate within a single entity. These participants are usually experts or traders and not ordinary investors.

Blockchain provides hedge funds with an open platform that allows more investors and strategists to participate. The objective of a hedge fund is to maximize the investor's returns and minimize risks. Blockchain technology is coming to impact investing. Impact tokens are integrated with smart contracts and are provided as rewards for certain activities.

10.1.9   Fundraising

Raising funds through venture capital is a common but complex process today. Most of the time entrepreneurs meet face-to-face with potential partners, hold several rounds of negotiations on valuation and equity, and eventually offer to exchange their company for payment.

Blockchain companies are speeding up the process by raising funds with multiple options. These include Initial Coin Offerings (ICOs), Initial Exchange Offerings (IEOs), Equity Token Offerings (ETOs) and Security Token Offerings (STOs).

The blockchain model of financing could eliminate access to capital from capital-raising services and firms. Although ICOs were more popular in the beginning, they are now considered unreliable. STOs are the more popular option, as they are considered legally safe. Projects will have to go through an organized diligence process to take advantage of this model.

10.1.10   Enhanced Security

Distributed ledgers can help banks to conduct safe and fast transactions. Each transaction is protected by a combination of unique digital signatures – a public key and a private key that are governed by stringent cryptographic measures. A public key is available for every user, while a private key is shared between the parties for a given transaction. Once data is entered in a block, it cannot be changed in retrospect. Since it is shared among a large number of users, it is difficult to hack, which makes the blockchain inherently secure. Blockchain involves the use of transactional value exchanges that rely on public as well as private decryption codes; hence, it reduces the risk of fraud.

10.1.11   Accountability

The primary advantage of blockchain is its method of verifying and tracking transactions, enabling individuals and organizations to process transactions without the need for a third party or central bank. Blockchain makes all transactions easy to examine and authenticate, which will ensure that banks process transactions more consistently.

Instead of everything being controlled by a single central authority, the blockchain creates a shared infrastructure by distributing rights among all peers in the transaction chain. It eliminates counterparty risk, and therefore, users can be assured that transactions will be executed in accordance with the protocol.

Banks can allow auditors and government officials to access their business through a blockchain ledger. Authorities can track transactions more quickly and identify errors in a timely manner. Banks and auditors can intercept doubtful transaction activities and streamline the audit process.

Smart contract code for lending and borrowing

```solidity
pragma solidity ^0.7.0 || ^0.8.0;
import "./IERC3156FlashBorrower.sol";

interface IERC3156FlashLender {

    function maxFlashLoan(
        address token
    ) external view returns (uint256);

    function flashFee(
        address token,
        uint256 amount
    ) external view returns (uint256);

    function flashLoan(
        IERC3156FlashBorrower receiver,
        address token,
        uint256 amount,
        bytes calldata data
    ) external returns (bool);
```

Borrower interface

```solidity
pragma solidity ^0.7.0 || ^0.8.0;`

interface IERC3156FlashBorrower {

    function onFlashLoan(
        address initiator,
        address token,
        uint256 amount,
        uint256 fee,
        bytes calldata data
    ) external returns (bytes32);
}
```

Code Cell 10.1 Smart contract code for lending and borrowing (Interface).

ERC 3156 code

```solidity
pragma solidity ^0.8.0;

//interfaces discussed above
import "./IERC3156FlashBorrower.sol";
import "./IERC3156FlashLender.sol";

interface IERC20 {
    function totalSupply() external view returns
(uint256);
    function balanceOf(address account) external view
returns (uint256);
    function transfer(address recipient, uint256 amount)
external returns (bool);
    function allowance(address owner, address spender)
external view returns (uint256);
    function approve(address spender, uint256 amount)
external returns (bool);
    function transferFrom(address sender, address
recipient, uint256 amount) external returns (bool);

    event Transfer(address indexed from, address indexed
to, uint256 value);
    event Approval(address indexed owner, address
indexed spender, uint256 value);
}

//borrower implementation
contract FlashBorrower is IERC3156FlashBorrower {
    enum Action {NORMAL, OTHER}
    IERC3156FlashLender lender;
    constructor (IERC3156FlashLender lender_) {
        lender = lender_;
    }

    // @dev ERC-3156 Flash loan callback
    function onFlashLoan(address initiator, address
token, uint256 amount, uint256 fee, bytes calldata data)
external override returns(bool) {
```

Code Cell 10.2 ERC3156 code.

```
        require(msg.sender == address(lender),
"FlashBorrower: Untrusted lender");
        require(initiator == address(this),
"FlashBorrower: Untrusted loan initiator");
        (Action action) = abi.decode(data, (Action));
        return keccak256("ERC3156FlashBorrower.
onFlashLoan");
    }

    /// @dev Initiate a flash loan
    function flashBorrow(address token, uint256 amount)
public {
        bytes memory data = abi.encode(Action.NORMAL);
        uint256 _allowance = IERC20(token).
allowance(address(this), address(lender));
        uint256 _fee = lender.flashFee(token, amount);
        uint256 _repayment = amount + _fee;
        IERC20(token).approve(address(lender), _allowance
+ _repayment);
        lender.flashLoan(this, token, amount, data);
    }
}

//Lender implementation
contract FlashLender is IERC3156FlashLender {
    bytes32 public constant CALLBACK_SUCCESS =
keccak256("ERC3156FlashBorrower.onFlashLoan");
    mapping(address => bool) public supportedTokens;
    uint256 public fee; //  1 == 0.0001 %.

    constructor(address[] memory supportedTokens_,
uint256 fee_) {
        for (uint256 i = 0; i < supportedTokens_.length;
i++) {
            supportedTokens[supportedTokens_[i]] = true;
        }
        fee = fee_;
    }
```

Code Cell 10.2 (Continued))

```
    function flashLoan(IERC3156FlashBorrower receiver,
address token, uint256 amount, bytes calldata data)
external override returns(bool) {
        require(supportedTokens[token], "FlashLender:
Unsupported currency");
        uint256 fee = _flashFee(token, amount);
        require(IERC20(token).transfer(address(receiver),
amount),"FlashLender: Transfer failed");
        require(receiver.onFlashLoan(msg.sender, token,
amount, fee, data) == CALLBACK_SUCCESS,"FlashLender:
Callback failed");
        require(IERC20(token).transferFrom(address
(receiver), address(this), amount + fee),"FlashLender:
Repay failed");
        return true;
    }

    function flashFee(address token, uint256 amount)
external view override returns (uint256) {
        require(supportedTokens[token],"FlashLender:
Unsupported currency");
        return _flashFee(token, amount);
    }

    function _flashFee(address token,uint256 amount)
internal view returns (uint256) {
        return amount * fee / 10000;
    }

    function maxFlashLoan(address token) external view
override returns (uint256) {
        return supportedTokens[token] ? IERC20(token).
balanceOf(address(this)) : 0;
    }
}
```

Code Cell 10.2   (Continued))

In short, blockchain technology can make a huge difference in banking and
finance. This could potentially help banks avoid fraud or scams. Blockchain transactions are by and large secure, and can easily be done in seconds instead of
waiting three days for settlement. The absence of middlemen and lower fees in
blockchain transactions also reduce the cost of money transfers.

10.2 Trade Finance

Another sector, which is well-equipped for the blockchain revolution, is trade finance. Trade finance relies heavily on paper-based business operations involving information transmission, asset transfer, goods transfer, and payment processes. Traditionally, business parties build trust with a centralized operating mechanism, such as invoices, letters of credit, or bills.

Trade finance plays a pivotal role in international trade and commerce. An international consignment involves three major flows – documentation, cash flow, and shipment (see Figure 10.1). It involves exporters (manufacturers, sellers, suppliers), importers (retailers, buyers, consumers), transporters (shippers, logistic movers), credit operators (banks, financiers), and insurance companies and their agents. Traders often select payment modalities according to diverse risk levels and strategic concerns, and create sales contracts between sellers and buyers. Among various payment methods (letter of credit, open account, telegraphic transfer, cash on delivery), a letter of credit is generally preferred by exporters due to its low risk potential (Garg, 2021a, 2022a). However, this includes unnecessary documentation, high bank fees, and the possibility of forgery.

Banks in the seller's and buyer's countries act as reliable intermediaries to handle cash in exchange for goods. The buyer asks his bank to issue a letter of credit to the seller's bank for the exchange of goods. Currently, there are several centralized trusted intermediaries acting as functionaries, such as Central Counter Parties (CCPs) to assure trades on exchanges, Central Securities Depositories (CSDs) to provide securities settlement; Society for Worldwide Interbank Financial Telecommunication (SWIFT) to work as an arbitrator in the global transfer of money, CLS Bank to handle the settlement of foreign exchange transactions, and so on. A handful of banks dominate correspondent banking and an even smaller number provide custodial services to a large number of investment institutions.

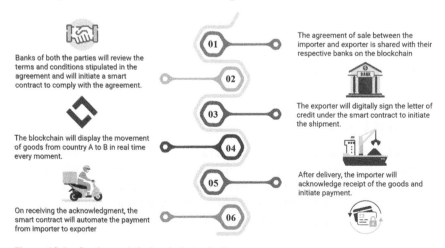

Figure 10.1 Parties and their role in trade finance.

In such trade finance systems, all participants are required to maintain their own database of documents related to transactions, and all these databases need to be continuously reconciled against each other. An error in one document may cause the same discrepancy in its replica or may create another disparity in other databases. Many order management systems want this to be done online, but the process consumes a lot of time. Blockchain-based trade finance can become a tool to streamline trade process by getting rid of such time-consuming manual processes, paperwork, and bureaucracy. With blockchain, there is no need to keep multiple copies of the same document. This is because the information can be integrated into a single digital file, which is updated in real time and can be accessed by all participants.

Reports show that distributed ledgers are able to process the entire trading day's volume at peak rates to perform at the levels required, which is equivalent to 115,000,000 daily trades, or 6,300 trades per second for five continuous hours during test conditions (Depository Trust and Clearing Corporation, 2018).

10.2.1 Smart Contracts

A trade contract is a business agreement, in physical or written form, between commercial minds in a complicated legal language, which either of the parties hardly understand. Instead of legal terms, these contracts can better be described by code in the Python programming language so that traders could understand them better. In 2010, the US Securities and Exchange Commission also recommended that the terms and conditions set forth in asset-backed securities be laid down in computer language (Securities and Exchange Commission, 2010).

In this milieu, blockchain provides an ideal platform for smart contracts. Smart contracts combine protocols with user interfaces to formalize and secure new relationships, such as business forms, contract law, and account controls. Though it is possible to share a database between two parties or deploy a smart contract even without the blockchain; nevertheless, who will build the trust in absence of a trusted intermediary? Neither of the parties will trust each other's data, formats, standards, and procedures nor let the smart contract run on the other's node. This is where the blockchain comes into being; it is not only a computer in the cloud but a shared platform across several nodes, backed by consensus algorithms and protected by cryptography. It is inherently designed to audit each transaction with no room for modification or omission.

By automating key contractual phases – search, negotiation, commitment, performance, and adjudication – transactions may be secured, overheads may be reduced, and petty transactions can be made viable. Today, many financial transactions, including stock trading, are largely done by algorithms that decide to buy or sell on the basis of price signals. A momentum-based algorithm may recommend a buy order, while another contrarian algorithm may recommend a sell order. The stock exchange's software, without any human intervention, makes decisions between the two algorithms on certain complex rules. Smart contracts deployed on a blockchain can achieve similar output in OTC markets without an exchange.

Thus, the blockchain, in amalgam with smart contracts, provides a secure, transparent, auditable, and automatic transactional environment for trade investors. Smart contracts may be automated in line with the terms of trade contract, logistics status may be updated as an event-driven mechanism, and payments may be activated as per predetermined procedures. This is how a blockchain network may alleviate the need of a central authority to verify transactions in a brick-and-mortar operation.

10.2.2   Enterprise Resource Planning

Organizations mostly use enterprise resource planning (ERP) software with a common database that provides a single version of the truth across numerous departments in real time. It ensures better management and internal controls (see Figure 10.2). Once again, blockchain itself is a distributed ledger that shares a common database and provides a single version of the truth to all participating nodes irrespective of any geographical or administrative precincts. An added advantage is that, in absence of a trusted intermediary, it would be easier for either of the parties to adopt a neutral platform like blockchain. At the same time, other players – clearing agents, insurance companies, shippers, and forwarding agents – will also have access to the same version of truth in real time. Thus, it is an area where the blockchain can leap from pilots to real-world applications (D'Monte, 2018; Sanghvi, 2018).

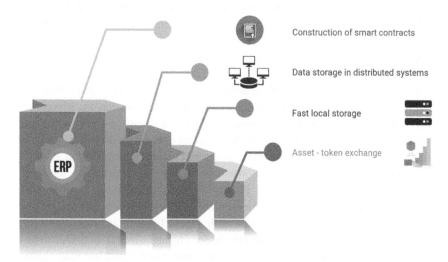

Construction of smart contracts

Data storage in distributed systems

Fast local storage

Asset - token exchange

Figure 10.2   Integration of enterprise resource planning with blockchain.

10.2.3 Data Repositories and Registries

After the Global Financial Crisis, 2008, trade repositories have been formed to make sure that regulators have requisite information about the risk and interconnectivity of the financial system. Post-2008 finance largely depends on data repositories (e.g., credit bureaus) and registries (e.g., loan registries) that provide verified data for a variety of transactions. Though such information is decisive for providing credit, the data stored by credit repositories contain inadvertent errors like duplication, and the system has been suffering from lack of accountability, loss of privacy, and excessive cost. Blockchain, being permanent and auditable, can provide a real solution.

10.2.4 Tokenization of Fiat Money

Finance is all about money, and over time, it can achieve better liquidity and scale, if fiat money (dollars, euros, rupees, etc.) in place of cryptocurrency is transacted directly on the chain. Initially, the central bank itself may issue a digital currency that flows on a blockchain. However, covering the initial operating cost and returns is not easy unless the issue is large enough.

It is evident from the reports that Blockchain has captured a vast landscape with 295 million crypto users across the globe. Japan, the harbinger of cryptocurrency trading, has announced a Payment Services Act to regulate cryptocurrencies and their use for trading purposes. After Japan, MasterCard, and the Bank of New York Mellon in the United States allowed users to transact in certain cryptocurrencies. Similarly, Amazon, Subway, Microsoft Store, Expedia, Overstock, etc. have started accepting payments in Bitcoin. By 2022, over 22,000 trade venues have adopted cryptocurrency payments.

In the European Union (following France in 2014), Germany has also legalized Bitcoin and remains a leader in blockchain solutions. In addition, Canada has validated Bitcoin exchanges but restricted its use to prevent money laundering. Australia is one of the countries that has effectively legalized cryptocurrency. The government has levied capital gains tax and recognized it as an asset.

According to the Global Consumer Survey conducted by the World Economic Forum (Statista, 2021), Nigeria is one of the top countries using cryptocurrency. The primary reason seems to be the high remittance fee to send money across borders. With relatively small legacy systems in the region, the prospects for emerging blockchain technology into a full range of financial products is highly possible, due to strong support from financial players and local governments. Stakeholders are slowly diagnosing blockchain as an emerging disruptor and enabler, and they are examining and fostering the technology to ensure that they are not excluded from its potential benefits.

The Philippines, as a big surprise, has the third largest number of crypto-users in the country after Vietnam. Despite the infrastructure challenges and rivalry, Ukraine and Russia are leaders in cryptocurrency adoption.

Asia is a global leader with 59 million crypto-users. There were nevertheless stark differences across Asian nations with China, Hong Kong, and Singapore leading the way. China's voracious thirst for blockchain went far beyond cryptocurrencies, as announced in its five-year plan, and was providing a conducive regulatory environment. Surprisingly, the Chinese government banned cryptocurrency trading and mining in one of the world's most swift actions. Despite this, the Chinese government is pursuing blockchain technology and other uses for nonfungible tokens as long as the technology remains under its control.

Other countries, such as Vietnam, Thailand, and Pakistan are also on the list, with India surpassing 100.7 million crypto-users. Asia has evolved the most comprehensive ecosystem for blockchain development with regulatory support and mobilization of capital from venture capitalists, as well as industry players. The Middle East is also catching up, despite the fact that many states in the region still do not allow activities related to blockchain.

In Latin America, abridged political uncertainty and risk mitigation effects are making blockchain-based financial products attractive. Some countries, such as Peru, Argentina, Brazil, and Chile, have begun, yet the entire region lacks technical infrastructure, adequate access to venture capital funding, and a regulatory sandbox for open adoption.

By the time cryptocurrency forms a substantial base as an alternative to fiat money, it is worthwhile to deliberate over and adopt regulated tokenization of fiat money.

10.2.5 Lightning Network

The Lightning Network, which relies on the underlying technology of the blockchain, can create a secure network of participants to conduct transactions at high volumes and high speeds, using its native smart-contract language. Suppose two participants want to transact multiple times a day. Initially, they will create a multisignature wallet that both of them can access using their respective private keys. Then, they will deposit a certain amount in that wallet, and after that, they can make unlimited transactions between them. Since all transactions will be confined only between the two, it will be more in the form of redistribution of funds within the shared wallet. For every transaction they make, both use their private key to sign the updated balance sheet. But, the actual distribution of funds will happen only when the channel is closed. Once the channel is closed, only information about the initial contribution and the final balance on the blockchain is transmitted. In this way, the Lightning Network enables users to make countless transactions outside the main chain and then record them as a single on the blockchain. In this way both volume and speed are accomplished with the confidence of on-blockchain enforceability.

10.2.6 Pre- and Post-trade Processes

Trading and settlement of securities takes place in three phases: (i) pre-trade authorization and approval; (ii) trade execution; and (iii) clearing and settlement. With enormous investments in technology infrastructure, trade execution has become highly automated to reduce latency to microseconds. The blockchain operates at a speed of seven transactions per second, and it would be nearly impossible for any blockchain to achieve the speed of a stock exchange. Therefore, exchanges may continue to work, but the pre- and post-trade processes, that involve inefficient and fragmented legacy systems, may be augmented by implementing blockchain.

Blockchain can remove ambiguity on cash and securities in pre-trade checks and trade confirmations. With dividends and stock splits being controlled by smart contracts, and settlements occurring on delivery versus payment basis, we will not require depositories, brokers, or custodians anymore. The novation – short selling, margin trading, and net settlement, provided by the central counter parties can be replicated through smart contracts, and the depository – could run the permissioned blockchain on which the settlement happens.

However, it is too early to predict things, as new protocols for business organizations and corporate governance may arrive in the coming days. It may be an algorithmic rule (Du Pont, 2017); an enterprise without entities (Verstein, 2017), or a Decentralized Autonomous Organization (DAO) with a foolproof code.

10.2.7 Accounts and Audit

Accounting has been a relatively slow area in terms of digitization. It needs to match the prevailing strict regulatory requirements regarding the integrity and validity of data. So accounting is potentially another area that could be replaced by blockchain.

Experts opine that the technology will simplify compliance and streamline traditional double-entry bookkeeping. Instead of keeping separate records based on transaction receipts, businesses can directly combine transactions into a combined ledger. All entries in the ledger will be distributed. As a result, records will be more transparent and secure. A blockchain will act like a digital notary who verifies all transactions. Blockchain smart contracts can be used to pay invoices automatically in such applications.

10.2.8 Latent Benefits

Blockchain can play a vital role in improving the activities of business organizations and financial institutions.

10.2.8.1 Decentralization

In conventional trade finance, if a centrally trusted institution shuts down for a period of time, the whole system comes to a standstill. In 2014, the Real Time Gross Settlement System (RTGS) of the United Kingdom experienced a downtime of nine hours (Deloitte, 2014). Though all the banks and other institutions were operational, the high-value transactions could not happen during this period. The advantage of using a distributed ledger is that the blockchain is partition resistant in that if some nodes fail or are disengaged from the network, the rest of the nodes continue to function since all nodes carry a copy of the same data.

10.2.8.2 Information Transmission

The vendor finance process requires a lot of manual documentation, from raising of purchase orders and bills of exchange by vendors to submission of invoices and transportation documents to banks. Blockchain allows trading parties – banks, transporters, agents, exporters, and importers – to share a common distributed ledger for trade practices. Business documents can be digitized to enable automatic implementation of trade processes through smart contracts. Since the flow of critical information between parties will be done through an event-driven mechanism, much of the trade friction and painful handover of goods can be turned into real-time response of workflow status. This will eliminate the repetitive manual checks used to verify business logistics, freight delivery, and payment references (see Table 10.1).

10.2.8.3 Incorporation of IoT

As there is no automation at any point of time in trade finance, it takes around four to five days for sellers to collect money from the bank against the relevant document. It blocks the working capital of the sellers until the process goes on. It is difficult for all the participants – banks, customers, and vendors – to track the movement of invoices and transactions in real time. The participants are informed about the status of the invoice only through mail.

This implies that payments are resultant upon shipment handovers, or notifications, and prevent smooth business practices. Blockchain provides parallel notification of the status of goods and documents in real time through the deployment of smart contracts (Wu et al., 2017). Furthermore, IoT-enabled operations, such as machine-to-machine transactions, source tracking, logistics, and shipping (Panarello et al., 2018) can facilitate business associates to perform accurate tracking of goods and supplies.

Table 10.1 Global trade pain points and potentials benefits of using blockchain platform.

S. no.	Issues	Global Trade Concerns	Blockchain Solutions
1	Trust mechanism	Rely on an authorized central party (e.g., banks) to deal with trade finance.	Immutable, consensus-based, and distributed ledger network for a conducive trade environment
2	Tampering issues	Malicious attempts may cause fraud and trade disputes; Authorities build trust among trade parties.	Preserve contract terms and amendments on blocks forever; Alleviate tampering issues.
3	Instruments used	Paper-based, manual process; Lengthy delivery across borders.	Digitized documents deployed on a secured and shared ledger.
4	Transaction risk	Risk-sensitive; Rely on authorized third parties.	Risk mitigation. Trust ensured through consensus mechanisms
5	Bill(s) of lading (B/Ls)	Intensive paperwork for presentation of B/Ls. Complex ownership transfer across handovers.	Digitized operation; Minimum time of transfer and delivery; Blockchain-based identification without presentation of B/Ls
6	Information transmission and cost-effect	Manual process, which takes time and cost; Centralized data, susceptible to cyberattacks or system malfunction.	Event-driven consensus with smart contracts; Cost-effective Tamper-proof features. Less security and privacy concerns on consortium chain
7	Traceability	Complex trade processes due to multiple participants; Uncertainties in tracking asset identities, ownership, and shipment status.	A member database, easily traceable; with provision of credit ratings, promises better user experience

10.2.8.4 Defense Mechanism

In the legacy trade process, the invoice passes through multiple hands during a transaction, leading to ample chances of document tampering and disbursement of funds to the wrong entity. In addition, cyberattackers lurk to perpetrate ambushes to inflict colossal damage to the system. Byzantine fault tolerance provides a strong defense against tampering or any malicious attack by virtue of (i) replication of data across a large number of nodes running on a fully isolated computer network and (ii) cryptographic integrity checks. Since, there is only one source of truth, the transaction can be processed only if all the concerned parties agree and authenticate it.

10.2.8.5 Transparency

Blockchain ledger is not only irreversible but trustworthy too. It averts any scope for malicious activity or fraudulence, thereby alleviating an obligation of any certified trusted party or a consensus mechanism. Further, it allows users to validate their identity, irrespective of any geographical border, and creates a traceable audit for authentication (Mainelli, 2017). Thus, transfer of ownership and verification of identity can be more accessible, transparent, and auditable (see Table 10.2).

10.2.8.6 Disintermediation

In trade practices, a number of intermediaries play their roles and eventually impede the process of transactions. The blockchain unites diverse trade groups into a single transactional network without intermediaries, automates the confirmation of trade documents, and expedites the process of cash settlements.

10.2.8.7 Corporate Lending

Corporate clients seeking loans coordinate and manage syndicate members with a lead arranger. The lead arranger performs KYC for the client, creating a syndicate

Table 10.2 Impact of blockchain on trade finance.

S. no.	Dimension	Blockchain's Impact
1.	Transparency	Auditable trail of transactions through global ledger
		Digitization of physical property and collaborative verification of critical transactions by participating nodes using a shared database
		Immutable transactions on the a common distributed ledger
		Lessen fake and counterfeit goods or documentation across transaction journey
		Providing participants with access to transaction records
2.	Information transmission	Enable broadcast of verified and time-stamped transactions
		Automatic execution of trade activities through smart contracts
3.	Traceability	Physical flow of goods
		Real-time notifications
4.	Disintermediation	Cash settlement and validity check of trade documents without intervention of third party
5.	Cost	Streamline administrative processes
		Shorten latency and curtail transaction fees
6.	Incorporation of IoT	Facilitate storage of tracking records

of members who are willing to fund a percentage of the loan and diversify the risk. Blockchain can facilitate instant KYC by lead arranger through digital identity for customers. It enables real-time financing through smart contracts.

10.2.8.8 Cost Efficiency

In Letter of Credit finance, trade-related administrative and logistic handovers, across shipping routes, obstruct the flow of business and make it less competitive under payment options, such as interfirm trade credit (Clark, 2014). Blockchain will streamline trade processes and reduce overheads by curtailing the cost of documentation and payments for central service providers.

10.2.8.9 Loyalty Rewards

Loyalty points are an integral part of customer retention strategies in the corporate culture. From banks to e-wallets and from wholesalers to retailers, each organization offers loyalty-based incentives in different ways. A variety of reward point schemes are offered by these institutions to redeem for a specific point of sale or group of sellers. Reward points help tokenize a portion of a customer's payout and keep him connected to the establishment.

The blockchain protocol creates an algorithmically generated standard loyalty token that is the basis for all kinds of rewards issued by participating nodes. This token can be used to initiate and execute any transaction – issuance, redemption, or exchange. The number of points and unique identifiers of loyalty tokens are updated on each participant's ledger and made available across the network. Blockchain platforms can accommodate different types of organizations and their loyalty programs, especially in terms of convertibility and exchange of their points. The network also facilitates coordination, consensus, and instant redemption among merchants, customers, and banks without any clearing-house.

10.2.9 Impending Challenges and Remediation

10.2.9.1 Security

Security is a prime concern with identity as well as finance. A participant, who has more than 50% mining capacity, can plan an attack by virtually having full control over the blockchain. Despite there being a fork on the blockchain, the attacker can perform stepwise counterfeit transactions by: (i) publishing a mining software with the expected value; (ii) by creating a pool with stickiness (Ponzi scheme); (iii) by forming unwanted alliances; (iv) by attacking other pools along with the cannibal pool; and (v) by eventually switching to members only.

In such circumstances, Wallet Security – a multiple signing process, known as MultiSig – can be adopted. Although creating scripts helps solve many problems, there is a possibility that transactions may not be configured correctly due to the complexity of the script. If it occurs, the Bitcoin that uses an incorrectly configured script would be discarded, since the unlocking script will not be able to generate (Park, 2017).

10.2.9.2 Storage Capacity

In the near future, there may be a problem with respect to storage capacity in blockchains as transaction histories are constantly intertwined with each other. The problem can be resolved by providing access to write information, but only to a central intermediary. This would reduce consensus needs (Mills et al., 2016).

10.2.9.3 Block Time

Currently, Bitcoin processes 4.6 transactions per second, and Visa processes approximately 1,700 transactions per second (150 million transactions per day), with a tiny fraction of the electrical power used by Bitcoin. The reasons for this passivity are cryptographic verification and blockchain consensus algorithms, which delay the amount of transfers (Del Rio, 2017).

Nowadays, the Bitcoin block puzzle is solved in a minimum of three seconds and a maximum of 50 minutes. Reducing the complexity of PoW will reduce the time spent, but blockchain forks can occur if the block generation time frame is too narrow (Chen, Jiang, and Wang, 2017). Lin et al. (2020) proposed an improved blockchain consensus algorithm based on a mortgage model instead of a probability model, a cross-chain protocol with transverse expansion capability, which will support message transmission between chains; and a high-performance cross-chain blockchain network structure, which can handle more than a thousand transactions per second by verification.

10.2.9.4 Privacy

Although transparency is one of the virtues of blockchain, it still poses a threat to privacy. The holder of the cryptocurrency can be tracked using the public key associated with his or her payment. Using software tools, one can access and create a behavior map based on the information collected via the public key, his/her purchase choice, spending ability, and the frequency of transactions.

To address privacy concerns, Del Rio (2017) proposed a notary-based blockchain system, in which no node in the system has a complete set of information. Since a trusted third party will contribute to validating the transaction, it will ensure greater confidentiality. The only disadvantage is that if one or more nodes contain any counterfeit information, the system will collapse, and verification will not be possible, as no one will have a complete copy of the ledger. In such cases, Bitcoin fog or dark wallets that promote anonymity through a series of scripts may be used as an alternative (Irwin and Turner, 2018).

10.2.9.5 Cyberattacks

Blockchain systems, in the absence of any central authority, enable transactions across the globe, without having to verify one's identity. This may encourage the development of illegal activities, such as drug trafficking, money laundering, and financial terrorism (Chen, Jiang, and Wang, 2017).

In recent years, ransomware attacks, such as WannaCry, have affected more than 300,000 computers in 150 countries. Investors can suffer huge financial losses if their cryptographic keys are lost, as the attack is immediate and irreversible in most cases (Mills et al., 2016). Irwin and Turner (2018) and Stefan (2018) pointed to the need for regulation processes to prevent fraud and money laundering activities.

10.2.9.6 Robustness

Trade and finance require 24/7 service to transact without downtime. Another concern for startups is to envisage increasing software requirements for blockchain-based products so that their business can grow seamlessly. This will require increased software capability for decision-making, higher levels of automation, and an upgrade of traditional software concepts to make them blockchain compliant (Almeida, Albuquerque, and Silva, 2019). Adapting smart contracts to the blockchain will help the network regain its strength (Kumar, Mookerjee, and Shubham, 2018).

10.2.9.7 Legal Enforcement

Blockchain systems have so far been dominated by ideologically motivated computer professionals or geeks who are not sufficiently meticulous about commercial aspects. In real-world finance, they have to face competition from incumbent players who are not only rich and powerful, but also well-rooted in the current legal and regulatory framework. Thus in order to push real-world finance into the blockchain, code and law must co-exist.

Policy makers are in a state of dilemma whether to continue with an unregulated state of affairs or to incentivize the new technology. An autocratic situation may embolden illegal organizations to make profits in absence of regulations that govern these activities (Ducas and Wilner, 2017). On the other hand, development of an adapted regulation could lead to loss of a country's competitive advantage, as FinTech start-ups may end up migrating to more favorable jurisdiction in some other part of the globe.

Other issues are associated with the darknet, financial risks (credit or liquidity risk), cybersecurity, and cryptocurrency volatility. However, the darknet escapes common users, as only one out of 3,000 web pages is visible to everyday search engines, and 80–98% of the information on the internet exists in the darknet. It is also necessary to address issues like instability of cryptocurrencies, which have experienced unprecedented growth, accompanied with violent volatility, during the last two years (Stefan, 2018).

The adoption of any new technology is often difficult to understand in terms of the path that it will take. History is replete with instances when there is a gap between early implementation and regulatory acknowledgment while dealing with significant market innovations. Legal compliance and regulation by the authorities, which depend on stable and optimal alternatives, is a prerequisite for any such innovation to make its way into the financial system. At present, this framework seems inadequate, especially when a disruptive technology, such as blockchain, is in equation.

However, recent market trends indicate that a proof-of-concept phase is happening across emerging markets, coercing governments and policy makers to observe and devise regulatory procedures for blockchain.

10.3 Auction Process

An auction is the process of selling or buying goods or services by inviting competing bids from multiple service providers or vendors. The competing participants may or may not know the identities or credentials of other competitors. Here is a smart contract to automate the auction process (see Figure 10.3; Code Cell 10.3).

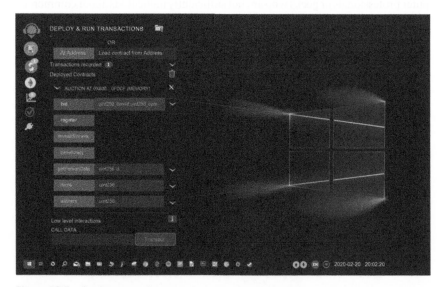

Figure 10.3 Deployment of smart contracts using remix IDE.

```solidity
pragma solidity ^0.4.17;
contract Auction {

    // Data
    //Structure to hold details of the item
    struct Item {
        uint itemId; // id of the item
        uint[] itemTokens;  //tokens bid in favor of the
item

    }

    //Structure to hold the details of a persons
    struct Person {
        uint remainingTokens; // tokens remaining with
bidder
        uint personId; // it serves as tokenId as well
        address addr;//address of the bidder
    }

    mapping(address => Person) tokenDetails; //address
to person
    Person [4] bidders;//Array containing 4 person objects

    Item [3] public items;//Array containing 3 item
objects
    address[3] public winners;//Array for address of
winners
    address public beneficiary;//owner of the smart
contract

    uint bidderCount=0;//counter

    //functions

    function Auction() public payable{    //constructor

        //Task 1. Initialize beneficiary with address of
smart contract's owner
        //constructor,"msg.sender" is the address of the
owner.
        // ** Start code here. 1 line approximately. **/
```

Code Cell 10.3   Auction process using smart contracts.

```
          beneficiary = msg.sender;
            //** End code here. **/
          uint[] memory emptyArray;
          items[0] = Item({itemId:0,itemTokens:emptyArray});

          //Task 2. Initialize two items with at index 1
      and 2.
          // ** Start code here. 2 lines approximately. **/
          items[1] = Item({itemId:1,itemTokens:emptyArray});
          items[2] = Item({itemId:2,itemTokens:emptyArray});
          //** End code here**/
      }
    function register() public payable{


          bidders[bidderCount].personId = bidderCount;

          //Task 3. Initialize the address of the bidder
          /the bidders[bidderCount].addr be initialized
      with address of the registrant.*/

          // ** Start code here. 1 line approximately. **/
          bidders[bidderCount].addr = msg.sender;
          //** End code here. **

          bidders[bidderCount].remainingTokens = 5; //
      only 5 tokens
          tokenDetails[msg.sender]=bidders[bidderCount];
          bidderCount++;
      }


    function bid(uint _itemId, uint _count) public
    payable{
        /*
            Bids tokens to a particular item.
            Arguments:
            _itemId -- uint, id of the item
            _count -- uint, count of tokens to bid for
      the item
        */
        /*
        Task 4. Implement the conditions below.
```

Code Cell 10.3 (Continued)

        4.1 If the number of tokens remaining with
the bidder is < count of tokens bidded, revert.
        4.2 If there are no tokens remaining with
the bidder, revert.
        4.3 If the id of the item for which bid is
placed, is greater than 2, revert.
        "tokenDetails[msg.sender].remainingTokens"
gives the details of the number of tokens remaining with
the bidder.
        */

        // ** Start code here. 2 lines approximately. **/
        if (tokenDetails[msg.sender].remainingTokens<_
count || tokenDetails[msg.sender].remainingTokens == 0
|| _itemId > 2) revert();

        //** End code here. **
        /*Task 5. Decrement the remainingTokens by the
number of tokens bid and store the value in balance
variable.
        "tokenDetails[msg.sender].remainingTokens"
should be decremented by "_count". */

        // ** Start code here. 1 line approximately. **
        uint balance=tokenDetails[msg.sender].remaining
Tokens - _count;
        //** End code here. **

        tokenDetails[msg.sender].remainingTokens=balance;
        bidders[tokenDetails[msg.sender].personId].
remainingTokens=balance;//updating the same balance in
bidders map.

        Item storage bidItem = items[_itemId];
        for(uint i=0; i<_count;i++) {
            bidItem.itemTokens.push(tokenDetails[msg.
sender].personId);
        }
    }
    // Task 6. Create a modifier named "onlyOwner" to
ensure that only owner is allowed to reveal winners

Code Cell 10.3 (Continued)

```
    // Use require to validate if "msg.sender" is equal
to the "beneficiary".
    modifier onlyOwner {
        // ** Start code here. 2 lines approximately. **
        require(msg.sender == beneficiary);
        _;
        //** End code here. **
    }

    function revealWinners() public onlyOwner{

        /*
            Iterate over all the items present in the
auction.
            If at least on person has placed a bid,
randomly select          the winner */

        for (uint id = 0; id < 3; id++) {
            Item storage currentItem=items[id];
            if(currentItem.itemTokens.length != 0){
            // generate random# from block number
            uint randomIndex = (block.number / current
Item.itemTokens.length)% currentItem.itemTokens.length;

            // Obtain the winning tokenId
            uint winnerId = currentItem.itemTokens
[randomIndex];

            /* Task 7. Assign the winners.
            " bidders[winnerId] " will give the person
object with the winnerId.
            you need to assign the address of the person
obtained above to winners[id] */

            // ** Start coding here *** 1 line
approximately.
            winners[id] = bidders[winnerId].addr;
            //** end code here*
            }
        }
    }
    assist:
```

Code Cell 10.3 (Continued)

```
    function getPersonDetails(uint id) public constant
returns(uint,uint,address){
        return (bidders[id].remainingTokens,bidders[id].
personId,bidders[id].addr);
    }
}
```

Code Cell 10.3 (Continued)

dApp Project Using Truffle

Truffle provides a world-class development environment, testing framework and asset pipeline for blockchain using the Ethereum Virtual Machine (EVM), which makes working as a developer easy. With over 1.5 million lifetime downloads, Truffle is widely regarded as the most popular tool for blockchain application development.

The code to test the smart contracts <truffle test> is shown in Figure 10.4; see Code Cell 10.4.

Figure 10.4 Truffle test for smart contracts.

```
let Auction = artifacts.require("./Auction.sol");

let auctionInstance;

contract('AuctionContract', function (accounts) {
  //accounts[0] is the default account
  //Test case 1
  it("Contract deployment", function() {
```

Code Cell 10.4 Truffle test for smart contracts.

```
    //Fetching the contract instance of our smart
contract
    return Auction.deployed().then(function (instance) {
      //We save the instance in a gDlobal variable and
all smart contract functions are called using this
      auctionInstance = instance;
      assert(auctionInstance !== undefined, 'Auction
contract should be defined');
    });
  });

  //Test Case
  it("Should set bidders", function() {
    return auctionInstance.register({from:accounts[1]}).
then(function(result) {
        return auctionInstance.getPersonDetails(0);
    }).then(function(result) {
      assert.equal(result[2], accounts[1], 'bidder
address set');
    })
  });

  //Test Case for checking if the bid is more than the
token amount
  it("Should NOT allow to bid more than remaining
tokens", function() {
    /**********
    Task 1:   Call bid method from accounts[1] of
Auction.sol using auctionInstance and
    pass itemId=0, count=6 as arguments
    To make a function call from account 1 use {from:
accounts[1]} as an extra argument
    **********/
    return auctionInstance.bid(0,6,{from:accounts[1]})
    .then(function (result) {
      /*
    This is to test for a negative condition and hence
this particular block will not have executed if test
case was correct. If this part is executed then throw an
error and catch the error to assert false
```

Code Cell 10.4   (Continued)

```
    */
    throw("Failed to check remaining tokens less than
count");
  }).catch(function (e) {
    var a = e.toString();
    if(e === "Failed to check remaining tokens less
than count") {
      /**********
      Task 2: An error that has been intentionally
thrown. Should you assert true or false?
      Use assert(false) to assert false
            Use assert(true) to assert true
      ***********/
      assert(false);
    } else {
      /**********
      Task 3: assert the opposite here
      ***********/
      assert(true);
    }
  })
});
  it("Should NOT allow non owner to reveal winners",
function() {
  /**********
  Task 4: Call revealWinners from account 1
  ***********/
   return auctionInstance.revealWinners({from:accou
nts[1]})
    .then(function (instance) {
      /*
      This is to test for a negative condition and
hence this particular block will not have executed if
the test case was correct. If this part is executed then
throw an error and catch the error to assert false
      */
      throw("Failed to check owner in reveal winners");
    }).catch(function (e) {
      if(e === "Failed to check owner in reveal winners") {
```

Code Cell 10.4 (Continued)

```
        /**********
        Task 5: It's an intentionally thrown error.
Should you assert true or false?
        Use assert(false) to assert false
                Use assert(true) to assert true
        **********/
        assert(false);
    } else {
        /**********
        Task 6: assert the opposite here
        **********/
        assert(true);
    }
  })
})


it("Should set winners", function() {
  /**********
  Task 7: Call register function from account 2
  **********/
  return auctionInstance.register({from:accounts[2]})
  .then(function(result) {
    /**********
    Task 8: Call register function from account 3
    **********/
       return auctionInstance.register({from:accounts[3]})
  }).then(function() {
    /**********
    Task 9: Call register function from account 4
    **********/
       return auctionInstance.register({from:accounts[4]})
  }).then(function() {
    /**********
    Task 10: Call bid method from accounts[2] of
Auction.sol using auctionInstance and pass itemId=0,
count=5 as arguments
    **********/
       return auctionInstance.bid(0,5,{from:accounts[2]})
  }).then(function() {
    /**********
```

Code Cell 10.4   (Continued)

```
       Task 11: Call bid method from accounts[3] of
Auction.sol using auctionInstance and
       pass itemId=1, count=5 as arguments
       ***********/
           return auctionInstance.bid(itemId=1,count=5,{from:
accounts[3]})
       }).then(function() {
       /**********
       Task 12: Call bid method from accounts[4] of
Auction.sol using auctionInstance and
       pass itemId=2, count=5 as arguments
       ***********/
           return auctionInstance.bid(itemId=2,count=5,{from:
accounts[4]})
       }).then(function() {
       /**********
       Task 13: Call revealWinners function from
accounts[0]
       ***********/
           return auctionInstance.revealWinners({from:accou
nts[0]})
       }).then(function() {
       /**********
       Task 14: call winners function from accounts[0] to
get the winner of item id 0
       ***********/
           return auctionInstance.winners(0,{from:accounts[0]})
       }).then(function(result) {
       /**********
       Task 15:  assert to see if the winner address is
not the default address
       Default address is '0x000000000000000000000000000000
000000000000'
             Use notEqual method of assert
             Parameters for notEqual : (result, default
address , message);
       ***********/
       assert.notEqual(result, '0x000000000000000000000000
00000000000000000', '')
```

Code Cell 10.4   (Continued)

```
/**********
Task 16: call winners function from accounts[0] to
get the winner of item id 1
**********/
return auctionInstance.winners(1,{from:accounts[0]})
}).then(function(result) {
/**********
Task 17:  assert to see if the winner address is
not the default address
Default address is '0x000000000000000000000000000
000000000000'
         Use notEqual method of assert
         Parameters for notEqual : (result, default
address , message);
**********/
assert.notEqual(result, '0x00000000000000000000000
00000000000000000', '')
/**********
Task 18: Call winners function from account 3 to
get the winner of item id 2
**********/
return auctionInstance.winners(2,{from:accounts[0]})
}).then(function(result) {
/**********
Task 19:  assert to see if the winner address is
not the default address
Default address is '0x000000000000000000000000000
000000000000'
         Use notEqual method of assert
         Parameters for notEqual : (result, default
address , message);
**********/
assert.notEqual(result, '0x00000000000000000000000
00000000000000000', '')
  })
 });
});
```

Code Cell 10.4   (Continued)

The dApp to implement Auction Smart Contract is shown in Code Cell 10.5.

```
App = {
  web3Provider: null,
  contracts: {},
  names: new Array(),
  url: 'http://127.0.100.94.1231',
  President:null,
  currentAccount:null,
  init: function() {
    $.getJSON('../proposals.json', function(data) {
      var proposalsRow = $('#proposalsRow');
      var proposalTemplate = $('#proposalTemplate');

      for (i = 0; i < data.length; i ++) {
        proposalTemplate.find('.panel-title').
text(data[i].name);
        proposalTemplate.find('img').attr('src',
data[i].picture);
        proposalTemplate.find('.btn-vote').attr('data-
id', data[i].id);

        proposalsRow.append(proposalTemplate.html());
        App.names.push(data[i].name);
      }
    });

    return App.initWeb3();
  },

  initWeb3: function() {
        // Is there is an injected web3 instance?
    if (typeof web3 !== 'undefined') {
      App.web3Provider = web3.currentProvider;
    } else {
      // If no injected web3 instance is detected,
fallback to the TestRPC
      App.web3Provider = new Web3.providers.
HttpProvider(App.url);
    }
    web3 = new Web3(App.web3Provider);
```

Code Cell 10.5 dApp to implement auction smart contract.

```
    App.populateAddress();
    return App.initContract();
},

  initContract: function() {
      $.getJSON('Ballot.json', function(data) {
      // Get the necessary contract artifact file and
instantiate it with truffle-contract
      var voteArtifact = data;
      App.contracts.vote = TruffleContract(voteArtifact);

      // Set the provider for our contract
      App.contracts.vote.setProvider(App.web3Provider);

      App.getPresident();
      return App.bindEvents();
    });
    },

  bindEvents: function() {
      $(document).on('click', '.btn-vote', App.
handleVote);
      $(document).on('click', '#win-count', App.
handleWinner);
      $(document).on('click', '#register', function(){ var
ad = $('#enter_address').val(); App.handleRegister(ad);
});
    },

  populateAddress : function(){
      new Web3(new Web3.providers.HttpProvider(App.url)).
eth.getAccounts((err, accounts) => {
      jQuery.each(accounts,function(i){
        if(web3.eth.coinbase != accounts[i]){
          var optionElement = '<option value="'+accounts
[i]+'">'+accounts[i]+'</option';
          jQuery('#enter_address').append(optionElement);
        }
      });
      });
    },
```

Code Cell 10.5   (Continued)

```
getPresident : function(){
  App.contracts.vote.deployed().then(function(instance) {
    return instance.President();
  }).then(function(result) {
    App.President = result.toString();
    App.currentAccount = web3.eth.coinbase;
    if(App.President != App.currentAccount){
      jQuery('#address_div').css('display','none');
      jQuery('#register_div').css('display','none');
    }else{
      jQuery('#address_div').css('display','block');
      jQuery('#register_div').css('display','block');
    }
  })
},

handleRegister: function(addr){

  var voteInstance;
  App.contracts.vote.deployed().then(function(instance) {
    voteInstance = instance;
    return voteInstance.register(addr);
  }).then( function(result){
    if(result.receipt.status == '0x01')
      alert(addr + " is registered successfully")
    else
      alert(addr + " account registeration failed due
to revert")
  }).catch( function(err){
    alert(addr + " account registeration failed")
  })
},

handleVote: function(event) {
  event.preventDefault();
  var proposalId = parseInt($(event.target).
data('id'));
  var voteInstance;

  web3.eth.getAccounts(function(error, accounts) {
    var account = accounts[0];
```

Code Cell 10.5 (Continued)

```
        App.contracts.vote.deployed().then(function
(instance) {
        voteInstance = instance;

        return voteInstance.vote(proposalId, {from:
account});
      }).then(function(result){
            if(result.receipt.status == '0x01')
            alert(account + " voting done successfully")
            else
            alert(account + " voting not done
successfully due to revert")
        }).catch(function(err){
          alert(account + " voting failed")
    });
    });
  },

  handleWinner : function() {
    var voteInstance;
    App.contracts.vote.deployed().then(function(instance) {
      voteInstance = instance;
      return voteInstance.Winner();
    }).then(function(res){
      alert(App.names[res] + "  is the winner ! :)");
    }).catch(function(err){
      console.log(err.message);
    })
  }
};


$(function() {
  $(window).load(function() {
    App.init();
    console.log('starting app.js');
  });
});
```

Code Cell 10.5 (Continued)

10.4 Decentralized Finance

Decentralized Finance (DeFi) is an emerging financial technology, based on blockchain, which is used by cryptocurrencies. It is different from existing financial networks by being open and programmable. Anyone with an internet connection can use it without the approval of any authority. It operates via peer-to-peer financial networks, which use security protocols, connectivity, software, and hardware advancements. It works automatically without a central authority through smart contracts and the conditions underlying them, allowing developers to build secure decentralized financial applications. It enables developers to conceptualize new models for payment, investment, lending, trade, exchange, etc. without the control of banks and institutions. DeFi companies such as Aave, Compound, MakerDAO, and Uniswap are already developing such products that permit peer-to-peer finance, computing interest on cryptocurrency holdings, and trading through decentralized exchanges, etc.

DeFi is a broad term that encompasses many different functions and applications. The current financial ecosystem falls under the category of a centralized finance, which includes centralized banks such as the Reserve Bank of India that fixes inputs around the repo rate. DeFi does not involve any such regulatory body or central bank and completely eliminates the control of banks and institutions over money, financial products, and financial services.

In centralized finance, your money is held with banks, financial institutions, or corporations, which act as guarantors of transactions. This gives them immense freedom to make money. The financial system is full of third parties that facilitate the movement of funds between parties, and each entity charges a fee for its services. In DeFi, a smart contract takes the place of a financial institution in the transaction. A smart contract here is an Ethereum account that can hold, send, or return money, subject to a predetermined set of conditions. Smart contracts are always programmed for automation and cannot be changed once they go live. Consequently, it becomes easier for sellers, buyers, lenders, and borrowers to conduct peer-to-peer transactions rather than the company or institution facilitating it. As such, a farmer sells their produce directly to the end user without any middlemen. They get fresh access to a new buying community, and they will earn more dividend.

DeFi applications give users more control over their money through trading services and personal wallets. Generally, when one buys cryptotokens and plans to hold them for some time, these coins are of no use in the pro tem. By using the DeFi lending protocol, one can put up his or her cryptoholdings in order to obtain loans. These loans are easier and more economical than loans taken from traditional banks. Users can keep their money in a secure digital wallet instead of in a bank and transfer funds as and when required.

10.4.1 DeFi Financial Products

Peer-to-peer financial transactions are one of the main premises behind DeFi. A P2P DeFi transaction is one in which two parties agree to exchange cryptocurrency for goods or services, without involving the third party. In a centralized bank system, when a customer visits the bank to apply for a loan, the bank checks his credit history, completes the Know Your Customer (KYC) process, and then calculates the value of the collateral, if any.

On the DeFi platform, a borrower uses a decentralized finance application (dApp) to enter his loan requirements, and an algorithm matches his conditions with that of lenders. Then, out of all the lending offers that come out, the borrower has to agree upon the terms of any one of those lenders to get the loan.

Now, the lenders and borrowers come together and execute smart contracts. The borrower gives his crypto as collateral and receives a loan from the platform, while the lender gives his fiat money to the platform to earn some interest. Once the transaction is recorded on the blockchain, you receive your loan amount on peer validation.

Peer-to-peer lending under DeFi does not mean that it is completely free of interest and fees. Once the customer has received the loan, the lender can start collecting payments from the customer at agreed-upon intervals. When you make a payment through your dApp, it follows the consensus process, again in the blockchain; and thus, the money is transferred to the lender.

If the trader has an internet connection, he can solicit, trade, and lend from anywhere using software that records and verifies financial operations in a distributed financial database.

10.4.2 Total Value Locked in DeFi

Total Value Locked is the sum of all cryptocurrencies that are staked, borrowed, pooled, or used for other financial activities on all DeFi platforms for financial purposes. It can also represent the sum of specific cryptocurrencies used for financial activities, such as Ether or Bitcoin.

10.4.3 Use Cases for Decentralized Finance

DeFi protocols have opened up vistas of new economic activities and opportunities for users around the world. It is an integrated and well-organized effort to build a parallel financial system on Ethereum that challenges centralized services as being more accessible, flexible, and transparent.

10.4.3.1 Asset Management

Users are the owners of their data in the DeFi space. They are the custodian of their own cryptofund and have the power to do everything from buying, selling, and transferring crypto to earning interest on their digital assets. Cryptowallets, such as Argent, Gnosis Safe, and MetaMask, help the user to securely interact with decentralized applications. MetaMask stores your seed phrases, passwords, and private keys in an encrypted format locally on your device so that only you have access to your accounts and data.

10.4.3.2 Tokenization

Tokenization is the core functionality of the decentralized finance and Ethereum blockchain. A token is a kind of network-operated instrument that is created, issued, and managed on a blockchain. Tokens are programmed with protective measures and built-in functionalities. Ethereum-based tokens have emerged as a secure and digital option for users around the world to use, trade, and store value.

10.4.3.3 Tokenized Derivatives

Ethereum-based smart contracts enable the creation of tokenized derivatives, whose value is dependent on the performance of an underlying asset. DeFi derivatives can represent real-world assets, such as fiat currencies, bonds, commodities, and the cryptocurrencies, as well.

10.4.3.4 Decentralized Exchanges

Decentralized Exchanges (DEXs) are cryptocurrency exchanges that allow users to conduct peer-to-peer transactions and maintain control over their funds. Being hooked on the blockchain, they are independent of central authority.

DEX gives tokens' projects access to liquidity that often rivals centralized exchanges. DEX minimizes the risk of price manipulation, hacking, and theft, as crypto-assets are never in the possession of the exchange. Popular DEXs in the DeFi space currently include AirSwap, Liquality, Mesa, Oasis, and Uniswap. Aggregators of DeFi liquidity data, such as MetaMask Swap, optimize trading experiences by providing unique insights to DeFi users, enabling them to identify the best price quotes.

10.4.3.5 Decentralized Autonomous Organization

A Decentralized Autonomous Organization (DAO) cooperates according to transparent rules encoded on the Ethereum blockchain. Several popular protocols in the DeFi space have launched DAOs for fundraising, financial operations, and decentralize governance to the community. Examples are Maker and Compound.

10.4.3.6 Data Analytics and Assessment

Due to their unmatched transparency over transaction data and network activity, DeFi protocols have the ability to discover, analyze, and make decisions on data related to financial opportunities and risk management. The explosive growth of new DeFi applications has led to the development of a number of tools and dashboards, such as DeFi Pulse, that help users to assess platform risk, track closing prices, and compare liquidity across the DeFi protocol.

10.4.3.7 Payments

Peer-to-peer payments are arguably one of the fundamental applications of the DeFi space and the blockchain ecosystem at large. DeFi payment solutions are leading the way in streamlining market infrastructure and better serving wholesale and retail customers by creating a more open economic system for the bankless population.

10.4.3.8 Lending and Borrowing

Peer-to-peer lending and borrowing protocols are some of the most widely used applications in the DeFi ecosystem. Compound DeFi is a compelling example of the exponential opportunity in space. It is an algorithmic-based autonomous interest rate protocol, integrated with DeFi platforms. It allows users to earn interest on crypto that they have provided to the lending pool by providing an interest rate market on Ethereum. The compound smart contract automatically matches borrowers and lenders and calculates interest rate based on the ratio of the assets to be borrowed. As more and more products continue to integrate the compound protocol, more and more crypto-assets will be able to earn interest even when they are inactive.

10.4.3.9 Identity

DeFi protocols combined with a blockchain-based identity system could help users with blocked accounts regain access to the global economic system. DeFi solutions can reduce collateralization requirements for those who do not have traditional data points, such as surplus funds, land ownership, or assets. It can help assess the credibility of users through such attributes as reputation and financial activity. Anyone with an internet connection can use the DeFi application while maintaining control over their data and assets.

10.4.3.10 Know Your Transactions

In the DeFi space, Ethereum's decentralized framework enables next-generation compliance analysis around the behavior of a participant's address rather than its participant's identity. These Know Your Transactions (KYT) help in conducting real-time, risk-based assessment and protect against frauds and financial crimes.

In traditional finance, compliance around Anti-Money Laundering (AML) and Countering-the-Financing-of-Terrorism (CFT) relies on KYC guidelines. In the DeFi space, Ethereum's decentralized framework enables next-generation compliance analysis around the behavior of participant's address rather than his identity. These KYTs help assess risk in real-time risk assessment and protect against financial irregularities.

10.4.3.11 Insurance

A number of new insurance options have hit the market to help users buy coverage and protect their holdings. However, DeFi is still an emerging platform, having risks associated with smart contract bugs and breaches.

10.4.3.12 Margin Trading

Margin traders in traditional finance often invest in their business by borrowing money from a broker, which then creates collateral for the loan; whereas DeFi margin trading is powered by a decentralized, noncustodial lending protocol.

10.4.3.13 Marketplace

DeFi protocols support a range of online markets that allow users to exchange products and services on a global scale.

The composability in the DeFi protocol allows different components of the system to easily connect and interoperate. Composable code creates a powerful network effect in which the community continues to build on what others have created. From Truffle's smart contract library and Infura's API suite to Diligence's security tools, Ethereum developers are now able to build and launch the DeFi protocol to suit their needs with full-stack tooling and security integration.

10.4.3.14 Gaming

DeFi composability has opened up new avenues for product developers in various verticals to build the DeFi protocol directly into the platform. Ethereum-based games have become a popular application for decentralized finance as a result of their underlying economies and innovative incentive models. PoolTogether, a no-loss audited savings lottery, enables users to purchase digital tickets by depositing the Dai Stablecoin, which are then pooled together and lend money to combined money market protocols to earn interest.

10.4.3.15 Yield Farming

Yield farming is one of the most promising use cases for DeFi in which users earn tokens by locking cryptocurrencies into smart contracts running on the exchange's trading platform. The protocol allows a cryptoholder to farm for more cryptotokens, using existing tokens, thereby saving time and money. This gives liquidity providers an incentive to stake or lock up their crypto-assets in smart contract–based liquidity pools (see Figure 10.5). These incentives can be a percentage of transaction fees, interest from lenders, etc.

Yield farming allows staking of crypto-assets in the form of additional cryptocurrencies to generate higher returns or rewards. There are many different strategies adopted for this type of farming, the most popular being Yearn.Finance. It continuously moves user tokens between multiple lending platforms to achieve higher returns on a blockchain, such as Ethereum.

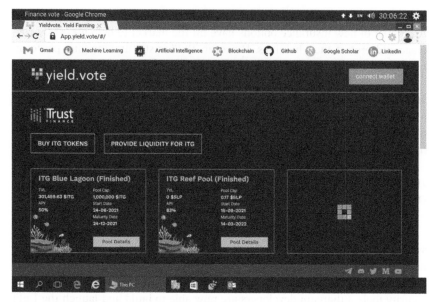

Figure 10.5 Yield.vote as a DeFi platform.

Operating Mechanism

DeFi is a code, and yield farming is a simple logic-based application. With the help of these smart contracts, your money is programmed to perform various functions. This creates a unique opportunity for anyone with a computer and internet connection to participate in the global economy. By applying DeFi to yield farming, users lock in their cryptotoken holdings and earn interest on them, based on pre-existing smart contracts. It is similar to betting cryptotokens, but the difference lies in the operating mechanism.

Yield farming operates using multiple smart contracts and Liquidity Providers (LPs). The Ethereum blockchain is the most popular underlying technology for these types of applications. Literally, LPs are users who provide money or liquidity to a smart contract, primarily in exchange for a reward in the system. This pool is used to create a marketplace where users using the smart contract system lend, borrow, or exchange their cryptotokens by paying a fee. A part of this fee is given to the LP as a reward (proportionate to the amount of reward). The rewards, thus earned, can also be reinvested in other smart contracts. The rewards that LPs receive are also a type of ERC-20 token.

However, there is a risk involved with DeFi, whereby the price of the assets locked in the liquidity pool changes after being deposited and incur an unrealized loss. Another risk is that the technology can have bugs, and you can lose your money.

10.4.4 Ethereum as a DeFi Platform

Ethereum is a new economic system that is code-driven and sets new standards for financial access, opportunity, and trust. Ethereum is the perfect ground for DeFi, owing to several reasons:

- No one owns or controls Ethereum or the smart contracts that reside on it. This gives everyone the right to use DeFi equally, subject to certain limitations.
- Many of DeFi's products work seamlessly together on the Ethereum platform. Participants or members can exchange interest tokens in different markets on entirely different applications.
- Ethereum is a wonderful step toward complete financial independence in which your funds are never governed by any third party.

10.4.4.1 Fast Money Transfer around the World
Like Bitcoin, Ethereum makes sending money around the world as easy as sending an e-mail. It is designed to perform global transactions in a secure manner. To send or receive payments, the user needs a wallet. He enters the recipient's Ethereum Name Service (ENS) or his account address from his wallet and the specified amount is transferred to his account in the blink of an eye.

10.4.4.2 Stream Money across the Globe
One can also stream money on Ethereum. It allows organizations to pay the salaries of their employees. Ethereum gives them access to their money whenever the employee (user) needs money. Alternative currencies, such as Stablecoins, are also accessible on Ethereum if users do not wish to send or stream ETH.

10.4.4.3 Programmable Money
Anyone can program logic into payments – a default feature of tokens that's possible only on Ethereum. This allows for the control and security of Bitcoin, mixed with the services provided by financial institutions. As a result, investing in index funds, lending, and borrowing, scheduling payments, and many more transactions that are not possible with Bitcoin can be done with Ethereum.

10.4.4.4 Access Stable Currencies
Cryptocurrency volatility is a problem for most financial products and general spending. The DeFi community has solved this with Stablecoins. The value of the Stablecoin is linked with another asset, such as the dollar. Coins, such as United States dollar coin (USDC), keep their value within a few cents making them appropriate for earning or retailing. Many people in Latin America have used Stablecoins to secure their savings in times of uncertainty.

10.4.4.5 Borrowing

Decentralized providers typically perform two types of transactions, peer-to-peer, where a borrower borrows directly from a specific lender; and pool-based, where lenders provide funds to a pool from which a borrower can borrow.

There can be many advantages of getting a loan from a decentralized lender:

- Borrowing from a bank, revolves around the persons involved in that transaction. Before lending money to a person by banks, it becomes obligatory to make sure whether there is a possibility of repayment of the loan by the concerned party or not. Decentralized lending conducts loan transactions on the borrower's collateral security without the identification of any party, which automatically accrues to the lender in the event of nonrepayment of the loan. Some lenders also accept nonfungible tokens as collateral. It allows one to borrow money without handing over the borrower's credit check or personal information like a unique asset.
- When one uses a decentralized lender, they have access to resources around the world, not just money deposited in a chosen bank or institution. This makes the loan more accessible at a reasonable interest rate.
- One can get access to the funds they need without having to sell their ETH. Instead of selling ETH, loanees can use ETH as collateral for Stablecoin loans.
- Flash loans are a more experimental form of decentralized lending that allows one to borrow without providing collateral or any personal information. It works on the premise that the loan is taken out and paid back within the same transaction. If it cannot be paid back, the transaction is rolled back as if nothing happened. Frequently used funds are kept in liquidity pools, which we know as large pools of funds used for borrowing. This creates an opportunity for someone to borrow these funds, do business with them, and repay them in full if they are not being used at a given point in time.

    There could be a possibility that someone can use flash loans to borrow more assets at the same price so that he can sell it on a different exchange where the price is higher. In such a situation the following events can happen in a single transaction, which might involve multiple logics:
    - A user borrows X amount of assets from exchange A at $1.00.
    - He sells the X assets for $1.10 on exchange B.
    - He refunds the loan to exchange A.
    - He keeps the profit, minus the transaction fee.
    - If supply drops suddenly on exchange B, the transaction will fail because the user is unable to purchase enough to cover the original debt.
- In traditional finance, these money-making strategies are only accessible to those who have plenty of assets or money. Flash loans are also available for people who do not have enough assets to make money.

10.4.4.6 Lending

Participants can earn interest by lending their crypto, and these interest rates are much higher than local bank interest rates. It allows clients to observe their funds growing in real time.

For instance, a participant pays his ten Stablecoins, such as Dai, for the product. He receives ten Dai Products (pDai), which is a token that represents his loan in terms of Dai. His pDai keeps on increasing, based on the interest rates which they can see as an increase in the wallet balance. Based on the APR, his wallet balance will increase after a few days or hours, like 10.01. He can withdraw the regular Dai amount equal to his pDai balance at any point of time.

10.4.4.7 No-loss Lottery

No-loss lottery like PoolTogether is a novel way to save money. Under this, the participant can buy ten tickets using ten Dai tokens, whereby the participant will receive ten lDai that represent his ten tickets. If the participant wins the lottery, his lDai balance will be increased by the amount he earned from the prize pool. And if he doesn't win, his ten lDai will remain in the pool, and he will have a chance to win again in the next week's draw. In the meantime, participants can withdraw the amount of regular Dai equal to his lDai balance at any time he wishes.

10.4.4.8 Exchange Tokens

DEXs allow a customer to trade different tokens whenever he wants. There are thousands of tokens on a platform like Ethereum, and it's like a currency exchange, albeit rather better. DeFi versions operate 24/7, 365 days a year. Hence the customer has seamless access to the funds. The DEX allows customers to swap their ETH for tokens as needed and get them back at any time.

10.4.4.9 Advanced Trading

When trading on a centralized exchange, the trader has to deposit his assets and trust the exchange to take care of his assets. Oddly, the asset belongs to the customer, and its security becomes the responsibility of the exchange. With decentralized trading you get access to global liquidity, and the trader's assets are always in his possession and control. In addition, for traders who prefer a bit more control, there are more advanced options such as limit orders, perpetual, margin trading, etc.

Basic Solidity Code for Implementing Limit Orders in Smart Contracts
(see Code Cell 10.6)

10.4.4.10 Fund Aggregation

A common investor needs a secure and well-organized platform to keep track of all his investments, loans, and trades. There are a number of products on Ethereum that are capable of coordinating all DeFi activity. Developers can build interfaces

```solidity
// SPDX-License-Identifier: BITS

pragma solidity 0.8.11;

import "@openzeppelin/contracts/utils/cryptography/
draft-EIP712.sol";
import "./OrderMixin.sol";
import "./OrderRFQMixin.sol";

contract LimitOrderProtocol is
    EIP712("1inch Limit Order Protocol", "2"),
    OrderMixin,
    OrderRFQMixin
{
    // solhint-disable-next-line func-name-mixedcase
    function DOMAIN_SEPARATOR() external view
returns(bytes32) {
        return _domainSeparatorV4();
    }
}
OrderMixin.sol
// SPDX-License-Identifier: BITS

pragma solidity 0.8.11;

import "@openzeppelin/contracts/utils/Address.sol";
import "@openzeppelin/contracts/utils/cryptography/
draft-EIP712.sol";
import "@openzeppelin/contracts/utils/cryptography/
SignatureChecker.sol";
import "@openzeppelin/contracts/token/ERC20/IERC20.sol";

import "./helpers/AmountCalculator.sol";
import "./helpers/ChainlinkCalculator.sol";
import "./helpers/NonceManager.sol";
import "./helpers/PredicateHelper.sol";
import "./interfaces/InteractiveNotificationReceiver.
sol";
import "./libraries/ArgumentsDecoder.sol";
import "./libraries/Permitable.sol";
```

Code Cell 10.6 Limit orders in smart contracts.

```
/// @title Regular Limit Order mixin
abstract contract OrderMixin is
    EIP712,
    AmountCalculator,
    ChainlinkCalculator,
    NonceManager,
    PredicateHelper,
    Permitable
{
    using Address for address;
    using ArgumentsDecoder for bytes;

    /// @notice Emitted every time order gets filled,
including partial fills
    event OrderFilled(
        address indexed maker,
        bytes32 orderHash,
        uint256 remaining
    );

    /// @notice Emitted when order gets cancelled
    event OrderCanceled(
        address indexed maker,
        bytes32 orderHash,
        uint256 remainingRaw
    );

    // Fixed-size order part with core information
    struct StaticOrder {
        uint256 salt;
        address makerAsset;
        address takerAsset;
        address maker;
        address receiver;
        address allowedSender;  // equals to Zero
address on public orders
        uint256 makingAmount;
        uint256 takingAmount;
    }

    // `StaticOrder` extension including variable-sized
additional order meta information
```

Code Cell 10.6 (Continued)

```
    struct Order {
        uint256 salt;
        address makerAsset;
        address takerAsset;
        address maker;
        address receiver;
        address allowedSender;  // equals to Zero
address on public orders
        uint256 makingAmount;
        uint256 takingAmount;
        bytes makerAssetData;
        bytes takerAssetData;
        bytes getMakerAmount; // this.staticcall(abi.
encodePacked(bytes, swapTakerAmount)) =>
(swapMakerAmount)
        bytes getTakerAmount; // this.staticcall(abi.
encodePacked(bytes, swapMakerAmount)) =>
(swapTakerAmount)
        bytes predicate;      // this.staticcall(bytes)
=> (bool)
        bytes permit;         // On first fill:
permit.1.call(abi.encodePacked(permit.selector,
permit.2))
        bytes interaction;
    }


    bytes32 constant public LIMIT_ORDER_TYPEHASH =
keccak256(
        "Order(uint256 salt,address makerAsset,address
takerAsset,address maker,address receiver,address
allowedSender,uint256 makingAmount,uint256
takingAmount,bytes makerAssetData,bytes
takerAssetData,bytes getMakerAmount,bytes
getTakerAmount,bytes predicate,bytes permit,bytes
interaction)"
    );
    uint256 constant private _ORDER_DOES_NOT_EXIST = 0;
    uint256 constant private _ORDER_FILLED = 1;

    /// @notice Stores unfilled amounts for each order
plus one.
```

Code Cell 10.6 (Continued)

```
    /// Therefore 0 means order doesn't exist and 1
means order was filled
    mapping(bytes32 => uint256) private _remaining;

    /// @notice Returns unfilled amount for order.
Throws if order does not exist function remaining(bytes32
orderHash) external view returns(uint256) {
        uint256 amount = _remaining[orderHash];
        require(amount != _ORDER_DOES_NOT_EXIST, "LOP:
Unknown order");
        unchecked { amount -= 1; }
        return amount;
    }

    /// @notice Returns unfilled amount for order
    /// @return Result Unfilled amount of order plus one
if order exists. Otherwise 0 function remainingRaw
(bytes32 orderHash) external view returns(uint256) {
        return _remaining[orderHash];
    }

    /// @notice Same as `remainingRaw` but for multiple
orders
    function remainingsRaw(bytes32[] memory orderHashes)
external view returns(uint256[] memory) {
        uint256[] memory results = new uint256[](order
Hashes.length);
        for (uint256 i = 0; i < orderHashes.length; i++) {
            results[i] = _remaining[orderHashes[i]];
        }
        return results;
    }

    /**
     * @notice Calls every target with corresponding
data. Then reverts with CALL_RESULTS_0101011 where
zeroes and ones
     * denote failure or success of the corresponding call
     * @param targets Array of addresses that will be
called
```

Code Cell 10.6 (Continued)

```
     * @param data Array of data that will be passed to
each call
     */
    function simulateCalls(address[] calldata targets,
bytes[] calldata data) external {
        require(targets.length == data.length, "LOP:
array size mismatch");
        bytes memory reason = new bytes(targets.length);
        for (uint256 i = 0; i < targets.length; i++) {
            // solhint-disable-next-line avoid-low-level-
calls
            (bool success, bytes memory result) =
targets[i].call(data[i]);
            if (success andand result.length > 0) {
                success = result.length == 32 andand
result.decodeBool();
            }
            reason[i] = success ? bytes1("1") :
bytes1("0");
        }

        // Always revert and provide per call results
        revert(string(abi.encodePacked("CALL_RESULTS_",
reason)));
    }

    /// @notice Cancels order by setting remaining
amount to zero function cancelOrder(Order memory order)
external {
        require(order.maker == msg.sender, "LOP: Access
denied");

        bytes32 orderHash = hashOrder(order);
        uint256 orderRemaining = _remaining[orderHash];
        require(orderRemaining != _ORDER_FILLED, "LOP:
already filled");
        emit OrderCanceled(msg.sender, orderHash,
orderRemaining);
        _remaining[orderHash] = _ORDER_FILLED;
    }
```

Code Cell 10.6 (Continued)

```
    /// @notice Fills an order. If one doesn't exist
(first fill) it will be created using order.
makerAssetData
    /// @param order Order quote to fill
    /// @param signature Signature to confirm quote
ownership
    /// @param makingAmount Making amount
    /// @param takingAmount Taking amount
    /// @param thresholdAmount Specifies maximum allowed
takingAmount when takingAmount is zero, otherwise
specifies minimum allowed makingAmount
    function fillOrder(
        Order memory order,
        bytes calldata signature,
        uint256 makingAmount,
        uint256 takingAmount,
        uint256 thresholdAmount
    ) external returns(uint256 /* actualMakingAmount */,
uint256 /* actualTakingAmount */) {
        return fillOrderTo(order, signature, making
Amount, takingAmount, thresholdAmount, msg.sender);
    }

    /// @notice Same as `fillOrder` but calls permit
first,
    /// allowing to approve token spending and make a
swap in one transaction.
    /// Also allows to specify funds destination instead
of `msg.sender`
    /// @param order Order quote to fill
    /// @param signature Signature to confirm quote
ownership
    /// @param makingAmount Making amount
    /// @param takingAmount Taking amount
    /// @param thresholdAmount Specifies maximum allowed
takingAmount when takingAmount is zero, otherwise
specifies minimum allowed makingAmount
    /// @param target Address that will receive swap
funds
    /// @param permit Should consist of abiencoded token
address and encoded `IERC20Permit.permit` call.
```

Code Cell 10.6   (Continued)

```
    /// @dev See tests for examples
    function fillOrderToWithPermit(
        Order memory order,
        bytes calldata signature,
        uint256 makingAmount,
        uint256 takingAmount,
        uint256 thresholdAmount,
        address target,
        bytes calldata permit
    ) external returns(uint256 /* actualMakingAmount */,
uint256 /* actualTakingAmount */) {
        require(permit.length >= 20, "LOP: permit length
too low");
        (address token, bytes calldata permitData) =
permit.decodeTargetAndData();
        _permit(token, permitData);
        return fillOrderTo(order, signature, making
Amount, takingAmount, thresholdAmount, target);
    }

    /// @notice Same as `fillOrder` but allows to
specify funds destination instead of `msg.sender`
    /// @param order Order quote to fill
    /// @param signature Signature to confirm quote
ownership
    /// @param makingAmount Making amount
    /// @param takingAmount Taking amount
    /// @param thresholdAmount Specifies maximum allowed
takingAmount when takingAmount is zero, otherwise
specifies minimum allowed makingAmount
    /// @param target Address that will receive swap
funds
    function fillOrderTo(
        Order memory order,
        bytes calldata signature,
        uint256 makingAmount,
        uint256 takingAmount,
        uint256 thresholdAmount,
        address target
    ) public returns(uint256 /* actualMakingAmount */,
uint256 /* actualTakingAmount */) {
```

Code Cell 10.6 (Continued)

```
        require(target != address(0), "LOP: zero target
is forbidden");
        bytes32 orderHash = hashOrder(order);

        {  // Stack too deep
            uint256 remainingMakerAmount = _remaining
[orderHash];
            require(remainingMakerAmount != _ORDER_
FILLED, "LOP: remaining amount is 0");
            require(order.allowedSender == address(0) ||
order.allowedSender == msg.sender, "LOP: private
order");
            if (remainingMakerAmount == _ORDER_DOES_NOT_
EXIST) {
                // First fill: validate order and permit
maker asset
                require(SignatureChecker.isValid
SignatureNow(order.maker, orderHash, signature), "LOP:
bad signature");
                remainingMakerAmount = order.
makingAmount;
                if (order.permit.length >= 20) {
                    // proceed only if permit length is
enough to store address
                    (address token, bytes memory permit)
= order.permit.decodeTargetAndCalldata();
                    _permitMemory(token, permit);
                    require(_remaining[orderHash] ==
_ORDER_DOES_NOT_EXIST, "LOP: reentrancy detected");
                }
            } else {
                unchecked { remainingMakerAmount -= 1; }
            }

            // Check if order is valid
            if (order.predicate.length > 0) {
                require(checkPredicate(order), "LOP:
predicate returned false");
            }

            // Compute maker and taker assets amount
```

Code Cell 10.6   (Continued)

```
        if ((takingAmount == 0) == (makingAmount == 0)) {
            revert("LOP: only one amount should be 0");
        } else if (takingAmount == 0) {
            uint256 requestedMakingAmount =
makingAmount;
            if (makingAmount > remainingMakerAmount) {
                makingAmount = remainingMakerAmount;
            }
            takingAmount = _callGetter(order.
getTakerAmount, order.makingAmount, makingAmount,
order.takingAmount);
            // check that actual rate is not worse
than what was expected
            // takingAmount / makingAmount <=
thresholdAmount / requestedMakingAmount
            require(takingAmount * requestedMaking
Amount <= thresholdAmount * makingAmount, "LOP: taking
amount too high");
        } else {
            uint256 requestedTakingAmount =
takingAmount;
            makingAmount = _callGetter(order.get
MakerAmount, order.takingAmount, takingAmount, order.
makingAmount);
            if (makingAmount > remainingMakerAmount) {
                makingAmount = remainingMakerAmount;
                takingAmount = _callGetter(order.
getTakerAmount, order.makingAmount, makingAmount, order.
takingAmount);
            }
            // check that actual rate is not worse
than what was expected
            // makingAmount / takingAmount >=
thresholdAmount / requestedTakingAmount
            require(makingAmount * requestedTakingA-
mount >= thresholdAmount * takingAmount, "LOP: making
amount too low");
        }

        require(makingAmount > 0 andand takingAmount
> 0, "LOP: can't swap 0 amount");
```

Code Cell 10.6 (Continued)

```
            // Update remaining amount in storage
            unchecked {
                remainingMakerAmount = remainingMaker
Amount - makingAmount;
                _remaining[orderHash] = remainingMaker
Amount + 1;
            }
            emit OrderFilled(msg.sender, orderHash,
remainingMakerAmount);
        }

        // Taker => Maker
        _makeCall(
            order.takerAsset,
            abi.encodePacked(
                IERC20.transferFrom.selector,
                uint256(uint160(msg.sender)),
                uint256(uint160(order.receiver ==
address(0) ? order.maker : order.receiver)),
                takingAmount,
                order.takerAssetData
            )
        );

        // Maker can handle funds interactively
        if (order.interaction.length >= 20) {
            // proceed only if interaction length is
enough to store address
            (address interactionTarget, bytes memory
interactionData) = order.interaction.
decodeTargetAndCalldata();
            InteractiveNotificationReceiver(interactionT
arget).notifyFillOrder(
                msg.sender, order.makerAsset, order.
takerAsset, makingAmount, takingAmount, interactionData
            );
        }

        // Maker => Taker
        _makeCall(
            order.makerAsset,
```

Code Cell 10.6 (Continued)

```
                abi.encodePacked(
                    IERC20.transferFrom.selector,
                    uint256(uint160(order.maker)),
                    uint256(uint160(target)),
                    makingAmount,
                    order.makerAssetData
                )
            );

            return (makingAmount, takingAmount);
        }

        /// @notice Checks order predicate
        function checkPredicate(Order memory order) public
    view returns(bool) {
            bytes memory result = address(this).function
    StaticCall(order.predicate, "LOP: predicate call
    failed");
            require(result.length == 32, "LOP: invalid
    predicate return");
            return result.decodeBool();
        }

        function hashOrder(Order memory order) public view
    returns(bytes32) {
            StaticOrder memory staticOrder;
            assembly {  // solhint-disable-line
    no-inline-assembly
                staticOrder := order
            }
            return _hashTypedDataV4(
                keccak256(
                    abi.encode(
                        LIMIT_ORDER_TYPEHASH,
                        staticOrder,
                        keccak256(order.makerAssetData),
                        keccak256(order.takerAssetData),
                        keccak256(order.getMakerAmount),
```

Code Cell 10.6 (Continued)

```
                keccak256(order.getTakerAmount),
                keccak256(order.predicate),
                keccak256(order.permit),
                keccak256(order.interaction)
            )
        )
    );
}

    function _makeCall(address asset, bytes memory
assetData) private {
        bytes memory result = asset.
functionCall(assetData, "LOP: asset.call failed");
        if (result.length > 0) {
            require(result.length == 32 andand result.
decodeBool(), "LOP: asset.call bad result");
        }
    }
    function _callGetter(bytes memory getter, uint256
orderExpectedAmount, uint256 amount, uint256 orderResult
Amount) private view returns(uint256) {
        if (getter.length == 0) {
            // On empty getter calldata only exact
amount is allowed
            require(amount == orderExpectedAmount, "LOP:
wrong amount");
            return orderResultAmount;
        } else {
            bytes memory result = address(this).
functionStaticCall(abi.encodePacked(getter, amount),
"LOP: getAmount call failed");
            require(result.length == 32, "LOP: invalid
getAmount return");
            return result.decodeUint256();
        }
    }
}
```

Code Cell 10.6 (Continued)

where investors can not only see their balance across products but also take advantage of all the features available on DeFi's open architecture.

10.4.4.11 Portfolio Management

There are a number of fund management products available on Ethereum that attempt to grow a client's portfolio, based on his customized strategy. It is open to all, incorporates a variety of strategies, and works automatically. There is no scope for a human manager to cut into the customer's profits. For example, the DeFi Pulse Index Fund (DPI) is a fund that automatically rebalances to determine whether a client's portfolio always includes the top DeFi tokens by market capitalization. The client can withdraw from the fund whenever he wants, and he never needs to manage any portfolio separately.

10.4.4.12 Quadratic Funding

Ethereum has developed an innovative fundraising model for quadratic funding. Quadratic funding stipulates that the projects that receive the most funding are the projects with the most singular demand that serve to improve the lives of the majority of people. It has the potential to improve the way money is made available for all kinds of public goods in the future.

A quadratic fund is a pool of donated funds from which begins with a round of public funding. Interested people can raise their demand for a unique project by donating some money. As the round ends, the pool money is distributed among the projects, and those with most unique demands grab the majority share from the matching pool.

At the core of quadratic funding is its matching pool. A matching pool is a model of public goods financing where a fund is provided by the government or philanthropic institutions that matches the individual contributions to a project. Quadratic funding strongly encourages people to contribute and ensures democratic allocation of funds. Matching amounts are calculated by using the quadratic funding formula, where the amount received by the project is proportional to the square of the sum of the square roots of contributions received.

Suppose, three projects of common interest are initiated as follows:

	Project A	Project B	Project C
Funds Received	10,000	10,000	10,000
Number of Donors	5	2	10
Per Unit Contribution	2000	5000	1000

Using the formula:

$$V_i^P \left(\left(\sum_j \sqrt{C_j^P} \right)^2 \right)$$

Matching amount for Project A:

$$\left(\sqrt{2000} + \sqrt{2000} + \sqrt{2000} + \sqrt{2000} + \sqrt{2000}\right)^2$$

$$= \left(5\sqrt{2000}\right)^2 = 25 \times 2000 = 50,000$$

Matching amount for Project B:

$$\left(\sqrt{5000} + \sqrt{5000}\right)^2$$

$$= \left(2\sqrt{5000}\right)^2 = 04 \times 5000 = 20,000$$

Matching amount for Project C:

$$\left(\begin{array}{c} \sqrt{1000} + \sqrt{1000} + \sqrt{1000} + \sqrt{1000} + \sqrt{1000} \\ + \sqrt{1000} + \sqrt{1000} + \sqrt{1000} + \sqrt{1000} + \sqrt{1000} \end{array}\right)$$

$$= \left(10\sqrt{1000}\right)^2 = 10 \times 1000 = 100,000$$

In a Matching Pool of US$ 100000

Share of A in the pool will be $= \left(\dfrac{5}{5+2+10}\right) \times 100,000 = 29,411.76$

Share of B in the pool will be $= \left(\dfrac{2}{5+2+10}\right) \times 100,000 = 11,764.71$

Share of C in the pool will be $= \left(\dfrac{10}{5+2+10}\right) \times 100,000 = 58,823.53$

	Project A	Project B	Project C
Funds Received	10,000	10,000	10,000
Number of Donors	5	2	10
Matched Grant	29,411.76	11,764.71	58,823.53
Percentage share (out of the initial fund)	**294.12%**	**117.65%**	**588.23%**

It optimizes matching funds by ensuring that projects are prioritized on the basis of the number of contributors. In this way, the money goes toward projects that actually benefit the public for a broader objective, not those that have the support of a few wealthy people.

10.4.4.13 Crowd Funding

Assuming that potential funders can come from anywhere, Ethereum and its tokens are open to anyone, anywhere in the world. It is an ideal and transparent platform for crowd funding, on which fundraisers can prove where the money is raised from, how much is raised, and how it is being spent. Fundraisers on Ethereum can set a specific time frame and a specified amount to ensure automatic refund.

10.4.4.14 Insurance

Decentralized insurance is a much cheaper and more transparent substitute. With automation, coverage is more economical, and pay-outs are much faster. Most insurance products are currently focused on protecting their users from loss of money due to the potential for bugs and exploits. Decentralized insurance can provide an affordable insurance alternative for farmers and retailers who do not have access to traditional insurance.

10.5 Prediction Markets

Prediction markets are exchange-traded markets where the outcome of events is traded. Market prices can indicate what the crowd thinks or what is likely to be the outcome of the event. It is a speculative market where participants do not bet on a product, option, or cryptocurrency, but rather, on information. Precisely, it's a platform for buying and selling futures contracts on binary events. The market is structured such that individual contracts are priced between $0 and $1. A participant buys a 50-cent contract for an outcome x, or its complement, y, and receives $1 if it results in x, or $0 if it does not. If we specify the contract price x as px, the price for y would theoretically be $1-px$. Although, in practice, owing to market dynamics, contract prices may be a little lower or higher in order to generate revenue for the exchange or a fee to purchase the contract, or a pay-out to maintain equilibrium.

For instance, will Ukraine survive the war between Russia and Ukraine? There are two possibilities here – it will survive or it will not survive. If you are confident that Ukraine will not survive, you can buy a number of "no" contracts. These can cost anywhere between $0 and $1. If Ukraine does not survive, the "no" contracts will be redeemable for $1, and the "yes" contracts would have no value. Contrariwise, if it survives, a "no" contract would be worth nothing, while a "yes" contract would be worth $1.

Meanwhile, there will be changes in the market sentiment, and the value of the contract will fluctuate accordingly. If Russia continues to dominate Ukraine, then the "no" contract prices will escalate, and if Russia initiates a reconciliation, it can be assumed that Russia is becoming weak and the "yes" market will start picking up. Unlike the speculative market, contracts in the prediction market exist as securities rather than as isolated bets. This allows for significantly higher liquidity, given that participants do not need to wait until the event occurs. This liquidity, in turn, helps in price search because participants with relevant insights can take leverage of temporary mis-pricing rather than remain locked in their bets. Though it works like a standard speculative market, prediction markets are more advanced than an average speculative platform. It can prove to be a powerful forecasting tool when used correctly.

James Surowiecki (2005), in his book, had expressed that a large sample of estimates of certain variables will likely be closer to the true value than most individual estimates. Prediction markets follow the same principle that the wisdom of the crowds will always be superior to the data known to a few experts. If individual estimates are based on esoteric knowledge and insight, a large-enough sample will be able to produce a desirable effect. However, participants' estimates are independent, reflecting different perspectives, and this is why crowds can sometimes be extraordinarily foolish, such as when the stock market suddenly jumps or falls. Nevertheless, the prediction market can work only if such a mandatory disqualification factor is present. If everyone believes in the same thing, no one will take the other side of the contract. The antithesis to the potential for profit is certainly the potential for loss, which is equally valuable. The potential for profit entices people with unusual knowledge to join the market, but it is not possible for all members of a group to have perfect intuition, so the community pushes the market toward a price that is closer to reality.

Prediction markets can be a formidable tool, provided they are decentralized. Whether due to local regulations or the reluctance of owners to list certain contracts, whatever centralized platforms offer today is inadequate. Users need a platform that is quick and doesn't levy charges for third parties. The traditional centralized model can be replaced by decentralized alternatives with a blockchain-based approach. This can provide a number of benefits such as censorship resistance, elimination of middlemen, and increased access.

10.5.1 Scope for Decentralized Markets

Experts believe that crypto-assets can play a role in improving these markets. Right now the markets in the US are highly regulated, and participating in them incurs relatively high fees. Proponents argue that cryptocurrencies can circumvent these issues. This is because with cryptocurrencies, users do not need to rely on a central entity. With Ethereum, the idea is that the rules contained in its code can guide certain actions in the project.

The best-known prediction markets in crypto are:

- Augur
- Gnosis's Omen
- Polymarket

Cryptocurrencies have no geographical limitations. Users around the world can buy Ethereum and other cryptocurrencies that support the prediction markets. They can be shipped anywhere in the world after purchase. Fees on centralized markets are higher than Ethereum fees most of the time, although now Ether fees have been rising recently as the network is becoming more popular and overcrowded.

Over the years, some prediction markets have been shut down by government authorities. In fact, prediction markets are generally run by one party. This means that government authorities or terrible entities can easily shut them down. One advantage of adding cryptocurrency to prediction markets is that users can create arcades on the blockchain. Decentralized platforms are out of the grip of the government, so they cannot be taken down so easily. When the system is governed by smart contracts, no user can edit or delete the programs that underpin the market. The system executes the contracts by default, without the need for an intermediary (Garg, 2021b, 2022b). In prediction markets, smart contracts pool the money put in by speculators, and then automatically distributes it among the winners at the end of each market. The flip side, however, is that smart contracts are a relatively new technology and have been observed to result in loss of money in the past due to bugs or flawed code.

Blockchain does not require administrators. As is expected with a centralized platform, users do not pay fees to any third parties, as transactions are conducted through smart contracts. It also rules out the counterparty risk.

With decentralized prediction markets, individuals around the world are free to place bets or make contracts available to users globally. So geographic and regulatory sanctions affecting erstwhile physical or digital platforms may no longer be a problem.

Oracle data services feed real-world data to smart contracts in prediction markets. Suppose a prediction market asks: will the price of gold rise tomorrow? One can use goldprice.com as an oracle source to predict what gold price is expected to be on the day of bet.

But the central oracles also have flaws. Let's say a betmaker has put a lot of money on "yes," and there is a possibility that goldprice.com can be hacked by him. If he succeeds in hacking goldprice.com, then he is almost certain to win.

There can be many options to avoid such troubles. One option may be to financially incentivize users to truthfully report incidents. Under this, a staking mechanism could be implemented, which would require users to forward tokens to report. If they report correctly, they will receive remuneration, but if they cheat, they will lose their stake. This model is being used by Augur, the first blockchain prediction market platform designed for dispute resolution (Augur, 2022).

Right now, the prediction market, Omen, is also trying to fix this with a decentralized oracle that compiles data from multiple oracles and eliminates oracles, which do not represent accurate data. The use of blockchain oracles in prediction markets is a relatively new concept. As a nascent technology, we have yet to see which type of oracle is best suited for different types of prediction markets. A few years ago, Binance Research, in its report, pointed out a design flaw attack along with some other flaws in a highly coveted implementation of prediction markets (Binance, 2019).

10.5.2 Real World Examples of Prediction Markets

10.5.2.1 Augur

Augur is a decentralized prediction market built on Ethereum's ERC-20 protocol that made its debut in 2014. Augur is an innovative protocol within the crypto prediction market space, which aims to democratize finance (see Figure 10.6). The first version of Augur was released at the public domain in July 2018.

Salient Features
User-generated Markets
With traditional prediction markets, each user is free to participate in trading shares of a prediction. With Augur, any user can create a market for a real world event by paying a small fee. The event price can be set between 0% and 50%, and the creator can earn from trading fees.

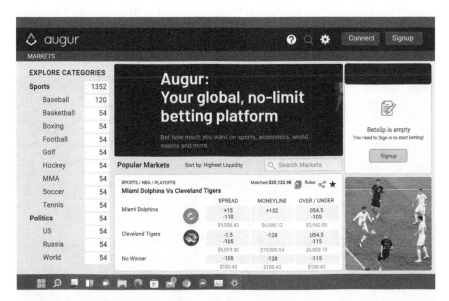

Figure 10.6 Augur betting platform.

Low Trade Fee

The trading fee on Augur is quite low (<1%) as compared to centralized prediction markets. Reputation tokens (REPs) also have a limited supply of 11 million, of which 80% were sold during the initial coin offering (ICO), in 2017.

Scope of Expansion

Augur remains the leading crypto prediction market, having raised over $5 million following a successful ICO launch in 2018. Augur launched its V2 on the mainnet, which supports the Dai Stablecoin. It effectively solves the issues around volatility.

10.5.2.2 TotemFi

TotemFi's platform is set to go live on the mainnet in a short time from now. It is a bet-based prediction market platform, which shows a lot of potential in the form of impending disruption in the space (see Figure 10.7).

Salient Features

Nonpunitive Predictions

TotemFi tokens offer nonpunitive predictions so users do not lose their initial stake if their predictions go wrong. It's the only platform in the market that provides such features. It strives to change the way asset classes and events are predicted, owns losses for inaccuracies, provides more incentive for users to stake and make predictions, and encourages users to say what they believe events will result.

BTC Rewards

TotemFi's platform offers native TOTM tokens as well as BTC rewards, for correct predictions, that evades native coin inflation. It is the only platform to offer this feature, which helps in providing real value to its users.

Figure 10.7 TotemFi prediction platform.

Collaborative Rewards

TotemFi uses the "wisdom of the crowd" concept in its truest sense. If the weighted average of the prediction pool comes close to accurately predicting the outcome of the event around which it is centered, those collaborators get the rewards. It promotes a true synergistic approach to prediction.

10.5.2.3 Finance.vote

In the coming days, Finance.vote aims to build a suite of dApps to equip DAOs with governance infrastructure and launch sustainable token economies (see Figure 10.8; Finance.vote, 2022). Finance.vote facilitates and fast-tracks the path to decentralization. This allows projects to focus on their use-cases and main business lines.

Through the Finance.vote dApp suite, projects are able to provide investors with fair token launches, incentives to participate in governance decisions, trustless vesting schedules, actionable market insights and trading signals, and decentralized liquidity mining (see Figure 10.9).

One of these is the dApp Market.Vote, which is a prediction market and collective intelligence tool. It uses quadratic voting and a decentralized identity system to curate emerging markets and reach consensus on the perceived future performance of assets.

Salient Features

Actionable Market Insights and Alpha Generation

Market.vote is the focal area of finance.vote architecture. It allows users to advance over the noise of permissionless systems and focus on their attention assets.

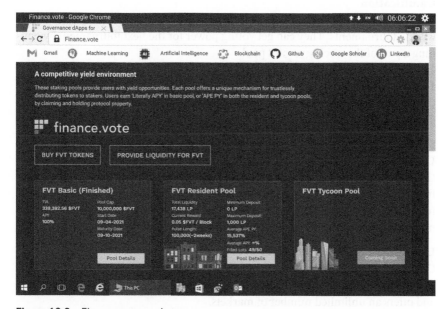

Figure 10.8 Finance.vote market.

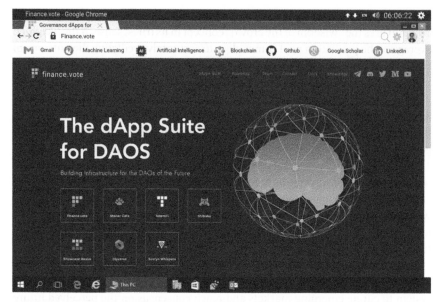

Figure 10.9 Finance.vote market.

Quadratic Voting
Quadratic voting is a method of collective decision-making in which a participant votes in favor or against, expressing how determined he or she is about it. It is in the interest of small groups of voters who care deeply about a particular issue.

Gamification
With Market.vote, users can vote on assets from the cryptospace to participate in weekly tournaments. They can get voting power for the next tournament by winning a part of the weekly reward pool.

10.5.2.4 OptionRoom
OptionRoom is a fully decentralized forecasting protocol that enables investors to guess on the outcome of real-world events (see Figure 10.10).

Salient Features
User-driven Oracle
OptionRoom is able to offer a user-driven Oracle due to their completely unique and innovative Oracle-as-a-Service, which introduces a human factor in data validation by resolving Oracle requests through user governance consensus. This enables them to process qualitative data requests as well as the quantitative ones (OptionRoom, 2022).

Unlimited Prediction Markets
OptionRoom is the only forecasting protocol on the market that lowers entry barriers for its users, streamlines access for users to the forecasting market landscape, and offers an unlimited number of markets.

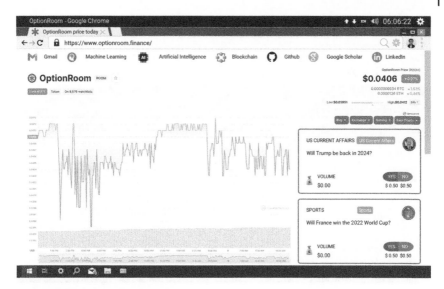

Figure 10.10 OptionRoom market.

Incentives and Rewards

OptionRoom provides users with industry-leading incentives to encourage the creation of forecast market offers and cater to the Oracle request criteria so that a strong and active community could offer unlimited prediction markets and verify Oracle requests successfully.

10.5.2.5 Polymarket

Polymarket was launched in 2020 on Ethereum's ERC-20 protocol. It is a decentralized market where users can trade the most debated events globally. Polymarket predictions are largely based around trendy real-world events with the ultimate aim of preventing the spread of misinformation.

Salient Features
Fiat-backed Trading

To trade the outcome of events, Polymarkets uses the US dollar-backed Stablecoin and USDC.

Simple User Interface

Polymarkets offer an opportunity to predict events to a wide range of users through their simple-minded platform that includes a step-by-step guide to financing and trading events across the globe (see Figure 10.11).

Smooth Resolution Process

Polymarkets platforms are able to automatically resolve the outcome of events without the need for a consensus mechanism.

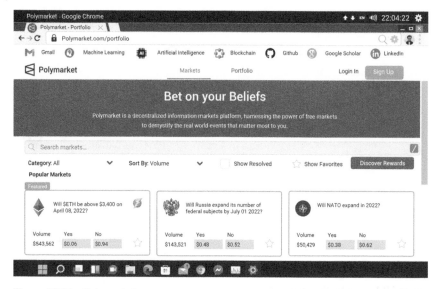

Figure 10.11   Polymarket.

10.5.3 Summary

- A prediction market implies betting on outcomes.
- Augur is a public blockchain-based solution for decentralized markets.
- Market creator posts market events on the platform.
- Market reporters speculate on the outcome of the event.
- Market participants can use their token/cryptocurrency for stake.
- If the predicted result is true/false, the participant will win/lose the prize.
- The tokens used are called Reputation Tokens (REP Tokens) and are used for the purpose of placing bets in case of dispute while the trading currency is Ether.
- An end-to-end marketplace of stocks, futures, products, ideas, etc. is facilitated by smart contracts.
- Oracle is used to resolve results that can be accessed by smart contracts.

Coming Up

The preceding chapter depicted how blockchain, along with smart contracts, provides a secure, transparent, auditable, and automated transaction environment for business investors, which has led to rapid adoption of the technology in banking, trade-finance, and decentralized finance. In addition, several use-cases, related to asset management, tokenization, decentralized autonomous organizations, payments, lending, insurance, margin trading, decentralized markets, such as Augur, TotemFi, Finance.Vote, OptionRoom, and PolyMarket, were also discussed at length.

While illustrating the growing fabric of blockchain, the upcoming chapter covers human resource management, e-Governance, supply chain management, e-Commerce, distributed resources, and Internet of Things.

References

Almeida S, Albuquerque A, and Silva A, 2019. An approach to develop software that uses blockchain. *Software Engineering Algorithms Intelligent Systems*, 763: 346–355.

Augur, 2022: https://www.kraken.com.

Binance, 2019. https://www.binance.com.

Chen PW, Jiang BS, and Wang CH, 2017. Blockchain-based Payment Collection Supervision System Using Pervasive Bitcoin Digital Wallet. Proceedings of the IEEE 13th International Conference on Wireless and Mobile Computing, Networking and Communications, Rome Italy, 139–146.

Clark J, 2014. Trade Finance: Developments and Issues. Federal Reserve Bank of New York, CGFS Papers No. 50.

D'Monte L, 2018. How Blockchain Puts Trade Finance Deals in Fast Lane. Mint. https://www.livemint.com/Money/aeuKOy0BpNrlFgXyjzTIqJ/How-blockchain-putstradefinance-deals-in-fast-lane.html. Accessed on 06 November 2018.

Del Rio CA, 2017. Use of distributed ledger technology by central banks: A review. *Enfoque Ute*, 8: 1–13.

Deloitte, 2014. Independent Review of RTGS Outage on 20 October 2014. Bank of England. bankofengland.co.uk.

Depository Trust and Clearing Corporation, 2018. DTCC announces study results demonstrating that DLT can support trading volumes in the US equity markets. https://www.dtcc.com/news/2018/october/16/dtcc-unveils-groundbreaking-study-on-dlt. Accessed on 16 October 2018.

Du Pont Q, 2017. Experiments in Algorithmic Governance: A History and Ethnography of the DAO, A Failed Decentralized Autonomous Organization. In *Bitcoin and Beyond*. Malcolm Campbell-Verduyn (ed), Routledge, Abingdon, 157–175.

Ducas E and Wilner A, 2017. The security and financial implications of blockchain technologies: Regulating emerging technologies in Canada. *International Journal – Canada Journal of Global Policy Analysis*, 72: 538–562.

Finance.vote, 2022. https://www.finance.vote.

Garg R, 2021a. Ethereum Based Smart Contracts for Trade and Finance. International Conference on Blockchain and Smart Contracts, Bangkok Thailand. doi: 10.5281/zenodo.5854730. https://www.researchgate.net/publication/357510533_Ethereum_based_Smart_Contracts_for_Trade_Finance.

Garg R, 2021b. Blockchain based identity solutions. *International Journal of Computer Science & Information Technology*. (In Press).

Garg R, 2022a. Distributed ecosystem for identity management. *Journal of Blockchain Research*, 1 (1). (In Press).

Garg R, 2022b. Decentralized Transaction Mechanism Based on Smart Contracts. 3rd International Conference on Blockchain and IoT, Sydney Australia. doi: 10.5281/ zenodo.5708294. https://www.researchgate.net/publication/325336102_ Decentralized_Transaction_Mechanism_based_on_Smart_Contracts.

Irwin AS and Turner AB, 2018. Illicit Bitcoin transactions: Challenges in getting to who, what, when and where. *Journal of Money Laundering Control*, 21: 297–313.

Kumar S, Mookerjee V, and Shubham A, 2018. Research in operations management and information systems interface. *Production and Operating Management*, 27: 1893–1905.

Lin T, Yang X, Wang T, Peng T, Xu F, Lao S, Ma S, Wang H, and Hao W, 2020. Implementation of high-performance blockchain network based on cross-chain technology for IoT applications. *Sensors*, 20: 3268.

Mainelli M, 2017. Blockchain Will Help Us Prove Our Identities in a Digital World. *In Blockchain: The Insights you need from*. Catherine Tucker (ed) Harvard Business Review Digital Article, 2–6.

Mills D, Wang K, Malone B, Ravi A, Marquardt J, Chen C, Badev A, Brezinski T, Fahy L, and Liao K, 2016. Distributed Ledger Technology in Payments, Clearing, and Settlement. *Finance and Economics Discussion Series, 1-34*. https://doi.org/10.17016/ FEDS.2016.095. Accessed on 19 June 2020.

OptionRoom, 2022. https://www.optionroom.finance.

Panarello A, Tapas N, Merlino G, Longo F, and Puliafito A, 2018. Blockchain and IoT integration: A systematic survey. *Sensors*, 18: 2575.

Park JH, 2017. Blockchain security in cloud computing: Use cases, challenges, and solutions. *Symmetry*, 9: 164.

Sanghvi N, 2018. The Truth about Reliance and India's First Blockchain Transaction. https://coincrunch.in.

Securities and Exchange Commission, 2010. https://www.sec.gov.

Statista, 2021. Global Consumer Survey: https://www.statista.com.

Stefan C, 2018. Tales from the Crypt: Might Cryptocurrencies Spell the Death of Traditional Money? A Quantitative Analysis. Proceedings of the International Conference on Business Excellence, Bucharest, Romania, 12: 918–930.

Surowiecki J, 2005. *The Wisdom of Crowds. Paperback*. Abacus Publishers.

Verstein A, 2017. Enterprise without entities. *Michigan Law Review*, 116 (2): 247.

The Wire, 2019. https://www.wired.com.

Wu H, Li Z, King B, Ben Miled Z, Wassick J, and Tazelaar J, 2017. A distributed ledger for supply chain physical distribution visibility. *Information*, 8: 137.

11

Growing Landscape of Blockchain

11.1 Blockchain Applications in Real World: An Overview

The legacy system allowed central authorities, banks, stock exchanges, and other trusted intermediaries to become indispensable in all spheres of life, from registration of birth to education, employment, finance, and land acquisition; and with the passage of time, they transformed from middlemen to gatekeepers. They restrict access, charge for everything, create friction, stifle innovation, and consolidate their dominance.

In such a setting, blockchain can neither promise to make a user a billionaire overnight, nor can it provide a way to protect his financial activities from politically motivated governments. But what is certain is that it can significantly reduce the cost of trust through a radical, decentralized approach to accounting and provides an innovative way to structure economic organizations.

Thus, blockchain has unlimited applications for almost every industry in the real world. Ledger technology can be applied to verify credentials or track one's past in education or finance; it can also securely share patient's medical records among health-care professionals and serve to track intellectual property for scientists, researchers, and authors. At present, blockchain is mostly used in the financial sector, but there are many traditional industries where blockchain-based solutions provide an exceptional functionality (see Figure 11.1; Table 11.1; Garg, 2021a, 2021b):

11.2 e-Governance

Many countries around the world have developed their own e-governance systems to facilitate vital services to their citizens. In most countries, these systems suffer from privacy and security issues. Although many scholars have attempted

Blockchain for Real World Applications, First Edition. Rishabh Garg.
© 2023 John Wiley & Sons, Inc. Published 2023 by John Wiley & Sons, Inc.

Figure 11.1 Applications of blockchain technology in real world.

to address the security challenges in the e-governance system, most of the existing frameworks and models do not meet the security requirements. Furthermore, the lack of trust in internet-mediated transactions and unauthorized access to the system by insiders cannot be discounted. In this view, the use of blockchain technology appears to be the only option to address these inadequacies. It assures safe, efficient, and better public service.

Over the past four to five years, hundreds of blockchain projects have been assembled to replace government systems (see Figure 11.2) in more than thirty countries. Estonia has implemented blockchain-enabled ID for identity verification of citizens (see Table 11.2). In Australia and Ukraine, it is being used to build electronic voting systems. The United States is using blockchain to securely share medical information, and the United Kingdom is improving public services. The distributed ledger is being used to manage land registers in Georgia and Honduras (Myungsan, 2018).

Estonia uses digital ID as:

- legal travel IDs for Estonian citizens traveling within the EU
- national health insurance cards

Table 11.1 Blockchain applications across the real world.

Domain	Growing Landscape
1. Identity management	Government can implement all-purpose digital IDs to replace discrete ones – Driver's licenses, Passport, Voter's ID, etc.
2. Document storage and retrieval	All IDs – birth certificate, academic credentials, employment history, medical and life insurance, marriage certificate, proof of ownership, notarized documents, death certificate, available on one ID. Encrypted but shareable records.
3. Human resource management	Streamline the vetting and hiring processes more quickly.
4. Cybersecurity	Eliminating the need for human intermediaries, reducing the threat of hacking, corruption, or human error.
5. Government services	Offers "smart cops" and upgrades the law department. Promises transparent administrative system.
6. Electoral process (voting)	Provides robust infrastructure for casting, tracking, and counting of votes. Eliminates the need for recounts, bogus voting, and foul plays.
7. Legal enforcements	Rationalizes evidence-handling process. Governments can monitor transactions and stop money laundering.
8. Public records	Lessens paper-based processes, minimizes fraud, and increases accountability. Government can keep records of all the legislation reports in a meticulous way.
9. Public assistance	Identifies poor, needy, or refugees and provides humanitarian assistance in a secure and private manner.
10. Welfare distribution and civil supplies	Plugs the system leakages for direct benefit transfer.
11. Postal services	Simplifies ID-linked QR codes and tracking system that reduces costs and saves time in sorting.

(Continued)

Table 11.1 (Continued)

	Domain	Growing Landscape
12.	Bills and payments	Government can automate the traditional billing and payment systems through smart contracts.
13.	Taxation	Government can expedite the tax process and bring transparency in solving tax issues.
14.	Medical and healthcare	Allows hospitals, payers, and other parties in the healthcare to share access to their networks. Speeds up diagnosis and preserves patient's information. Offers better clinical support, more accurate diagnoses, more effective treatments, and more cost-effective care.
15.	Genomics	Shares raw DNA data files for research, stripping away the personal identifiers and sensitive information.
16.	Clinical trials	Finds better solutions during treatment phase through research and clinical trials.
17.	Pharmacology	Faster innovation, better-regulated production, and smarter medical data security. Creates a more efficient system.
18.	Vaccination and community health	Enables real-time visibility on supply management. Authenticate vaccine certificates.
19.	Medical claim settlements	Automates claim submission, review, approval or denial, and settlement.
20.	Insurance	Improves operational efficiency. Eliminates the risk of forgery. Drives down processing time and costs.
21.	Banking	Expedites the key services – clearance, cross-border payments and settlements, with enhanced accuracy. Stockades: annuities, bank deposits, bonds, equity, stocks, and derivatives in personal vaults. Eases transactions, like crowd funding, personal loans, mutual funds, provident funds, salaries, and pensions
22.	Loans and credits	Allows tokenized debts, P2P lending, and decentralized finance. Manages identity, risk, and credit scoring

23.	Stock trading and hedge funds	Automates and fortifies the process of buying, selling, and trading of the stocks more efficiently.
24.	Crowd funding	Supports Initial Coin Offerings (ICOs).
		Disintermediates capital formation, direct fund creation.
25.	Trading	Provides a safe platform for cryptocurrency trading.
		Provide a higher level of security for assets.
26.	e-Commerce	Connects users with better merchandise.
		Promotes fairness in the digital markets.
		Maintains a shared, time-stamped record of flow of goods during shipping and delivery.
		Ensures proof of delivery and tracks contract details without the risk of data being altered.
27.	Accounts and Audit	Mechanizes accounting services using AI.
		Helps auditors to accurately vet digital assets.
		Verifiable transactions make business accounting more transparent.
28.	Loyalty programs	Allows loyalty incentives to facilitate exchange across multiple sectors and myriad point of sales.
29.	Retail and Consumer Packages Goods (CPG)	Collaborates manufacturers, brands, retailers, third-party sellers, content providers, and consumers, without a middleman.
30.	Prediction markets and forecasts	Applies machine learning algorithms to cultivate targeted predictions and insights.
31.	Shipping and goods transport	Improves transactions and shipment tracking
		Protects assets and increase fleet efficiency.
32.	Public Transport, travel and mobility	Stores and shares information on vehicle efficiency.
		Maintains timeline.
		Connects passengers with better quality transport.

(Continued)

Table 11.1 (Continued)

	Domain	Growing Landscape
33.	Ride hailing	Creates a more user-driven and value-oriented marketplace.
34.	Air travel	Keeps accurate logs of aircraft maintenance. Prevents overbooking.
35.	Distributed resources and Internet of Things	Support devices to connect, interact, and transact without a central authority. Manages software updates, bugs, or energy management. Better system to deal with operational challenges
36.	Information and communication	Implements sharing models for the leasing of networks. Manage contracts to co-build 5G infrastructure. Automates the negotiation, settlement, and implementation of service-level agreements with roaming coverage partners in multiple countries.
37.	Messaging	Eliminates third-party surveillance.
38.	Hospitality	Eases booking and selling process. Removes middlemen. Seamless access to hotel rooms, banquets, and rental cars.
39.	Entertainment	Modernizes entertainment channels and ensures better artist value. Enables encoding, storage, and distribution via streaming.
40.	Gaming	Provides high-end technology for gaming. Offers uniform fields for competitions, rewards, and exchanges across digital spaces.
41.	Food and beverages	Tracks the origins of food through a QR code. Reveals a product's full journey from farm to fork.
42.	Fishing	Makes the industry more sustainable, eco-friendly, and legally compliant. Divulges full life-cycle from bait to plate.

#	Category	Description
43.	Animal husbandry	Unveils animal's genomic profile, the feed it was provided, and its medical history. Improves food safety, traceability, and sustainability. Advances breeding and raising of livestock.
44.	Agriculture and natural resources	Safeguards transactions, market expansions, and product-specific logistics throughout the supply chain. Digitizes buying, selling, and storage of grain.
45.	Infrastructure and energy	Promotes decentralized energy generation schemes. Allows people to generate, buy, and sell energy to their neighbors.
46.	Manufacturing	Enables smart manufacturing. Optimizes time, speed, and reduces costs.
47.	Real estate (Land registration, title-ownership, and transfer)	Preserves Land and property titles, registration, business license. Tracks and transfers land titles, property deeds, liens, etc.
48.	Construction	Tracks the source of material and construction progress across multiple teams. Automates timely payments as per project milestones.
49.	Automotives	Tracks vehicle's history, including lease and insurance. Verifies genuine spare parts on the basis of product life cycle.
50.	Wills and Inheritances	Automates compliance of an inheritance trust to beneficiaries upon confirmation, eliminating the need of courts. Executes power of attorney, contracts, trusts, mortgages, and wills.

Figure 11.2 Applications of blockchain technology across government departments.

Table 11.2 Use of blockchain across different countries.

United Nations	Distribution of aid
Georgia	Land registration
UK	Welfare payments
Estonia	Identity management, e-voting, health records
Singapore	Interbank payments
United States (Delaware)	Smart contracts, public archives

- proof of identification when logging into bank accounts
- digital signatures
- an instrument for i-Voting
- a tool to e-Prescriptions, check medical records, submit tax claims, etc.

11.3 Supply Chain Management

There are billions of products being manufactured and supplied daily through complex supply chains spanning every corner of the globe. However, little is known about when and where these products are originated, manufactured, and used through their life cycle. Even before reaching the end-consumer, goods travel through a vast network of retailers, distributors, transporters, warehousing facilities, and suppliers, who participate in the design, production, distribution, and sale. However, in almost every case, this journey remains an unsolved riddle to the consumer (Jessi, Jutta, and Wood, 2016).

Supply chains are becoming increasingly more complex, more elaborate, and more global. An event in one corner of the world can stop production, distribution, or supply in another corner. When service delivery is disrupted or affected due to a critical factor (natural phenomenon, infrastructure failure, or counterfeit products), not only the supply chain, but the entire economy collapses. Not only do producers, sellers, distributors, consignees, and warehouses suffer financial loss, but it also affects the daily life of a consumer.

Thus, supply chain visibility is a major business constraint that causes most companies to have little or no information about their second- and third-tier suppliers. Incorporating transparency and visibility into the end-to-end supply chain can help in the flow of products from raw materials to manufacturing, testing, and supply of end products. This can lead to remedial measures by performing new types of analysis for operations, visibility, and sustainability.

However, operations and visibility, i.e. maintaining the flow of information about each product among all relevant parties requires a high level of accuracy in data collection and security in data storage. Currently, this responsibility is performed by a handful of government entities, nonprofit organizations, or a third party with a centralized information depository. As a unit of manufacturing system, such organization may misuse information with intent to coerce or harm either party. In addition, such agencies must have the technical capabilities to effectively store and handle the sensitive business information.

Sustainability standards and certifications pose another concern for supply chain management. Certification marks, such as ISO, ISI, FPO, Eco-mark, Organic, and Fair-trade are becoming vital tools to provide consumers with a better understanding of the product life cycle (Baier, 2005; Elder, Zerriffi, and Le Billon, 2013). However, the end result is just a hallmark or logo of certification printed on the products, assuring the common consumer that the government and the company have manufactured the product with utmost integrity. Although the cost of this certification is also borne by the consumer out of his own pocket, the consumer neither understands the meaning of such authentication nor can verify this information as the veracity of such claims made by these certificates is a costly affair, which requires rigorous auditing. Besides, such standards may exemplify an abuse of trust in the event of collusion between certification agencies and business establishments.

The adoption of blockchain technology in the supply chain can promise better output. A shared, consensus-based public ledger can be deployed for the supply chain to track the origins and processes associated with the product (Zhao et al., 2018). Blockchain can provide certification and documentation, including product lifecycle data, used in supply chain management, and make them accessible to all parties at once. Products can be tracked from factory to storage, transit, delivery, and sale. This can streamline the processes of product tracking and timely payment, and build trust between suppliers and customers.

A blockchain may have several types of authorities and trade associates. The registrar provides a unique identity by registering the participants on the network. The standards organization sets or defines the standards for a product to be supplied by a manufacturing agency. An authenticator provides certificates based on their credentials to participants, such as manufacturers, distributors, consignees, warehouse in-charges, retailers, and waste management organizations, which allows them to write about the product specific data onto the blockchain. An overview of the proposed application of blockchain in the supply chain for manufacturing systems is shown in Figure 11.3.

In a manufacturing system, as the product progresses through its life cycle, it passes through different trade holders or business entities – manufacturer, supplier, producer, distributor, retailer – and finally reaches the end-consumer. Each of these units can write the relevant information of the product on a real-time

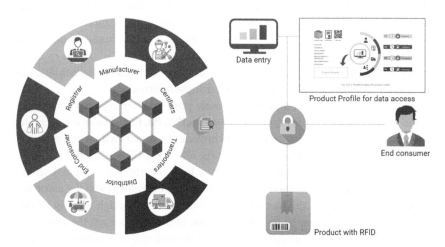

Figure 11.3 Blockchain for supply chain management.

basis on the network. This will create a unique digital profile of each product, and the pertinent information shall be displayed, from time to time, during every stage of the product life cycle. In order to streamline this process, a barcode, RFID, or QR code may be printed on each item, giving the product a virtual identity on the network. The code will be generated from a unique digital cryptographic identifier that will represent the digital profile of the product on the system software.

Trade holders can register themselves as blockchain participants on the network through a registrar, to obtain credentials and a unique identity. Consequent upon registration, a pair of public and private cryptographic keys is generated for each participant – the public key identifies the participant within the network, and the private key authenticates the participant to transact with the system. Trading parties can interact with the network only by cryptographically authenticating themselves with their private keys. This ensures each product to be digitally signed by the concerned business party while being exchanged or moved forward in the supply chain.

The digital profile of business entities on the network that they may have created at the time of registration will display information, such as business identity, location, and certification of the entity concerned. While the system allows participants to remain completely anonymous to maintain the confidentiality of their profile, the entity shall be authenticated by a registrar or an auditor in order to maintain trust in the system. Now, whenever a business partner puts its signature on the product, it will be linked to the profile of that business entity.

Each stakeholder using the system can access a specific network of blockchain through a user interface. The software application used by the stakeholder may be developed by a group of trusted parties and configured to suit the specific requirements of the product. Each consumer will have a customized version of the user interface from which they can access data pertaining to the product. The system software, through the options provided, can surf a new product or access the existing one. This software can run on a blockchain that allows program code to be executed, such as the Ethereum blockchain (Buterin, 2014).

The set of rules governing the system, written in code, determine how stakeholders in the network will interact and how data will be shared between networks. Once rules are stored on the blockchain, they perform in strict compliance and cannot be changed. All transactions are stored on a blockchain and after verification, the participants of the system are allowed to access the data, depending on their jurisdiction and nature of work.

Under the certification and standards program, certifiers and auditors will visit the industrial unit and service area to inspect whether regulatory measures are being complied with or not. After physical testing and verification of the product, the auditor can digitally sign the profile to endorse the product. The entry so made will be accessible to all the participants after verification and will also maintain transparency in the system while preserving the integrity and security of the data.

11.3.1 Data Logging on Ledger

Each physical product in the proposed system can be digitally represented on a blockchain network so that all stakeholders of that product can have direct access to the product's profile. Data can be added by trade parties using their private keys. A software application allows stakeholders to write new entries for products, which may vary, depending on the nature and specifications of the product. Product-specific information may be shared to reflect certain features of the product or to communicate performance data to producers, manufacturers, and quality controllers. It may have information about the modern industrial process, nonharmful effect on the environment, carbon footprint, etc.

At a given time, a product can be in possession of only one unit. Only that entity can enter new information into the product's profile or collaborate with another party to perform the assigned task. When products are transferred from one participant to another, both parties sign a digital contract to authenticate the exchange. To sign this digital contract or registry, related parties use their private key, which helps to track a certified source of each information recorded on the blockchain.

The network will then refer it to its next stakeholders. Also, the former party's access to the product will be terminated, and now only the new party can create a new entry and update the product details. The transaction details will be updated on the blockchain after all parties sign the contract. In this way, the network will be able to create a complete history and transfer of each product on a real-time basis, which will be accessible to all the participants.

Thus, a chronological list of events can be logged on the blockchain network for the entire life cycle of a product, beginning with the merchant who supplied the raw material to the end-consumer (Verhoeven, Sinn, and Herden, 2018). Whenever a product is exchanged between two parties, the system creates a new entry in the product's profile to record the details of the transacting parties, and records the time of that entry as well. Since the system contains the location details of all the registered participants by default, it also records the location of the product every time a new entry is made. This information can typically be a unique location ID, or dynamic GPS data that can be applied across supply chains to determine the actual location of the product. In this way, blockchain provides a see-through window to everyone, from farm to fork, sharing comprehensive information on product specification, quality, real time, and location.

Some products can be programmed during their functioning span to broadcast their performance data on the blockchain. For example, a sports utility vehicle may be connected to the internet, autonomously uploading information related to its mechanical efficiency, sensor performance, high-speed driving, and maintenance costs to the blockchain. This information can help engine designers to make informed decisions about engine performance, electronic gadgets, and other equipment to make it cost-effective and improve the overall driving experience. Also, the customers will also get access to the performance of the vehicle in the long run.

11.3.2 Access to a Ledger

The ensuing image illustrates the template of a product profile, in which each entry is time stamped and digitally signed by business parties. Product-related certificates, time, location, and specific product details can all be recorded in the product's digital profile (see Figure 11.4). Certain terms and conditions may be embedded with the product profile in order to maintain control over access to the information. It allows each participant to authenticate themselves using their private key to access a product's profile, and the system allows that participant to access the profile to a specified extent.

For example, a product like tribal handicrafts may have a profile that details when the item was manufactured and where it was made. A distributor, retailer, or consumer who acquired the item would have access to these details but would not have the specific names of the tribe that produced the item. Whereas, a dealer or quality controller will have access to more information, such as the identity of the tribal group, the city where they carried out the crafting work, and the place from where they bought their raw materials.

In this way, business organizations involved in the design, manufacturing, production, and supply chain can integrate smart contracts to create a better ecosystem. This allows the system to detect fraud while securing transactions at all levels.

Figure 11.4   A sample template of a product profile.

11.4 e-Commerce

Data security is important for companies to obtain sensitive information like names, addresses, phone numbers, and other pertinent details of customers. Blockchain-based e-commerce platforms offer comprehensive security at every level, including wallet security.

The most widely used blockchain technology in e-commerce is Ethereum. It is a platform for e-commerce brands who want to manage their own blockchain through apps that accept Bitcoin payments. Blockchain ensures the security of millions of users of the e-commerce platform with private and confidential data. The rise of blockchain in the global financial landscape could disrupt the retail market as decentralized markets will be able to leverage large-scale pricing, real-time logistics, and cryptocurrency transactions on blockchain. Perhaps this is the reason why many companies encourage startups to come forward and strengthen the brand management system of retailers, secure the flow of international trade, reduce the ubiquitous fees associated with financial transactions, and introduce loyalty programs on blockchain-based e-commerce. The introduction of block-chain technology into the supply chain will help users to track their purchase orders, store products, and service warranties, and gain access to the data.

One of the major benefits of blockchain technology is that it allows retailers to combine services, such as payment processing, inventory management, product detailing, etc. to save on the expense of purchasing and maintaining separate systems. It also deducts charges levied by banks for debit transactions or for payment processing by credit card companies. Since blockchain transactions are basically instant and do not go through traditional banks, purchases can be made directly, which means faster order fulfillment for customers.

Blockchain is also known as chain code. It can store smart contracts, which can automate tasks based on predetermined rules and statements, such as automated payments or inventory management. It is helpful especially for those products that have a limited time frame, such as food products or medicines. Blockchain can ensure the validity and quality of inventory and assure customers that they are getting the value of their money.

For example, you buy an LED TV and pay its price through a blockchain. You get a receipt in the form of a virtual contract. Accordingly, the retailer sends you the LED by a specified delivery date, and if it does not arrive on time, the blockchain issues a refund of your deposit. If you receive the LED, the blockchain issues your entire payment to the retailer. In return, the blockchain stores the cash-receipt and warranty proof it receives. In case of LED failure, it becomes easy to verify owner-ship and warranty based on the bill and warranty card stored on the blockchain.

Thus, blockchain appears to be a promising technology for e-commerce mar-ketplaces as it provides round-the-clock security to online databases. In a time where cybercriminals are highly innovative, this new age technology can provide a collaborative and user-friendly platform to traders and customers.

Blockchain based e-Commerce App

11.4.1   Backend

Sample database

```
const mongoose = require('mongoose');

mongoose.connect(
    'mongodb+srv://rishabh1234:rishabh@blockchain-ecommerce.
up78i.mongodb.net/blockchain-ecommerce?retryWrites=truea
ndw=majority', { useNewUrlParser: true,
useUnifiedTopology: true }
);

const paymentSchema = new mongoose.Schema({
    id: String,
    itemId: String,
    paid: Boolean
});

const Payment = mongoose.model('Payment', paymentSchema);

module.exports = {
    Payment
}
```
Code Cell 11.1   e-Commerce app (Backend).

Server

```
const Koa = require("koa");
const Router = require("@koa/router");
const cors = require("@koa/cors");
const ethers = require("ethers");
const PaymentProcessor = require("../frontend/src/
contracts/PaymentProcessor.json");
const { Payment } = require("./db.js");
```
Code Cell 11.2   e-Commerce app (Server.js file).

```
const app = new Koa();
const router = new Router();

router.get("/api/getPaymentId/:itemId", async ctx => {
    const paymentId = (Math.random() * 10000).
toFixed(0);
    await Payment.create({
        id: paymentId,
        itemId: ctx.params.itemId,
        paid: false
    })
    ctx.body = {
        paymentId
    };
});

const items = {
    '1': { id: 1, url: 'http://UrlToDownloadItem1' },
    '2': { id: 1, url: 'http;//UrlToDownloadItem2' }
}

router.get("/api/getItemUrl/:paymentId", async ctx => {
    const payment = awaitPayment.findOne({ id: ctx.
params.paymentId });
    if (payment andand payment.paid === true) {
        ctx.body = {
            url: items[payment.itemId].url
        }
    } else {
        ctx.body = {
            url: ''
        }
    }
})

app.use(cors()).use(router.routes()).use(router.
allowedMethods());
```

Code Cell 11.2 (Continued)

```
app.listen(4000, () => {
    console.log("Server started");
});


const listenToEvents = () => {
    const provider = new ethers.providers.
JsonRpcProvider('http://localhost:9545');
    const networkId = '5777';

    const paymentProcessor = new ethers.Contract(
        PaymentProcessor.networks[networkId].address,
        PaymentProcessor.abi,
        provider
    );

    paymentProcessor.on('PaymentDone', async(payer,
amount, paymentId, date) => {
        console.log(`
        from ${payer}
        amount ${amount}
        paymentId ${paymentId}
        date ${(new Date (date.toNumber()*1000)).
toLocaleString()}
        `);

        const payment = await Payment.findOne({ id:
paymentId });
        if (payment) {
            payment.paid = true;
            await payment.save();
        }
    });
}
listenToEvents();
```

Code Cell 11.2 (Continued)

11.4.2 Smart Contracts

Cryptocurrency (Dai) minting

```solidity
// SPDX-License-Identifier: BITS
pragma solidity ^0.8.0;

import '@openzeppelin/contracts/token/ERC20/ERC20.sol';

contract Dai is ERC20 {
    constructor() ERC20('Dai Stablecoin', 'DAI')
public {}
    function faucet(address to, uint amount) external {
        _mint(to, amount);
    }
}
```

Code Cell 11.3   Smart contract for currency minting.

Migrations

```solidity
// SPDX-License-Identifier: BITS
pragma solidity >=0.4.22 <0.9.0;

contract Migrations {
  address public owner = msg.sender;
  uint public last_completed_migration;

  modifier restricted() {
    require(
      msg.sender == owner,
      "This function is restricted to the contract's
owner"
    );
    _;
  }

  function setCompleted(uint completed) public
restricted {
    last_completed_migration = completed;
  }
}
```

Code Cell 11.4   Deployment of smart contract by the owner.

Payment processor

```solidity
// SPDX-License-Identifier: BITS
pragma solidity ^0.8.0;

import '@openzeppelin/contracts/token/ERC20/IERC20.sol';

contract PaymentProcessor {
    address public admin;
    IERC20 public dai;

    event PaymentDone(
        address payer,
        uint amount,
        uint paymentId,
        uint date
    );

    constructor(address adminAddress, address
daiAddress) public {
        admin = adminAddress;
        dai = IERC20(daiAddress);
    }

    function pay(uint amount, uint paymentId) external {
        dai.transferFrom(msg.sender, admin, amount);
        emit PaymentDone(msg.sender, amount, paymentId,
block.timestamp);
    }
}
```

Code Cell 11.5   Smart contract for Payments (transferring money to admin).

11.4.3   Ethereum Front-end

```javascript
import React from "react";
import { ethers, Contract } from "ethers";
import PaymentProcessor from "./contracts/
PaymentProcessor.json";
import Dai from "./contracts/Dai.json";
```

Code Cell 11.6   Ethereum (Frontend).

```
const getBlockchain = () =>
    new Promise((resolve, reject) => {
        window.addEventListener("load", async () => {
            if(window.ethereum) {
                await window.ethereum.enable();
                const provider = new ethers.providers.
Web3Provider(window.ethereum);
                const signer = provider.getSigner();

                const paymentProcessor = new Contract(
                    PaymentProcessor.networks[window.
ethereum.networkVersion].address,
                    PaymentProcessor.abi,
                    signer
                );
                const dai = new Contract(
                    Dai.networks[window.ethereum.
networkVersion].address,
                    Dai.abi,
                    signer
                );
                resolve({provider, paymentProcessor, dai});
            }
            resolve({provider: undefined, payment
Processor: undefined, dai:undefined})
        })
    })
    export default getBlockchain;
```

Code Cell 11.6   (Continued)

11.4.4   Currency Store

```
import React from 'react';
import {ethers} from 'ethers';
import axios from 'axios'
import { darkviolet } from 'color-name';

const API_URL = 'http://localhost:4000';
const ITEMS = [
```

Code Cell 11.7   Transacting on the dApp using Currency store.

```
    {
        id: 1,
        price: ethers.utils.parseEther('100')
    },
    {
        id: 2,
        price: ethers.utils.parseEther('200')
    }
];
function Store() {
    const buy = async item => {
        const response1 = await axios.get(`${API_URL}/
api/getPayment/${item.id}`);
        const tx1 = await dai.approve(paymentProcessor.
address, item.price);
        await tx1.wait();

        const tx2 = await paymentProcessor.pay(item.
price, response1.data.paymentId);
        await tx2.wait();

        await new Promise(resolve => setTimeout(resolve,
5000));

        const response2 = await axios.get(`${API_URL}/
api/getItemUrl/${response1.data.paymentId}`);
        console.log(response2);
    }
}
```

Code Cell 11.7 (Continued)

11.5 Distributed Resources and Internet of Things

On a blockchain-enabled IoT platform, one can select the data that is to be managed, analyzed, optimized, and shared among permitted customers and partners.

Smart devices in the IoT can be connected with each other through a distributed blockchain network (see Figure 11.5). Many functions have used blockchain to enable peer-to-peer communication in IoT. There has been a lot of research into designing blockchain-enabled IoT, from trade and finance to the synchronization of industrial and academic activities.

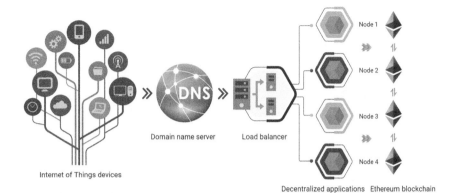

Figure 11.5 Blockchain enabled internet of things.

In blockchain, participants (miners) are required to solve a cryptographic puzzle through complex algorithms. Only the winner can write the block and reach a consensus with the rest of the miners. Such an approach is optimally scalable and secure but at the cost of computing resources and consensus speed.

Nodes in IoT are highly resource-limited, especially for computing and networking resources, making it extremely challenging for them to solve such complex puzzles and propagate blocks among all miners. In order not to degrade system performance, miners themselves can act as mining agents for nodes in the IoT, they can offload mining operations to nearby cloud-computing servers, or they can dynamically access networking resources on a hired basis. In this way, the usability of miners can be improved to enhance the performance of blockchain-enabled IoT.

If system performance is constrained due to users' service demands, computing capabilities, and networking resources, it can be increased by formulating users' access selection, computing resource allocation, and networking resource allocation as a combined optimization problem. A deep reinforcement learning approach can also address this problem.

The integration of blockchain and IoT systems can effectively assure efficiency as well as data security in IoT applications. To facilitate the use of blockchain on resource-limited IoT end devices, an algorithm can be used with a new leader selection scheme. The leader selection scheme is generated by a Deep Q-Network (DQN), which can select the leader in a variety of situations by taking advantage of limited system resources and balancing the load of the consensus mechanism across multiple IoT end devices.

This distributed consensus algorithm is based on RAFT, which helps reduce the disparities between different types of IoT end devices. This allows block consensus across a variety of IoT end devices and makes the consistency of the blockchain network more robust.

- It works on the idea of Distributed Energy Resources (DER).
- It can enhance system performance while maintaining system safety under high load conditions.
- Fifty percent of cost is due to administrative overheads in the supply chain mechanism
- It operates at the energy retail stage (energy generation, transmission, distribution, out of retail) of the power supply chain.
- It aims to move energy transfer and payment transactions via cryptotokens on a blockchain architecture.
- Market participants other than power companies own power plants and transmission lines.
- Companies sell electricity to these participants who, in turn, supply electricity to the end users.
- Grid+ uses smart agent, i.e. a computing device that hosts software for blockchain transactions, multisig cryptowallet with PKI security.
- Intelligent electricity is harnessed by coding efficient price options using smart contracts. The integration with IoT devices further strengthens the process.
- The ERC20 (fungible) token called BOLT is used for payment purposes
- To sign a transaction, two signatures out of MS1, MS2, MS3 are required.
- MS2 and MS3 are used to control smart agent.
- Smart agent escrow is used to hold tokens with some security deposit (in case of extra power consumption).

A few other use-cases of blockchain-based distributed resources and Internet of Things are enumerated as follows:

11.5.1 Tracking and Compliance

The ability to track products in transit is important for both safety and regulatory compliance. IoT data stored in shared blockchain ledgers facilitates all parties to see component provenance throughout a product's life cycle. This makes it safe, easy, and cost-effective to share all relevant information with regulatory agencies, shippers, and manufacturers.

11.5.2 Delivery Consignment

Freight transportation is a complex process involving different parties with different priorities. An IoT-enabled blockchain can store the temperatures, position, arrival times, and status of shipping containers as they move. An immutable blockchain helps all the parties to move products reliably, quickly, and efficiently by providing a uniform source of truth.

11.5.3 Maintenance Record

IoT devices also track the security status of critical machines and their maintenance. Blockchain provides a tamper-free ledger of operational data and consequent maintenance. Maintenance partners can continuously monitor the blockchain for preventive care and log their work directly on the blockchain. Operational records can also be shared with government entities and certification agencies to verify compliance.

11.6 Decentralized Streaming

Videos are engaging, educational, and empowering, but for companies, their streaming is extremely expensive, and live streams are even more expensive because broadcasters who distribute video over the internet have to transcode it first. This is the reason why video streaming accounts for 80% of all internet bandwidth.

The biggest cost video broadcasters incur is transcoding, which is the process of converting and reformatting raw video to ensure that it can be played on multiple devices and wide network bandwidth for an immersive experience. This process, for a cloud service like Amazon, costs from about US$3 per stream per hour to US$4500 per month for a media server. With the advent of 4K video, VR streaming, Ultra-HD, etc. the demand for video services has grown rapidly, replacing traditional and broadcast channels on the Internet. Video infrastructure needs more scalable and affordable solutions to keep pace with the upcoming demands.

Livepeer aims to revolutionize the video transcoding market by giving broadcasters access to a myriad of distributed processors, allowing app developers to produce video within an accessible, secure, and cost-effective architecture. It is a scalable platform for those who want to make their projects more captivating and engaging by adding on-demand or live video; those who want to stream content, such as educational clips, coding, gaming, video, entertainment, etc.; and those with larger audiences and higher streaming bills or infrastructure overheads. The company provides a decentralized video streaming infrastructure built on the Ethereum blockchain that aims at a market similar to Amazon's Twitch and Google's YouTube, to increase the reliability of video streaming and reduce the associated costs up to 50 times.

Central to its dogma is a Livepeer Token (LPT) used for video transcoding and distribution over the network. The more LPT a user has, the more work he can perform on the network against a fee. LPT is used to secure the Livepeer network and coordinate tasks for participants that support the video encoding process.

11.6.1 Operative Mechanism

There are two major components in the Livepeer network that ensure the quality of the live stream – the orchestrator and the delegate.

11.6.1.1 Orchestrator

Any user who operates the software by connecting to Livepeer's network is called an orchestrator. The orchestrator contributes his computer resources to serve broadcasters and developers for video transcoding and distribution. To do this, they are paid in the form of cryptocurrencies, such as ETH, or a stablecoin pegged to the US dollar, such as Dai. But in order to earn the right to perform this type of work on the network, the orchestrator must first earn Livepeer Token. It is important to note that LPT is a protocol token, which coordinates the distribution of work over the network. It is not a means of exchange tokens to pay for services within the Livepeer protocol.

11.6.1.2 Delegators

Livepeer (2022) believes that not all LPT holders may have the expertise or computing power required to perform the role of orchestrator. Thus, another group of participants in the Livepeer protocol, called Livepeer delegators, play a lesser but equally important role within the protocol. Delegators choose to stake their tokens on the orchestrator they believe is contributing to quality and honest work in the video-transcoding process. Tokens once placed are locked in for some time and then can be withdrawn after some time or spent on betting for another orchestrator. This helps in ensuring the security of the network.

11.6.1.3 Participation Rewards

When a user pays a fee to the network for a video broadcast, both the orchestrator and the delegator earn a portion of that fee as a reward. This earned fee, payable in ether or a stablecoin, such as Dai, is directly proportional to the stake of LPT orchestrators and delgators in the Livepeer protocol. Livepeer also mints new tokens over time, much like Bitcoin and Ethereum block rewards, which are divided among delegators and orchestrators after every 5760 Ethereum blocks, which Livepeer refers to as a round. In Ethereum, one block is mined at an average of 15.21 seconds, which means one Livepeer round lasts about 24.33 hours (a little more than a day).

According to livepeer.org, if the rate of inflation is 0.02185% as on March 2022 and there is a total supply of 24,918,514.38 Livepeer tokens, all participants will receive a total of 5,444.7 newly minted Livepeer tokens during the next round. In Livepeer, the inflation rate is adjusted automatically, depending on how many tokens are at stake out of the total circulating supply. As of March 2022, the total supply of Livepeer tokens is 24,918,514.38, and 12,559,303.81 of them have a participation rate of 50.4%. For a healthy trade-off between network security and token liquidity, the protocol encourages participation by raising the inflation rate to 0.00005% in each round if the participation rate is below 50%, and so does a reduction of 0.00005% for each round, if the participation rate is above 50%.

11.6.2 Video Mining

How does video mining work?

Run a node on the Livepeer network that advertises the price it will charge for video transcoding. Continue your cryptocurrency mining with your GPUs (see Figure 11.6).

When video encoding jobs come your way, the Livepeer node routes the tasks to your GPUs, and the encoding leverages a different part of the GPUs than the mining, so the mining can also continue with minimal hashrate loss. No opportunity cost!

Pre-requisites: in order to become a video miner, one must have a GPU with video-encoding chips; access to affordable bandwidth from an internet service provider; and the ability to run a blockchain-enabled Livepeer node continuously (24/7).

Most of the media server solutions available in the market are proprietary and not open source. Being developed by a single company, these come with a high

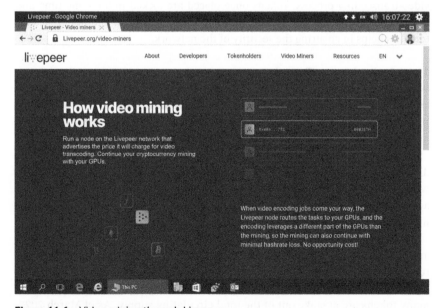

Figure 11.6 Video mining through Livepeer.

cost or license fee. If open-source solutions are available, they are usually incomplete, outdated, or require an upgrade to a proprietary service package to get the full set of features.

Livepeer Media Server is an open-source media server capable of taking input streams of live video and audio and transcoding them into alternate encodings. It translates live videos into different bitrates, and transmuxes them into various delivery formats. This is necessary so that the recorded video in one format and bitrate can stream over any platform and any device, irrespective of format and bandwidth specifications.

Because the Livepeer media server is a core component of the economically efficient protocol and network, its development is financed by the protocol itself. The media server can be used as a standalone component in any media-streaming application. In fact, it is a powerful tool that operates within the Livepeer network. Features like peer review and community contributions make it truly open source and transparent.

11.6.2.1 Dual Mining

Dual mining is the technique of completing two sorts of work with the same hardware. The term first appeared in the context of PoW mining, where it refers to the simultaneous mining of multiple cryptocurrencies using the same GPU to execute PoW hashing algorithms. Dual mining may still be viable on the Livepeer network, which entails using GPUs to mine cryptocurrency like Ethereum while also using the GPU to transcode video as a video miner on the network.

Dual mining can be used to first, increase GPU utilization, which is especially important for Livepeer video miners because, unlike other blockchain networks, the GPU does not always have work to do in the Livepeer network, and second, using existing GPUs creates a new revenue stream. One of the advantages of employing transcoding as a second strain in dual mining is that it uses less GPU cores than other possible workloads because much of the heavy lifting is done by the GPU's hardware encoder and decoder. More information on the separation of video encoding and decoding from GPU cores may be found in the Nvidia video encoding and decoding documentation (Nvidia, 2022).

11.6.2.2 Trade-offs and Considerations

When dual mining, there are a few considerations and issues to consider:

- VRAM is likely to be the limiting constraint for transcoding capacity in most circumstances. The more VRAM utilized by the other activity (ethash mining), the fewer streams that can be transcoded at the same time. When dual mining, GPUs with higher VRAM will have more transcoding capacity.
- Between the two workloads, there is still a performance trade-off. For example, as more streams are transcoded at the same time, the hash rate for ethash

mining will fall linearly. The usage of CUDA MPS with newer generation GPUs can assist lessen the rate at which hash rate drops – for more information, read the dual mining tutorial (Livepeer, 2022).

- If you're only transcoding right now, dual mining another cryptocurrency will take more power on your GPU, particularly if the second cryptocurrency employs a PoW hashing algorithm. When contemplating dual mining, the cost of electricity and cooling for your GPU should be taken into account.
- Based on past tests, if you're just mining a cryptocurrency like Ethereum right now, transcoding is unlikely to boost your GPU's power consumption.

11.6.2.3 Earnings
Orchestrators are compensated for video transcoding services with LPT awards and ETH fees. Note that transcoders who participate in pools are reimbursed according to the pool's rules.

11.6.2.4 Rewards
Every day, an orchestrator collects incentives, depending on its total stake (which includes its own self-delegated stake as well as the stakes of its delegators). The block reward in PoW blockchains like Bitcoin is equivalent to these incentives.

- Staking more LPT is one way to gain greater prizes.
- Stake delegation from delegators might be attracted by performing well on the leaderboard at https://explorer.Livepeer.org and performing efficiently in the network and earning money from broadcasters.
- Setting commission rates to distribute rewards and fees with delegators.

11.6.2.5 Fees
Fees are paid to orchestrators for the video transcoding services they give to broadcasters. An orchestrator will receive more money if it does more transcoding. These charges are similar to transaction fees on PoW blockchains like Bitcoin.

Staking more LPT or attracting stake delegation to provide more economic stability to broadcasters requires minimizing latency by providing access to hardware and bandwidth resources, and expanding geographic coverage – all ways to generate more fees.

11.6.2.6 Costs
Ethereum transaction fees, hardware costs, bandwidth charges, and electricity costs are all the costs incurred when working on the network.

11.6.2.7 Per Pixel Pricing
The value of payments is based on the number of pixels of video transcoded. Off-chain, orchestrators offer a price per pixel. Broadcasters filter and choose

orchestrators, based on a maximum price per pixel for transcoding that they are willing to spend.

The quantity of pixels transcoded will be affected by the video profiles requested by broadcasters. A greater number of video profiles, or more complicated video profiles, will necessitate more pixel transcoding and, as a result, more fees.

11.6.2.8 Probabilistic Micropayments

A probabilistic micropayment protocol is used to make payments.

Broadcasters offer orchestrators "lottery tickets" in exchange for transcoded results. Each "lottery ticket" has a face value, which is the amount paid to the orchestrator if the ticket wins, and a probability of winning.

Each ticket is viewed as a micropayment of the ticket's estimated value (calculated as: face value multiplied by probability that the ticket will win).

Orchestrators describe a necessary ticket expected value (EV) as the amount of work they are willing to undertake before requesting a ticket. If the ticket EV is 1000 gwei, for example, the orchestrator is willing to accomplish 1000 gwei of work before needing a ticket. Because the default ticket EV in Livepeer is set to be reasonable (1000 gwei), orchestrator operators are urged to stick with it for the time being. Using a nondefault number may result in broadcasters eliminating an orchestrator from consideration due to the broadcaster's maximum ticket EV (which has a default that is set based on the default ticket EV).

Winning tickets will be redeemed on-chain by orchestrators for the face value of the tickets.

11.6.2.9 Automatic Price Adjustments

Orchestrators' default practice is to modify their advertised price per pixel automatically based on the projected overhead for redeeming a ticket. The expected transaction cost of a redemption transaction divided by the face value of the ticket expressed as a percentage is the overhead for redeeming a ticket. Given a 1000 Wei base price per pixel, for example:

The advertised price would be 1010 Wei if the overhead is 1%.
The advertised price would be 1200 Wei if the overhead is 20%.
The advertised price is 1500 Wei if the overhead is 50%.

The goal of this automatic price adjustment technique is to allow orchestrators to alter their prices dynamically to compensate for greater ticket redemption overheads when gas costs are high.

11.6.2.10 Transcoding Pools

Transcoding pools can be created thanks to the split orchestrator and transcoder architecture. These pools are similar to PoW mining pools, which delegate PoW hashing to one or more individual miners. Pool operators are orchestrator operators in the Livepeer network, while pool participants are transcoders. Because transcoding pools are not part of the core protocol, the specifics of how work in a pool is tracked and transcoders are reimbursed are up to the pool implementation.

Private and public pools are the two sorts of pools.

11.6.2.11 Private Pools
Only known transcoders are allowed to join in private pools depending on a set of criteria provided by the pool operator.

- Only transcoders run by the pool operator
- Only transcoders run by entities partnered with the pool operator
- Only transcoders that go through an identification process

11.6.2.12 Public Pools
Public pools allow any transcoder to participate.

11.6.2.13 Selection
The Livepeer network is an open marketplace where broadcasters can choose which orchestrators they want to send their work to, based on their preferences. The algorithm for picking orchestrators varies per broadcaster implementation, but all selection algorithms, including the default implementation in Livepeer, take into account the following factors:

- Economic security
- Latency

11.6.2.14 Economic Security
An orchestrator's economic security is evaluated by its total stake, which includes both its own self-delegated stake and the stakes of its delegators. Because the stake might be trimmed if the job is performed improperly, the more stake an orchestrator has, the more economic protection it provides to a broadcaster.

The default broadcaster implementation will favor orchestrators who provide more economic security, with the likelihood of an orchestrator receiving work proportionate to the orchestrator's stake in relation to the rest of the network's orchestrators. However, just because an orchestrator receives work does not guarantee that it will keep it; if the orchestrator does not fulfil the broadcaster's requirements for other selection considerations, the orchestrator can lose the work after being initially selected.

11.6.2.15 Latency
An orchestrator's latency is the whole time it takes for it to return transcoded results to a broadcaster. This includes the time it takes the broadcaster to upload

a segment to the orchestrator, the time it takes the orchestrator to transcode the segment (which includes network transit time between the orchestrator and transcoder in the case of a split orchestrator and transcoder), and the time it takes the broadcaster to download the transcoded results from the orchestrator. An orchestrator's latency is determined by its geographical closeness to the broadcaster, as well as its hardware resources, which influence transcoding speed and bandwidth resources, which influence upload/download speed.

After initial selection, the default broadcaster implementation will evaluate an orchestrator's latency to determine whether or not to continue transmitting work to the orchestrator. The default criterion is that the transcoded results be received in real time, which means that the round-trip time must be less than or equal to the segment duration. If an orchestrator who was initially chosen fails to achieve this condition, the broadcaster may discontinue working with them, allowing other orchestrators a chance to earn employment.

11.6.2.16 Other Considerations

The Livepeer selection method is improving over time, and the network may use a variety of selection techniques in the future. Selection algorithms may also take into account the following factors:

- Fees earned
- Reputation

Coming Up

Based on the growing fabric of blockchain, this chapter outlines applications of blockchain in all major real-world areas, including human resource management, e-governance, e-commerce, tracking, compliance, maintenance, goods delivery, etc.

We shall make an effort to comprehend its functionality in the following chapter. We will also discover how a blockchain network may be built to safeguard people's identities against hacks and theft, also how technology might make it possible for people to construct encrypted digital identities rather than having to come up with several usernames and passwords – and how these identities might facilitate chores in the real world.

References

Baier A, 2005. Organic Certification Process. *Review Literature and Arts of the Americas*, 8.

Buterin V, 2014. A Next-generation Smart Contract and Decentralized Application Platform. *Etherum White Paper*, 1–36.

Elder SD, Zerriffi H, and Le Billon P, 2013. Is fairtrade certification greening agricultural practices? An analysis of fairtrade environmental standards in Rwanda. *Jounal of Rural Studies*, 32: 264–274.

Garg R, 2021a. Global Identity through Blockchain. International Webinar on Blockchain. Scholars Park, India, 01–60. https://doi.org/10.13140/RG.2.2.27803.18728 https://zenodo.org/record/5122164#.YwIvD6BBzIU.

Garg R, 2021b. *Identidades de Soberania Própria*. Edições Nosso Conhecimento, Portuguese, 01–104. doi: 10.5281/zenodo.5647905.

Jessi B, Jutta S, and Wood G, 2016. Provenance White Paper. provenance.org. https://www.provenance.org/whitepaper.

Livepeer, 2022. https://docs.livepeer.org/video-miners/guides/dual-mining.

Myungsan J, 2018. Blockchain government – a next form of infrastructure for the twenty-first century. *Journal of Open Innovation: Technology, Market, and Complexity*, 4(1): 7. https://doi.org/10.1186/s40852-018-0086-3.

Nvidia, 2022. https://developer.nvidia.com/nvidia-video-codec-sdk.

Verhoeven P, Sinn F, and Herden T, 2018. *Examples from Blockchain Implementations in Logistics and Supply Chain Management: Exploring the Mindful Use of a New Technology*. Berlin Institute of Technology, Berlin Germany, 2 (3): 20.

Zhao H, Bai P, Peng Y, and Xu R, 2018. Efficient key management scheme for health blockchain. *CAAI Transactions on Intelligence Technology*, 3: 114–118.

12

Functional Mechanism

Blockchain can be used to create a platform that shields user identities from hacks and theft. Instead of having to generate numerous usernames and passwords, it might enable people to construct self-sovereign and encrypted digital identities.

12.1 Software Requirements

In blockchain applications, almost all of the software are open-source. However, most of these are intended to run on the Linux operating system. The most appropriate way to run these software on Windows is to use virtual machines or Docker containers, which enable such programs to run by providing a Linux environment. This does not hinder business applications in any way because financial services enterprises are already using a large number of Linux/UNIX-based servers for other applications (Garg, 2022a).

The most popular software platforms for permissioned blockchain applications are R3 Corda, an open-source platform with a commercial version, and Hyperledger Fabric, an open-source collaborative project by a group of major banks and technology giants. Due to the intrinsic constraints like Proof-of-Work, permissionless blockchains find it difficult to achieve high throughput; however, the permissioned systems do not face any difficulties on this score.

The technical elements and interfaces required for blockchain-based identity management are suggested by Garg (2022b) as follows:

- Native Android or Apple's mobile OS that runs on an iPhone. The app may be required for the user only or for verification by third-parties.
- IPFS for storing personally identifiable information (PII) of the user.
- NodeJS-programmed microservices.
- Public blockchain element.

Blockchain for Real World Applications, First Edition. Rishabh Garg.
© 2023 John Wiley & Sons, Inc. Published 2023 by John Wiley & Sons, Inc.

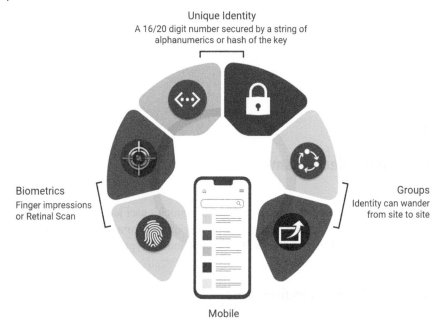

Unique Identity
A 16/20 digit number secured by a string of
alphanumerics or hash of the key

Biometrics
Finger impressions
or Retinal Scan

Groups
Identity can wander
from site to site

Mobile

Figure 12.1   Blockchain-enabled identity.

Thereafter, an account address can be created, using a unique private key to participate in the blockchain. The private key may be an alphanumeric password coupled to a random number, employing complex mathematical algorithms (see Figure 12.1). Though biometrics can be applied for identification, they can never be used to generate private keys, as fingerprints and retinal blood vessels may change over time.

12.2   Installing a Mobile Application

- The user must download the mobile app from the Google Play or Apple App Store.
- After installing the app on a smartphone, the user will create a profile on the app.
- Once the profile is created, the user will receive a unique ID number from the UDI authority, which will enable organizations to submit documents or request access to the identity documents of the user.

12.3 Fetching or Uploading the Documents

- On having the unique ID number, the user needs to fetch the government-issued IDs through the app that will be preserved in IPFS and have their hashed addresses retained in the blockchain (see Figure 12.2).
- In order for the user to self-certify their information, the program will reclaim personal information from these IDs.
- The users will now have the possession and control of their own data. It would help users to choose what information is to be shared with organizations. In order to share the specific details or required information, he will encrypt the information (hash of the credentials, in this case) and share the relevant public key to which it may concern (the government organization/service provider or verifier) for decryption. No information can be shared with any third party without the explicit consent of the user.
- In case of a newborn baby, the registrar of births and deaths would record the birth details and provide a 16-digit unique digital identification number (UDI).
- The family details viz. name of the child, date of birth, place, parents' name, address, and so on; together with biometric information (DNA map, finger impressions, retinal image, blood group, etc. as feasible) of the child shall be fetched from UDI database (in case of existing citizens) or may be uploaded through authorized service-providing agency (in case of newborn babies) and

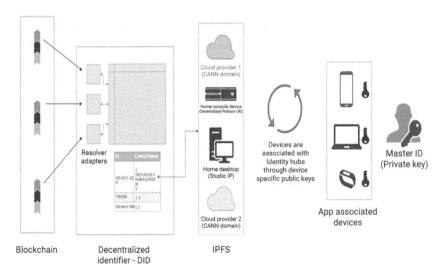

Figure 12.2 Blockchain for recording citizen data.

saved on IPFS. The biometric details would be updated after every five years until the child attains 15 years of age.

- Now, wherever he or she moves, may it be to school, medical center, job or market, this 16-digit ID number would serve as their roll number, enrollment number, registration number, bank account number, driver's license number, vehicle registration number, mobile number, LPG gas number, etc. No additional number would be required for any purpose (Garg, 2016). Even if the 16-digit ID becomes public, it cannot fetch the documents/information from the app unless gets access to the password. Further, the hacker cannot generate the private key from the password, as the former contains a random number that is autogenerated by the system.

- To share specific credentials, two approaches can be adopted: (i) One can send the respective hashes of all the credentials to the receiver, or (ii) they can compile the credentials into an object on the IPFS and send the root hash of the object. The root hash is generated by hashing the object entities employing the Merkle tree hash method.

- For example, if a child is to be admitted into a school, the parents (on behalf of the child) would share child's public key, along with the hashes of the respective credentials, with the school administration to allow access to the relevant details (name, father's name, mother's name, date of birth, nationality, etc., duly encrypted). The school will write all accomplishments, viz. participations, scholastic grades, add-ons, extracurricular attainments, sports, etc. of the candidate on the blockchain.

- On seeking transfer from one institution to another, the previous school would generate a transfer certificate through its authority key. An authority key is a private key, specific to an official holding a position of authority, which would be different from their individual private key (see Figure 12.3). As soon as the

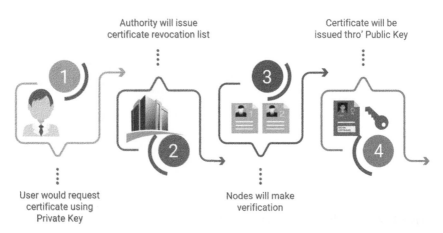

Authority will issue
certificate revocation list

Certificate will be
issued thro' Public Key

User would request
certificate using
Private Key

Nodes will make
verification

Figure 12.3 Endorsement of documents on user's profile.

child is admitted into the successive institution, their parents would share their public key with all pertinent details, and the new school administration would start writing on the blockchain. The school would write a revocation registry, which would prevent the student from being admitted in two institutions at a time.

- Often the postal department finds it difficult to provide quality service on time due to incomplete or incorrect addresses on the post or parcel received. If every citizen has a unique identification number, which can be entered on the portal of the Department of Posts, then the department will never require the name and address of the consignee or recipient. They can decode the address on the basis of that identification number and provide services at the registered address. Such services are already being used in a limited territorial range by the aviation department, supply-chain management, etc.

- During periodical censuses, the government can issue a notification to all citizens of the country to share their hashed data (encrypted with their private key), comprising most pertinent information, such as name, parent's name, address, date of birth, and educational qualifications with a public key to decrypt the same. The government should avoid gathering redundant information, which may serve as a honeypot for hackers.

- On attaining maturity, as per census records, the individual would automatically get the right to vote. Evidently, they would not require any separate EPIC (Garg, 2019). Since the blockchain would verify the electoral rights of those who have attained 18 on a day-to-day basis, no extra procedure would be required. On the day of polling, any citizen, who has attained 18 years of age, can log in through their password on dApp, anywhere in the world. Once they cast their vote, the account address would be disabled.

- For barely a few services like passports, where documents may be essential in paper form for visa or immigration procedures, there seems to be no valid argument for having a hard copy. For other services, this will simplify the procurement procedures too. As soon as the document is digitally issued by the authority, it will appear on the blockchain, and the user can store it in their IPFS. Since most of the services would be available online, clerks or proxies will seldom get an opportunity to make delays or expect bribes.

- If one visits a hospital, either as an outpatient or gets hospitalized, all chronic and major ailments shall be entered into IPFS so that doctors would be able to study the entire medical history of the patient, if required. This will help the patients to get better treatment (Garg, 2018).

- For all financial transactions, your UDI will be linked to only one object. Hence, it would be a matter of seconds to get the details of all deposits and borrowings, using the tree root hash. Wherever you go, be it a restaurant, club, shopping mall, or fly abroad, the ID-linked IPFS object would carry a statement of every penny you earn or spend. This would enable an honest taxpayer to display all their assets and liabilities before the income tax (IT) authority; even the IT authorities would have no reason to doubt their integrity. However, dishonest taxpayers would have bad days.

- In a similar way, documents pertaining to the property, occupation, financial history, medical records, health insurance, etc. can be maintained by creating a Distributed Hash Table (DHT) on a unique ID linked IPFS; and the hashes of the same can be encrypted using the public key of the user. These encrypted hashes will be operated, accessed, or retrieved through a Multipurpose Digital ID card.

One World – One Identity

- The multipurpose ID would carry the user's name, a QR code, and the user's photograph (see Figure 12.4). The card, on insertion into a card reader or a customized machine, shall display the DHT, comprising all the encrypted, hashed information of the objects and its sub-objects. The user can make access to the online documents using their private key.
- If somebody loses their multi-purpose ID, they can request the appropriate authority to issue a clone. This clone will be a vegetative copy (because no mutation is possible in blockchain) of the original ID. If an offender tries to steal

Figure 12.4   One World – One Identity.

someone's identity or reap the benefits thereof, they will not be able to do so as the entire information is encrypted through a private key (Garg, 2022c).

- On death, the registrar of births and deaths shall be informed. They would deactivate the unique ID for further use. In such cases, only the legal heir would be entitled to draw claims through nomination or power of attorney.

12.4 Government or Third-party Access

- The people who hold the identity will be notified whenever a government agency or other third party needs to access certain information about them for authentication purposes (see Figure 12.5).
- Once the user allows the third party to access their specific details, the said authority or entity can use the identifiable information only for authentication, and the user can track how their PII has been used.
- Blockchain does not hold any personal data or information of the user. The information is stored in the user's IPFS, and the transactions that are made between identity holder and third-party will only be visible on the blockchain.

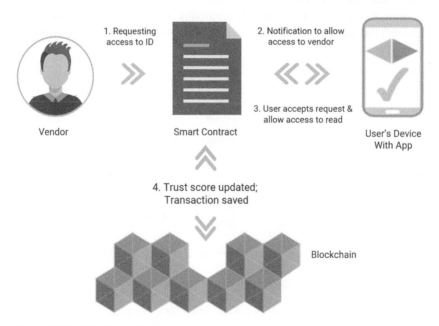

Figure 12.5   Third party access.

- For instance, if a passport authority uses a public key or an app to confirm a person's identity, that transaction will be published to the blockchain and made available to all associated nodes. Let us say "A" is a person who needs to prove their identity in order to apply for a visa. He will provide the hash of the object that contains all the required credentials (duly encrypted by A's private key and the authority's public key) to the authorities, enabling them to make access to the information. The authority will decrypt the hash of the object, using their authority key and A's public key. Now the verifying authority can examine the applicant's documents and record the outcome on blockchain. This is how the authorities can validate their identity instantly.

12.5   Credibility Through Smart Contracts

- Smart contracts with business logic can determine a credibility or trust score from the information provided by a user to form a self-sovereign identity. The higher the trust score, the higher the credibility of the individual. This can help organizations validate a user's identity on a real-time basis (see Figure 12.6; Garg, 2021).
- An initial user may be kept under observation for the initial semester (six months); allowing them to build the credibility. Through this period, they may furnish the required information and upload relevant credentials to establish

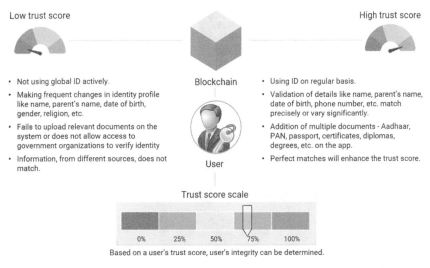

Figure 12.6   Rise and fall of trust score.

their identity. By uploading numerous documents to the app/IPFS, a user can raise their trust score.

- The system will verify if the details like name, parent's name, date of birth, etc. match precisely or vary significantly. Perfect matches will enhance the trust score.
- On the contrary, a user's trust score will decrease if he fails to upload the necessary documents into the system, denies access to government agencies for identity verification, or frequently changes their identity profile, particularly their name, parent's names, date of birth, gender, and religion.
- A user's trust score can also serve as a tool to determine whether their account is legitimate or suspicious.
- For instance, if a bank has to verify a person's credibility before lending them money, it can do so by looking at the user's trust rating. It will save time, money, and provide an insight to user's credibility.
- Since the object containing all information or transactions, would be protected by the user's private key, it's only the user who would be able to make access to the entire information. In the wake of suspicion or illegitimate activities or suppression of information, a competent authority, duly appointed as per provisions of law, shall ask the user to share the requisite hashed information, duly encrypted, along with the public key. If the user fails to share the pertinent information in a specified time period (say 15 days), the system will start dipping the user's trust score @ 20% for every ten days. As the trust score drops down, the users will find it difficult to make transactions. He'll have no alternative except to share the key. No sooner do they share their public key, the trust score would automatically be restored.

12.6 User-Optimized Features

- Each user who enrolls in the Blockchain Identity Management System will be provided with a unique ID that they can keep on their device with IPFS support.
- Since blockchain identity management systems employ smart contracts to share personal information rather than storing any user data, it completely rules out the possibility of any data manipulation. No exchange of user information can take place without the express permission of the user. It adds a layer of security to identity management.
- A blockchain identity management system does not store any user's data; rather it uses smart contracts to share the personal information, and hence data manipulation is not possible on the blockchain. No transaction of user's information can occur without the explicit consent of the user that adds security to identity management.

- No personal identity document of the users is stored in a centralized database. All documents that establish a user's identity are stored on their device, supported by IPFS, leaving sensitive information out of reach of hackers. Decentralization permits the propagation of data on every single node in the system, which decreases the likelihood of a single point of failure (SPoF).
- Irrespective of geographical boundaries, the users can get their identity verified across the globe.
- Blockchain ecosystem is user optimized. It is both cost and time effective.
- Blockchain allows every individual on its network to trace the transactions. Every transaction recorded on the blockchain has a verifiable authenticity. However, the identity of the person involved in transaction remains obscure.

References

Garg R, 2016. *Generic Information Tracker*, 2nd India International Science Festival, New Delhi, India, 2:1-34. doi: 10.5281/zenodo.4762602. https://zenodo.org/record/4762602#.YwG8_qBBzIU.

Garg R, 2018. Digital ID with Electronic Surveillance System. Innovation registered with National Innovation Foundation, Autonomous Body of Department of Science & Technology, Government of India. doi: 10.5281/zenodo.4760532. https://www.researchgate.net/publication/325247403_Digital_Identity_with_Electronic_Surveillance_System.

Garg R, 2019. Multipurpose ID: One Nation – One Identity, Annual Convention – Indian Society for Technical Education (ISTE). National Conference on Recent Advances in Energy, Science & Technology, 39. doi: 10.6084/m9.figshare.16945078. https://www.researchgate.net/publication/337398750_Multipurpose_ID_One_Nation_-_One_Identity.

Garg R, 2021. Blockchain based identity solutions. *International Journal of Computer Science & Information Technology*, (In Press).

Garg R, 2022a. Distributed ecosystem for identity management. *Journal of Blockchain Research*, 1 (1) (In Press).

Garg R, 2022b. Decentralized transaction mechanism based on smart contracts. 3rd International Conference on Blockchain and IoT, Sydney Australia. doi: 10.5281/zenodo.5708294. https://zenodo.org/record/5708294#.YwI5Z6BBzIU.

Garg R, 2022c. A Technological Approach to Address Deficiencies in UID (Aadhaar). 3rd International Conference on Big Data, Blockchain and Security, Copenhagen Denmark. doi:10.5281/zenodo.5854732. https://www.researchgate.net/publication/325247615_A_Technological_Approach_to_Address_Deficiencies_in_UID_Aadhaar.

Appendices

Full forms (elaborations) of the acronyms used in the book.

Abbreviation	Full form or Meaning
ABFT	Asynchronous Byzantine Fault Tolerance
AI	Artificial Intelligence
AML	Anti-money Laundering
APB	Advanced Peripheral Bus Bridge
API	Application Programming Interface
ASA	Authentication Service Agency
ASCII	American Standard Code for Information Interchange
ATM	Automated Teller Machine
AUA	Authentication User Agency
AWS	Amazon Web Services
B2B	Business-to-Business
B2C	Business-to-Consumer
BAT	Basic Attention Token
BCH	Bitcoin Cash
BCT	Blockchain Technology
BGP	Byzantine Generals Problem
BIP	Bitcoin Improvement Proposal
BLI	Breach Level Index
BNB	Build and Build (previously known as Binance Coin)
B/L	Bill of Lading
BTC	Bitcoin
BTC-SV	Bitcoin Cash – Satoshi Vision

Blockchain for Real World Applications, First Edition. Rishabh Garg.
© 2023 John Wiley & Sons, Inc. Published 2023 by John Wiley & Sons, Inc.

Abbreviation	Full form or Meaning
BTM	Bitcoin Teller Machine
CaaS	Containers as a service
CBS	Content-Based Storage
CCA	Central Competent Authority
CCP	Central Counter Parties
CDC	Centers for Disease Control and Prevention
CFT	Countering the Financing of Terrorism
CIDR	Central Identity Data Repository
CIS	Computer Information Science
CLS	Continuous Linked Settlement
CNN	Convolutional Neural Network
CPU	Central Processing Unit
CSD	Central Securities Depository
CSS	Cascading Style Sheet
CTOR	Canonical Transaction Ordering Route
CUDA	Compute Unified Device Architecture
CV	Curriculum Vitae
DAA	Difficulty Adjustment Algorithms
DAC	Decentralized Autonomous Corporations
DAG	Directed Acyclic Graph
DAO	Decentralized Autonomous Organization
dApps	Decentralized Applications
DBT	Direct Benefit Transfer
DDoS	Distributed Denial-of-Service
DeFi	Decentralized Finance
DER	Distributed Energy Resources
DES	Data Encryption System
DEX	Decentralized Exchange
DG	Digital Government
DHT	Distributed Hash Tables
DID	Decentralized Identifier
DLT	Distributed Ledger Technology
DNA	Deoxyribonucleic Acid
DNS	Domain Name System

Abbreviation	Full form or Meaning
DoS	Denial-of-service (attack)
DPI	DeFi Pulse Index
DPKI	Decentralized Public Key Infrastructure
DPoS	Delegated Proof-of-Stake
DQN	Deep Q-Network
DS	Directory Service
DSI	Digital Service Infrastructure
ECC	Elliptic Curve Cryptography
ECI	Election Commission of India
EDA	Emergency Difficulty Adjustment
EHR	Electronic Health Records
ENS	Ethereum Name Service
EOA	Externally Owned Account
EPIC	Electoral Photo Identity Card
ERC20	Ethereum Request for Comment 20
ERP	Enterprise Resource Planning
ESC	Enterprise Smart Contracts
ETH	Ethereum
ETHUSD	Ethereum USD cryptocurrency
ETO	Equity Token Offering
EU	European Union
EV	Expected Value
EVM	Ethereum Virtual Machine
EWF	Energy Web Foundation
FAO	Food and Agriculture Organization
FCA	Fabric Certificate Authority
FDA	Food and Drug Administration
FHIR	Fast Healthcare Interoperability Resources
FINTECH	Fusion of Finance and Technology
FIQ	Fast Interrupt Request
FIR	First Information Report
FPO	Follow on Public Offer
FPV	Full Payment Verification
GB£	Great Britain pound

Abbreviation	Full form or Meaning
GDPR	General Data Protection Regulation
GHOST	Greedy Heaviest Observed Subtree
GMP	GNU Multiple Precision Arithmetic Library
GPU	Graphics Processing Unit
HD	High Definition
HEI	Higher Education Institution
HIPPA	Health Insurance Portability and Accountability Act
HPL	Hyperledger Fabric
HTML	Hyper Text Mark-up Language
HTTP	Hyper Text Transfer Protocol
IA	Identity Attributes
IAM	Identity and Access Management
ICO	Initial Coin Offering
ID	Identity or Identifier
IDE	Integrated Development Environment
IDS	Intrusion Detection System
IEO	Initial Exchange Offering
IETF	Internet Engineering Task Force
IIT	Indian Institute of Technology
INR	Indian National Rupee
iOS app	iPhone Operating System
IoT	Internet of Things
IP	Internet Protocol
IPFS	Interplanetary File System
IPS	Intrusion Prevention System
ISI	Indian Standards Institute
ISO	International Standardization Organization
ISTE	Indian Society for Technical Education
JAM	Jan Dhan-Aadhaar-Mobile (trinity)
K	Thousand
KRW	South Korean Won
KSI	Keyless Signature Infrastructure
KYC	Know Your Customer
KYR	Know Your Resident

Abbreviation	Full form or Meaning
KYT	Know Your Transactions
LED	Light Emitting Diode
LP	Liquidity Provider
LPG	Liquified Petroleum Gas
LPT	LivePeer Token
MB	Megabyte
MIT	Massachusetts Institute of Technology
MITM	Man-in-the-middle (attack)
ML	Machine Learning
MP	Media Processing Service
MS	Multi-Signature, viz. MS1, MS2, MS3
Multisig	Multi Signature
N2N	Node-to-Node
NAT	Network Address Translation
NDI	National Digital Identity
NFT	Nonfungible Tokens
NGO	Nongovernment Organization
NIAI	National Identification Authority of India
NIF	National Innovation Foundation, Government of India
NIMC	National Identification Numbers (Nigeria and Georgia)
Nonce	Number only used once
NPR	National Population Register
NRI	Nomura Research Institute
OCI	Overseas Citizenship of India
OEM	Original Equipment Manufacturer
OOP	Object Oriented Programming
OSS	Open Source Software
OTC	Over-the-Counter/One Time Consent
OTP	One Time Password
P2P	Peer-to-Peer
PAN	Permanent Account Number (like US FTIN)
PBFT	Practical Byzantine Fault Tolerance
PID	Personal Identification Data/Proportional Integral Derivative
PII	Personal Identifiable Information

Abbreviation	Full form or Meaning
PIN	Personal Identification Number
PIOC	Person of Indian Origin Card
PKC	Public Key Cryptography
PKI	Public Key Infrastructure
PoA	Proof of Authority
PoS	Proof-of-Stake
PoW	Proof-of-Work
PP or PPC	Peercoin
QR	Quick Response
QRL	Quantum Resistant Ledger
RAFT	Reliable, Replicated, Redundant, and Fault-Tolerant
RBD	Registrar, Births and Deaths
RBF	Replacement-by-Fee
REP	Reputation Tokens
RFC	Remote Function Call
RFID	Radio Frequency Identification
RPC	Remote Procedure Call
RSA	Rivest Shamir Adelman
RTGS	Real Time Gross Settlement
RTI	Right-to-Information
SaaS	Software-as-a-Service
SCM	Supply Chain Management
SCP	Stellar Consensus Protocol
SDK	Software Development Kit
SHA	Secure Hash Algorithm
SLA	Service-Level Agreement
SPoF	Single Point of Failure
SPV	Simple Payment Verification
SQL	Structured Language Query
SSI	Self-Sovereign Identity
SSN	Social Security Number
STO	Security Token Offering
SUT	System Under Test
SV	Satoshi Vision

Abbreviation	Full form or Meaning
SWIFT	Society for Worldwide Interbank Financial Telecommunications
TOTM	TotemFi
TPoA	Tolerated Power of Adversary
TPS	Transactions per second
UAE	United Arab Emirates
UDI	Unique Digital Identification
UDID	Unique Disablity Identity
UID	Unique Identification (Project)
UIDAI	Unique Identification Authority of India
uint	unsigned integer
UN	United Nations
UNL	Unique Node List
URL	Uniform Resource Locator
US$	US dollar
USDC	USD Coin or Tokenized US dollar
USDT	Tether
USSEC	US Securities and Exchange Commission
UTXO	Unspent Transaction Output
VC	Verifiable Credentials
VOUT	Vector Output
VRAM	Video Random Access Memory
WHO	World Health Organization
WWII	World War II
XKP	Zero-Knowledge Proof
XRP	Cryptocurrency of Ripple

Glossary

Explanation of the technical terms used in this book:

Term Used	Meaning or Explanation
Aadhaar	Aadhaar number is a 12-digit random identification number issued by the UIDAI to the residents of India after completing the prescribed verification process.
Aadhaar holder	A person to whom an Aadhaar number has been issued under the UIDAI Act, 2009.
Accelerator	A type of incubator for tech start-ups that usually lasts for three months, with mentorship and other support provided in exchange for equity.
Adware	Adware is a form of malware that displays or downloads advertising material, such as banners or pop-ups when a user is online. Certain adware also monitors user behavior online to target them with specific advertisements.
Algorithm	An algorithm is a set of well-defined instructions to solve a particular problem. It slashes down the time required to do things manually.
All-inclusive identity	A digital ID comprising a 16-digit unique identification number for citizens of a country. Alternatively, it can also carry 20-digit universal identification number, unique to all denizens of the world.
Altcoin	Altcoins are similar to bitcoin, but a somewhat different type of cryptocurrency. For example, Litecoin, Monero and Zcash.
Anonymity	Transactions on the blockchain are recorded using public and private keys, allowing people to keep their privacy intact while verifying their identity to third parties.
Arbitrage	Arbitrage is the process of simultaneous purchase and sale of the assets (in equal amounts) at different platforms, or locations, to capitalize on small price differences. Arbitrage trade allows an investor to make a profit by buying and selling a commodity in two different markets.

Blockchain for Real World Applications, First Edition. Rishabh Garg.
© 2023 John Wiley & Sons, Inc. Published 2023 by John Wiley & Sons, Inc.

Term Used	Meaning or Explanation
Asset management	Asset management is a systematic approach to growing wealth by acquiring, maintaining, and trading investments that can increase in value over time. This applies to both tangible assets and intangible assets.
Asset transfer	Asset transfer means the sale, lease, or disposal of one or substantially all the assets of one person or company to another.
Asymmetric cryptography	Asymmetric cryptography, also known as public-key cryptography, is a process that encrypts and decrypts a message using a pair of keys – the public and private keys – to protect against unauthorized access or use.
Attribute-based authentication	Attribute-based authentication (ABA) is a method of authenticating users by their attributes, in order to validate their identity along with protecting their privacy.
Auditability	Every transaction on the blockchain is validated and recorded with a timestamp, allowing users to access a full copy of the record.
Augmented reality	The user continues to experience real life, in an enhanced form, through the superimposition of graphics or text.
Authentication	Authentication in cryptography refers to the process of proving the identity of the counterparty and the existence of an asset by means of a private/public key. The process of authentication within an identity system involves the verification of an individual's demographic information or biometric information, on the basis of information available with the Central Identity Data Repository.
Authentication-based identities	Many providers of online services, such as Google, LinkedIn, Facebook, etc. allow users to access their accounts using the same username and password (also known as login credentials).
Authentication devices	The host devices/electronic gadgets that collect personal identity data, encrypt PID blocks, transmit authentication packets, and receive authentication results.
Authentication facility	The facility provided by the authority to verify the identity information of the Aadhaar number holder through the process of authentication, by providing e-KYC data, or a yes/no response, as applicable.
Authentication protocol	Authentication Protocol is a type of computer communication protocol or encryption protocol specially customized for the transfer of authentication data between two entities.
Authentication service agency	Authentication service agency is an agency that offers the required infrastructure to provide secure network connectivity and identity authentication services in order for the requesting entity to be able to undertake authentication using the authentication facility given by the authority.

Term Used	Meaning or Explanation
Authentication user agency	Authentication user agency can be a government/public/private agency registered in India that sends authentication requests to enable its services/business functions using the Aadhaar authentication services of UIDAI.
Bearish	A bearish trend is a particular attitude of investors toward declining stock prices in a market, which could be an accumulation of various fundamental and technical factors, including price history, economic reports, seasonal factors, and national and world events.
Bill of lading	A bill of lading is a legal document issued by a carrier to a shipper that details the type, quantity, and destination of the goods. It serves as a shipment acknowledgment when the carrier delivers the goods to a predetermined destination. Although historically, the term only referred to carriage by sea, today a bill of lading can be used for any type of carriage.
Biometric system	A biometric system is an instrument that allows a certain characteristic of a person to be recognized using mathematical algorithms and biometric data. It enables better handling of criminal cases, defense of national borders, access control, etc.
Bitcoin	Bitcoin is the world's first decentralized digital currency that is traded directly between users, without a central administrator or third party, through a publicly distributed ledger, called blockchain.
Bitcoin Cash	Bitcoin Cash is a cryptocurrency that originated from a fork of Bitcoin. In November 2018, Bitcoin Cash further split into two cryptocurrencies: Bitcoin Cash and Bitcoin SV.
Block	A block is the largest contiguous amount of disk space that can be allocated to a file and is, therefore, the biggest amount of data that can be accessed in a single input-output operation.
Block time	Block time is a measure of the time taken by a miner or validator within a network to verify a transaction within a block and add a new block to that blockchain. The block time of bitcoin is ten minutes.
Blockchain	A blockchain is a type of distributed ledger or database, where transaction records are saved in a page of the ledger, called a block. Each block has a hash code that identifies the block immediately preceding it, sequentially adding the blocks, and tethering them together to form a chain.
Blockchain 1.0	Blockchain 1.0 was the first generation of blockchain technology that focuses on cryptocurrency and decentralization.
Blockchain 2.0	The concept of Blockchain 2.0 was a forward-thinking version of Blockchain 1.0 to enable automated computerized protocols, known as smart contracts, that are used to digitally facilitate, verify, or enforce an agreement.

Term Used	Meaning or Explanation
Blockchain 3.0	Blockchain 3.0 is dedicated to transcend the purely financial application and offer new perspectives in areas, such as education, health care, real estate, transportation, and logistics.
Blockchain 4.0	Blockchain 4.0 envisions blockchain as a business-friendly ecosystem for building and operating applications in the real world. The system can achieve infinite scalability by exploring the possibilities of virtual blockchains within the blockchain.
Borrowings	The long-term liabilities of the company or individual which have to be paid back to the lender after a certain period of time are called borrowings or loans.
Botnet	Botnets are used to perform Distributed Denial-of-Service attacks, steal data, send spam, and allow the attacker to access the device and its connection through command and control software.
Bull run or bullish	A bullish trend or bull run refers to a period of time when most investors buy stocks in line with market sentiment, demand exceeds supply, market confidence becomes high, and prices show an upward move.
Byzantine fault tolerance	Byzantine fault tolerance is the ability of a computer system to continue working even if some of its nodes fail or act maliciously.
Byzantine generals problem	The Byzantine army problem is a riddle in which several divisions of the army, camped at different locations, receives the same piece of information to ensure that all loyal commanders choose the same course of action and that a few traitors should not force the loyal generals to accept an evil plan.
Caesar cipher	The Caesar cipher technique is one of the earliest and simplest method of encryption technology, in which each letter of the plaintext is replaced by a letter, some fixed number of positions down the alphabet.
Card reader	A gadget that can be used to access the document or information saved in the multipurpose ID.
Cash flow	Cash flow is a real or virtual movement of money that reflects the net balance of cash going into and out of a business at a specific time.
Cash on delivery	Cash on delivery, also referred to as cash on demand or collect on delivery, is the sale of goods by mail order, where payment is made upon delivery rather than in advance.
Central Identities Data Repository	A consolidated database in which personally identifiable information, demographic data, biometrics, or other related facts of users are stored for a specific purpose.
Centralized identity	Centralized identity management refers to the workspace setting where the user makes a single sign-in to access all the applications and tools.

Term Used	Meaning or Explanation
Clearing	Clearing in the banking system is the process of settling transactions between banks.
Coinbase transaction	A coinbase transaction is the first transaction in a block. Miners use this to collect the block reward for their work and any other transaction fees collected by the miner in this transaction.
Collaboration	Collaboration is the process of two or more people or organizations working together to achieve a goal.
Commit	In commit chain, non-custodial and untrusted operators facilitate communication between transacting parties by sending periodic updates to the parent blockchain about a user account balance status.
Consensus	Consensus is a reliable method of authenticating and validating value or transactions on a blockchain or a distributed ledger in the absence of a central authority.
Consortium blockchain	Consortium blockchain is a semi-private system in which a group of like-minded companies leverage cross-company and cross-discipline solutions to improve workflow, accountability, and transparency.
Content (coinbase transaction entry)	Content is an entry that, unlike other cryptocurrency transactions, is not linked to the address of any other holder or sender. This entry is called Coinbase and is responsible for creating new currencies within the blockchain as a reward to miners.
Credentials	Credentials are a set of identifying attributes that refer to the verification of identity or tools for authentication.
Credit	A credit is a contractual agreement or trust that enables one party to provide money or resources to the other party, and the latter agrees to return it in the future, usually with interest.
Credibility score	Credibility score is a measure that determines the fidelity of an identity user on the basis of his activities and consistency of information provided by him on a technology platform, such as blockchain.
Credit operator	Credit operator is an organization or an individual, which operates a system for clearing and settling transactions in which it capitalizes its credit for the purchase of goods or services or for obtaining cash advances.
Crowd funding	Crowd funding is a practice in which large groups of people syndicate small individual investments together to raise the capital needed to get a company or project off the ground.
Cryptocurrency	Cryptocurrency is a digital currency, created, stored, and exchanged on the blockchain, using encryption techniques. Bitcoin and Ether are the best-known examples

Term Used	Meaning or Explanation
Cryptocurrency exchange	A cryptocurrency exchange, or a digital currency exchange, is a business platform that allows customers to trade cryptocurrencies for other assets, such as traditional fiat money or other digital currencies.
Cryptographic keys	In cryptography, a key is a string of alphanumeric characters that encodes a secret value or information into a cryptographic text by means of encryption algorithms.
Cryptographic signature	A cryptographic signature is a mathematical scheme to verify the authenticity of digital credential or documents.
Cryptography	Cryptography, or cryptology, is the practice or discourse of techniques for secure communication, which allows only the sender and intended recipient of a message to view its contents.
Cyberattacks	A cyberattack is a forceful maneuver that targets computer networks, infrastructure, or personal equipment with the aim of disabling the system or pilfering data. These could be denial-of-service, malware, man-in-the-middle attack, phishing, ransomware, etc.
Cybersecurity	Cybersecurity is the practice of protecting computers, servers, mobile devices, digital systems, networks, software, and data from theft and malicious attacks.
Data integrity	Data integrity refers to the accuracy and consistency of data stored in a database, data warehouse, data mart, or other silos and is an important aspect to the design, implementation, and use of any system that stores, processes, or retrieves data.
Data portability	Data portability is the ability to move data among different applications, programs, or cloud services that allows data and applications to migrate between users.
Data repositories	Data repository refers to an enterprise data storage unit or entity in which data is stored for a specific purpose.
Decentralized identity	A Decentralized Identity or a distributed digital identity is an identity deployed on a blockchain that allows users to share it on demand in a secure manner, while providing users full control over their personal information.
Decentralized autonomous organization	Decentralized autonomous organization is a member-owned community with no centralized leadership that leverages smart contracts on the Ethereum blockchain. It is a new type of self-governing organization, which runs on a peer-to-peer network by computer programs and is represented by transparent rules encoded in the form of computer programs.
Decentralization	Decentralization refers to the transfer of control and decision-making from a centralized entity to a distributed network and eradicates many-to-one flow of information to avoid a single point of failure.

Term Used	Meaning or Explanation
Decentralized applications	Decentralized applications are distributed open-source software applications that can operate autonomously on a peer-to-peer blockchain network, rather than on a single computer, through the use of smart contracts.
Decentralized finance	Decentralized finance is an emerging financial technology, based on a secure distributed ledger, called blockchain, using smart contracts, without relying on intermediaries, such as banks, exchanges, or brokers.
Decentralized identifiers	Decentralized identifiers are important components of decentralized web applications, typically associated with cryptographic keys in order to secure decentralized digital identities.
Decentralized storage	Decentralized storage means the encrypted files are stored on multiple computers (nodes) on a decentralized network. As the data is being encrypted, no one can access the data except the owner of the data who has the private encryption key.
Decryption	Decryption is the process of converting data back to its unencrypted form, which has been made unreadable through encryption. This is usually a reverse process of encryption.
Delegated proof-of-stake	Delegated proof-of-stake is a verification and consensus mechanism in the blockchain that competes with other proof-of-work and proof of stake models as a way to verify transactions and promote blockchain organization. Voting and delegation mechanism makes DPoS more democratic.
Delivery/sale consignment	Consignment is an arrangement in which goods are left to a third party for delivery or sale, who receives a flat-rate fee or commission as a part of the service or profits after the goods are delivered or sold.
Denial-of-Service attack	Denial-of-Service (DoS) attack is a spasm designed to disrupt a machine or network by flooding it with traffic or sending information that triggers a crash, making it inaccessible to its intended users.
Digital signature	Digital signature securely associates a signer to a document or a recorded transaction through a coded message. It uses a standard, universally accepted format called Public Key Infrastructure (PKI) to provide the highest level of security.
Digraph cipher	A digraph cipher encrypts by substituting each digraph, i.e. pair of letters, in the message with a different digraph or symbol.
	They are similar to monoalphabetic substitution ciphers, except that instead of replacing individual letters in the plaintext, digraph ciphers replace one pair of letters with another pair or digraph.

Term Used	Meaning or Explanation
Directed acyclic graph	A directed acyclic graph is a directed graph with no cycles. It consists of vertices and edges, and each edge is directed from one vertex to the other in such a way that following those directions will never form a closed loop.
Disintermediation	Disintermediation is the outright denial of the need for a central controlling authority or third party to manage transactions or keep records.
Distributed ledger	A distributed ledger is a record of replicated, shared, and synchronized digital data that exists across several locations or among multiple participants.
DNA	DNA digital data storage is the process of encoding and decoding binary data to and from synthesized strands of DNA
Documentation	Documentation may be any communication material – paper, online, digital or analog media – which is used to describe, record or provide evidence of an object, system or process.
Downtime	The term downtime is used to refer to the period during which a machine, especially a computer, is not working or is unavailable for use.
DPKI	Decentralized public key infrastructure is an alternative approach to design PKI systems in a distributed framework.
Dridex	Dridex is a vicious form of malware that targets the banking credentials of its victims. It is also known as Bugat and Cridex.
e-Commerce	e-Commerce (electronic commerce) is the buying and selling of products or services, and transmission of funds or data, over an electronic network, primarily the internet.
Electronic identities	Some governments or organizations issue electronic identities to their citizens or employees as a tool for identification, daily attendance or other online uses.
Electronic signatures	An electronic signature, or e-signature, is data that is associated to a recorded transaction through a coded message. It uses a standard and universally accepted format called Public Key Infrastructure (PKI) to provide the highest level of security.
Emotet	Emotet, also known as Heodo, is a Trojan strain that spread primarily through spam emails, malicious scripts, macro-enabled document files.
Encryption	Encryption is the process of encoding information, which converts the original representation of information (plaintext) into an alternative form (ciphertext) that only authorized parties can decrypt with the private key and decipher.
Enterprise resource planning	Enterprise Resource Planning is an integrated management of core business processes, such as accounting, manufacturing, sales, and marketing, often in real time through software and technology mediation.

Term Used	Meaning or Explanation
Ether	Ether is a transactional token that drives smart contracts for all programs and services connected to the Ethereum network.
Ethereum	Ethereum is a decentralized platform, developed as a custom-built blockchain with shared global infrastructure, where each node (computer) in the network runs an operating system called the Ethereum Virtual Machine (EVM). EVM understands and executes software, called a smart contract, written in the Ethereum-specific programming language.
Ethereum backend	Ethereum introduced the concept of smart contracts that allows developers to use its network to run backend applications. The code is entirely open source, and anyone can check how it works.
Ethereum frontend	Transactions with Ethereum, such as signing messages, sending transactions, and managing keys, are often conducted through web browser extensions, such as MetaMask.
Ethereum requests for comment	Ethereum requests for comments (ERC) are application-level standards for Ethereum, which may include token standards, name registries, package formats, and more.
Ethereum wallet	Ethereum wallet enables a user to write, deploy, and use smart contracts as well as holding Ether and other crypto-assets built on Ethereum.
Event	Multiple transactions on the same timestamp can be stored on the ledger, which are stored in a parallel structure. Here each record in the ledger is called an event.
Exchange tokens	Exchange tokens are digital assets native to a cryptocurrency exchange. Exchange tokens carry a high value, and they help in fundraising as well as smooth operation of the exchange.
Facial recognition	Facial recognition is a biometric solution capable of matching a human face from a video frame against a digital image or database of faces. It is usually employed to authenticate the identity of users.
Fault tolerance	Fault tolerance is a property of a computer system, cloud cluster, or network, that enables a system to continue operating efficiently, even when some of its components fail.
Federated Byzantine agreement	Federated Byzantine agreement is a method of achieving consensus, in which nodes can share another node and reach consensus without directly knowing all other nodes.
Federated identity	A federated identity is an agreed-upon process of authentication of a user's identity between multiple identity management systems – an organization or service provider and an external party or identity provider.
Fiat currency	Fiat currency is a type of money that is not backed by any commodity, such as gold or silver, and is usually declared as legal tender by a decree of a government.

Term Used	Meaning or Explanation
Fingerprints	Tiny ridges, whorls, and valley patterns on the tip of each finger that are altogether unique to the individual.
Forex counter	A forex counter converts one currency into another whose exchange rates often change regularly, based on fluctuations in global trading markets. For international money transfers, the difference is calculated, based on the prevailing market rate at that point of time.
Fork (hard fork)	In blockchain, a fork develops when a blockchain moves along two possible paths or when two or more blocks have the same block height.
Fundraising	Fundraising is the process of receiving and collecting voluntary financial contributions for business activities involving individuals, businesses, or government agencies.
Fungible tokens	Bitcoin and other cryptocurrencies are prime examples of fungible tokens because each coin has the same value as any other coin of the same type at any given time.
Gamification	Gamification is the strategic effort to enhance systems, services, organizations, and activities to create a game-like experience by adding game-like elements to a task to motivate and engage users.
Gaming	Gaming refers to the playing of electronic games, whether from a console, computer, or mobile phone, and involves interaction with a user interface or input device, such as a joystick, controller, keyboard, or motion-sensing device, to generate visual feedback.
Genesis block	The genesis block is the name given to the first block on which a cryptocurrency, such as Bitcoin, was ever mined.
Genetic profile	Genetic profile refers to detectable nucleotide variations on DNA, particularly in the exons.
Genomics	Genomics is a study of the structure, function, and expression of genomes. A genome is an organism's complete set of DNA.
Gossip protocol	Gossip protocol is a peer-to-peer communication mechanism, based on the way epidemics spread, in which nodes periodically exchange information about themselves and other nodes at random about whom they know.
Halving	Bitcoin halving is the process of halving the rewards of Bitcoin mining after each set of 210,000 blocks has been mined. By reducing the rewards of Bitcoin mining, the Bitcoin halving limits the supply of new coins, so increasing demand could reinforce the potential for price increases.
Hard cap (Bitcoin cap)	A hard cap is a limit placed by a blockchain's code on the absolute maximum supply of a particular cryptocurrency.

Term Used	Meaning or Explanation
Hash	Hashing is a cryptographic process that converts data into unique outputs of a fixed length to form a digital fingerprint.
Hash function	A hash function is a function that fits a set of inputs of any arbitrary size into a table or other data structure that contains elements of a fixed size. The values returned by a hash function are called hash values, hash codes, or hash digests.
Hashgraph	A hashgraph is a data structure that keeps a record of who gossiped with whom and in what order. It is a distributed ledger technology that has been described as an alternative to blockchain.
Hashrate	The number of hashes that can be performed by a Bitcoin miner in a given period of time, usually a second.
Hedge funds	A hedge fund is an actively managed investment pool whose managers use risky, aggressive, or esoteric investment options, such as short selling, leverage, and derivatives, in search of outsized returns.
Hill cipher	The Hill cipher, invented by Lester S. Hill (1929), is a polygraphic substitution cipher based on linear algebra, in which each letter is represented by a number modulo 26. It was the first polygraphic cipher in which it was possible to operate with three symbols at a time.
Holochain	Holochain is an open-source framework that provides self-owned data, a distributed database, and peer accountability.
Hybrid blockchain	Hybrid blockchain is a unique type of blockchain technology that amalgamates components of both public and private blockchains to harness the potentials of both the blockchain solutions.
Hyperledger	Hyperledger, hosted by the Linux Foundation, is a global, multi-project open-source collaborative effort that provides the framework, standards, guidelines, and tools needed to build open-source blockchains and related applications for use in a variety of industries.
Identifiers	All internet interactions include the use of identifiers, such as IP addresses, to help internet functions, identify devices, and track users' online interactions.
Identity attributes	Personal identification attributes such as name, date of birth, social security number (SSN), address, etc. are reckoned as personal identifiers that are commonly used to differentiate an individual from others.
Immutability	Data on a blockchain is replicated continuously on different nodes across multiple organizations so once written and stored, it becomes permanent and immutable.

Term Used	Meaning or Explanation
Incentives and rewards	On the blockchain, miners are rewarded for solving complex mathematical problems using cryptographic hash algorithm, which speeds up transactions and enables them to take wise decisions while processing the full transaction safely. Miners are rewarded in two different ways. One represents brand-new coins that are minted with each new block, and the other represents transaction fees from all of the transactions in the block.
Interledger protocol	A protocol that connects legacy ledgers of the past with the distributed ledgers of the future.
Intermediary	An intermediary is a third party or a trusted authority, such as a bank, agent, or arbitrator that provides mediation services between two parties, which involves trust, preventing direct contact, and potential escalation of the issue.
Internet of Things	The Internet of Things (IoT) is a network of machines or physical objects that are embedded with sensors, software, and other technologies to connect and exchange data with other devices and systems over the internet.
Interplanetary file system	Interplanetary file system is a protocol designed to be a permanent and decentralized method of storing and sharing files. IPFS uses content-addressing to uniquely identify each file in the global namespace that links all computing devices.
IOTA	IOTA does not use the traditional blockchain design used by most cryptocurrencies. Instead, it has developed a new platform called Tangle, which uses a mathematical concept known as Directed Acyclic Graphs.
Iris scan	Iris detection or iris scanning is a mathematical pattern-recognition technique of using visible and near-infrared light to take a high-contrast picture of a person's iris.
Know Your Customer	Know Your Customer (KYC) is an essential measure to verify identity and suitability to assess the risks involved in maintaining a business relationship. The procedures fit within the broader scope of a bank account opening or a bank's anti-money laundering policy.
Know Your Transaction	Know Your Transaction (KYT) is about those financial institutions that have fully granular, data-centric information about the transactions done by the customer. It is part of a legislative arsenal that aims to complete the KYC process by identifying risky transactions, especially by improving regular monitoring of customer relations.
Leader-based consensus	Leader-based consensus is a mechanism in which a leader is elected, who validates transactions and sends data to other nodes and remains in control until a vote is decided on a new leader.

Term Used	Meaning or Explanation
Ledger	A ledger is a book of accounts in which classified and summarized information from the journals is posted as debits and credits. It is an append-only record store, where records are immutable and may hold more general information than financial records.
Letter of credit	A letter of credit, also known as a documentary credit or a bank's commercial credit, is a payment system used in international trade to provide an economic guarantee from a trusted institution that the buyer will pay full amount to the seller on time.
Lightning network	The Lightning Network is a layer-2 payment protocol of the Bitcoin blockchain, which enables rapid transactions between participating nodes, by creating a micropayment channel between the two parties. It has been proposed as a solution to the Bitcoin scalability problem.
Light-weight client	Light-weight client or light node is a piece of software that connects to full nodes to interact with the blockchain. Unlike their full node counterparts, light nodes do not have to run 24/7 or read and write a lot of information on the blockchain.
Liquidity provider	A liquidity provider is a financial entity or a market broker that acts as an intermediary in the securities markets. Providers buy securities in large quantities directly from companies, and they distribute them in batches to financial institutions which, in turn, make them available to retail investors.
Loan	A loan is usually an advance provided by a corporation, financial institution, or government organization to an individual, group, or organization with the expectation of repayment, along with finance charges and interest.
Logical clock	A logical clock is a mechanism for capturing chronological and causal relationships in a distributed system, as it may not be possible to have a physically synchronous global clock in such a system.
Logistics	Logistics refers to the management and implementation of a complex operation during acquisition, storage, transportation, and distribution, involving the flow of resources between a point of origin and a point of consumption.
Loyalty rewards	A loyalty reward is a marketing strategy sponsored by retailers and other business establishments designed to attract and retain customers to continue to purchase products or use the services of the business, associated with the program.
Malware	Malware is a file or malicious software designed to intentionally interfere with security and privacy; damage computers, servers, clients, or computer networks; leak personal information; obtain unauthorized access to information or systems; or deny access to users. It could be a computer virus, worm, Trojan horse, ransomware, or spyware.

Term Used	Meaning or Explanation
Man-in-the-middle attack	Man-in-the-middle, also known by many other names, such as monster-in-the-middle, machine-in-the-middle, monkey-in-the-middle, medlar-in-the-middle, or person-in-the-middle attack, is a spasm in which a perpetrator hides or impersonates each endpoint to eavesdrop in a conversation between a user and an application, in such a manner that appears like a normal flow of information.
Margin	Margin is the collateral that the holder of a financial instrument has to deposit with a counterparty so that the holder can cover some or all of the credit risk for the counterparty.
Margin trading	Margin trading is the process in which a person can potentially earn more money on his investment by buying and selling stocks or other instruments from borrowed money.
Merkle tree	A Merkle tree, also known as a binary hash tree, is a data structure that serves to encode blockchain data more efficiently and securely. It is a tree in which each leaf node is labeled with a cryptographic hash of the data block, and each nonleaf node is labeled with a cryptographic hash of the labels of its child nodes.
Metacoin	Metacoin is a coin built on top of the Bitcoin blockchain with additional functionality that allows a small amount of Bitcoin to represent another asset.
Metal pay	Founded by Marshall Heiner (2017), Metal Pay develops a blockchain-based payment and rewards wallet for digital assets.
Miners	The miner, as an auditor, authenticates the validity of a blockchain transaction, and in return, receives incentives in the form of tokens. Blockchain mining is a metaphor for the computational work that a node performs.
Modulus	Modular arithmetic is a system of arithmetic for integers, where the values are reset to zero and rise again after reaching a certain predefined value, called the modulus (modulo). Modular arithmetic is widely used in computer science and cryptography.
Multipurpose ID	A digital ID, advocated by Rishabh Garg (2016), comprising a 16-digit unique identification number for citizens of a country or 20-digit universal identification number for all denizens of Earth.
Multisig	Multi-signature is an authentication function that allows a group of users to sign a document with more than one private key. It is a multi-signature algorithm that generates a joint signature, which is more compact than a collection of discrete signatures of individual users.

Term Used	Meaning or Explanation
Network protocols	Network protocols govern the end-to-end communication of data across the network in a timely, secure, and seamless manner. Network protocols are used to access the internet, transfer files between devices, transmit messages over internet, and automate processes on the network.
Node	A node is actually a computer, laptop, or server device that functions to store, spread, and protect blockchain data.
Node-to-node	Node-to-node, or N2N, data transfer is the movement of data from one node of a network to another.
No-loss lottery	A no-loss lottery is a gamified savings account that incorporates the concept of a traditional lottery system with cryptocurrency bets, where participants forgo a portion of the generated yield to pursue a potential jackpot opportunity.
Nonce	A nonce is an abbreviation for "number only used once," which is a number added to a hashed or encrypted block in a blockchain that, when rehashed, meets difficulty level restrictions. The nonce is the number that blockchain miners solve in order to obtain the cryptocurrency.
Nonfungible tokens	Nonfungible tokens are cryptographic assets on a blockchain with unique identification codes and metadata that cannot be traded or exchanged for equivalence.
Online identity	An online identity is the identity that an internet user creates on social platforms and websites.
One World – One Identity	*One World – One Identity* is a 20-digit universal identification number (UID), propounded by an Indian scholar, Rishabh Garg (2016), that serves as a unique digital ID for every citizen of the world. This blockchain-enabled, all-encompassing global ID replaces any document that a person may have obtained over his lifetime and shields personal data from breaches, hacks, and unauthorized access.
Participant or peer	Participant, or peer, is the fundamental element of the blockchain network, who has an access to the ledger, reads, or appends records, maintains the integrity of the ledger, and hosts smart contracts.
Peer-to-peer network	Peers are the participants in the network, who have the same privileges and powers in the ecosystem. Blockchain consists of a series of computers (nodes) and servers in a P2P network that share tasks, tasks, or files among peers.
Peercoin	Peercoin, also known as PP coin or PPC, is a peer-to-peer alternative cryptocurrency that uses both proof-of-stake and proof-of-work systems. It was launched in August 2012.
Permissioned blockchain or private ledger	Permissioned Blockchain is a private network of vetted participants, which operates with predefined rules regarding access, consensus mechanisms, governance, participation, etc. A permissioned ledger is usually faster than a permissionless ledger.

Term Used	Meaning or Explanation
Permissionless blockchain or public ledger	Permissionless blockchain is a public network that is open to everyone, and where any user, whosoever wishes to transact with the network, can participate and write on the blockchain. Bitcoin is the most familiar example of an unlicensed network.
Persistence	A blockchain is a decentralized and globally distributed ledger, shared over a public or private network, where data, once committed, can never be manipulated or hacked.
Personal identifiable information	Personal identifiable information is the data or information about a person or citizen that can, either directly or indirectly, disclose the person's identify.
Phishing	Phishing is a form of social engineering whereby an attacker attempts to gain confidential information by sending mails that resemble emails from reputable companies to induce the target person to reveal personal information, such as passwords or credit card numbers.
Playfair Cipher	The Playfair Square or Playfair Cipher, proposed by Charles Wheatstone (1854), is a manual symmetric encryption technique, which is reckoned as the first literal digraph substitution cipher.
Polymarket	Polymarket is a decentralized information market platform that harnesses the power of free markets to demystify the real-world events that matter the most to you.
Portfolio management	Portfolio management is the selection and monitoring of appropriate investment tools that meet an investor's long-term financial goals and risk tolerance. Its objective is to balance the overall maintenance of the business while optimizing the return on investment in line with the strategic objectives of the investor.
Practical Byzantine fault tolerance	Practical Byzantine fault tolerance is a consensus algorithm introduced by Barbara Liskov and Miguel Castro in the late 1990s, which has a great potential to break the performance bottleneck of proof-of-work–based blockchain systems, which hardly support a dozens of transaction per second. It is optimized for low overhead time.
Prediction markets	Prediction markets are exchange-traded markets created for the purpose of trading the outcome of events. These contracts are similar to bets on uncertain events, where people trade contracts that pay based on the outcomes of unknown future events.
Privacy	Privacy is the protection of one's personal information, whether demographic or biometric, from those who may cause economic or social harm to the individual concerned by having an unauthorized access to such data, or derive economic benefit from that information.

Term Used	Meaning or Explanation
Privacy leakage	Privacy leakage is the access of personal information of a citizen or user, whether due to system error, misconfiguration, negligence, or willful attempt by the data custodians, into unauthorized or undesirable hands.
Private blockchain	A private blockchain only allow nodes coming from a specific organization to participate in the consensus process. These are also called permissioned blockchains. Being fully controlled by one organization, they are often considered as centralized networks.
Private key	A private key is a string of alphanumeric characters that encode a secret value or information into a cryptographic text by means of encryption algorithms, and decode the encrypted data back into plaintext using decryption algorithms. It is secretly held in a digital wallet.
Product tracking or tracking shipment	Package tracking is the process of tracking shipping containers, mail, and parcels in real time to verify their provenance during sorting, warehousing, and package delivery; and to determine when, where, and by whom the goods or product parts were manufactured, processed, stored, transported, used, or disposed of.
Programmable money	Programmable money refers to a digital form of currency that is programmed to work in a certain way, based on certain predetermined criteria. A well-known form of digital money is the cryptocurrency Bitcoin, which is accounted for and transferred using online systems.
Proof-of-stake	The proof-of-stake protocol is a category of blockchain consensus methods that chooses validators based on the number of holdings in each coin. This is regarded as an alternative to the computational expense associated with proof-of-work plans. PoS algorithms leverage the collateral staking mechanism to encourage users to validate network data and maintain security.
Proof-of-work	Proof-of-work is a decentralized consensus mechanism that compels peers of the network to put effort into solving an arbitrary mathematical puzzle to prevent anybody from gaming the system. It is a technique for attaining network consensus where the computational power of the miner determines their ability to mine currency.
Public blockchain	Public blockchain is a permissionless blockchain in which all records are visible to the public, and each node can participate in the consensus process. Any user, whosoever wishes to transact with the network, can participate and write on the blockchain.
Public key	Public key is a cryptographic code – a large numerical value used to encrypt data. The key may be generated by a software program, but typically, it is provided by a designated authority, who makes it available to one and all through a publicly accessible repository or directory.

Term Used	Meaning or Explanation
Public key infrastructure	Public key infrastructure is a system for the creation, storage, and distribution of digital certificates, which verifies that a particular public key belongs to a certain entity. It uses public key cryptography (PKC) for secure data transmission and authentication.
Quadratic funding	Quadratic funding is mathematically a more scalable way to fund public goods in a democratic community. Public good can be a commodity or service valuable to large groups of people or accessible to the general public.
Quantum resistant ledger	A quantum resistant ledger is the first blockchain of its kind – a future-proof, post-quantum value store and decentralized communication layer that protect cryptocurrencies from the impending threats of quantum computing in the years to come.
Random gossip	The random gossip process is a classical strategy for spreading messages through a peer-to-peer network in which communication nodes randomly select connection partners from among their eligible neighbors and exchange useful information.
Ransomware	Ransomware is a malware that threatens to destroy user's personal data or permanently block the user's access to the data, using a technique called cryptoviral extortion, until a ransom amount is received.
Rate of transactions	A new block is mined in the blockchain every ten minutes. Based on previous assumptions, Bitcoin can do an average of 2,759.12 transactions per ten minutes = 600 seconds, which equates to 4.6 transactions per second.
Remote procedure call	Remote procedure call, also known as a function call or subroutine call, is a protocol that a program can use to request a service from another program located in a remote computer, without knowing that it is remote. RPC is not a transport protocol but a method to transparently use existing communication facilities.
Reputation systems	A reputation-based system is a system that formalizes the process of gathering, accumulating, and dispensing information about the past behavior of individuals.
Retinal scan	It's a process to scan an intricate network of blood capillaries as an image, by means of a high-definition camera or scanner that casts a low beam of infrared light. It can be converted and saved into a database, using appropriate algorithms.
Revocation	Identities are dynamic, and hence, the possibility of revoking a credential for an issuer in an identity infrastructure becomes crucial. Deleting or updating a credential is called revocation.

Term Used	Meaning or Explanation
Ripple	Ripple is a blockchain-based, real-time gross settlement system, currency exchange, and remittance network with its own cryptocurrency, XRP. As an alternative to the SWIFT payments, Ripple offers a much faster, cheaper, and hassle-free way to exchange currencies and send money across borders.
Root hash	Root hash, or Merkle root, is a special type of hash with an interesting computing structure, designed to facilitate verification of data within a Merkle tree.
Round	Round refers to the time it takes to find a new block. This is the time elapsed since the last time the pool received the block. For instance, if a block is found and added to the blockchain nine minutes after the previous block, that was a nine-minute round.
RSA algorithm	The RSA algorithm is an asymmetric cryptography algorithm that uses two distinct but mathematically associated keys – a public key and a private key. The public key is publicly shared, while the private key is secret and is not shared with anyone.
Scalability	Scalability is the capability to withstand and perform increased throughput and maintain or even increase its level of performance when tested by large operational demands.
Schema	Schema is a conceptual framework that describes the structure of different types of data.
Schnorr signature	Schnorr is a signature scheme that allows multi-signature functionality for BTC transactions with less data required than the older elliptic curve signature scheme. For example, if three parties wish to sign a transaction, they can combine their individual public keys to form one public key. Then, using each of their three private keys, they can sign the same message.
Security	Blockchain uses cryptographic algorithms involving public and private keys to maintain virtual security. Encryption keeps private data confidential, while digital signatures ensure authenticity, data integrity, and nonrepudiation.
Self-sovereign identity	Self-sovereign identity allows users to establish their own identity while maintaining control over the storage and management of their personal data.
Selfish mining	Selfish mining, also known as a block-withholding attack, is a malicious attempt to discredit the integrity of the blockchain network. It occurs when someone in the mining pool tries to hold back a valid block from being broadcast to the rest of the network.
Server	Servers, such as home media servers, web servers, print servers, file servers, or database servers, are computers that run services to serve the needs of other computers.

Term Used	Meaning or Explanation
Settlement	Settlement can be defined as the process of transferring funds from payer to payee through a central clearing agency with participation of their respective banks or custodians of funds.
Sharding	Sharding is a method of distributing a large dataset into several smaller data chunks, thereby increasing the total storage capacity of the system by storing the data on multiple machines. Sharding divides the entire network of a blockchain into smaller divisions, known as shards. Each shard carries its own data, which makes it independent and distinct from other shards.
Shipment	It is the physical movement of goods from one point to another, such as the moving merchandise from the warehouse to the customer. The shipping process follows the manufacturing and the packing of goods and is controlled and overseen by a shipping or logistics company.
Sidechain	A sidechain is the transfer of assets from one mechanism to a separate pegged mechanism; special-purpose ledger.
Single point of failure	A single point of failure is such a nonredundant part of a system that, when itself idling, causes the entire system to fail. It is a barrier in achieving high availability in a computing system, network, software application, business practice, or any industrial system.
Smartphone	A smartphone in the present context is a device which can be used to get instant OTP or to enter security pass-word, biometric details (fingerprint, retinal scan), and to track the geographical location of the person.
Smart contract	A smart contract is a contractual agreement built on a computer protocol whose terms can be automatically enforced without the possibility of downtime, censorship, fraud, or third-party intervention.
Software	Software is a collection of instructions that includes a complete set of programs, procedures, and routines associated with the operation of a computer system.
Spyware	Spyware is software with malicious behavior that aims to collect and transmit information to another entity, infringing on the user's privacy or jeopardizing the security of his device.
Stakeholder	A stakeholder, such as an investor, employee, customer, or supplier, is a party who has an interest in a company or business and who may influence or be affected by the business.
Storage optimization	Storage optimization is the collective process, framework, and technology that enable efficient use of storage infrastructure and resources.

Term Used	Meaning or Explanation
Structured query language	Structured query language (SQL) is a domain-specific language used for databases that allows a database to handle the information, using tables, and shows a language to query these tables and the other related objects – views, functions, procedures, etc.
Supply chain management	Supply chain management is the management of the flow of goods and services between businesses and locations from origin to end consumption – the procurement of raw materials, warehousing, work-in-process, finished goods, and end-to-end order fulfillment.
Symmetric key cryptography	Symmetric key cryptography is a function that leverages cryptographic algorithm for the encryption of plaintext as well as the decryption of ciphertext. The key is called symmetric because the same key is used to encrypt and decrypt the data.
Tempo	Tempo, apart from being a distributed ledger, is an underlying consensus protocol, as well. The consensus part of tempo is based on the notion of logical clocks in which each node has a counter that increases, and never decreases, with every new request.
Tendermint	Tendermint is a type of blockchain stack that consists of two main technical components: a blockchain consensus engine and a generic application interface. The consensus engine or tendermint core ensures that identical transactions are recorded on each machine, in the same order.
Thermal map	A thermal map consists of infrared radiations (about 12 microns) emitted by a human body to distinguish between man and a robot.
Timestamp	Timestamp is the exact point of time when the block was mined and validated (data stored in each block as a unique serial) in the blockchain network.
Tokens	Tokens are digital assets prescribed by a project or smart contract and built on a specific blockchain. Tokens can be utility tokens (consumer or incentive tokens) or security tokens.
Tokenization	Tokenization refers to the process of converting tangible and nontangible assets into a token that can be transferred, stored, or recorded on a blockchain. It is a process of replacing sensitive data with unique identifiers that retain all the necessary information about the data without compromising on its security.
Tokenized derivatives	A derivative is a contract or product whose value is determined by the underlying asset. Tokenized derivatives are mathematical models that speculate on the price of an underlying security token that may represent an alternative asset, such as art, commodity, currency, gold, stock, real estate, or others.

Term Used	Meaning or Explanation
Trade finance	Trade finance represents financial institutions, instruments, and products that are used by companies to facilitate domestic as well as international trade and commerce.
Trade-off	The trade-off is a situational decision to achieve a balance between two desirable but incompatible characteristics. It is a simple settlement that involves losing a less desirable asset in exchange for a more desirable one.
Transaction	Transaction refers to a change in the state of funds between two or more businesses or individuals, in compliance with an agreement or by exchange of goods, services, or assets.
Transaction throughput	Transaction throughput is the rate at which valid transactions are carried out across the entire blockchain system under test over a specified time period. This rate is expressed as transactions per second (TPS) in a network size.
Transcoding	Transcoding is the direct digital-to-digital conversion of one type of encoding into another (video, audio, and text file) to adjust the amount of data according to the carrying capacity of the target device.
Transparency	All transactions in a public blockchain network are transparent and visible to all market participants. This increases the reliability of the system and gives participants access to the data at all times.
Transposition cipher	The transposition cipher is a cryptographic algorithm where the order of alphabets in the plaintext is permuted to form a ciphertext.
Trojan horse	A Trojan horse is a malware that acts as an authentic application to trick the user and steal his data or damage his network. The term is derived from the ancient Greek story of the deceptive Trojan horse that led to the fall of the city of Troy.
Trust	Trust is an environment that gives people sufficient trust in the technology or platform being used to make payments or transactions. In this context, blockchain, being based on a shared consensus between different parties, is considered a reliable platform.
Trust score	Trust Score is a measure that determines the credibility of an identity user on the basis of his activities and consistency of information that user has provided on a technology platform, such as blockchain.
User-driven Oracle	Oracle provides service-enabled public integration interfaces by providing an infrastructure for the deployment, consumption, and administration of web services.

Term Used	Meaning or Explanation
User-centric identity	User-centered identity management allows users to select their credentials when responding to an authentication or attribute request, thus giving users greater authority and control over their identity information.
Validation	Validation is the process of checking the accuracy and authenticity of source data before it is used, imported, or processed otherwise.
Venture capital	Venture capital is a form of private equity financing provided to venture capital firms or startups, early stage, and emerging companies that demonstrate high growth potential along with associated risk.
Veracity	Multiple copies of the ledger's historical records are stored in a network of nodes, and each record is verified by consensus. This improves accuracy to a high level, and fraudulent entries are identified and fail to reach consensus.
Vigenère cipher	Vigenère Cipher is a type of substitution cipher used for data encryption that employs a form of multi-alphabet replacement by using a series of interwoven Caesar ciphers based on the letters of a keyword.
Virtual reality	Virtual reality, similar to or completely different from the real world, is a three-dimensional, computer-generated world that uses computer technology to provide the user with an immersive and simulated experience.
Virus	Computer virus, a metaphor derived from biological virus and first defined by Fred Cohen (1983), is a malevolent software program that replicates itself on execution by modifying other computer programs and inserting its own code. If the replication succeeds, it performs malicious actions.
Wallet	Wallet is a small software program that contains addresses and their associated keys; permits online purchases, transactions, sending and receiving coins by connecting to the network; and also allows Bitcoins to be spent while holding credentials that proves one's ownership.
Whales	Whales are giant traders who stockpile large amounts of cryptocurrency in anticipation of making huge profits or who have the ability to manipulate valuations due to their large reserves of currency. Their movements create turbulence in the water in which small fish swim, hence they are called whales.
Withdrawal	Withdrawal means removal or redemption of money from a bank account, savings plan, pension, or trust.
Yield farming	Yield farming is an investment strategy under DeFi in which cryptocurrency coins or tokens are lent or staked in order to receive rewards in the form of transaction fees or interest.

Term Used	Meaning or Explanation
Zero downtime	Zero downtime deployment is a method in which the web server does not begin serving changed code until the entire deployment process is complete so that the user's website or application is not likely to be shut down or unstable at any time during the deployment process.
Zero knowledge proof	Zero knowledge proof, or zero-knowledge protocol, is a method by which, without sharing original credentials or evidence, one party can prove to the other party that a given information is true.

Index

Printed and bound by CPI Group (UK) Ltd, Croydon, CR0 4YY

27/10/2024

14580670-0003